Material Architecture

Material Architecture

Emergent Materials for Innovative Buildings and Ecological Construction

John Fernandez

AMSTERDAM • BOSTON • HEIDELBERG • LONDON • NEW YORK • OXFORD
PARIS • SAN DIEGO • SAN FRANCISCO • SINGAPORE • SYDNEY • TOKYO

Architectural Press is an imprint of Elsevier

ELSEVIER

Architectural
Press

Architectural Press is an imprint of Elsevier
Linacre House, Jordan Hill, Oxford OX2 8DP, UK
30 Corporate Drive, Suite 400, Burlington, MA 01803, USA

First edition 2006
Reprinted 2006

Notice
No responsibility is assumed by the publisher for any injury and/or damage to persons
or property as a matter of products liability, negligence or otherwise, or from any use
or operation of any methods, products, instructions or ideas contained in the material
herein. Because of rapid advances in the medical sciences, in particular, independent
verification of diagnoses and drug dosages should be made

British Library Cataloguing in Publication Data
A catalogue record for this book is available from the British Library

ISBN–13: 978-0-7506-6497-4
ISBN–10: 0-7506-6497-5

For information on all Architectural Press publications
visit our website at www.architecturalpress.com

Printed and bound in *Italy*

06 07 08 09 10 10 9 8 7 6 5 4 3 2

Working together to grow
libraries in developing countries

www.elsevier.com | www.bookaid.org | www.sabre.org

ELSEVIER   BOOK AID
International   Sabre Foundation

for my mother and father – in return for their many gifts

Contents

Prologue - Building Design

While the most fundamental goal of architecture - providing buildings to shelter human activities - is as pressing as ever, the balance between functional services and the intangibles of delight is constantly evolving. The Prologue explores these issues as they are related to the physical making of building systems in a contemporary material world.

I   Time

Part I establishes the intellectual context for the remainder of the book by addressing architectural research and the emerging issues of ecological construction.

1   Matters of Research

Chapter 1 offers an outline of the historical background and disciplinary distinctions that have emerged from the changes that technology and academic institutions have prompted.

2   Time and Materials

Material flows, buildings lifetimes, designing for obsolescence and disassembly are discussed as an emerging understanding of the ecological and environmental ramifications of construction materials.

II   Material

Beginning with an outline of material properties and families in Chapter 3, Part II is the technical heart of the book - presenting the five material families in detail. Sections 3.1-3.5 include historical and technical background for each material family, typical properties of those families, emerging new materials and implications for future architectural design.

3   Material Families and Properties

An introduction to the science of architectural materials including a survey of their use in building systems, a discussion of intrinsic and extrinsic material properties, and a detailed description of individual properties and the behavior of individual materials from the array of families.

For Sections 3.1-3.5: properties, architectural applications and new materials.

3.1   Metals

Ferrous and non-ferrous alloys.

3.2   Polymers

Thermoplastics, thermosets and elastomers.

3.3   Ceramics

Concrete, fired clays, glasses and other ceramics.

3.4   Composites

Glass, carbon, kevlar fiber reinforced polymers and other composites.

3.5   Biomaterials and Loam

Natural fibers, wood, earth and other materials of biological and geochemical origins.

III   Design

Part III proposes that material selection methodologies and research can be brought to bear in the assessment and comparison of traditional and non-traditional architectural materials for better design.

4   Material Selection

Multi-objective optimization is presented as a proven technique for making informed choices between the vast array of available materials for any design situation.

5   Material Assemblies

Three research projects that merge design and technical matters are described.

Epilogue - Building Ecologies

An overview of the theories and methods of industrial ecology and the opportunities for incorporating this new science into an understanding of the paths that responsible construction make take for the future.

Acknowledgements

As all writers inevitably become, I am now deeply indebted to many individuals for inspiration, constructive criticism, unwavering support and - most importantly - unconditional patience.

The MIT Class of 1957 made this book possible with their generous support these past three years. *Material Architecture* is a direct result of their kind and generous gift and I am hopeful that my ambitions to contribute to the mending of the artificial rift between the technology and design of buildings will be well-received. Clare Hall provided the wonderful space and the University of Cambridge the perfect environment for thinking and writing. To my colleagues in the Building Technology Program here at MIT - who have been supportive of my work of the past five years and whose steady encouragement I have readily accepted - Leon Glicksman, Les Norford, Andrew Scott and, most recently, John Ochsendorf and Marilyne Anderson. Also, to those colleagues from other institutions whose conversations and collaborations I have enjoyed and benefited from greatly - Daniel Schodek, Mike Ashby, Koen Steemers, Charles Kibert, John Habraken and many others - thank you all. Also, it has been my pleasure and privilege to present a good portion of the contents of this book to the students in my Emergent Materials Workshop at MIT these past couple of years. For your contributions, I hope you will find this volume a useful collection of thoughts and information. And to my publishers, Architectural Press of Oxford, England, for allowing the freedom and granting complete acceptance to pursue the idea of this book as deeply as possible.

Kisses forever to my children, Vita and Lorenzo, whose brave patience has regularly threatened to break my heart. And finally to my wife, Malvina, who is the only person to know how totally I have depended on her for completion of this work. Many years ago she suggested that the materials of architecture was a subject worth pursuing - the seed was planted then. More than anyone, I hope she finds this book worthy of the youthful aspirations that initiated these interests.

John Fernandez is an Associate Professor and registered
Architect in the Department of Architecture at the
Massachusetts Institute of Technology in the USA. His work
addresses the physical systems of contemporary buildings.
He has most recently been involved in the study of construction
ecology and the opportunities afforded by a comprehensive
description of the material flows dedicated to the making of
our built world.

Building Design

The engineer and architect must go back to basic principles, must keep abreast with and consult the scientist for new knowledge, redevelop his judgment of the behavior of structures and acquire a new sense of form derived from design rather than piece together parts of convenient fabrication... His work will then be part of his age and will afford delight and service for his contemporaries.

Louis Kahn, 1944

Material Works

Figure P.1

Morning rush hour at Grand Central Terminal in New York City, a grand civic space like no other for its intense service to the city and the region, performed within a constructed canopy of the heavens. Transportation buildings are particularly good examples of the nexus of functional and architectural relations.

Grand Central Terminal, New York City, USA (1913).
Whitney Warren, Architect.

To "afford delight and service" is an optimistic phrase that captures well the best aspirations for making buildings. In articulating this pair, Kahn gives us a remarkably succinct statement of the ultimate goals of architecture. In doing so, he also enlivens a practice that concerns itself with the symbiotic linking of the pragmatic and the poetic - the technical and the intuitive - in the material works of our built environment. We are reminded of the articulation of the essential parts of architecture by Vitruvius; *firmitatis* and *utilitatis* define the service rendered by buildings and *venustatis* the delight, or grace, that results.

The results of the linkage between service and delight are readily apparent in our great spaces. Grand Central Terminal in New York City is alive with use everyday. This building serves the city, the region and the imagination of its commuters through its simplicity of form and the splendor of its scale. Like many great works of architecture, separating its function from its form is a reduction of its enduring presence, for only in its material reality does it become a landmark of our mind's eye of the city.

Buildings that *delight* their users endeavor to enhance daily routines and timeless built landscapes. Buildings that provide reliable *service* ensure the safe, comfortable, reliable and durable shelter needed to fulfill the basic requirements of our species. Achieving this pair of conditions through time has been the driving force behind much of architectural design and building construction. The balance between the two depends on the priorities of society and the flux of economic and cultural forces. These are often substantially modulated locally by the needs of the building type, its particular location, owner, users and many other factors specific to a particular time and place.

Through the ages, the desire for delight in architecture and the constituent elements of that delight have continually evolved. The intricacies of revelatory spatial organization and volumetric elaboration, astounding qualities of light and the movement of air, fidelity to stylistic codes and ornament and the suggestive import of all kinds of material surfaces are only a few of the ways in which design has led to the making of some of the most extraordinary cultural artifacts ever conceived. The Alhambra, the Louvre, King's College, Cambridge, Grand Central Terminal are among many thousands of buildings that extend their utility toward poetic expression. The elements of design used to achieve these extraordinary spaces have changed over time. The materials have changed as well.

Buildings are meant to fulfill the diverse aspirations of a complex society. When delight and service are coupled together into a symbiotic whole, the built environment becomes a richly varied mosaic of design invention and engineering creativity achieved through the materials of the time. Today we are equally impressed by the lightness of a cable-stay structure as the Egyptians were by the solidity and intended permanence of their pyramids and tombs. Partly guiding these fascinations are the various cultural productions that have contributed to the pluralism of contemporary aesthetics.

Figure P.2a, b

Construction photographs showing window units produced with advanced CAD/CAM systems delivered to site and placed within the superstructure of the building (above) and elaborately curved structural steel framework of laboratory space.

Stata Center, Massachusetts Institute of Technology, Massachusetts, USA (2004).
Frank O. Gehry, Architect.

While aesthetics - that collection of codes, theories and manifestos that orbits the making of all kinds of forms - has become an esoteric subject verging on a quaint irrelevance, the underlying fascination that drives it persists. We are still taken aback by new forms and the evolving forces - technological and otherwise - that drive their conception.

This evolution - the changing nature of delight - has been driven by many factors including cultural diversity and global economic interdependence, the increasingly fluid global exchange of information and images, structural changes to the knowledge and practices of design and construction and many technological changes, such as material innovations. Of course we also live in a time of frenetic expressive heterogeneity in which aesthetic codes have intermingled, mutated and spawned every kind of architectural proposition: occasionally simultaneously. It is this intermingling with technological discovery and invention that gives rise to the surprising forms of contemporary architecture.

The continuing search for architectural form has always captivated the imagination and led to remarkable buildings and structures in every time period. From the first tall buildings in Chicago to Frei Otto's tensile net surfaces in Munich to Santiago Calatrava's bridges, novel form has a presence unmatched by any other physical objects produced by society. The technology of these objects can overwhelm and obscure their cultural and civic value and a mere fascination with technique can trivialize their contribution to design. Caution is wise when praising the technical over the lyrical because we know that trivializing and discounting the value of the character of form, the meaning of shapes and surfaces, colors and materials, inevitably leads to a process bankrupt in spirit and impotent in fully capturing the imagination. And yet, we know that technical changes have prompted many new design approaches, and surprisingly novel forms, in the making of large and complex buildings and elements of infrastructure.

Figure P.3

Supporting structure and panel arrays for photovoltaic cells serving simultaneously as solar shading, partial enclosure to an egress stair, major facade material and energy - producing vertical surface. This type of inventive construct, using elements that aspire to address emerging concerns - in this case the need and ability to tap into renewable energy sources - is one of the most exciting leading edges for contemporary architecture.

Colorado Court, Multi-Unit Housing,
Santa Monica, CA, USA (2003).
Pugh + Scarpa Architecture.

3

Figure P.4

Float glass treated with a spectrally selective metal oxide coating and aluminum extrusion mullions comprise a high performing building enclosure providing both daylighting and thermal comfort reliably.

London, UK.

Similarly, the nature of service has also changed, evolved and progressed through time, especially during the industrial revolution and since the early 19th century. Despite the fact that our physiological needs, as a species, have not fundamentally changed over time, we do have greater expectations for higher comfort levels and the technologies used to satisfy them have evolved dramatically. The primary domain of these changes has been in the engineering of building systems required to support and deliver the acceptable performance of the building. We have come to expect a constancy and unfailing reliability over structural performance, precise control over the interior environment, predictability in the integrity of the building enclosure and a general level of performance from all other building systems at a level never before attempted, but now often realized and routinely expected. Contemporary buildings are safer than ever before. Structural engineering and standardized structural members, fire suppression technologies and alarm and communication capabilities, noncombustible materials and regulatory mandates of every kind have made contemporary buildings very safe and reliable.

As a result, we now expect - especially in the developed west - a level of service never before achieved or sought after in the history of buildings. In the United States, with its multitude of contrasting climates, mechanically assisted ventilation and air conditioning can be found in most buildings and almost all commercial office buildings. Our contemporary airline terminals provide moving walkways to spirit harried passengers through their extensive corridors. Our buildings reliably serve us with steady supplies of light, water and air and now broadband streams of data. And yet, the haste with which buildings have fundamentally changed their systems and adopted the latest technologies has also led to notable problems. Indoor air quality, high energy consumption, unpredictable failures in durability, have all contributed to

Figure P.5

An airport terminal - another example of a transportation building serving both functional and nonfunctional needs. In this era of frenetic travel these buildings have acquired a central place in the modern experience of millions of people.

Bilbao Airport, Spain. Santiago Calatrava, Architect.

situations in which contemporary buildings have failed to improve people's lives. An example of this is the commercial office building, particularly in the United States. Processed air, artificial lighting, acoustic monotony, the off-gassing of materials and the general environmental tedium of office interiors, while serving economic goals, cannot generally be considered an improvement in the lives of its users. These kinds of buildings serve narrow economic interests and ignore value that falls outside of the harsh criteria of corporate accounting. Many of the problems of these buildings have arisen by virtue of the fact that the inclusion of seemingly beneficial new technologies (in any situation) is almost always accompanied by unforeseen negative consequences (Tenner 1997). However, the constant refinement of service continues and the balance between it and the priorities to enhance the well-being of people is in constant negotiation. Some change has been beneficial - some not. The very basis of a humane and appropriate architecture is the impassioned search for materials and methods to achieve an optimal mix of delight and service. This is why there is no real separation between technique and form - technique and design.

Understandably, it is sometimes necessary to emphasize one concern over another, delight over service or otherwise, for the benefit of advancing architecture generally. The discourse that is necessary in pursuing this negotiation for the benefit of a humane built environment is a pluralistic endeavor born of the diversity and scope of the architectural mission. Topics both technical and nontechnical bear the weight of a contemporary mission to serve and delight in ways that both belong to and transcend our times. Architectural design is irreversibly stitched together by the desire for enhanced delight and the search for better service to occupants. So, it is not surprising that this pair of interests, forming as they do the foundation of design, has *co-evolved* over time (Basalla 1988). This evolving balance has been the hallmark of

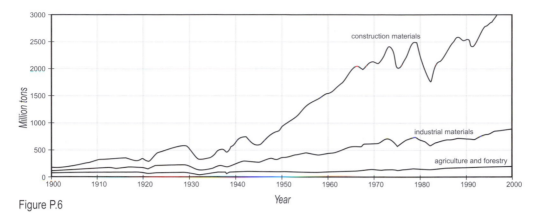

Figure P.6

Materials use for construction, industrial, agriculture and forestry in the United States between 1900 and 2000.

Source: Matos and Wagner, USGS.

the transaction between engineering and architecture; between analytical examination and design synthesis (Daniels 1997,1998). Technological advances inevitably alter the path for design and continually supply new and unanticipated opportunities for architectural form - as the changing nature of the material world has been a prime source of new opportunities for design (Timberlake 2001).

Material Ecology

Using contemporary materials in the best possible ways involves both technical understanding and design invention. It is reasonable to suppose that enhancing the knowledge of materials, traditional and novel, will improve the ability of designers to better respond to contemporary needs and produce a more humane built environment that also serves the contemporary imagination.

Today, improving the environment requires a reconsideration of the contribution of new materials in this process. One such issue is the relationship between the production and consumption of materials and the service lifetimes of buildings. The material reality of typical buildings is not the static and unchanging permanence that monumental architecture aspires to. Yet, buildings do constitute an enormous store of materials used in construction - primarily due to their long lives. Understanding and designing within an organized ecology of the built environment, and not just for a single project's needs, requires more information about the material flows for construction. Therefore, the ecology of the built environment becomes one aspect of the study of materials for buildings.

Buildings are among the very largest and most complex artifacts that our species has ever produced. The sheer size, weight and volume of many buildings are far larger than the

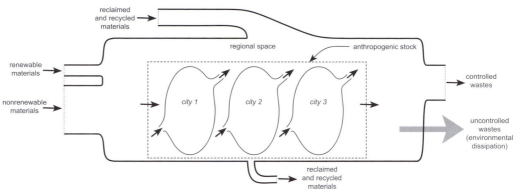

Figure P.7

A simplified diagram of material flows devoted to contemporary construction within a regional spatial boundary during a period of one year. Cities are the primary beneficiaries of the *anthropogenic stock* that is comprised of all existing buildings.

Source: Based on various diagrams from a variety of industrial ecology sources, see Graedel, Kibert, Ayres, Bringezu among others.

vast majority of other modern industrial artifacts. The construction of these buildings, their long lives and their aggregation into enormous cities has permanently altered the earth's landscape. The modern city is the largest accumulation of materials and harnessed energy ever assembled. It is estimated that our cities, past and present, existing and dissolved have together consumed and retained upwards of *75 percent of all materials ever extracted* by humans. This anthropogenic stock is now the material legacy left to us by all previous generations, Figure P.7.

The enterprise of organizing materials into our buildings and cities has been the historical responsibility of construction technique and, recently, building technology. The history of that technology and the continuing story of its developments are critical aspects of the legacy left to us by the act of building.

Material Intuitions and the Intellectual Dangers of *Materiality*

The emergence of novel technologies has always held a central place in the creative efforts of designers (Auer 1995;Beukers 1998;Cornish 1987;Gregotti 1996). The materials of architecture have always been pivotal in the development of its form and the implication of future form. Ancient concrete and masonry construction, Gothic stonework, the standardized steel bar joists of modern buildings, the reinforced concrete of bridges and tall buildings have shaped the direction of design and the production of novel forms of architecture. Whether experiments in materials yield successful buildings is still dependent on the individuals involved and the rigor of the effort. As in any field of technology, the development of technologies for buildings has been littered with false starts. And yet, some of the primary developments in architectural form have been prompted by the introduction of new materials

(Cowan and Smith 1988; Schwartz 1996; Turner 1986). The reinforced concrete frames of Auguste Perret's Theatre des Champes-Elysees (Paris, 1911-13), LeCorbusier's Dom-ino (1914-15) and Albert Kahn's Ford Motor Company Factory (Highland Park, Michigan, 1909), are among the very many that have initiated the novel forms of a new architecture.

Regulating these developments are the assemblies that comprise contemporary buildings. These building systems have been segregated into several discrete and interdependent assemblies, each with its own set of performance requirements, lifecyles, maintenance needs, replacement protocols and specialized professionals, engineers and others to design, construct and maintain them. As a result, the materials used to fulfill the range of performance requirements of the foundation, superstructure, building services (HVAC, lighting, plumbing and others), exterior envelope, interior furnishings and other systems has become widely diverse (Wigginton 2002). Every material class is represented in most building systems, see Chapter 3 Material Families and Properties.

Through rapid advances in a wide variety of materials for many industries, including construction, the question of the nature of these materials has continued to provoke commentary from practitioners and theorists alike (DiTomas 1996). This questioning has supported a provocative engagement with architectural materials and placed the *facts* of these materials at the center of the inventive moment. The properties of architectural materials have been mingled with the traditions of building construction resulting in a discourse of the tectonics of assemblies (Groak 1992;Frampton 1995,1999).

Also, from time to time, the question of the use of materials in the design project has been framed in terms of a true "nature of materials" (LeCorbusier 1931). Architects have, in the past, repeatedly stated their

Figure P.8

Stone facade detail that clearly demonstrates the "particulate" nature of many ceramics that results in relatively high porosities.

London, UK.

8

Figure P.9

Concrete surface detail showing the numerous "micropores" in what seems, at arm's length, a very smooth surface.

Los Angeles Cathedral, CA, USA. Rafael Moneo Architects.

own views on the appropriate use of certain materials in terms of their generalized properties. Whether a material has a grain, or originates from inorganic or organic sources, is highly processed or relatively untouched - this is the language of a good deal of the discourse that attempts to formulate the nature of materials in architectural assemblies. While these views have achieved certain positive results that focus on the integrity of purpose and a heightened sensibility for the physical presence of architectural forms, they are not generally robust to the point of promoting an inventive interaction with materials. The danger in the adoption of subjective viewpoints over all other concerns lies in attempting to perceive a nature of materials primarily through visual (and some other sensory) experience. Textural qualities tend to obscure, or at least diminish, the importance of material properties. The selection and use of materials too often becomes an exercise in two-dimensional composition, based on a generally uninformed set of notions about the unique attributes of those materials.

However, it is not reasonable to assume that quantitative knowledge of properties can fully engage a designer in defining the nature of the materials used for an architectural assembly. Computational methods for selection, while powerful tools underutilized by designers, can only augment a broader exposure to the qualities of materials for construction. It is necessary to enliven this analytical knowledge with the messy process of construction, the multi-sensory familiarity of personal contact within the context of the synthetic process of design.

For example, it is inconceivable that Eladio Dieste would have been able to conceptualize his reinforced masonry structures without a tactile, personal connection to the material of brick, mortar and steel tensioning. It is equally difficult to believe that Felix Candela would have been able to form concrete and find the proper shell geometry with the same subtlety of detail and complexity of form in his buildings had he not been a contractor responsible for the construction of a number of his own designs. A mere familiarity with the properties of materials is only enough to inform one of the ways in which to assess discrete behaviors of that material under restricted conditions. The hint of the full range of creative possibilities in any design situation cannot reasonably be perceived through a mere listing of the mechanical and physical properties alone.

And while it may seem that a certain inevitability determines certain inventions in form and material, especially those born of deep experience and substantial technical knowledge, it is not useful to simply advocate that a material has a "nature" all its own, prescriptive of a limited set of forms. The physical and mechanical properties that describe a material are not intended, and do not have the capacity, to be a reductive plan for a limited number of predetermined forms that arise with the use of that particular material, see Chapter 4 Material Selection.

And besides, the state of architecture today precludes such moral judgments about any "right" way to use materials. While sustainable design advocates may argue this point, it is still irrefutable that overwhelming plurality is the nature of our contemporary world. An intractable and singular position denies the overwhelming richness of contemporary design and negates the undeniable fact of the need to optimize a selection of material for any particular use, because there is no such thing as the perfect material for any particular application. Therefore, design intention and the material world coexist as an animated assertion of possibilities made physical. Designers understand that a fundamental step in design involves the translation of intention into material form. This critical leap requires the optimization and selection of materials that can satisfy the needs and desires that the designer has formulated. While intuition is central to this effort, technical knowledge is absolutely necessary. And today, with more material choices available than ever, this process has become a monumental challenge of data management.

One reaction to this challenge has been the formulation of an alternative "soft narrative" of materials. A keystone of this self-compromised discourse is the use of the word "materiality"; a term that has gained a stubborn foothold in schools of architecture and come to encapsulate all too well the many indistinct notions of the physical "character" of a design proposal. Not surprisingly absent from inclusion in the *Oxford English Dictionary*, the word has persisted and spread like a mild cold, not enough to cause fatal illness, but enough to muddle the mind (Mori 2002).

The notions that seem to constitute the *materiality* of an entity are often limited to the narrow goal of a heightened sensibility toward the use of materials within an architectural context, that is, the applied material *qualities* of a thing. Implicit in the general character of the word is the fact that a significant swath of contemporary designers are not able to discuss a material in terms that extend beyond the general and immediately sensory-oriented. The haptic and visual aspects of materials clearly dominate discussions of materiality and while these discussions may be rich, useful and inspirational, they are limited in the coverage of the topic in light of its potential. The disciplines of materials science and engineering can add to this discussion - not to overtake or subsume in the specter of determinism or reductive analysis but by strategically contributing facts, data, sets of values, that may lead to an inventive idea. The broad use of the word materiality is an indication of the need for a simple effort of augmenting the general knowledge platform from which architects may launch design proposals. Without this effort, overly general discussions will continue to prevail and design innovation will suffer.

And yet, it is almost needless to point out that the effort to yield truly innovative forms and spaces can only be achieved if the design process involves knowledge offered by the sciences and engineering of mechanics, materials and structures (Elliot 1992). These disciplines are an entry into another kind of invention. Through this dynamic it is not unreasonable to think that we may be on the cusp of a new age of design in which an energetic contemporary craft of new and old materials may play a central role.

For example, it is now estimated that the average time necessary for a new construction material or system to proceed from laboratory success to production and distribution by the building construction industry in the United States is 17 years. This is a much slower process of invention and diffusion of innovation than comparably sized industries. In fact, it is widely believed that construction is the slowest of all industries of such scale in implementing proven, scientifically sound technological innovation. While this pace is understandable in terms of the certification necessary for ensuring the safety and health of the occupants of buildings using new materials and systems, it is surprising to know that it is generally easier to introduce a new material into the human body by way of biomedical engineering than it is to introduce a new material into buildings. The reasons for this include the decentralized nature of the US construction industry, the relative paucity of research funding, the conservative nature of the building trades, the extreme pressure on least cost solutions and a general set of cultural ideals that have consistently undervalued the more subtle aspects of architectural invention.

However, the reasons run deeper than these observations imply. There exist deep cultural reasons for the discrepancy between technological innovation in the United States and comparisons with Western Europe, for example. The differences - in sensitivity to environmental issues, workplace quality, materials and energy resource management - point to a fundamental divergence in underlying values. The construction of architectural form and material innovation are necessarily no less distanced from these values and ideologies of society than any other large-scale enterprise. Therefore, efforts to investigate materials should be set within a well-conceived notion of the interests and goals of society. The amount of construction material consumed in the US alone should be considered reason enough to support and carefully evaluate innovations in construction technologies. In any case, the ubiquity of discussions of "materiality" speaks to a pressing need for a more complete understanding of materials and their properties. Doing so is not difficult. Ideally, this effort

Figure P.10

Metals, especially ferrous alloys, are used in high stress applications in both tension and compression. Approximately 50 times more steel is needed to resist compression than is required to sustain the same stress in tension.

The Louvre, Paris, France, IM Pei Architect.

should originate from within architecture as the best way in which to place the specialized knowledge of materials immediately within the context of architectural design.

Becoming Familiar: A Personal Clause

Therefore, the central premise of this book is that becoming familiar with new materials is a richly promising avenue in the continuous search for architectural form. In particular, engaging those materials that have been developed through the workings of industry, science and society over the past decades is a worthwhile effort for designers wishing to improve the built environment - a central goal of this book. However, several points should be emphasized here.

First, this book should not be seen as another attempt to distill an essential meaning from materials themselves. The desire to do so would be unappealing to this author and simply an incorrect use of the book. I contend here that meaning springs from human constructions focused on thoughtful and humane values and the spirit of the creative moment - intuitive, rational, irrational, associative and *informed*, all at the same time. A mere search for meaning in the vagueness of an "essence of materials" is not the intent here. Therefore, it should be clear that I do not intend to present a book to the design community that places value on the nature of material itself. This would, again, lead to a naive fetishism - just another aesthetic obsession with the technical. Conversely, it is in a material's use that value is struck and intention is fulfilled - that is, transformation toward meaning from lowly material to humane buildings is achieved through the action of deep values (Calvino 1988;Manzini 1989; Pallasmaa 1994).

Figure P.11

Ceramics are generally limited to low stress applications in compression only. Most ceramics are not recommended to carry tensile loads because of the nature of their failure mode - sudden and catastrophic.

Bedell Mills Residence, Fernandez Lampietti Architects.

Second, the offering of information in the following chapters and the description of methods, primarily for materials selection, is not meant to preclude the most important process of learning about materials by the designer. Actual physical, tactile contact, cannot be replaced by the numerous graphs, tabular listing of properties, photographs or any other medium meant to contribute - but certainly not replace - a deeply intuitive sense of the behavior and presence of a material. The contemporary architect needs to step outside of the office often and visit manufacturers, assemblers, workshops and other sites of material manipulation. There are too few examples of real interaction between designers and material experts. For illustration here, I am drawn to a description given by Billie Tsien and Tod Williams regarding the casting of the bronze panels that cover the 53rd Street facade of the American Folk Art Museum in New York City. In discovering the opportunities and the limitations of casting various bronze alloys, the two architects engaged in a timeless shaping of design ideas through a material experience. The building facade benefited greatly from their trials. I also offer this example because I want to stress the fact that I am not advocating the creation of technophiles either. Williams and Tsien could never be accused of that, and yet they are adventurous and enthusiastic designers that challenge the filtered and marketed information about materials that most architects settle for (Pearson 2001).

Third, the motivation behind the writing of this book is quite simple. I believe that a design community, better informed about materials, can produce a vastly improved built environment. The aspiration is simple. To deliver on this aspiration, the range of knowledge necessary for real change is vast and, currently, wildly decentralized and widely dispersed. In its barest outline, the knowledge base requires information of material properties and processing technologies as well as knowledge of the characteristics and performance mandates of contemporary building systems. Today it is also critical for designers to be eminently informed about the environmental and resource consequences of their decisions. Linking knowledge of material properties, requirements of building systems and ecological ramifications of resource use will foster a design ethic that is appropriate to the times in which we live. Large portions of this book attempt to improve the depth of knowledge of materials available to the designer by centralizing this information and making it relevant to the needs and desires of architects and students of a better architecture.

Fourth, while it may strike the reader as stridently dogmatic, this book is not about materials. I am not a material scientist or engineer. I am an architect and this is a book about architecture - material architecture. The relationship between traditional and nontraditional materials and the processes and aspirations of design and construction are central to every section of this book. This is the reason that each chapter begins in a "discursive" style, outlining the historical, cultural, social and environmental topics to examine in the use of materials for contemporary buildings. A primary motivation in writing this book is the belief that architects should be making more of the knowledge that is available, both technical and nontechnical and fusing this knowledge with our own expertise in fulfilling the aspirations of society in the making of vast and complex systems for inhabitation. Writing about the systems of architecture necessarily involves addressing the materials of those systems. I believe there is general resignation in design communities to the prospect of gaining useful technical knowledge of new materials - so much so that important opportunities are being lost. But, I also believe in the adaptability and intelligence of the contemporary architect - especially the younger generation. This book is not beyond the realm of understanding of interested students and practitioners - and it is in this spirit that I offer it.

Finally, the writing of this book works against the notion that a mere fascination with the materials of today is satisfactory, or even responsible. Obsession without knowledge makes unimportant, misguided and sometimes dangerous buildings. I strongly believe that a simple allure of contemporary materials is not only superficial at best but, in light of the enormous material expenditure of construction, critically irresponsible at worst. Equally, I hold to the ideal that technical knowledge of contemporary materials without a foundation of values to guide a passionate viewpoint for design is no better. Materials, in and of themselves - however novel - will never make us better designers.

Therefore, if you are strictly interested in reading about the properties of materials, it is best to consult a book written by a scientist or engineer of materials. If, on the other hand, you are interested in reading about materials that can be employed in the ongoing evolution of humane, optimistic and spirited design, then I sincerely hope this book is in some way useful to you.

Matters of Research

The greatest invention of the 19th century was the invention of the method of invention.

Alfred North Whitehead, 1925

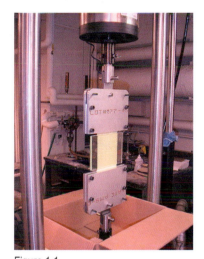

Figure 1.1

Tensile test setup for a structural fabric laminated glass sample proposed for a new kind of curtainwall assembly (see Chapter 5 for full explanation). While the testing of many materials for the purpose of establishing definitive values for all mechanical and physical properties has been substantially completed, the testing of original assemblies - new configurations of components - will never be complete as long as inventive and novel ideas spring forth from the architecture and engineering disciplines.

Building Technology Program, MIT.
Principal investigator: author.

Gated Communities

Technical innovation comes by way of the accepted procedures of science-based engineering, and no small measure of creative thought. The "invention of the method of invention" has fundamentally changed the nature of the relationship between the contemporary designer and the materials of architecture - as it has affected every other intellectual discipline of inquiry, research and development. Formulating a hypothesis, organizing a research plan, articulating a new viewpoint, advocating for a shift in perspective requiring further work and engaging with a community of interested individuals through the dissemination of results constitute the basic conditions for innovative work - the method of invention (Bernal 1954;Kuhn 1962;Latour and Woolgar 1986;Latour 1987).

Critical to this enterprise, for any discipline that supports a serious research community, is the effort of communicating with others engaged in similar pursuits. The nature of the distribution of information in research has changed a great deal over the ages because the nature of research has changed. From the lone inventor-gentleman in England and France of the 18th century to the richly subsidized laboratories of today's multi-national corporations and research universities, the breadth and depth of technical inquiry has greatly increased. As a result, the proliferation of means of communication - peer-reviewed journals, web-based collaborations, conferences and symposia - has responded to the enormous explosion of output from these research engines. Specialization has driven communities of expertise toward the refinement of research methods that produce strict delineations between a proliferation of subdisciplines. These intellectual "gated communities" of distinct core competencies characterize the landscape of research today.

Research in architecture and its array of associated disciplines have also changed dramatically from the time of the emerging manufacturing and technical production of the industrial revolution to the current firewall between much of technology research and design work. The shifts in its modes for communication - also journal and periodical based, web-based and spawning numerous specialized gatherings - have reflected the larger changes in research.

Many of the changes reflect the intensity of specialization that has become the conservative structure of architecture schools everywhere. No less assertive are distinctions made in architectural practices in which designers and technical staff may work together but understand the subdisciplinary delineation of their roles. Clear and strong divisions between design and technology (and, by the way, criticism, history and visual studies and others) have resulted in both productive and debilitating shifts away from the generalist center of design. In some contexts this has created the disciplinary equivalent of "gated communities".

The establishment of a separate camp further and further away from the most energetic discourses of design is arguably most pronounced in the architectural (or building) technologies. On the one hand, specialization

Figure 1.2

Barker Library at MIT is the repository for the dozens of peer-reviewed journals used to assess advances in the areas of materials, civil engineering, computer science and many other science and engineering fields.

of and within the building sciences has provided society with a much deeper understanding of the mechanics of all manner of phenomena related to the behavior of buildings. From the study of structures, strength of materials, energy flows, the physics of light and many other "practical" matters, we have come to be in much greater control of our buildings and, therefore, expect much higher levels of service than in the past. These scientific and engineering-based studies have delivered the tools and methods for engineering and constructing safer, more comfortable, more reliable buildings in greater numbers than ever before.

Conversely, the intensity for specialization has fueled the enduring tendency for a growing segregation of technologies from design. While many notable exceptions to this trend can be easily invoked (the work of Santiago Calatrava, integrated design at Ove Arup and Partners, the work of a number of European architects, and a number of schools that consciously work against distinctions) globally the trend is readily discernible. That is, the diffusion of technologies away from the generalist and synthetic center of design has resulted in distinct and mutually exclusive groupings of researchers whose primary allegiance is no longer architecture per se, but a specific technology of building.

The modes of communication used by this group closely reflects the science and engineering heritage of the subdiscipline. Peer-reviewed journals act as the vehicle of communication as they do for all the sciences and engineering fields. This contrasts greatly with much of the communication that is carried out by architects, through the publication of built work, essays and other writings in reviewed and non-reviewed periodicals, magazines and trade journals. The cultural distinction between the building sciences and the design field is also reflected in the work spaces used by these two populations. For the most part, the building technologies model their spaces after those in engineering. In contrast, the architects still retain a spatial organization more akin to

Figure 1.3

Rotch Library, Department of Architecture, MIT, showing a selection of the periodicals that constitute the primary vehicle for international communication in design.

Figure 1.4

The Building Technology Program graduate student space at MIT. This is the type of space in which much of the research conducted in building technology today is accomplished. The tools are computational, the media electronic, communication is web-enabled and the space is closely related to those in engineering. Desks are tightly arranged and suffice for the generally quantitative and analytical work accomplished here.

the work studios of the fine arts than to any office or lab environment. As a reflection of the self-identity of these two distinct intellectual cultures, their spaces of work speak volumes of their aspirations, beliefs and interests. This trend, of specialization and segregation, has been noted many times (Watson 1997;Allen 2004). Why is it important to raise here? Have we not benefited more from the creation of productive satellites of specialization while maintaining the very high expectations for architectural design that characterizes construction globally?

It is not the intention of this book to address these questions in a general way. This first chapter traces key shifts in the modes of research and communication in architecture and other disciplines for the dual purpose of offering the background to our current state of affairs and demystifying the path back to a more integrated practice of architecture.

The Built Word

The written word has always been used to advance communication and advocacy in the design arts. Since the beginning of the coordinated enterprise of construction, expert knowledge of building materials and supporting technologies have been conveyed from one cultural context to the next - often through the written and printed word. Transfer through time, across geographic and societal boundaries and from knowledgeable practitioners to novices in building construction, has accelerated with improved methods for disseminating the myriad types of technical advances generated within the last several centuries. A variety of media has facilitated this transfer. Among many methods employed through the ages, the buildings themselves have been primary artifacts along with architectural treatises, published papers and a continuing legacy of the instruction in craft and trade skills.

Figure 1.5

The Department of Architecture design studio spaces. The enduring spatial configuration, while transformed somewhat by the use of computers, attests to the commitment of educators to continue the legacy of the *atelier* environment. Work tables are suitable for the messiness of model-making, sketching and other media and the space closely relates to studio spaces in the fine arts.

While innovation in construction has always been, and to some extent continues to be, the result of the local confluence of a great diversity of economic, technological and cultural forces, the context for that innovation, and its mode of dissemination, has steadily shifted from a synthesis of architectural priorities and proven techniques to a process of increasing intellectual specialization within separately guided scientific disciplines. Beginning in the mid-18th century, the locus of innovation in construction and building crafts slowly began to shift from the trade guilds, craft workshops and construction site itself to the nascent production plant of the industrial revolution, and later the corporate-sponsored scientific laboratory (Frampton 1996). Also, with the rapid growth of the European city, the responsibility for building began to rest with specialists - the early contractors (Heyman 2002). For the first time, the process of the development of materials for construction was displaced to entities - the research laboratory and industrial production facility - whose primary modes of investigation are regulated, not by the multifaceted discourse of architectural thought and construction logic, but by newly emerged procedures of the scientific method and industrial capacities organized according to their own logic and needs.

> ...what, if any, is the organizational influence of technique upon a specific work of art? In other words, how important is professional skill and its specific use for a defined aim; but also how much does it matter that technique is a means toward something else, and at the same time carries the significance of its own history as an instrument? And finally, what place does the question of technique (by no means a technical problem) occupy in the process of forming a work? Naturally, all this began when distinctions were drawn between practical and conceptual action, between heights of ability and depths of reflection, which in the ancient world were united in the concept of techné.
>
> (Gregotti 1996)

The advances of architectural technologies, as a particular body of technical and design knowledge, have also been transmitted through the ages in a great variety of ways. These methods have also changed dramatically over time and continue to evolve and the type of communication media used has been very much related to the type of architecture in question. Knowledge of the architecture of the ruling classes and governing institutions has always traveled through privileged conduits; published treatises, monographs, pamphlets, paintings, sketches and measured drawings. Knowledge of vernacular, popular and regionally distinctive architecture, especially that of residential and agrarian buildings of the feudal, agrarian and working classes, has been transferred by the multifarious workings of tradition.

Early in the development of construction technologies and throughout the pre-industrial world, buildings themselves played the dominant role in exemplifying accepted practice and transmitting techniques to a select design audience (Fitchen 1994;Mark 1993). Throughout the ancient world, into the medieval period and the Renaissance and continuing through the industrial revolution, the most widely recognized buildings were most instrumental in providing knowledge of architectural technologies to successive generations of engineers and architects. During those periods, the master mason, the builder, and the architect were most indebted to the knowledge gained from previous built work (King 2000).

And yet publications dating back to ancient Rome have also played a role in teaching, proselytizing and attempting to persuade interested individuals of the benefits of a particular point of view. Both design philosophies and construction directives have been the subjects of these publications. Augmenting the buildings as primary sources for architectural thinking, the architectural treatise and associated publications have played an important role in documenting advances in construction technique, codifying best practice and disseminating findings geographically and temporally. Beginning with Vitruvius, the techniques of construction and the properties of building materials have been an important component of architectural learning - included in the same volumes that discussed mathematical proportion and aesthetic ideals, city planning, infrastructure placement, military fortifications and many other "building-related" topics (Vitruvius 1999a,b). For example, while venturing far beyond mere construction topics in his famous books, Vitruvius stressed the importance of understanding the relevant physical properties of the primary materials of construction as a fundamental aspect of the act of building.

> Hence I believe it right to treat of the diversity and practical peculiarities of these things as well as of the qualities which they exhibit in buildings, so that persons who are intending to build may understand them and so make no mistake, but may gather materials which are suitable to use in their buildings. (Vitruvius, Granger 1999a)

The treatise, through much of history, was engaged in presenting a more or less complete picture of the discipline of architecture; design principles and building techniques. The topics typically addressed included technical discussions of methods of construction, strategies for good practice on the construction site, descriptions of useful material properties and many other facts regarding the process of realizing a building. However, the technical information gathered within these documents spoke to a set of generalized and descriptive relations rather than results gathered from empirical studies of the kind that characterize modern science. The relations illustrated within treatises produced before the 18th century did not contain the kinds of investigations that would characterize the scientific revolution of Galileo and Copernicus and the regulated process of the scientific method. Therefore, early treatments of the technology of construction were presented as a set of relations based in "common sense", construction experience and rules of beauty or notions of propriety. Only later, and through the eventual proliferation of specialized publications, did the science of building and construction emerge.

The writings of Alberti, Palladio, Carlo Fontana and others demonstrate the character of the treatment of construction issues quite well (Palladio 1570). For example, Fontana, writing in 1694 (Fontana 1694), addressed problems in the cracking of St. Peter's dome through a postulation of solutions that used geometric relations to establish the requisite needs of *solidity* (Perez-Gomez 1994). Fontana used this rationale for uncovering divine relations in the physical construct and design conception of the church. Alberti, also intent on providing useful information on building includes diagrams of typical masonry wall construction, timber details and other mundane construction details as well as suggestions on construction that depend quite a lot on common sense, or at least reasonable conclusions.

> The ancients used to say, "Dig until you reach solid ground, and God be with you."
>
> (Alberti 1550)

And while the 18th century was to bring a revolution in the nature of technical knowledge and the methods of investigation, the descriptive treatise was to survive through many centuries, not as a more integrative document of design and technology but as a statement of architectural design motivation and intention. Technical communication began to be pursued elsewhere. For example, in the early 18th century, parallel to advances in science, several efforts were under way to inaugurate a newly revived renaissance sensibility in architecture quite apart from the technological advances of the day. Writing in his *Vitruvius Britannicus*, Colen Campbell (1676-1729) argued the right of British architecture to assume the mantle of the ancient and renaissance orders (Campbell 1967). He raised Indigo Jones to the position of rightful heir to the perfection of Palladio's architecture. This kind of treatise has come to typify what we know of today as architectural writing. In fact, the writings of architects today strongly continue to argue for the legitimacy of particular forms and design approaches primarily based on nontechnical issues. During the passage of centuries, one type of knowledge did not fully succumb to another; while science was developing its own methods and beginning to publish findings, the architectural treatise did not lose its power to establish artistic authority.

However, individual thinkers and vanguard scientists of the time were initiating an irreversible germination of principles based on observation and experimentation. During the early 18th century discoveries made of the strength of materials began to find their way into scientific papers and a selection of architectural treatises. These discoveries, while still presented very much in the tradition of Vitruvius, Alberti and Palladio, used a nascent scientific method and newly developed empirical strategies for reaching conclusions directed toward rapid introduction into engineering and architectural applications. These efforts were fundamentally influenced by the mathematical formulations brought to the study of the strength of materials and statics by Galileo. While the direction was a productive one, it would be some time before the most fundamental problems in statics and strength of materials were to be solved. Eventually novel solutions surfaced to replace the "pronounced failure in the normal problem-solving activity" of predicting the performance of structural elements (Kuhn 1962). The intent of these writings was still clearly toward augmenting the tools available to builders in achieving physical constructs. The methods used to reach these conclusions were of a very different kind than ever used before, that of the construction of a world fully described in terms of abstract geometry and numerical quanta.

As a clear shift toward scientific principles, Gautier of the newly formed *Corps des Ponts et Chausees* published a treatise on bridges during the first third of the 18th century. His *Traité* (Gautier 1727) went so far as to advocate that architecture was founded on principles of mechanics and empirically determined strength of materials. His eclipse of previous methods for establishing the "correct" proportions of individual structural members helped to bring forward the idea that form was dependent on physical phenomena rather than "rules" of ideal proportion or beauty.

That is, the description of architecture, both as a process of production and the embodiment of physical proportional perfection was achieved through a treatment of subjects as varied as mathematical constants of the ancient orders and specific recommendations on the processing, placement and finishing of building materials. For many centuries, the discussion of architecture could not be considered in terms in which this synthesis was not referred to. While this clearly led to extraordinary results, especially in terms of advances reached through a combination of construction experience as well as an enhanced intuition aided by the learning that comes from a first-hand knowledge of the properties of building materials, it could not advance a generalized understanding of the forces that contributed to the performance of buildings through their individual components. It would take a search of several centuries, beginning with Galileo's attempts to mathematically describe the essential elements of statics and the strength of materials, to arrive at the beginnings of a concerted effort to understand the underlying forces affecting architectural components (Heyman 1998;Timoshenko 1953).

An Industrial (not Technological) Revolution

It is useful to remind oneself that since the very beginnings of human existence, technology - as a measure of the human ability to configure tools and develop processes - has always assisted our daily activities. Science has not. Science is only the relatively new result of formulations of methods and conclusions reached through the application of the scientific method. Also, it is important to note that the industrial revolution was a revolution for society, industry and national economies but not a revolution, in the true sense of that word, for technology or science. Contrary to popular understanding, the scientific and technological progress of that time was clearly incremental (Basalla 1988). Improvements in machinery design, the harnessing of useful work from energy with the development of the steam and internal combustion engines, the rise of organic chemistry, the invention of electric lighting and communications, all contributed to revolutionary social changes through incremental scientific and technological advances. Likewise, massive shifts away from the traditional fuels of wood, other biomass, wind and water power and towards coal and, eventually, oil and other fossil fuels radically changed the nature of production and industry output. As a result, during the industrial revolution the manufacture of architectural materials and components (and most other physical implements) was transferred from the agrarian setting of the nonindustrial countryside and the artisanal workshop of the skilled craftsman to workplaces of the urban factory filled with legions of hired low-skilled workers displaced from that same countryside (McClellan and Dorn 1999).

Above all else, the industrial revolution was an expansion of manufacturing capacity, a dramatic increase in industrial productivity and a proliferation of incremental technical advances *for the purpose of meeting the demands of a surging population.* The real revolution lay in the transfer of productive capacity from the fields to the factories as an absolutely necessary condition to feed and clothe a great deal more people than ever before. As a result of better hygiene and more productive agricultural practices European populations were exploding; in England alone, the population grew from 2 to 9 million between the middle of the 15th century to the end of the 18th. During that same time energy consumption per capita increased by a factor of ten. Between 1830 and 1870, coal production increased from 24 to 110 million tons and iron production from 70,000 to 4 million tons. During that same time, worker production also doubled (McClellan and Dorn 1999; Stearns 1993).

While a social revolution was displacing centers of production and expanding industrial capacities through the centralization of manufacturing facilities, the contributions by scientists and technologists were incremental and slow. However, the contributions of Mariotte, Musschonbrek, Gautier, Soufflot and later Perronet and others brought architectural technologies, especially those concerned with statics and the strength of materials, toward consensus for efficient form and use of materials. Before the work of these individuals, the truths inherent in geometric relations – defined as originating in notions of both correct form and divine representation – dominated the work of leading architects and engineers. As a result of a reconsideration of the deterministic import of geometry, and a newly gained set of empirical and theoretical tools, the forms of architecture were now to be substantially influenced by a growing articulation of physical principles. Culminating in the presentation, to the Royal Academy of Science, of Charles-Auguste Coulomb's paper "On the Application of the Rules of Maximums and Minimums to Some Problems of Statics Relative to Architecture" (Coulomb 1773) the aspirations of many engineers and architects intent on applying mathematical relations to real-world scenarios was finally achieved (Nicolaïdis and Chatzis 2000). By the end of the 18th century the science of architecture and engineering had finally overtaken the philosophy of form and the invocation of construction intuition. As Perez-Gomez writes in *Architecture and the Crisis of Modern Science*,

> Finally, architectural reality could be truly functionalized, allowing for an effective substitution of mathematical rules for the experience derived from building practice. Building practice could now be effectively controlled and dominated by "theory."

> (Perez-Gomez 1994, 266-267)

These advances led to the establishment of two conditions that were to change the nature of the relationship between the architect, construction techniques and the materials of construction. First, the delineation of the discrete domains of study for the inventor of construction techniques and materials meant that the nonarchitect could make strides forward in improving, and profiting, from new technologies for realizing buildings. This continues today. Many individuals involved in building sciences are not architects and the proportion of nonarchitects is only likely to grow. Second, these individuals would begin the process of the founding of two of the dominant organs for research, development and manufacturing of building materials; the private corporation and the academic building science research department. This quickly led to the development of separate and distinct disciplinary languages focused on rapidly diverging interests. As a result, today, the practice of writing architectural treatises that rigorously address technical issues as well as propose serious design positions is rare, if not completely absent from the literature. Most of the serious writing on architecture today segregates the technical from the nontechnical (Pacey 1992;Stearns 1993).

Research Engines

In delivering the fruits of the theoretical work of the 18th century, researchers of architectural and engineering subjects were still occupied, as they are today, with the need to synthesize the lessons of quantitative analysis with the messy reality of the real, constructed, world. To achieve this synthesis, the researchers of the time needed to employ the regulated steps of the scientific method (Jacob 1997). Independent inventors sought, through the scientific method, an unassailable strategy for entering into new and potentially profitable enterprises. The individuals that took over control of the development of building materials were those entrepreneurs and inventors that were often only mildly associated with the technology of building. The likes of Aspdin, Monier, even Paxton were concerned with the development of materials through experimentation and eventually characterization. The methods of science were the methods employed by this group of inventors.

With the use of the scientific method the slow shift toward empirical research for architectural materials began. These individuals and others came to be the front wave of the establishment of the large modern multinational corporation. As a result, these large corporations have become the stewards, and the owners, of real material innovation - including that applied to architecture. The companies most responsible for changing the materials landscape of contemporary architecture have been the larger chemical companies, steel and aluminum refiners and fabricators and glass companies. Owens Corning, Dupont, LaFarge, Pilkington, Saint-Gobain, Bethlehem Steel and many others have been setting the pace for the invention and development of new materials and enhancements of existing materials for industry. The primary vehicle for achieving this sustained dominance has been the corporate research laboratory (Jacob 1997;Latour and Woolgar 1986;Latour 1987). Architecture has seen a great deal of transfer of materials and techniques from an assortment of industries bolstered by the fruits of this research and development.

Beginning with the rise of the scientific method, an interesting and influential process began to overtake traditional methods for making incremental improvements in architectural technologies and capturing these innovations within the knowledge base of the architect. The laboratory, rather than the construction site, began serving as the primary location for the development of innovative material formulations for buildings. Increasingly through the latter half of the 19th century and into the 20th, materials conceived of at a distance from the construction site, and in the research lab, and for applications not related to architecture were being redirected toward building components. The construction industry has always been too large for corporations to ignore. This began the long slide that has led to a general disassociation between the designers of buildings and the invention of materials for buildings. During the early 20th century, the research laboratory has clearly become the primary location of this kind of innovation.

The modern research laboratory began its history as a corporate sponsored facility born of the activities of individual inventors and entrepreneurs. Many of them were the founders of research-active companies. The first research laboratories were established in Germany during the last half of the 19th century to serve synthetic dye manufacturers. England and the United States were to follow closely behind with a number of labs established by the first quarter of the 20th century. Thomas Alva Edison's workshops at Menlo Park (established 1876) and West Orange, New Jersey (established 1887), were the precursors to the modern industrial research laboratory and would come to spawn the General Electric Corporation. In 1901 General Electric founded its research laboratory and within the next 12 years Kodak,

Dupont, the Bell System and others followed suit (Cowan 1997). By 1930, 526 American companies had established research facilities. IBM's first research lab was established in 1945. By the early 1980s, 11,000 American companies supported laboratory facilities (Basalla 1988;Hughes 1989;Holton 1996).

These early labs established the precedent for diversification of products and an initiation of corporate sponsored invention. They also initiated an era in which patent law became a prime insulator from competition. The argument that these facilities accomplished as much in terms of sheltering commercial rights as catalyzing original research is a strong position bolstered by significant research. However, these labs did continue to accelerate changes in the physical components of buildings. In particular, advances in metals, ceramics (including glass) and synthetic polymers have caused a virtual revolution in the nature of architectural assemblies over the past 75 years (Hughes 1989;Jacob 1997). These changes are noteworthy not only for the physical changes they have brought to contemporary architectural systems but also for the altered processes of production that are necessary in their application to buildings (Strike 1991;Robbin 1996;Beukers 1998;Sebestyen 1998).

The Fruits of their Labors

For example, aluminum was the first metal to be introduced into buildings since the late ancient period and it has now become second only to steel. In 1935, Le Corbusier wrote "The airplane is the symbol of the new age… The aluminum framework of an airplane – search for economy of material, for lightness, always the fundamental, the essential law of nature." (LeCorbusier 1935). Aluminum is now produced in dozens of alloys and many extruded and cast forms. A recent invention is the production of a foamed aluminum (stabilized aluminum foam, SAF) for use in lightweight structural surfaces (Ashby et al. 2000). Between 1910 and 1915 stainless steels were produced through the combination of iron and chromium. The use of stainless steels has significantly improved the durability of exterior envelope components and superstructures (Abbott 1996;Markaki et al. 2002;Markaki and Clyne 2003a,b). Entire facade assemblies have been made of stainless steel sheet; the Petronas Towers of Kuala Lumpur being one recent example, see Section 3.1.

Ceramics have been much improved in the last 100 years as well. These materials, classified into three groups – glasses, clay-based materials and cementitious mixtures – have existed for the duration of the making of building components. Most of the materials contained within the ceramics grouping contain silica (SiO_2). Portland cement, arrived at through a series of individual experiments by Smeaton, Parker, Frost, Aspdin and Johnson, was patented in England by Joseph Aspdin in 1794, and used extensively in construction beginning in the early 20th century (Moavenzadeh 1990). Reinforced concrete was invented in 1849 by Joseph Monier, who received a patent in 1867. It is important to note that Monier, a gardener by trade, was extremely important in continually inventing further applications and enhancements of reinforced concrete. Concrete now accounts for roughly 75 percent (by weight) of all construction materials used worldwide annually.

Recent improvements in concrete have been largely due to the range of additives, including synthetic polymers, silica fume and other pozzolans that have enhanced properties such as strength and ductility, decreased curing periods, decreased weight, improved durability and ease of workability (Sivakumar 2002;JNMR 1998). Fibrous reinforcing and alternative rebar materials, both internal to the matrix and applied to the surface of the cured concrete, have also improved its performance (Magee and Schnell 2002;Yoshino 1990). In addition, cellular concrete has become a commonly used material in both block and panel forms. These new, higher strength and more durable concrete formulations are fueling a renaissance of cast architectural and civil forms (Bentur 2002). Glass has been improved in diverse ways, from better production techniques to the introduction of various methods for strengthening the pane itself to developing various forms of the material such as fibers, silica foams and ultra-thin sheets. Glass coatings made of thin metallic films have dramatically increased the thermal performance of insulated glass assemblies and high-performance windows and large-scale glass walls are now routine, see Section 3.3.

Synthetic polymers represent the clearest example of discoveries born of the laboratory, far from the messy chaos of the construction site. In 1934, Wallace Carothers, director of research at Dupont, invented nylon 66. Since then polymer science has produced a virtual mountain of synthetics polymers. Silicones and neoprenes, urethanes and EPDM, ETFE and many other synthetic polymers are used extensively in contemporary architectural assemblies. Polymer and engineered wood composites have been a subset of this field of research (Keller 2003). Structural insulated panels, particle boards, polymer lumber and other types of cellulose reinforced materials have become a significant market of building products, see Section 3.2.

These and many other examples illustrate the effect that the research laboratory has had on the physical components through which contemporary architecture is made (Bakis et al. 2002;Bentur 2002;Fridley 2002;Hillig 1976;Jacob 1997;Kranzberg and Stanley 1988). All of these material classes have been substantially altered through the work of a corporate research lab, sometimes in collaboration with an academic group (Intrachooto 2002). As these materials are developed and placed in the marketplace they inevitably change the relationship between the contemporary designer and the building itself. "While the language of architecture and the nature of construction can never coincide, neither can they go their separate ways" (Ford 1996). The plurality of architectural practice allows for a proliferation of forms and approaches to a point in which classification may seem impossible if not extremely difficult. The immense range between an architecture that acts as the simple resultant of technological forces and architectural form that productively captures innovation from other industries explains the diversity in building to be seen today.

Technology Flows and Design

Changes occur because consequential forces evolve or entirely new factors arise. These new issues may be obstacles, or new requirements, enabling techniques and technologies, improved methods, wholly novel tools and newly discovered or invented materials (Williams 2000). In certain industries tracing cause and effect from new developments is an easy task. Not so with architecture.

The making of buildings is unkempt, difficult, and costly. It is a messy and fragmentary business involving huge resources and an array of technical specialties. The existence of "intermediate stages and intermediaries" clearly separates it from the production of art with its enduring legacy of the intellectual at its center (Hill 2003). The relationship between prevalent architectural form and the materials used in construction is a matter of innumerable negotiations, both knowable and unknowable, between those in charge of the alternatives and possibilities for production, the economic requirements of the project and the analysis of the engineer-specialist. It is also, in no small measure, dependent on the ephemeral preferences of the immediate client and society at large. Local acceptance of certain architectural form is also another set of negotiations that undoubtedly affect the design. It is the habit of the architect to bemoan these negotiations and yet it can be argued that these particular transactions form the center of the creative impulse. All of these negotiations occur at all stages of the project and involve the numerous "intermediaries" engaged in the building's production. The link between materials and form is, therefore, decentralized and the object of fierce contention - the result of a fluctuating collection of often competing forces.

Naturally, though, it is undeniable that a link exists between new materials and changing building form, just as it does with any human artifact (Basalla 1988). The nature of this link is not simple. Establishing unassailable schema of cause and effect is a problematic effort, steeped as it is in the difficulties of historical analysis (Kuhn 1962). But, this kind of link may not be necessary. It is certainly not the goal here. Revealing the links that exist between several interested groups, without need for definitive causal flows, reveals the primary types of transactions that shape both material and form. This kind of analysis can generate renewed efforts and novel methods for further development and better collaboration between these groups. The first step involves establishing that technical developments do affect building form, sometimes in dramatic ways (Turner 1986;LeCorbusier 1927). The potential in new materials cannot be denied in light of the inventions in structural form that come as direct results of the development of new structural materials (Von Meiss 2000;Pevsner 1968;Peters 1996, 2003). Constructing tall buildings, for example 30, 50 even 80 floors tall, is not only inconceivable but physically impossible without high strength steel and concrete (Elliot 1992). The stochastic failure mode of ceramic materials (for example, fired clays, brick, stone) is a very real problem when reaching the higher levels of internal material stress necessary for tall buildings (Moavenzadeh 1990). Therefore, masonry materials are generally used in situations

Figure 1.6

A mountain-top production facility for the manufacture of a range of fiberglass products for buildings. As a result of the enormous costs of building, maintaining and tooling such facilities, major corporations are forced to seek out markets that closely align with the production capabilities already in place. This inherent conservatism of production places very high thresholds for proving the economic opportunities for real innovation in building materials.

of very low internal stress levels for buildings of relatively limited heights (Heyman 1995). The notion of making such a building of masonry - while not, strictly speaking, impossible - is certainly dubious. Therefore the modern tall building has required the development of high strength steel alloys. Many other similar examples can be made. The forms of suspension bridges, thin shells, even reinforced ceramic tile vaults, are all fundamentally influenced by material properties and system behavior.

Even in our technically advanced age, the task of architecture remains firmly vested in a profoundly humane aspiration. Its medium for doing so has also not changed; ultimately it is a material medium. LeCorbusier's statement that "The business of Architecture is to establish emotional relationships by means of raw materials" is as true now as it has ever been (LeCorbusier 1935). But what is the range of design impulse when new raw materials become available?

With the development of the specialization of the material scientist out of the broadening scope of metallurgy came the necessary exclusion of nonscientists from the actual development of new materials. Architects were no exception. This is a change brought about by greater knowledge, and therefore more intensive specialization, since the 19th century. It is not, however, the beginning of the distancing of the architect from the materials of architecture. As previously noted, that process started during the renaissance and the first few intellectual architects of the Italian Renaissance (Hill 2003). When the diversity of materials was much more restricted to the basic metals, earthen, clay-based ceramics and other natural materials, glass, and primitive concrete, namely at the end of the 19th century, the disciplinary distance between architectural design and construction and materials science was rather small in comparison.

Today, the sheer proliferation of materials, theory and analytical methods has thankfully exploded the subject of materials science and added to the depth of specialization of that field. The insulation between it and the rest of the world is intense, as it is with so many of the scientific disciplines of the 20th century (Kuhn 1962;Basalla 1988). However, the depth of learning has also irreversibly set materials science at a very great distance from the concerns of architectural design and building construction. So, there is a very real disjuncture between the expertise of architects and that of materials scientists (Allen 2004). Material innovation, application, improvement and diversification, while occurring as an oscillation between the development of materials and the design of buildings, does not encounter a smooth transition between the needs of architectural assemblies and the interests or methods of materials scientists. This is, of course as it should be. Each discipline works within its own paradigms. However, this disjuncture promotes an often incomplete and mistranslated set of instructions between the two.

However, the situation does not suggest a declining design influence in the use of new materials in contemporary architecture. The architect continues to be the specialist that is needed to address the very particular issues of performance and integration between the various building systems of contemporary architecture. The material scientist, or any other nonarchitect, cannot make this kind of assessment. This may be a gap in the collaborative stream between specialists and architects, but it is a potentially fruitful separation (NMAB 2000;Restany 1997;Hartoonian 1986). In fact, in any disjuncture, there is a real opportunity for leaps of design speculation (Hurley 1982;Zambonini 1988). This is an integral part of the architectural design moment. This discontinuity offers opportunities because it allows the architect to leap into speculation without the knowledge of potential obstacles, and it also allows the materials scientist to propose wholly new approaches in seeking out applications for new materials without being discouraged by the idiosyncrasies of the processes of construction or the behavior of architectural systems. The relationship clearly remains an uneasy, but sometimes productive, discontinuity.

Time and Materials

The US economy produces millions of tons of industrial materials and, almost as rapidly, it consumes and discards them. A recent study of the country's materials use estimated that nearly 2.5 billion metric tons of nonfuel materials moved through the economy in 1990. Over 70 percent of these materials were used in construction.

Kenneth Geiser, 2001

Creative (Re)construction

Figure 2.1

Debris field remaining after the explosive demolition of the Seattle Kingdome brought down in a carefully planned series of detonations over the brief period of 16.8 seconds. The 4,728 pounds of explosives generated enough energy to mimic an earthquake of magnitude 2.3.

Seattle Kingdome, Seattle, WA (1976).
Skilling Helle Christiansen Robertson, Structural Engineers.

On March 26, 2000 in the city of Seattle in the United States, a subcontractor hired by Turner Construction Company set off a series of explosions that resulted in one of the largest coordinated events of progressive structural collapse ever engineered and realized. The assembled crowd watched in awe as the gigantic concrete frame and thin shell buckled under the assault. As the gray cloud of dust settled, a circular pile of debris only 23 feet high remained.

The demolition experts hired to implant and detonate 5,905 explosive charges in the superstructure of the Kingdome had been engineering the event for more than 18 months, taking into account issues as diverse as the resulting terrestrial vibrations from 25,000 tons of concrete roof falling to the ground, possible damaging effects on surrounding structures and infrastructure, the subsequent complex series of tasks necessary for removing the collapsed structure and the political and public relations ramifications of destroying one of the largest buildings in the city. At the end of that spring day the deed was successfully done and work began on the next phase in the recycling and removal of 125,000

31

Figure 2.2

A demolition site. The existing building stock is in a constant state of material flux - however, the growth of modern cities has placed ever greater stocks of materials into a semi-permanent situation.

tons of concrete debris left by the demolition. The site was to be quickly prepared for the construction of a new stadium (Liss 2000). The last stage in the stadium's life was now over as a result of its creative destruction.

When the Kingdome was completed in 1976, it became the latest in a distinguished and long line of spectacular concrete domes beginning with the Roman Pantheon. In fact, the Kingdome and the Pantheon were structural cousins, each having had the distinction of being the largest concrete dome structure of its time. The Pantheon spans 142 feet in a thick concrete dome - the Kingdome had achieved a clear span of 661 feet using a combination of radial rib beams and transversely spanning thin shells of only 5 inches in thickness.

The structural engineers of the Kingdome, Skilling Helle Christiansen Robertson (the same engineers of the ill-fated World Trade Center in New York City), had delivered a building design that would eventually cost $67 million to construct. Once completed, the stadium was used extensively - hosting 3,361 events and 73,130,463 spectators in total - until in 1994, four ceiling tiles fell from the underside of the concrete roof, precipitating the closing of the stadium for, what was to become, a four month and $70 million dollar repair.

The Pantheon still stands in Rome, built between 118 and 125AD; it is now 1,879 years old.

Figure 2.3

Material recovery from construction is now commonplace and contributes significant amounts of metals to the greater industrial economy. This building had been designed for easy reclamation of structural steel members by minimizing welding.

The Kingdome was demolished in its 24th year of operation and during its service life of two dozen years had incurred normal maintenance costs plus the $70 million repair expenditure in its 18th year - only 6 years before its purposeful destruction. While the cost of this short service life can be calculated in monetary terms, the larger *complete* cost of the building including the total environmental costs, associated material resources, energy in construction and operation, dissipation of useful materials and other "unaccounted"-for expenditures are almost inestimable.

The replacement structure, completed in 2001 and named the Seahawks Stadium, cost the state of Washington and the city of Seattle $430 million dollars, including cost overruns. This level of expenditure is controversial for the substantial public funds committed, $300 million in taxes and other public funding mechanisms (in addition to substantial private monies). But, as part of a recommitment to a civic sports franchise, and more generally to urban economic development, the creative reconstruction of the stadium played a pivotal role.

Originally, the Kingdome had been designed with an anticipated lifetime of 75 years, possibly as long as 120 years with good maintenance. While it served its basic purpose well, architectural and functional deficiencies were articulated soon after its opening. Of course, as with any building, its lifetime could have been extended indefinitely given the appropriate level of material and financial investment. But, it was considered a "mean" space, partly due to the overwhelming amount of unfinished concrete and the tight spaces of its circulation. It was also faulted for the paucity of its amenities and a general feeling of stingy architectural design. It must also be noted that the economics of American team sports were rapidly changing during the 1980s and 1990s and the easy movement of lucrative teams from one city to another was becoming routine. Many American cities that could claim a professional sports team were facing the prospect of losing it to another city unless substantial commitments were made. This often included the construction of a new stadium.

In fact, my previous use of the phrases *creative destruction* and *creative reconstruction* were carefully chosen to invoke the basis for the modern transformation of our cities - the workings of capitalism. Creative destruction - the process that defines the "essential fact about capitalism" (Schumpeter 1950) - is a primary motivator in the assessment of obsolescence for all manner of capitalism's products. Continually cycling through the economy new, and ostensibly better, products requires discarding the old artifacts of production and recalibrating modes of consumption. This incessant throughput establishes one of the principal rhythms of the business cycle - product-oriented introductions driving ever-increasing consumption patterns. Maintaining this heady flow of materials requires technology and production advances as well as generally accepted socioeconomic ideologies primed to legitimize consumption at the very high levels that citizens of the developed world are now accustomed to.

The driver of creative destruction - essentially, *in with the new and out with the old* - has had a major influence on our assessment of the worth of buildings in society today. The discussion of obsolescence (see "Obsolescence as the Anti-permanence" below) will explore the relationship between self-consciously constructed notions of obsolescence and the actual lifetimes of buildings. The case study of the Kingdome offers one example of the recalibration that we have undergone in assessing the useful lifetime of our buildings and our willingness to dip into material resources to better satisfy our present needs. Placing the history of the notion of obsolescence adjacent to the resource pressures that our societies are facing, several questions arise.

How is it that we have reached so prolific a level of material consumption that we so boldly discard even the largest of our buildings? What are the environmental ramifications, but also - and just as importantly - what are the design and construction opportunities? Has engaging in a cycle of willful obsolescence and the resulting intensified material consumption made even our buildings easily dispensable and vulnerable to financial bottom lines and ideologies of the superiority of all things new?

One of the best ways in which to engage these questions involves invoking some of the pioneering work of the relatively new science of industrial ecology. Essentially a science of flux, this discipline has assumed the enormous task of accounting for material and energy flows at all physical and temporal scales, for all societal activities industrial and otherwise (Ayres 1994;Allenby 1999;Graedel and Allenby 2003). The purpose of the kinds of analyses that result is a better understanding - more accurate and current - of the ways in which we, as a species, interact with the physical world (Kibert 1999b, 2003). Using the analogy of ecological systems places the emphasis, and the research mandate, on examining the relationships that exist and those emerging between human activities and the environment. In addition, industrial ecology - by implication, but sometimes remaining unstated - endeavors to use this knowledge in proposing alternative relationships that improve our material and energy resource use while minimizing deleterious impacts. Later in this chapter, various elements of industrial ecology - both in terms of technological and design proposals - will be used to clarify relationships between the lifetime service of buildings and their use of materials.

In transferring certain concepts and tools from industrial ecology to architectural design and construction it is critical to embrace the broad coverage of topics, and sometimes obsessions, that architectural design has come to invoke as part of its discourse. Acknowledging the fact that theories of contemporary design do not recoil from selectively mining the intellectual content of disciplines as diverse as post-structural philosophy, literary criticism, conceptual art, genetics, biomechanics, material science and many other - probably most other - highly intellectual pursuits is the first step in approaching the contemporary design context in a positive way. This is relevant to our effort to transfer knowledge and tools from industrial ecology in very specific ways. In particular, this chapter focuses on two aspects that are exclusive to material flows in construction; the long and uncertain *actual* lives of buildings and the dominance of intangible, ephemeral and non-physical forces in the determination of building obsolescence.

(Re)merging Time and Space

Architects have clearly been neither masters nor servants of the material flows of their time. Designers and builders from ancient antiquity to the present have assumed the roles of both innovators and simple consumers of the material flux that flowed through their societies and settled into their buildings. Materials use in most buildings - artifacts of large volumes wed to specific sites - have always been determined by local availability, current practice and experience, cost and construction expediency, and to a lesser extent, design and aesthetic preferences. Buildings have always benefited from the opportunism of resource exploitation whether or not architects or designers were directly involved. For example, one need only travel to any one of dozens of European cities to find evidence of the reuse of materials from dismantled Roman buildings. For example, the Catholic Church of Cordoba, situated as it is in the middle of a Moorish mosque, reuses Roman masonry as part of the mosque that serves as a portico for the Christian church.

In broader terms of both temporal events and architectural type, the realities of time have been inextricably linked to the exigencies of using materials in buildings. For example, many people today attend to the urgent needs of materials for basic shelter on a regular basis. That is, for many "vernacular" or "indigenous" material systems, service lives are relatively short and the consideration of lifetime predictions for both assemblies and the building as a whole is intimately linked to the material reality of the architecture itself, and sometimes to a matter of survival. For example, many earthen material systems, such as pisé and sun-dried bricks covered in a mud finishing layer, are dependent on seasonal and annual cycles and are interwoven with the material durability and the investment necessary to keep the building viable. This situation can become tragic when the effort involved can become a critical opportunity cost preventing communities and individuals from using scarce resources for improving other aspects of their lives. In addition, these kinds of buildings are known to contribute to the compromised health and welfare of its occupants from collapse during earthquakes and disease from insufficient ventilation. It has been estimated that at least 1 billion people live in earthen structures today. The buildings are seasonally maintained and adjusted by their occupants. Design lifetimes are short term and closely monitored.

On the other hand, many architects designing buildings for the developed world default their lifetime service expectations to a general design life of 50 years or so. However, it is clear that there is considerable uncertainty regarding a building's actual lifetime and the forces that the building will encounter during its service life. It is also clear that this uncertainty contributes to the flux of materials used in construction of all kinds including renovation, adaptive reuse, deconstruction, new build and every other kind of building effort. This situation is curious, given the inevitably temporal nature of any material use and the seeming complexity of predicting *anything* in 50 years. That is, it is impossible to understand the use of materials in any human activity without gauging the various temporal scales of application to the artifacts of that activity (Lynch 2001;Daniels 2002). It is also impossible to assess the opportunity costs of committing large-scale volumes of materials to building projects without this same examination of the actual forces that compel change over time.

In the influential book *The Tower and the Bridge*, Professor David Billington makes a strong case for the moral obligation of a structural and building art consisting in equal measure of inventive form and technical innovation and including economic sobriety (Billington 1985). Mobilizing huge material and economic resources, the civil engineer invents the structural form of a society's "infrastructure". Appropriate form and responsible structural practice do not solely arise from the tenants of theory but are steadfastly rooted in the physical, economic and social opportunities and constraints. The amount of material used, the overall cost, the placement of that material to achieve a safe and reliable structural span and the opportunity cost of the use of those same resources defines the depth with which the engineer (and designer) engages with the material world. Professor Billington reminds us that the substantial resources devoted to these kinds of projects are inescapably diverted away from other endeavors, and so should be considered in light of these lost opportunities.

Yet, does society qualify its considerations of the use of vast amounts of material in such a rational way? It seems that building to economic ends, using the art and science of modern engineering, is only the best first step. The duration of the actual service lives of these structures and buildings, and therefore a primary component of the "final" measure of their worth to our society, is substantially determined by a plethora of unruly and intangible forces arising from independent actors. A building's lifetime is often determined in arenas not directly related to the design of the buildings themselves; real estate and financial markets, urban planning and zoning code agencies, corporate and governmental owners and building managers. As a result, the actual service life of a building is not only independent of its design life but quite removed from it. There is very little in the process of building design today that addresses the uncertainty of its likely service life. Yet, the overall flux of material into and out of construction is inextricably linked to the amount of time materials are enlisted in the physical systems and assemblies of buildings. It hasn't always been quite like this.

For example, with the widespread industrialization of architectural components and the standardization of primary structural materials in the developed world, like steel and concrete, a broad swath of buildings built today possess generally higher durabilities than in the past. This is because buildings built in these economies do not use high maintenance, low performance materials like earth and natural fibers. Therefore, seasonal maintenance and short-term durability - and therefore regular material inputs - have become a thing of the past. Today, no longer do homeowners need to patch their thatch roofs every spring because material alternatives (asphalt tiles, standing seam metal etc.) have come to completely replace that system (and substantially improve lifetime durability).

Curiously then, the actual lifetime profiles of contemporary buildings are ruled less by material and component durability - a dominant factor in the past and the "traditional" measure of service life - than by a series of intangible forces including aesthetic discrimination, user preferences, market-related fluctuations and evolving social norms for work and living (Brand 1994). These *constructs of value* have evolved substantially, and often fitfully, over time. A useful survey of the changes between these various factors can be accomplished by considering a concept mentioned briefly above; *obsolescence*. Obsolescence is a concept that has dramatically influenced the making of new buildings and the destruction of existing building stock in the name of aesthetics, planning efficiency, real estate value and the ideals of modernity.

It is not possible to render a comprehensive history of the array of variants of the idea and use of obsolescence in architecture. However, it is useful to discuss certain aspects in the evolution of this notion that have directly affected the determination of the end-of-life for buildings, and even large portions of cities.

Figure 2.4

A section of the Chicago Loop at twilight. In 1930, the National Association of Building Owners and Managers estimated that much of the Loop district in Chicago had been demolished and rebuilt twice since the Great Fire of 1870. Many of the buildings that were taken down were substantially less than 50 years old and quite large. Several were the earliest skyscapers built in the United States (Abramson 2005;BNABOM 1930).

Obsolescence as the Anti-permanence

The end of life of any human artifact is popularly considered to be when it reaches a state of substantial uselessness. But reaching a consensus on the definition of utility can be difficult. Real estate economics places the end of utility as generally that point in time when a property no longer commands rent at a level commensurate with comparable properties in the immediate area. But because the rent potential for buildings and land itself can be considered separately, one can reasonably distinguish two types of rent (Marx 1984;Houghton 1993;Bryson 1997). The first type of rent is "a function of the advantages offered by the site of a property, and which do not depend on any action by the owner" (Lamarche 1976). A building situated in one location will draw a very different rent if located in a very different location in that same city. We can call this type of rent location-dependent rent (LDR). The second type is dependent on the state of the building itself and is independent of the location. Therefore a new, up-to-date building will draw the highest rent for its location. Obviously, once a building is constructed the potential to draw the highest rent diminishes with the passage of time. This type of rent is called building-dependent rent (BDR).

Figure 2.5

Anthropomorphic analogies have been applied to cities for the sake of creating a discourse of building "health" that contributed to the general formulation of building obsolescence. Creating cities that could "breathe" and streets that eliminated the urban disease of blight led to violent excisions of buildings and resulted in the demolition and reconstruction of entire neighborhoods.

Pine Street, New York City, NY (2005).

Each one of these types of rent, LDR and BDR, is related to similarly defined types of obsolescence. LDR is influenced by the state of the location within its context. In urban contexts, a location may suffer through radical changes including the deterioration of its infrastructure, increases in crime, building abandonment due to suburban flight and other forces that result in a lowering of the level of rents that can be achieved at that location and the immediate vicinity. This *locational obsolescence* is independent of the state of the building itself.

Similarly, BDRs are highly influenced by the state of the building; the performance of its various systems, the aesthetic state of its facades, interior finishes etc. (and not the state of the location). The aging of these systems will contribute to *building obsolescence*.

However, embedded within these ideas of building and locational obsolescence are various qualitative factors that contribute to the overall assessment of both the state of the location and the separate state of the building. When we delve deeper into the useful service of a building there is no question that the utility of architecture is a concept that wanders far and wide beyond the strict boundaries of function. With even a simple notion of architecture, it is clear that a service is provided by simply providing a measure of delight (compounding L. Kahn's terms discussed in the Prologue). Therefore, a loss of utility cannot always be directly linked to prescribed assessments of value especially when those values include incommensurable elements of the experience and use of buildings by people.

For example, objects hold sentimental value for all of us even after their useful lives have finished. A broken down car, old furniture, keepsakes, all speak to a complex relationship that humans retain to physical objects of all scales. In fact, there is an aspect to historical preservation that speaks to the value of buildings, not as functional architecture but as unique historical artifacts with a value that extends well beyond any reasonable use of their spatial volumes or building systems. Most architects would agree that these values are important and have a place in our assessment of the investment society should devote to these less-than-useful architectural artifacts. Nevertheless, there have been periods when notions of the utility of things has been consciously constructed by interest groups intent on pursuing ideologies of change. These ideologies often had their basis in the opportunistic economic rewards of real estate development.

In recent work, Daniel M. Abramson of the Department of Art and Art History at Tufts University has begun to shed light on the convoluted history of building utility and obsolescence and the relationship to a burgeoning capitalism of land development (Abramson 2005). Abramson notes that, as part of an evolution of modern capitalism generally, the United States (and subsequently most developed western economies) have in the past adopted a diverse collection of criteria for the determination of end-of-life and loss of utility for buildings, notably commercial buildings and then many other objects of industry (automobiles, household appliances, clothing etc.). Certainly diverse and originating from a variety of sources, these criteria have been amazingly consistent in one respect; for the most part, the central determination of utility was constructed from external "causes outside the physical condition of the building itself" (Roberts 1930;Abramson 2005).

This is not surprising given the context - social, economic and cultural - in which buildings operate. Their physical states are merely one small aspect of their larger service to society. Obvious examples come to mind, such as the "utility" of the Empire State Building in New York City as well as other landmark buildings like the John Hancock in both Boston and Chicago, the Transamerica Tower in San Francisco, the Sears Tower in Chicago. Aside from its local service to its tenants, the Empire State is a symbol (both collectively and on an individual level) of the city and its residents. In other words, the economic utility of the building can be affected by but not fully defined by the physical state of its systems because its service can be considered very broadly and very differently depending on your viewpoint (and particular stake).

Similarly, a building in very good working order may be deemed not to be serving its main purpose (generally, the purpose being reduced to revenue generation). Its aesthetics may be detrimental to attracting new rental tenants or its location may have become less than attractive for the type of tenants necessary for a profitable return on investment. Its materials and systems may possess substantial service life remaining while the determination of a complete loss of utility may not be out of the question. In this circumstance, one option available to the owners is the removal of the building; its physical demolition and replacement.

Therefore, if functional utility and the overall assessment of value can be so dramatically influenced by a constructed notion like obsolescence, and that notion may change over time, how much do we really understand about the character of building lifetimes and especially the condition of the end-of-life? Furthermore then, how much do we really understand the mechanisms that control the enormous material consumption of construction based as it is on shifting notions of utility? The Kingdome is only one example, albeit dramatic, of the uncertainties engendered and the material costs borne in realizing a large physical object, having it become part of the functioning building stock of a contemporary American city and meeting a surprising and unpredictable early demise. Its demolition and replacement is evidence of the multifaceted and multifarious elements that contribute to a working definition of utility.

Closely related to utility and a prime determinant of end-of-life conditions has been the recurring notion of obsolescence - the condition of passing out of use and becoming archaic and readily replaced by a more effective or sophisticated thing. Obsolescence has maintained a central position in our assessment of architectural function throughout the 20th century. The idea of obsolescence has changed in various ways; through an evolution of popular usage and through organized initiatives, as a point of advocacy for change and in the service of generating consumption momentum. The notion has remained stubbornly resilient and continues to represent an enduring set of concepts about the role of architecture in society.

As a historically mutating concept, obsolescence can be considered in terms of the various discourses that were instrumental in formulating the notion and changing it. Abramson has defined three separate "discourses" during the period of time from roughly the 1910s until present day; the Financial Discourse, the Urban Discourse and the Consumer Discourse. Each had its purpose and its assembled groups of stakeholders and proponents (Abramson 2005).

The *Financial Discourse* had its origins in the growing sophistication of early 20th century real estate development in the central business cores of Chicago and New York. In need of methods for evaluating the potential for return on investment on property and in search of explanations regarding the increasingly common phenomenon of the demolition of relatively new (and very large) buildings in these cities, several attempts were made to define and closely examine the "financial decay" of buildings (Bolton 1911). At the time, both cities were witnessing the unfamiliar and troubling spectacle of the dismantling of very large and relatively new buildings and their replacement with equally large buildings. There is good documentation showing that many, if not a vast majority of these buildings were in very good states - with little or no problematic deterioration of their building systems before demolition (Abramson 2005;Roberts 1930;Gray 2005). Buildings in the Loop of Chicago, including the cavernous Marshall Field Wholesale Store (architect: H.H. Richardson) declared obsolete after only ten years and demolished in its 44th year, the 41 year old Tacoma Building (a skyscraper designed by Holabird & Roche) completely demolished and replaced by a similar tall building, the Singer Building of New York City also 41 when demolished in 1967, and many other buildings dating to the early 20th century are examples of what has been characterized as "the useful or economic existence of all classes of buildings, in the rapid march of modern conditions, is constantly shortening" (Bolton 1911). Even at this early time of modern development in America's fastest growing cities, developers and others were remarking on the extreme shortness of life of many of the largest buildings in urban centers. Several researchers at the time stated that building lifetimes were likely to remain at an average of between 30 and 40 years (Burton 1919;Klein 1922;Bryson 1997).

The Financial Discourse of obsolescence has been preoccupied with developing models that explain the vast flux of buildings (and associated materials of construction). However, despite the tabulation of actuarial tables for building lifetimes and the linkages between these predictors of life expectancy and the evolving tax code of the United States, the seemingly precise analytical tools produced over the decades belie our inability to get very close to a holistic understanding of the nature of building lifetimes.

Lately it has been remarked that the speed of obsolescence is now tightly related to the global economy; a more restless and frenetic set of financial and social relations (Bryson 1997). Speculation has raised the spectre of a permanent pressure on buildings to respond faster and more dramatically to the forces leavened on their ability to deliver a level of service demanded by this global context.

While the tools of the Financial Discourse were intent on an analytical explanation of unexpected demolition and rebuilding, the Urban Discourse has been responsible for some of the most egregious planning and urban design projects in the US - often placed under the sweetening moniker of "urban renewal". This discourse has been marked by the adoption of an anthropomorphic metaphor of the city and the building as living, breathing organisms. Blight, the urban diseases of crime, squalor, poverty and racial and ethnic tension were attributed to antiquated and substandard urban form. The solutions of the surgical removal of structures, renewal of neighborhoods and the complete replanning of entire districts of cities were considered to be appropriately bold measures to combat the malaise of the modern city. Obsolescence of urban form meant that physical solutions could be brought to bear as social and economic "cures". As Abramson notes, the Financial and Urban Discourses are closely related to each other both in their notions of the effects of the loss of utility and their application to architectural and urban form. The Consumer Discourse extends beyond architectural form to encompass essentially the whole of modern consumption today.

Obsolescence, as a determinant of utility, heralds both the cessation of use for that artifact and the commencement of use for something new. The pair essentially defines the most direct route to the dilemma of obsolescence. This dilemma is not only an opportunity for but the raison d'être and a primary engine of capitalism. The Consumer Discourse focuses on this particular facet of obsolescence.

During the first third of the 20th century, simultaneous with the modern development of financial tools for real estate speculation, several phrases entered into the vocabulary of corporate business planning and marketing including *progressive obsolescence*, *planned obsolescence* and *creative waste*. During the next several decades various sectors of the American business community were to discover the opportunities afforded by advocating a cyclical consumption pattern based on the certainty of continual improvements in technology, materials and, therefore, products themselves. Yearly issues of automobile models, appliances, electronic products, and many other items infused the consumer market with a strong belief in the advantages (and personal satisfactions) of staying up to date. The benefit to business was obvious - a built-in reason to decouple the end of life of an item from its actual utility and a recoupling of its lifetime to a design and production outside of its physical state. This inevitably resulted in greater overall "churn" of consumer items. Eventually this frenzied consumption settled into what we now have - a market with select hot spots of planned obsolescence (such as automobiles) and a general infusion of the strategy across all product types and industry sectors.

All three of these discourses of obsolescence have had an impact on the character of contemporary building lives and the associated material expenditures of modern buildings. Particularly relevant for our discussion here is the way in which the history of obsolescence has been modulated by a combination of economic and social forces driven by the direct advocacy of business interests and the indirect influence of cultural norms. Both direct interests and indirect norms continue to evolve over time. Therefore, establishing a definitive character of building lives is complicated by the fact that we cannot ignore the significant contributions from unpredictable actors and intangible forces that change.

And finally, as we've seen, obsolescence has been used to assemble related sets of beliefs for the purpose of analyzing diminishing utility and advocating for a kind of anti-permanence position for architecture. Whether invoked by accountants and real estate developers to argue for escalating demolition and construction of buildings and urban districts entirely or used as the foundation of a new paradigm for disposable, adaptable architecture, the various discourses are essentially ideologies for facilitating change - ideologies against permanence.

Of course, these ideologies of accelerated obsolescence contrast sharply with recent advocates for the design and construction of very long lived buildings (Brand 2000). The long-life loose-fit ethic of sustainable design calls for a general lengthening of the durability of buildings and their systems despite good evidence that building lifetimes are not deterministically linked to the physical state of these assemblies. The 150, 500, even 700 year building is not just a passing fancy of the "paper architecture" of intellectuals and nonbuilding academics any longer. Long life has been an accepted position of several of the founders of the latest version of building responsibly. The Cathedral of Los Angeles, recently completed and designed by the Spanish architect Rafael Moneo, uses a concrete technology engineered specifically for a 500 year lifetime with minimal maintenance, Figure 2.18. The financial premium for this effort is considered safe, applied as it is to an institution whose continued existence is believed to be assured, even over several centuries (Roberts 2003; see Section 3.3 Ceramics for a discussion concerning long-life concrete). In fact, long-life design has become a central mantra of the sustainable design movement - based, as it is, on the rationale that extending the useful service life of nonrenewable materials is a fundamental goal of resource savings by reducing the extraction of virgin materials.

However, as we have seen, and will see again later in this chapter, material durability is only one small, and often insignificant, component of the assessment of prolonged value in service. Discussions of utility and obsolescence have tended to dominate and make more complicated the simplistic notions of designated service lifetimes used by most practicing architects leading to new research and design opportunities (Fernandez 2004). Before treating these issues in more detail and relating them to current design strategies, it is useful to review the composition of construction materials used in contemporary buildings in the following sections.

Material Change

During the time between the construction of the Pantheon and the demolition of the Kingdome, the material world has changed quite dramatically. A look around you now will almost certainly confirm this. Glass, aluminum, plastics, plywood, latex paints - all of these materials have been born of modern, and mostly very recent, developments. While it is true that the construction of buildings still includes traditional materials such as brick, stone, concrete and timber, albeit many substantially altered and improved, nontraditional substances such as neoprene and silicone, glass and aramid fiber reinforced composites, polycarbonates and polymer concretes are now routinely used.

This prolific augmentation of the materials available for construction has altered the design and construction of buildings in too many ways to specify here. In fact, it is important to note that these new materials have also fundamentally altered the construction process as much as the completed building. Consider, for example, the prodigious use of construction fabrics used to enclose large structural frames for the purpose of establishing a temporary weather screen and protecting surrounding structures and pedestrians from miscellaneous debris (see Section 3.2 Polymers). The aspects of the change that most concerns us here are the ways in which these materials have brought about significant shifts in the kinds and amounts of materials that flow into and out of the industrial enterprise of contemporary construction.

First, we consider the actual changes in the types of materials available to the architect. Much of this analysis relates specifically to the United States. However, similar sequences of events have also shaped the material reality of architecture in most European nations and portions of both Asia and Latin America. A brief survey of some of the most important material changes follows. Following this survey, a discussion of building lifetimes brings us back to the intention of merging material and temporal considerations.

In tracking the intensity of use of the major materials used in construction, let's begin by considering the 100 years of the 20th century. Figure 2.6 also includes the 150 years before, for the purpose of clarifying the context that was established upon the arrival of 1900. Figure 2.7 illustrates the percentage concentrations of select materials used in construction at two points in time, 1900 and 2000. During the 20th century, the US population grew from a little over 76 million in 1900 to over 286 million in 2000. The home ownership rate increased from 46 percent to over 60 percent in the same period (US Census 2000). During the 200 years between 1800 and 2000 the country experienced a great urbanization transforming a nation of farm owners into one of city dwellers. In 1800, 93.9 percent of the population lived in rural areas. By 1990 that figured had dropped to only 24.8 percent (US Census 2000;Mines 1991). At the beginning of the 20th century overall material consumption per capita in the United States was 2 metric tons. In 1995, despite the increase in the absolute number of people in the US, a corresponding increase in per capita consumption now amounted to 10 metric tons. Therefore, along with the population growth the total consumption of materials in the United States grew by a multiple of almost 19 times in the 20th century. With 5 percent of the population on earth, the United States consumes roughly one third of its materials (during the period from 1970 to 2000). However, between 1970 and 2000, the rate of increase at which the rest of the world consumed materials far outstripped that of the US (1.8 percent versus 1 percent). During this period US consumption increased from 2 to 2.8 billion metric tons, and world consumption from 5.7 to 9.5 billion metric tons, Figure 2.8. Even so, half of the bulk of materials consumed in the US during this past century occurred during the last 25 years (Matos and Wagner 1998;Kesler 1994).

The vast mechanization of many industries was one of the main causes of these increases in consumption and shifts in population. As described in Chapter 1, the shift from an agricultural to an industrial economy and then, in the 1950s and 1960s, to a service economy drove great changes in material consumption. Similar changes were also transforming northern Europe (Adriannse et al. 1997). A cause and consequence of this industrialization was the invention, improvement and commercialization of new materials; steels, better concretes, aluminum and other light metals and synthetic polymers through the concerted efforts of new research engines. These new materials were critical to the development of methods for increased productivity in all industries. They allowed for designs that were lighter, stronger and faster to construct, made of materials that facilitated faster industrial throughputs and tapped into less expensive and more readily available mineral feedstocks.

While changes to the material composition of the economy were dramatic, Figure 2.6 shows that during the 20th century, traditional materials (for our purposes here, those materials that were used in architecture before 1900) not only continued to be used but were used in increasing quantities during the expansion of the American economy, also see Figure 2.7. Between 1900 and 2000 the use of brick increased by a multiple of 5, glass by 10, steel for nonresidential use by 20, and copper by an astounding 2000 (Moavenzadeh 1990;Brown 1998;Matos and Wagner 1998). These "traditional" materials continue to provide the majority of primary materials for buildings today, while the addition of aluminum and polymers in all forms will continue to affect the overall diversity of materials used in buildings.

Therefore, despite anecdotes to the contrary, buildings do contain many of the same materials that were used before 1900. However, important improvements to those materials, changes in their placement within architectural assemblies, overall mass of the material used for particular purposes, and the nature of the craft used during the process of construction have all changed dramatically. In addition, while many traditional materials are used, their proportional contribution to the mass of contemporary building has radically changed. The change in the proportion of various materials used in buildings has resulted in some important trends, including the increased use of nonrenewables and the emerging priority to account for the embodied energy of architectural assemblies.

For example, a consequence of these new materials is a significant increase in the consumption of nonrenewables, see Figure 2.9. In 1900, 42 percent (by weight) of the materials consumed in the US were renewable (all industries). By the end of the century this had decreased to 5 percent (Matos and Wagner 1998). Nonrenewables are those materials that do not regenerate (within one or, at most, two generations) and are extracted from the natural capital of the earth, such as metals, petroleum fuels, minerals, etc.

In order to gain a better understanding of the ways in which contemporary materials have altered construction, three topics are addressed in more detail; dematerialization, substitution and technology transfer (Grübler 1996).

Dematerialization, Substitution and Technology Transfer

These three subjects play important roles in catalyzing and sustaining material changes to the physical constitution and form of architecture. Throughout history, it is clear that all three transformative modes have contributed dramatically to fundamentally changing the process and forever altering the result of the construction of buildings. Since the industrial revolution, the pace of change has quickened. Examples of all three are easily identified. The slender iron columns of Henri Labrouste's Bibiliotheque Ste-Genevieve in Paris of 1843-50 is an ideal example of dematerialization through the substitution of iron for stone as a technology transferred from the new civil projects of towers and bridges.

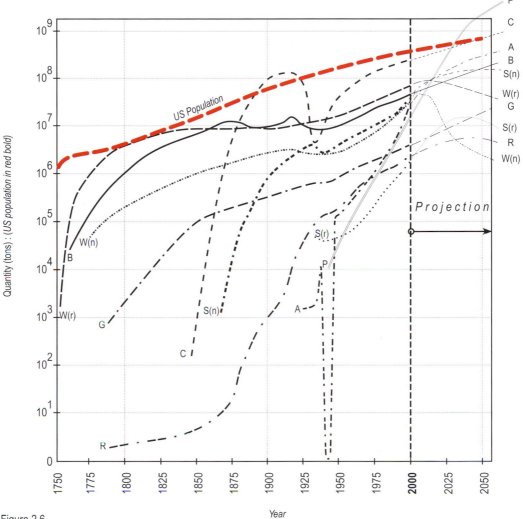

Figure 2.6

US materials use in construction showing general trends of materials use over time. Note that the projected levels for metals (with the exception of aluminum) is predicted to decline over the next several decades due to increasing fuel costs, depletion of ores and the resulting increase in pricing. On the other hand, polymers will continue to substitute for other materials resulting in an increase of its proportional contribution to the architectural construct. Also notice that concrete will continue to be a primary structural material due to its relative affordability, almost comprehensive local and regional availability, ease of application at most scales and versatility.

A:	aluminum	R:	copper
B:	brick	S(r):	steel
C:	concrete	S(n):	steel, nonresidential
G:	glass	W(r):	wood, residential
P:	polymers	W(n):	wood, nonresidential

Sources: Adriannse et al. (1997), Moavenzadeh (1990), Matos and Wagner (1998), Mines (1991), Wagner et al. (2002), Wernick et al. (1996), Smith (2003), various USGS and US Minerals Reports.

In this example, and in many others like it from around the industrial revolution, all three modes are present. This is often the case, as dematerialization will cause a ripple through system design that prompts both material substitution and technology transfer. Similarly, a material substitution and technology transfer may result in dematerialization and technology transfer opportunities as with the introduction of synthetic polymer sealants for building glazing seals (transferred from automotive technologies) by Albert Kahn in the 1930s. This technology transfer allowed for a substantially lightened glass wall and began the process of the complete substitution of sealing materials in buildings from natural rubbers to synthetic polymers.

But in considering these topics, it is necessary to acknowledge an overwhelmingly ideological basis of the respective architectural positions on dematerialization, substitution and technology transfer. That is, architects have been as involved in advocating the "correctness" of their aesthetic preferences by invoking the inevitability of dematerialization and substitution trends, for example, as they have been in analyzing the actual mechanisms behind the broad material changes affecting contemporary architecture. This should not be surprising or alarming. Architects have always been - and have always needed to be - part artist, part technician and part politician. Having large technosocial themes to wrap around building proposals is an inevitable facet of the business of building.

Yet, we can discern certain clear changes in the material reality of our buildings that indicate irreversible dematerialization and substitution apart from the chatter of the designing classes. The substitution of asbestos with other fibrous insulating materials, like e-glass, is an irreversible material substitution (at least for the western developed nations but, alas not many countries of Latin America and Asia where asbestos is still used in a variety of building products). This substitution is the direct result of establishing the mechanism that links the fibers to detrimental health effects.

Similarly, dematerialization has clearly played a significant role in the transformation of the use of stone in buildings from the once massive structural blocks of masonry construction to the plated veneers of nonstructural stone curtainwalls pinned to structural frames (using stone panels of 1⅝ inch thickness and less).

Dematerialization

Dematerialization is a well-documented force in the transformation of material flows in the making of human artifacts. The reasons for this are self-evident; that is, the search to satisfy a need with less material - and therefore reduce one's cost and effort - is a purely rational adjustment based as it is on self-interest. However, one can define dematerialization in many ways; as the reduction in the volume of resource use per economic unit, as the overall reduction of materials used in society, as the reduction of wastes generated per unit of industrial product, etc. (Cleveland and Ruth 1999;Wernick 1996;Herman et al. 1989;Bernardini and

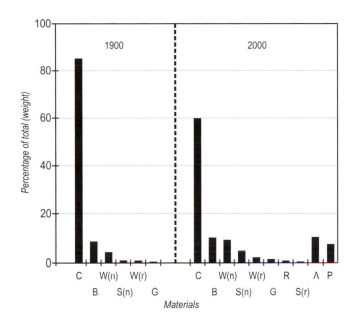

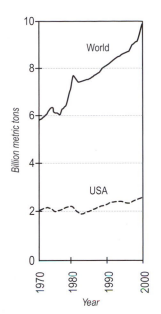

Figure 2.7

Proportion of materials used in construction: 1900, 2000.

Sources: Same as in Figure 2.6, including material legend.

Figure 2.8

Amount of materials consumed in the US and the World.

Sources: same as in Figure 2.6

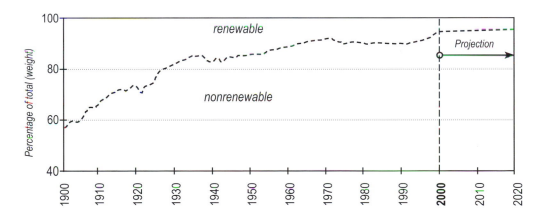

Figure 2.9

Percentage of renewable versus nonrenewable materials consumption in the US. Since the beginning of the 20th century the use of renewable resources in the economy as a whole has decreased from 42 percent to less than 5 percent today (not including fossil fuels - a nonrenewable resource).

Sources: Matos and Wagner (1998).

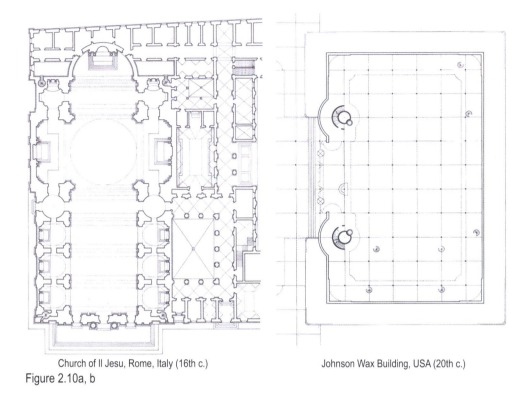

Church of Il Jesu, Rome, Italy (16th c.)   Johnson Wax Building, USA (20th c.)

Figure 2.10a, b

Dramatic dematerialization can be seen in this simple juxtaposition of two buildings at the same scale. The superior performance of steel reinforced concrete of the Johnson Wax Building can be seen to be a technology that dramatically dematerializes the overall material used in the structure.

Galli 1993;Labys and Waddell 1989). The resultant increase in "resource productivity" leads to the idea of resource-light economies, a known trend in the developed industries of today and an aspiration of many resource researchers for the global economy (Goodland and Daly 1993;Sachs 2000;Bartelmus 2002).

Many diverse factors may contribute to an event of dematerialization, but five distinct conditions often play significant roles. First, technical progress may offer a material, process or configuration that significantly reduces material use per unit of service. Second, resource pressures, such as diminishing ore quality, may prompt development of material efficient practices. Third, supply or distribution interruptions may compel a search for efficiencies, as in the short-lived shift to fuel-efficient compact cars during and after the OPEC oil embargo of the 1970s. Fourth, the emergence of security concerns, including the break-out of war, may spur reduction in the consumption of materials that reveal nascent efficiencies in the overall material use of societies that then become accepted norms long after the security problem has passed. And finally, economics is almost always a factor - gaining the same economic return from investing in less material is a powerful compelling force.

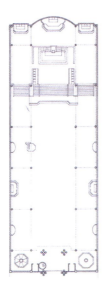 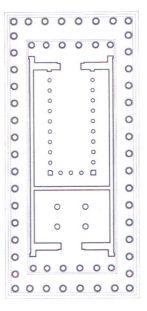

Church of Notre Dame, Raincy, France (20th c.)   Parthenon, Athens, Greece (5th c.)

Figure 2.11a, b

Another comparison showing the intense dematerialization of modern structures (again, both structures are shown at the same scale for correct comparison purposes).

Sources: Plans shown in Figures 2.10 and 2.11 based on drawings published in Sacriste Jr., E. (1959) Building Footprints: a selection of 45 building plans, all drawn at the same scale. School of Design, Raleigh N.C., Vol. 9, No. 1.

Dematerialization has been a steady interest and periodic obsession of a series of architectural schools of thought in the 20th century, from the dematerialized cable nets of Otto Frei to the polygonal structural surfaces and latticeworks of Buckminster Fuller and Kenneth Snelson to the current fascination with polymer films, high-strength fibers, aerogels, translucent structural materials and other "light" materials (Beukers 1998;Mori 2002;Riley 1995;Kahn 2005;Krausse and Lichtenstein 1999;Kronenburg 1997). The idea of lightness has been irresistible to the architect enamored of industrial analogs (the dirigible, airplane, automobile, laptop, cell phone) but less so for those interested in an ecology of construction that reveals the totality of material use. For it can be readily demonstrated that the lightness of the finished artifact is little indication, and often misleading, of the overall material use (consumption and dissipation) that results from the making of that object. For example, a heavy and massive traditional stone building constructed today would require less material overall, than the same building in aluminum and glass. The reason resides in the dramatic differences in the amounts of material that result as wastes (mine tailings, industrial wastes, fuel expenditures in processing and transportation) between the stone and aluminum and glass. Buckminster Fuller was keen to know how much a building weighed. A better question would now be, how much material resides in the building plus how much material was *displaced and energy consumed* in the making of the building (Wernick et al. 1996;Weizsacker 1998)?

A measure of this displacement is the *rucksack*, a quantification of the materials and their volumes that serve in the making of a desired material (Schmidt-Bleek 1993). Sometimes the rucksack is used to pursue and identify material expenditures outside of a region and sometimes it is used to quantify material expenditures that are not accounted for in standard economic accounting. In any case, the rucksack is a measure of the amount of material not represented in the material volume of the artifact itself. The rucksack for a common construction material may be many times in weight that of the material itself. For example, today the production of one unit in weight of aluminum (from virgin ore) requires 300 units in weight of a variety of materials (including mine tailings, fuel consumed etc.).

Using measures such as the rucksack calls into question the responsibility of advocating light forms without a consideration of the "weight" of the processes of extraction, processing, manufacturing, transportation etc. In other words, the *physical accounting* of a unit of service is a better measure of materials use than a standard monetary accounting. More on this point in "Industrial Ecology of Buildings", below.

Substitution

Like dematerialization, substitution has always been a dynamic that has prompted the evolution of architectural form. The substitution of steel for structural masonry materialized the modern architectural typology of the skyscraper. The substitution of concrete for stone, steel for timber, plywood for timber planking, thin wood veneers for lumber, gypsum and paper wall boards for plaster, and countless other examples illustrate the pervasiveness and persistence of the process of substitution. Also, similar to dematerialization, substitution is prompted by a complex assortment of factors of which a handful are almost always present; technical advances, resource pressures, supply or distribution interruptions, security concerns, and economics (Cornish 1987).

Material substitutions are our concern here. Therefore, our working definition is the substantial replacement of one material or material *system* for another material or system such that the performance of the assembly is equaled or improved. While it is possible, and fairly common, for performance to suffer (as in the replacement of exterior stucco with Exterior Insulated Finishing Systems, EIFS) this kind of substitution is not considered legitimate as it decreases the performance of the material system.

Substitution plays a significant role in generating ideas and forms for contemporary architecture while providing alternatives for construction. Polycarbonate replacing glass (Caples and Jefferson 2005), pultrusions replacing aluminum (Strongwell 2005), aerated autoclave concrete (AAC) replacing regular concrete masonry units (Hebel 2005), carbon fiber and epoxy resin reinforcing bar replacing steel rebar in precast concrete (DelMonte 1981;Chen and Chung 1996), and many others incrementally change the material choices and construction practices that characterize contemporary architecture and facilitate the proposal of new forms.

Substitution is rarely perfect - that is, the substitution of one material for another almost always entails a change of some kind in the performance situation (Reynolds 1999;Tilton 1983). For example, the seemingly one-for-one substitution of cold-rolled steel studs for wood studs seems, at first, seamless. The dimensions of the steel studs mimic those of the wood members, the fasteners are the same and the steel acts in precisely the same way to support the remainder of the assembly (usually gypsum board wall panels). However, because of its much higher thermal conductivity (50 W/m.K versus 0.25 W/m.K for pine) it is clear that thermal bridging between the inner and outer layers of an exterior wall increases greatly and detailing that minimizes this thermal flux should be prioritized. In addition, resource management issues should also be considered given the fact that US forests are some of the most closely managed silviculture anywhere in the world (since 1950, US forest cover has actually increased). One should question the benefit of replacing a renewable resource with a nonrenewable material. And while there are good points to be made regarding the increasingly anemic biological diversity of many of our national forests, the state of the renewable resource of wood is a positive attribute of the material.

Substitution and dematerialization are often present simultaneously and sometimes working in concert to produce changes in the material content of buildings. However, neither force acts by default to improve the responsible use of materials in construction. The results of both of these forces may actually worsen the environmental impact, introduce new health hazards, and corrode the social fabric of communities. Yet, an awareness of these forces is the first step along the path of formulating a comprehensive strategy for ecological construction.

Technology Transfer

Finally, the third mode for change of the material content of contemporary buildings is the process of technology transfer. Just as substitution and dematerialization are readily explained in terms of materials and performance, the nature of technology transfer is similarly reducible. In the search for improved methods and materials to accomplish any particular task, *importing* techniques and materials from other disciplines and industries may improve the efficiency with which materials are used while improving (or not compromising) performance. One often hears the caution of "not reinventing the wheel" as one of the basic checks in any creative process. Transferring a technology that successfully satisfies one set of performance requirements in one industrial context into a different context defined by a different, but similar, set of issues may prove a useful strategy. Therefore, technology transfer can be defined as the substantial adoption, with likely modifications, of an existing technology or material for a purpose for which it was not originally intended.

While this process may seem simple, achieving real success through technology transfer is another matter altogether. The application of one technology in a context of new performance requirements often gives rise to all kinds of unintended effects - both positive and negative. A simplistic application that involves little reengineering or redesigning is not often successful. The usual trajectory of such transfers involves the transposition of certain key technological elements into systems that already exist in the new context.

In this sense, successful technology transfer is a rather messy enterprise, involving as it does the grafting of assemblies and systems onto, or in substitution of, unfamiliar constructs. The history of architecture - especially the history of the unbuilt - is full of examples of the desire to import complete systems to be used as architectural constructs. Bucky Fuller again presents us with a good example of this in the failure of his Dymaxion houses to achieve the promise of mass standardization and production so successful in the automobile industry. Given the fact that the profession is intensely attentive to the visual qualities and formal characteristics of constructed things, the irresistible temptation to procure entire assemblies and call it architecture has led many architects far from the fundamental mandate of the making of buildings and down disastrous paths of nonfunctioning curiosities. This is not true substitution as the use of materials with large rucksacks is not true dematerialization.

It will be useful to keep in mind these three kinds of forces as we continue with the discussion of building lifetimes, construction ecologies and the introduction of materials and their properties.

The World's Largest Material Repository

The accumulated mass of construction from all extinct and extant human civilizations constitutes the largest material repository that we currently possess. All of the buildings and dams and bridges and roads, museums and opera houses, tunnels and towers, mosques and cathedrals, supertall buildings and all other architectural and large-scale engineering constructs hold in their possession the vast resources of extracted material wealth of the past.

When one considers the compounding effects of the long life of buildings (and infrastructure) and their large and material intensive bulk, it is not surprising that construction has resulted in sprawling landscapes of assembled mineral resources. The extraordinary efforts of previous societies to mine and process the mineral wealth of the world have left us with a huge bounty of material embodied within the structure, skin and internals of our buildings.

Much of this material is essentially part of the permanent fabric of the building. Not much of the material bulk of buildings is recycled during its lifetime - finishes may be altered, walls moved, but the structure, foundation and much of the exterior skin and interior partitions will likely remain. The great proportion of this material is contained within the protective envelope of the building's skin. Spared the fluctuations of temperature and the other deleterious forces of the weather, much of the bulk of these materials live a pampered, protected life within the stable interior environment of their building's shell.

This material store now forms our cities and highways, our civil infrastructure and residential architecture. A good deal of material flux - material flows devoted to new and existing buildings - contributes to the expansion of this semi-permanent material store. While it is true that nothing lasts forever, many of our cities have begun to solidify a central core, highly valued for its historical and economic values and considered immutable. The central arrondissements in Paris, parts of Midtown Manhattan, much of Beacon Hill in Boston, sections of London and many other mature cities - these districts have reached a semi-permanent state of completion in which major construction has essentially ceased and further material investment will be devoted to maintaining existing structures. If these city districts are essentially immutable - carefully maintained and highly valued - then what can one say about the service lives of the buildings contained within them? Are they extended indefinitely into the future?

Time Change

This question and others bring forth the topic of building lifetimes. How do contemporary buildings live out their lives? How do different kinds of materials contribute to the trajectory of those lifetimes? In fact, the relationship between the changes that have been brought about by materials research for buildings and the way in which we use buildings prompts an essential question; what is the nature of the lifetime of a contemporary building?

Building Lifetimes and Uncertainty

This is not the same as asking about service and design lives for buildings, their components and systems. These topics are attended to by a growing assortment of regulating organizations and standards groups. These technical bodies concern themselves with the need to establish clear guidelines for product and material lifetimes under a variety of service conditions. This work, while useful and necessary, fulfills the needs of the insurance industries and manufacturing sector, while the designer and engineer are most mindful of the demands of service in light of warranty limitations and risk calculations. While these activities are essential, they are not at the core of the nature of building lifetimes.

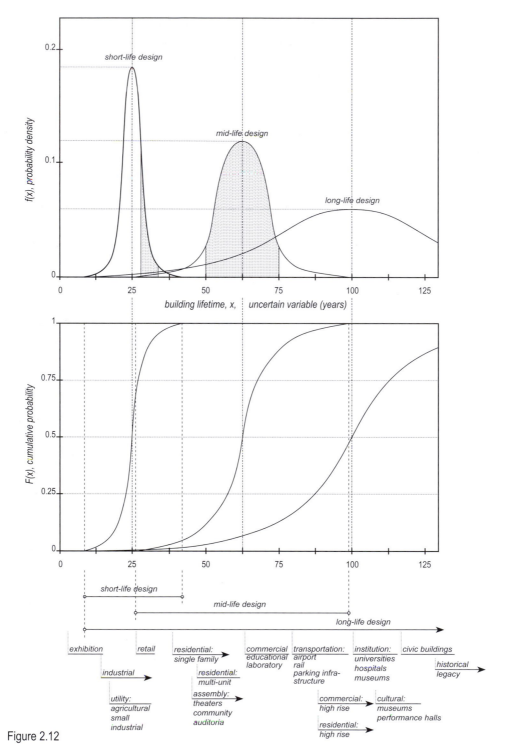

Figure 2.12

Probability distributions, cumulative probabilities and building types for short-, mid- and long-lived buildings.

The distinction between component and system service and design lives and *building lives* is based on the understanding that buildings serve out their lives in unpredictable ways, dependent on the vicissitudes of changing cultural values, aesthetic norms, patterns of use and economic forces. It is all very well to design to *allow* for a certain lifetime by designing to that level of durability, but the uncertainties of use often contribute unanticipated factors that fundamentally affect the lifetime of the building. Narrowly defined, the design life of a building is the expected cumulative service life that results from the properly maintained set of components and systems (Nireki 1996;Soronis 1996). The service life is the actual life of the component, assembly or building.

The primary contention here is that the actual lives of buildings are significantly affected by forces that are outside of the control of the original designers or lifetime operators of the building (Douglas 2002;Brand 1994). Rather, control over the service lives of individual buildings is most often exercised by an array of forces independent of the building fabric itself and the original designers and engineers. These forces, generally the economic and social conditions within which the building is situated, unwittingly conspire to create situations in which the design lives of buildings do not generally correlate with their actual service lives (Soronis 1996;Nireki 1996). Therefore, actual building lifetimes are best represented as probabilities, Figure 2.12.

These forces tend to introduce types of uncertainty not generally considered during the design or operation of most types of buildings. In addition, it can be shown that this uncertainty is more likely to affect a building of long life (+75 years) than one of short (0< x <10 years) or mid-life duration (10< x <75 years). In the presence of this uncertainty, buildings are required to accommodate new scenarios. Most buildings can easily accommodate some scenarios, such as a new tenant or changes in ownership. Others, such as a structural shift in the surrounding economy or shifts in aesthetic preferences, may be much more difficult to accommodate. Most building types affected by this kind of shift may be dramatically disturbed. These shifts can often render impotent the lifetime projections based on component service lives and the design life targets used in the original design and construction of the building. The presence of uncertainty may also lead to the premature obsolescence of a building. Despite significant service life remaining in the fabric of the building, its location, particular use, materials, systems or other aspect of its original design may lead to a decision for demolition rather than reuse or adaptation of some kind (Prins et al. 1993;Patterson 1998;Maury 1999;Keymer 2000;Slaughter 2001;Douglas 2002).

Industrial Ecology of Buildings

The previous sections have highlighted broad trends in the physical composition and lifetime behaviors of contemporary buildings. Dematerialization and the uncertainty inherent in building lives combine to produce complex new material realities. Linking observations about the physical and the temporal afford the contemporary designer a new way of viewing the modern architectural proposal (Daniels 2002). In fact, linking these in the context of a variety of industries has been the preoccupation of the emerging science of resource extraction, processing and consumption; that is, industrial ecology (Ayres 1994;Ayres 2002;Balkau 2002;Bringezu 2002;Graedel and Allenby 2003;Kibert 2002;Wernick 2002). This section will explore the real opportunities that may be gained by associating the architectural enterprise with the appropriate tools and methods of industrial ecology.

As an integral aspect of the continuous weathering and aging of individual components and assemblies and the constant adjustment of value based on aesthetic, social, economic and environmental concerns, buildings become an important part of the industrial ecology of the planet. Buildings use and discard materials in huge quantities. Modern construction, based less and less on any interest in permanence, uses and then releases large materials flows at faster rates than ever before. Many industrialized societies count construction as one of the largest materials consumers and waste producers in their economies. Using industrial ecology theories to map out the material flows in architecture clarifies the idea that buildings can and should play a role in the greater ecology of the planet.

Balancing the needs for development and construction with the reality of materials consumption in the making of buildings, the contemporary architect can play a more active role in designating responsible materials paths. We live on an earth of limited material resources. Coordinating the use of construction materials towards more sustainable paths requires a better knowledge of the opportunities and the costs inherent in construction. In addition to these forces, the level of consumption for construction varies greatly the world over. The extraction and consumption of materials is accomplished at varying rates from region to region. The industrialized, wealthy regions of the world consume more than their proportional share of the materials wealth of the globe. These issues will also affect the way in which architecture continues to use resources; especially the nonrenewable resources of the planet.

Two general realms can be said to exist for examining the analogy of ecology in construction. The first is typical of the application of industrial ecology to any industry - that is, it involves an examination of the material and energy flows devoted to this enterprise and research intent on developing better ways in which to satisfy the needs of society while managing material and energy flows. Using the analogy compels conceptual shifts that define the challenge; for example, considering waste as a potentially useful "residue", closing material cycles, understanding the network of material and energy exchange relationships, protecting endangered resources and inventing processes that can deliver on the promise of a true ecology of human activities.

The second realm seeks to engage in an assignment of "living agency" on the physical assemblies and systems of architectural things. Whether anthropomorphic or simply relating to biological connotations, this use of the analogy places emphasis on the autonomy of the building, as a physical "living and breathing" organism that requires materials and energy to be brought into being (constructed), live out its life (operation, maintenance and repair) and pass away (demolition, adaptive reuse or underuse). This use of the analogy is focused on the opportunities inherent in having the ability to control the actual material composition of a building. With actual living things, we can only engage in the study of material and energy exchange between them and the natural world. With buildings, we are able to specify their materials and design the configuration of their assemblies that fundamentally affect their interaction with the larger environment (see the Epilogue; Wolman 1967).

Making this distinction is important to the enterprise of architecture because, as it stands now, architects are primarily concerned with the design of individual architectural things; additions to buildings, alterations, adaptive reuse or new build. Currently, the discipline is not directly involved in the design of processes, or the determination of the overall industrial relations that serve construction (McDonough 1992). However, the discipline is intimately involved in the physical specification of buildings and while this may change, and has begun to change (especially in the realm of sustainable design and advanced production technologies like CAD/CAM processes), these shifts will most likely not affect the primary mission of the field of design.

This may seem limiting to the profession's ability to affect fundamental change in the "ecology" of industrial relationships that govern the making of architectural components and materials, but it is heartening to remind oneself that architects still retain the primary role in decisions regarding the material content of these massive societal artifacts. In other words, architects are the primary actors in determining the material composition of our buildings and therefore assume the role of primary drivers in the extraction, recycling and processing of specific materials, the manufacture and assembly of components and the construction of our buildings.

And, in delving deeper into the analogy of buildings as "living agents" of architecture, the material expenditure devoted to these buildings is fundamentally affected by the uncertain character of their lifetimes, as shown above. Therefore, design may soon commit a certain attention to the engineering aspects and design opportunities of the lifetimes of buildings for the purpose of capitalizing on the potential for the formulation of a holistic ecology of construction.

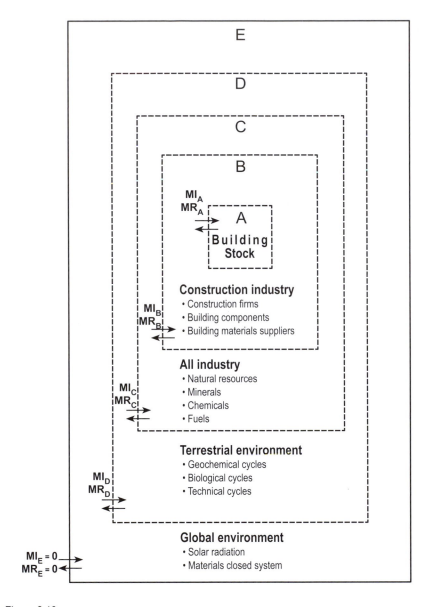

Figure 2.13

The industrial context (or construction ecology) of the built world showing schematic material flows as inputs (MI, material investment) or outputs (MR, material residuals) between the various *organizational domains* of consumption. Levels A, B, C and D are contained within the closed system of the global environment (closed except for the daily input of solar radiation). Material residuals (commonly referred to as *waste*) include both the controlled and regulated flows of construction and demolition waste (CDW) and the uncontrolled flows of unregulated material dissipation into the environment.

Sources: Adriannse et al. (1997), Ayres (1994,2002), Balkau (2002), Bringezu (2002), Graedel and Allenby (2003), Kibert (1999a,b, 2002), Matos and Wagner (1998), Mikesell (1995), Sachs (2000), Schmidt-Bleek (1993), Tilton (1979), Wermick et al. (1996, 2002).

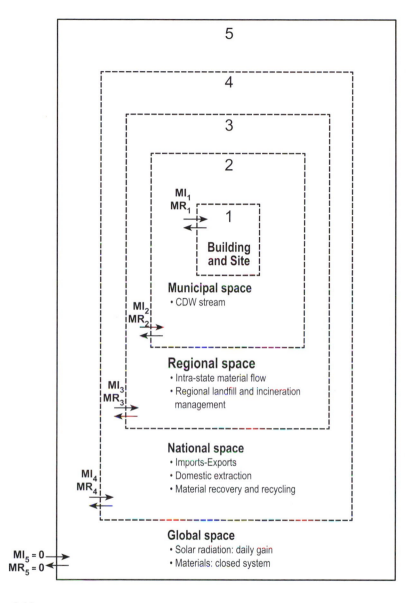

Figure 2.14

The spatial context of the built world showing schematic material flows as inputs (MI, material investment) or outputs (MR, material residuals) between the various *spatial domains* of consumption. Levels 1, 2, 3 and 4 are contained within the closed system of the global environment. A unique characteristic of buildings is the fact that their location is fixed - essentially immutable - over their entire service lifetimes, thereby requiring that material flows traverse many of the boundaries between these spatial domains during the lifetime of the building. Doing so requires both material and energy expenditures that, besides other effects, results in increased irreversible dissipation of material into the environment.

Sources: Adriannse et al. (1997), Ayres (1994,2002), Balkau (2002), Bringezu (2002), Graedel and Allenby (2003), Kibert (1999a,b, 2002), Matos and Wagner (1998), Mikesell (1995), Sachs (2000), Schmidt-Bleek (1993), Tilton (1979), Wermick et al. (1996, 2002).

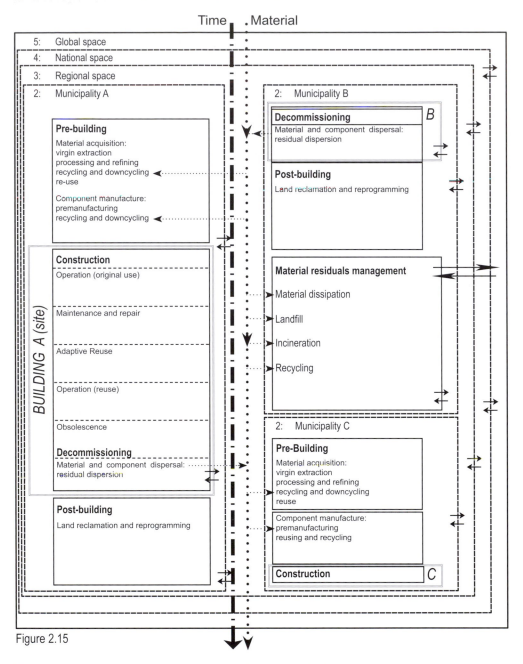

Figure 2.15

The diagram conflates several processes and distinct building artifacts in a linked set of material relationships in time and space. These material flow processes are contained within the spatial domains illustrated in Figure 2.14. Despite the tendency to use cyclical diagrams to illustrate the movement of materials through society in both the industrial ecology and sustainable design literature, both time and the unavoidable dissipation of materials into the environment are irreversible (one-way and entropy-increasing). Therefore, the diagram shows time moving from the top to the bottom and includes the various lifetime phases of three buildings; A, B and C as they contribute material to one another. The entire lifetime of Building A is shown, the end of life of Building B and the initial phases of Building C. Transfer of materials occurs between buildings and every geographic study boundary (municipalities, regions, nationalities and the global environment).

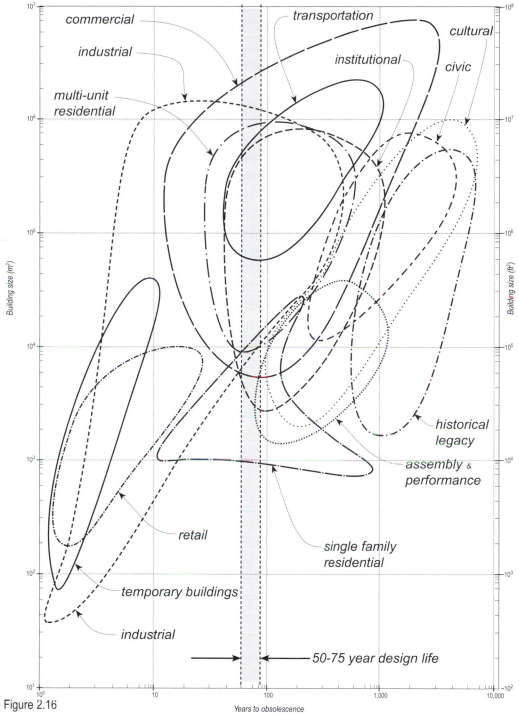

Figure 2.16
Building use occupancies graphed with respect to their size and lifetime ranges. The central shading designates the narrow band for 50-75 years, the typical design lifetime range for contemporary buildings. Clearly, many buildings and building types fall outside of this range.

Source: Building Lifetimes Research, MIT.

The previous pages show a series of figures illustrating material, spatial and temporal relationships. Because buildings exist within these various contexts, some insight can be derived from correlating the transfers that are compelled by and accomplished in each.

Figures 2.13, 2.14 and 2.15 outline the material relationships between various spatial and organizational domains that situate the industry of construction and the actual artifact of the contemporary building. As noted in the caption for Figure 2.14 - buildings are unique human artifacts in that they are wedded to a particular location for the duration of their service lives. Additionally, buildings are unique for the fact that their service lives are very long - relative to other human artifacts. Buildings may last several generations, hundreds, even thousands of years, or a building may be built to last one year, or six months. Coupling the complexity of material transfers to the unique lifetime characteristics of contemporary buildings is one of the richest challenges for an ecology of construction.

For example, Figures 2.16 and 2.17 are the result of an ongoing survey of thousands of buildings in the Boston metropolitan region in the American state of Massachusetts. By examining the construction and demolition records for a diverse array of building types and sizes, several illuminating correlations can be made.

First, the typical design service life used to specify new buildings today - from 50 to 75 years - registers as a small sliver of the actual lifetimes of buildings that form the anthropogenic building stock that is contained in our cities, see vertical shaded area in Figure 2.16. It is clear from this diagram that buildings tend toward a very wide range of lifetimes - from the very premature demise of retail, industrial, some commercial and some residential buildings to the very long lifetimes of buildings that are generally regarded as representing enduring cultural, historical or civic value. These buildings can

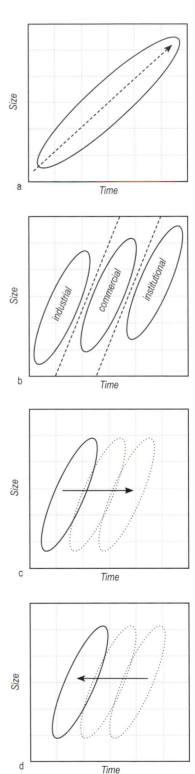

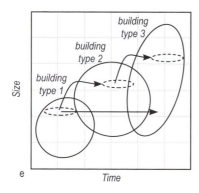

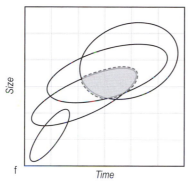

Figure 2.17a, b, c, d, e, f

A series of diagrams illustrating correlative tendencies between building size, occupancy use and designated design lifetimes. The following can be generally concluded:

a: actual lifetime and size tend to be directly proportional,

b: occupancy use is generally segregated into three classifications,

c: in successful contexts, actual building lifetimes are extended through additional investment,

d: in declining contexts, actual lifetimes decrease,

e: use migration occurs between similarly sized building types (e.g. adaptive reuse),

f: significant overlaps between expected lifetimes and size envelopes (shaded area) prompts significant use migration from one to another over the lifetimes of buildings, especially if these buildings are located within a dense urban fabric.

extend into the hundreds and thousands of years - and some buildings may have their service lives extended indefinitely (through renovation and repair). Some of the most important conclusions from Figure 2.16 are described in the series of diagrams of Figure 2.17.

Design Strategies

As is sometimes the case with changes in the relationships between technologies and the needs of society, businesses have sensed the emerging opportunities brought about by the substantial flux of materials into and out of buildings. Apart from the ideology of "Creative Destruction", business opportunities have arisen from the need to attend to the many facets of buildings' uncertain lives.

Existing Building Stock

The existing building stock is in constant need of attention both for normal maintenance and repair and at thresholds between one use and another. Several strategies have been flourishing around the opportunities to be had in reclaiming and reusing the materials and components from existing buildings. These strategies have been at work in the field for some time now in Europe and Asia and have had a great deal of recent interest in the United States. They include initiatives to organize the segregation and assessment of construction and demolition waste (CD&W) and the organized deconstruction of buildings and parts of buildings.

Programs to monitor and regulate the composition and quantity of CD&W have come primarily from government regulation at a variety of levels depending on the country and region. These efforts are important as an immediate solution to some of the most pressing environmental issues that arise with the movement of materials onto and off a construction site. In the United States, the most effective measures are established by

Figure 2.18

With the use of massive concrete, a dedicated research initiative and a willingness to pay for the capability, this building aspires to a 500 year lifetime free of any significant repair or replacement needs.

Cathedral of Los Angeles, Los Angeles, CA.

Rafael Moneo, Architect.

local governing authorities. Given the fact that 15-30 percent of the municipal waste stream is due to construction, attention paid to this issue has the potential for real reductions within short periods of time (Formoso et al. 2002).

Deconstruction is a broad effort to bring into being a culture and industry of reclamation of the valuable materials and components that reside in the existing building stock. Its many forms and practices, while diverse and spread throughout the globe, are all intent on accessing any remaining useful service life that building materials and components possess even after the utility of the building itself may be in question. Therefore, the breadth of deconstruction includes the smallest of refurbishment and renovation projects to the largest of civil structures.

Much deconstruction already occurs. For example, the reclamation and recycling of many metals is supported by an industry of deconstruction that targets assemblies as diverse as copper tubing and wiring, aluminum window mullions and frames, entire steel bridges and other civil structures, steel reinforcing bar from concrete, zinc and tin roofing and many other metal components. These salvage and recycling industries are taking advantage of

Figure 2.19

Extending the useful life of reclaimed freight containers, this building has adapted these premanufactured metal boxes into dwelling units in the making of a multi-unit residential building just outside of central London.

Container City, Trinity Buoy Wharf, London.

the economics of the production of metals and the savings to be gained from avoiding the substantial energy costs from the processing of primary metals.

The effort to organize deconstruction efforts globally go beyond this existing patchwork of reclamation, salvage and recycling industries. Currently the International Council for Research and Innovation in Building and Construction (CIB) sponsors Task Group 39 which holds the mandate for working out the framework necessary for establishing international cooperation in the effort to reap the greatest benefits from the careful use of the existing building stock. Under the Agenda 21 initiative meant to coordinate efforts in sustainable construction, Task Group 39 has completed a comprehensive report of the types and intensity of ongoing global deconstruction efforts (Kibert 1999a,b).

New Build

With the design and construction of new buildings, opportunities that are not possible with the existing building stock are apparent. The range of these possibilities should be carefully analyzed to identify those that would bring greatest benefit.

For example, given the changes in the materials used in construction and the prospect that current trends of increasing lightness, more synthetics and composites, tighter assemblies of multiple layers will continue, then the value of recycling many building materials becomes questionable. However, the benefits of recycling certain materials, such as metals and wood, will continue to be an important part of demolition reclamation. In addition, because components themselves are also being engineered for a minimum of materials with the use of many more adhesives, the growth in the reclamation of components is not likely (Kibert 2003). Concentrating on stipulating that certain materials should be easily recycled is a better strategy than insisting on wholesale component reclamation and reuse. Therefore, in considering the potential contribution that new buildings bring to the issue of increasing material efficiencies in construction, the issue of design becomes primary. Designing buildings such that they can best accommodate change and contribute to an organized material management initiative is the basis for the following strategies:

1. Designing for Disassembly and Deconstruction
2. Premanufactured Building Modules
3. Temporary and Moveable Buildings
4. Extended Producer Responsibility for Buildings
5. Long-Life Buildings
6. Buildings of Diversified Lifetimes

Each one of these focuses on a distinct aspect of the need, environmental and economic for providing technologies and methodologies to access the opportunities inherent in changes during a building's lifetime.

Designing for Disassembly and Deconstruction
As a subset of the larger effort to organize deconstruction strategies generally, several groups of researchers and designers are attempting to formulate guidelines for the design of buildings for their eventual deconstruction. This design and engineering for disassembly is intended to improve the rate of materials recovery from all of our manufactured artifacts.

Premanufactured Building Modules
A subset of the premanufactured module industry includes the manufacture of modules for buildings of the more typical lifetimes of 20 to 50 years. Hospitals, office buildings, warehouses and other types of buildings are served by this kind of construction. Interestingly, a market has

emerged for the reclamation and refurbishment of these building modules (see Foremans Buildings Ltd.). This secondary market is only concerned with existing module stock - not with the production of new stock.

Temporary and Moveable Buildings

A small but significant sector of the construction market premanufactures modules for a variety of uses. Most uses are temporary and the history of these kinds of buildings is rich in invention. The mobile food trucks of 19th century America became the diners of today. In Europe, the premanufactured building module industry is composed of several large companies all bidding for the business of specialty buildings and temporary structures.

Extended Producer Responsibility (EPR) for Buildings

With the advent of the premanufacture of buildings and a secondary market for the products of these companies, the issue of extended produced responsibility has an opportunity to flourish. While the idea of coupling EPR for their products is nearly impossible in today's construction environment, applying the principles of this environmental strategy may show potential with the growing prefabrication market (Schwartz and Gattuso 2002).

Long-Life Buildings

Longer life means greater risk that the building will encounter an unanticipated condition rendering it obsolete because of its greater exposure to a variety of changing scenarios over time.

Buildings of Diversified Lifetimes

Currently, primarily a theoretical position, designing buildings to possess a diversified set of lifetimes has been suggested as a method for minimizing the risk of dysfunctional utilization during its service lifetime (see "Two Research Projects" below). While in practice the implantation of a diversified set of lifetimes throughout a single structure may be complicated by the interdependence of building systems, the theory is quite simple. A building, designed with a single service lifetime, is subject to inefficiencies born of the uncertainties of its use. This has been adequately covered previously in this section. One of the issues that becomes problematic within a dynamic and uncertain context is the optimum service lifetime for the building. Also, as shown before, lifetimes are best represented by probability areas and therefore are not easily reduced to a singular obsolescence date. Diversified lifetimes proposes that, for a building of a certain size and type, designing the building with a set of distinct lifetimes (long, medium and short) will act as a hedge against the inefficient use of the building in a variety of eventual circumstances (Fernandez 2004). This theory proposes that, in addition to the diversity of component lifetimes embedded within the building's assemblies, there is good reason to segregate certain sections of a building from one another and assign distinct lifetimes such that the building may better respond to a greater range of possible futures.

Figure 2.20

This building module, used primarily for temporary and moveable buildings and produced by Yorkon of England, is transported to a variety of locations within the European Union.

Yorkon production yard, York, UK (2003).

Final Thoughts

It would seem that despite the ability to determine the material composition and assembly configuration of buildings, architects have a limited role in steering the lifetimes of buildings in one direction or another. Designing such that the lives of buildings and structures are most productive requires some understanding of the forces that affect and sometimes dramatically alter those lives. Associating lifetimes with their material consequences is not only an interesting academic question but a path that yields surprising and useful opportunities for contemporary architectural design. While it has been productive to consider the physical dimensions of the environmental impact of our buildings, it is also instructive to examine the temporal aspects of the use of materials for buildings. Correlating specific relationships between time and materials promises the potential for elucidating better the nature of the use of physical resources in contemporary society.

The next section describes two research projects undertaken in the Department of Architecture at MIT that examine the opportunities for design as basic assumptions about building lifetimes are reconsidered.

Figure 2.21

A short life pultruded structure temporarily occupying a dense urban parcel.

South Boston Temporary Building Proposal, Adaptable Buildings Research Project, MIT (2004).

Figure 2.22

A typical Boston parcel awaiting development.

South Boston Temporary Building Proposal, Adaptable Buildings Research Project, MIT (2004).

9.0 Two Research Projects

Currently, in south Boston a great deal of land is vacant. Great swaths are owned by the city, others by an array of private investors and real estate developers. Several large buildings have been located in this area of the city, including the new convention center and a courthouse. However, it is common to see undeveloped parcels of land idle for long periods of time, sometimes generating some income as a parking surface. In these locations, uncertainty about the various zoning, financial, ownership and infrastructure issues is very high. However, it is known that the city is in a planning phase for the area and that substantial change will be forthcoming. Certainly, the lack of a binding plan has generated a great deal of uncertainty about the status of all of the major factors, financial, physical and otherwise. This has placed a threshold for development that is much higher than typical and created a scenario in which a "wait and see" option is common (Cheng et al. 2003). As a result, a part of the city remains mute, unused and lacking vitality. This research project proposed the construction of buildings that would serve to "test" the viability of program uses on these various sites without permanently committing the parcel to a particular building. Temporary, or short-life, construction was sought as an appropriate solution because these kinds of buildings are inherently at a lower risk of losing a substantial portion of their lifetimes to the uncertainties in this context. Providing the site with a temporary building allows the option to the owner to extend the life of the building by investing in more permanent building systems at some point in the future. It also allows the owner to take the option of disassembling the building after only a short period of time.

In fact, this particular building scenario brings forth the possibility of alternative owner arrangements including the possibility that the owner of the development parcel simply "leases" the building just as one would lease an automobile - with an option to purchase parts or all of it at some future time. The leased building could then act as an urban full-scale trial of the possible highest uses that the building could serve. The developer would be generating income from the site while providing the city with much needed productive space in an area in transition.

Therefore, the scenario provides a buffer against the kind of uncertainty that plagues many cities today. Allowing for a less permanent physical construction provides a lower investment threshold while gathering useful information about the success of particular uses. The building is organized into autonomous volumetric constructions with distinct material and tectonic attributes. They act collectively to set in motion the staged settlement of the site. Figure 2.23d is a diagram showing the five portions of the building pulled apart for clarity. The five act together to facilitate a range of occupied densities and built framework on this parcel. Also, the five represent diverse lifetime potential due to their ease of assembly and disassembly and the inherent durability of their respective materials. The building is organized in descending permanence beginning with structure A through C.

Physical change is assisted by the incorporation of two cranes, structures A and D, capable of handling construction equipment and materials to assemble components or disassemble portions of the building. Structure A contains a tower crane that handles materials from the street level up to each floor of the building. This materials handling wing also accommodates the storage of materials going into and coming out of the building. Therefore, structure A serves as the onsite materials workshop for the building.

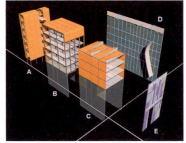

Figure 2.23a, b, c, d

A series of images showing the variety of configurations allowed by the pultruded structure and fabric exterior envelope of a temporary "trial" building for speculative development of unused urban development parcels. The images show several alternative configurations for the adaptable structure and reconfigurable exterior skin of the building.

South Boston Temporary Building Proposal.

Adaptable Buildings Research Project, MIT (2004).

Structure D is a horizontal crane capable of moving material from structure A to all parts of the building. Structure B is constructed of bolted steel structural columns and beams supporting ductile concrete precast or aerated concrete slabs. Structure C is a frame of pultruded fiber reinforced polymer structural sections, columns and beams, supporting a pultruded monocoque section floor slab. Section C is extremely lightweight for the purposes of quick construction and disassembly as needed. Both structures are enclosed using a multi-layered textile envelope (see Chapter 5). The plane labeled as E is a composite fabric and polycarbonate exterior envelope acting as the main street elevation.

The second research project serves to illustrate the idea of *diversified lifetimes*. Diversified lifetimes intends to more easily allow a building to adapt over time through an embedded diversity of permanence and impermanence built into the systems of the building. This is done by carefully specifying and detailing assemblies such that they can provide a diversity of expected service lives. Providing buildings with such diversity reduces the risk that the building's configuration will not be able in some future context. These principles were applied to the conceptual design of a new Exploration Headquarters Building for British Petroleum. Located in Dyce, just outside of Aberdeen, Scotland, the building is intended to house the various business units that are responsible for operations in the North Sea region. The new building will replace the existing headquarters, now deemed unusable by the current management because of its inflexibility, and provide 180,000 square feet (17,000 m^2) of office space. The project brief stipulated that the building was to be designed in accordance with typical lifetime expectations. Normally, such a building is expected to provide reasonable performance over a period of approximately 50 years with regular maintenance, repair and replacement of certain components. And yet, due to its continuing reduction in operations in the area, BP was projecting a dramatic workforce reduction within the next 15 to 20 years. The population of the building would be affected accordingly with a decrease in staff of close to 90 percent within 15 years. Therefore, there is a very high probability that the building would not be needed after less than half of its service life had been exhausted. Clearly, these kinds of projections are always difficult to fully accept, especially in an area in which BP has considerable political and economic commitments. However, the possibility of constructing facilities that would soon be underutilized was quite high.

Scotland is an ideal context in which to develop an experiment in ecological construction using diversified lifetimes. The Scottish Parliament has placed sustainable development high in their listing of priorities as early as December 1999, with adoption of the Scottish National Waste Strategy. Construction is a very large part of the Scottish economy and accounts for a great deal of the environmental impact of industry overall. The gross output of construction is valued at 5.6 billion pounds per annum, 6.5 percent of Scotland's gross domestic product. Almost half of this activity is dedicated to the repair and maintenance of existing buildings. In the United Kingdom as a whole, 40-50 percent of carbon emissions can be attributed to the activities of construction. The current UK target for industrial and commercial waste reduction is landfill flows at 85 percent of the 1998 levels by 2005. While this may seem conservative, it will take a significant commitment to achieve changes in typical practices, especially in construction.

This case study illustrates one mode of change - that of staged contraction. Given BP's predictions, the overall state of the regional economy, and the high vacancy rate for commercial office buildings, economic contraction may be the future reality of Dyce and Aberdeen. The site for the new building is located 300 yards southwest of the complex of buildings that houses the current headquarters. The buildings are located in the heart of the industrial sector of Dyce. The regional airport is within ½ mile and Aberdeen is 8 miles to the southeast.

Applying these discrete lifetimes to building subunits yields two distinct scenarios for contraction. The first is staged in a linear fashion in which the building recedes serially, eventually leading to a contraction of the building down to a core of 20 percent of the original built area. This core can then be sold or let to a much smaller single tenant. It can also be adapted to an alternative use distinct from commercial office space. The second scenario allows for subtraction and addition of building volume leading to an overall contraction and reconfiguration of the building layout for multi-tenant rental.

The building facilitates disassembly by enlisting the superstructure as a mechanism for disengaging components and moving materials from their original locations within the building back to the onsite materials reclamation workshop, Figure 2.24a,b,c,d. This workshop serves as the primary materials handling facility, including storage, sorting of materials and components, recycling and repairing and reusing for building needs on site and off. Eventually materials are brought back to the workshop for reclamation, recycling and distribution to continued use on site or transfer off site (Fernandez 2004).

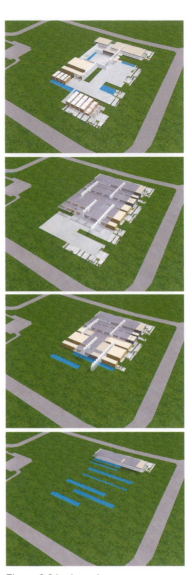

Figure 2.24a, b, c, d

A contraction sequence from the top image to the bottom showing the graduated removal of building mass over time. Removal of foundation slabs and temporary structural frames of various materials (depending on the particular "lifetime" of the portion of building) allow the site to be reclaimed after the building is no longer needed.

BP Headquarters Building, Aberdeen Scotland.
Diversified Lifetimes Research Project, MIT (2003).

Material Families and Properties

Because the influence of materials and structures upon almost every aspect of our lives is so great, the fact that we now at last understand, pretty well, how materials work and have some idea of how to invent new ones, is important indeed. So far the implications of this new knowledge have not been sufficiently widely appreciated.

J.E. Gordon, 1988

Figure 3.1a, b

Green (Atlantic) sea urchin "test" and detail of stone wall. Ceramic assemblies are characterized by relatively small pieces and a multitude of joints assimilating a complex "network" of load transfer.

3.1a Cranberry Island, Maine.

3.1b Getty Center, Los Angeles, Richard Meier, Architect.

Material Systems

The exoskeleton of a green sea urchin and the plated surface of a contemporary stone wall both consist of substances that belong to the ceramic material family. What links the calcareous shell (called the "'test") of the sea urchin to the assembly of discrete units of the stone wall is not only the general need for a physical barrier between a fragile interior environment and a harsh exterior climate, but the hard brittle ceramic material that comprises each assembly. And yet, these two material constructs are quite dissimilar in actual function and dimensional scale - neither are they closely related by origins. The sea urchin test is exclusively the result of biological processes, the stone wall a combination of geological and other natural forces and human activities of extraction, processing and assembly. Still, the primary components of each belong to the same material family because the designation "ceramic" does not strictly indicate a material or even a set of materials - it designates a set of closely related *material properties* that best describes a grouping of unique substances in the physical world.

That is, when we speak of materials, we are inevitably drawn to articulate distinctions in terms of material

75

properties. Therefore, when we refer to a material we are actually referring to the set of unique properties that characterize that one material. Learning about material properties, identifying precise and measurable differences in behavior, is the most essential step in gaining valuable knowledge for usefully articulating distinctions between various substances. In this chapter we will review a set of useful material properties - their definitions and applications - that are most relevant to the performance requirements of architectural building systems. This listing, and the explanations within, are certainly not a comprehensive treatment of the subject; however, it will certainly serve to begin the process of advancing disciplinary knowledge well beyond what most contemporary designers possess.

The diversity of materials is only rivaled by that of the natural world (DiTomas 1996;Hondros 1988). Animate and inanimate matter share an uncanny diversity that is spawned by the various ways in which just a few particles of crystalline or molecular - or other discrete material components - are arranged and massed. The DNA of organisms is able to manifest extraordinary variety from the alternating placement of only four base nucleotides along the backbone of a deoxyribose sugar molecule. Similarly, the variation in the number and geometric relations of just a few elemental particles and their electromagnetic bonds generates the wealth of material variety that constitutes the physical world. In both cases, the simplicity of the fundamental components belies the complexity of behavior that is so generously manifest. Making definitive causal links between the behavior of the material itself and the microstructural entities of which it is composed is the domain of materials science and engineering. While our interests as designers do not exclude micromechanical behavior and its causes, we are most concerned with the definition and measurement of properties and their appropriate application to building systems.

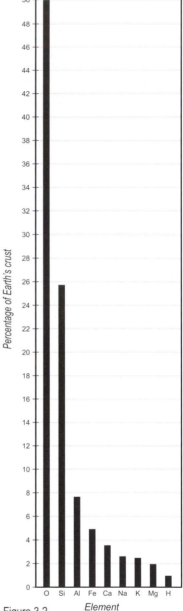

Figure 3.2

Element

The nine most common elements found in the Earth's crust.

O: Oxygen	Fe: Iron	K: Potassium
Si: Silicon	Ca: Calcium	Mg:Magnesium
Al: Aluminum	Na: Sodium	H: Hydrogen

Sources: Various including Everett (1998), Pascoe (1978), Kingery et al. (1976), Walker (2001), and the web sites of the USGS and ASM International.

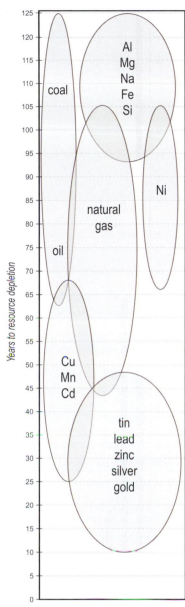

Figure 3.3

Depletion time estimates for a number of selected elements and materials, represented as areas because of the substantial uncertainty involved in such predictions. Some depletion times refer to the mineralogical barrier, see Epilogue.

Sources: various, including Graedel and Allenby (2003), British Geological Survey, US Bureau of Mines, Brown (1998), Kesler (1994).

In many design situations, utilizing the diversity of materials to accomplish all types of necessary and sometimes unnecessary tasks is not critically dependent on a full understanding of the link between molecular composition, arrangements of crystals and other formations and behavior that interest us. As designers, we are, however, enriched by and emboldened by a good understanding of the property groupings that distinguish one material family (metals) from another (ceramics). Material families have been classified and their properties defined, standardized and grouped so that their uses can be easily understood and quickly put to use. Engaging in this diverse wealth, using it wisely and responsibly, and making it the primary medium of technological innovation has been the task and joy of designers since the earliest making of tools.

Today, designers engage a material at the level of its behavior as defined by the science of materials and codified by the various building specialists such as structural, mechanical, acoustical, electrical and other building engineering specialists (Lesko 1999). These behavioral definitions assist in answering questions like, how does a particular material react under certain circumstances and what materials are attractive candidates if I am seeking a certain behavior? These questions can be partially answered by using what is known about the commonalities between large groupings of materials like metals, ceramics, polymers and so on and provides methods for an understanding of the behavior of materials under various conditions. The science of materials and the associated engineering disciplines have formulated the terms of precisely defined material properties through established standardization from research and disciplinary consensus. An example of a well-established set of standards are those produced by ASTM International, see Figure 3.8.

However, many material properties are essentially probabilistic. The values often used have been arrived at through statistical analysis and repeated testing.

Figure 3.4

The seemingly immutable solidity of masonry construction belies its actual adaptability and resilience over long spans of time.

York Minster, York, UK.

While this subtlety does not fundamentally affect most architectural considerations, there are notable exceptions. For example, glass does not allow for an easy dismissal of the probabilistic nature of its load transfer and mechanical energy absorbing properties. The failure of glass under loading is stochastic - relatively unpredictable - primarily due to Griffith flaws; small surface cracks that initiate explosive failure. The actual failure value requires a statistical determination, and therefore the use of glass as a structural material requires a great deal of care (Block 2002; see Section 3.3).

But in architectural design simply applying some knowledge of material properties and classifications is not enough to produce effective and responsible building systems. Because architecture is composed of systems that act to address sets of performance requirements, considering only material properties will not yield a complete understanding of the behavior of that system nor will it lead to an infallible design for that particular system (Reid 1995). Material properties and their collective behavior can only be fully assessed for a particular application when considered within the macroscopic behavior of the entire system itself. For example, the system of structural masonry exhibits the ability to alter its form and accept changing loading conditions over time - sometimes great expanses of time - and demonstrates an amazing flexibility for an assembly that nevertheless uses a brittle (or "inflexible") material (Heyman 1995;Ochsendorf 2002). So, designing with particular material properties in hand as well as precisely defined system requirements in mind (at the micro, meso and macro scales) prompts the necessary linkages that results in truly creative design. One without the other is not particularly useful to the architect.

Of course, this is simply an articulation of the difference between micromechanical behavior (micro), component behavior (meso) and system behavior (macro). A property clearly expressed at one scale is not necessarily present, or relevant, in another. A brittle ceramic

Figure 3.5

Structure and envelope merge in this assembly designed by the architect and engineer Santiago Calatrava.

Milwaukee Art Museum (completed October 2001), Milwaukee, Wisconsin, USA. Santiago Calatrava, Architect. Photograph courtesy of David Foxe, M.Arch. MIT.

material (an expression of micro behavior) exists within a system comprised of many individual blocks (meso) that displays significant ability to deform, redirect loads and move over long periods of time, due to the many joints between masonry units (an expression of the macro behavior of the structural system).

In addition, we have finally arrived at a cultural and scientific crossroads in which the environmental and ecological ramifications of our material decisions must be explicitly addressed by all those charged with committing our resources for current societal needs. Designing with materials that have indisputable depletion dates (such as copper, Cu), or massive expenditure of associated materials as wastes (as illustrated by rucksack measures), or uncertain long-term effects of all kinds, engenders serious and informed reconsideration (discussed at length in Chapter 2 and the Epilogue). And, of course, the consideration of materials for architectural applications is a process that is integral to the design moment; the actual creative act. Conceiving of form and material separately is sometimes unavoidable but often only a symptom of a less than ideal design process.

However, there are exceptions to this holistic view. Many engineering design situations call for making a choice of material a singular step, often determined through a combination of quantitative selection and subjective judgment born of experience. The architectural design process is somewhat different in that the selection of materials is immersed in a never-ending flux of all kinds of interrelated and disassociated concerns, many of them unquantifiable and intuitive. While this process is never at a standstill in architectural design, it is useful to define methods that can augment a designer's knowledge and provide a tool for wading through a great mass of material information. Chapter 4 outlines one process for selecting materials, the method of multi-objective optimization.

Therefore, in the spirit of establishing a clear and organized beginning to the introduction of contemporary materials, as applied to contemporary building systems, the following sections proceed first from a discussion of building systems and then to material family classifications and properties.

Structure and Enclosure

Any building is an assemblage of systems to accomplish some very simple tasks. First is the need to provide a stable, reliable and strong structure. The building must transfer loads, vertical, horizontal, static and dynamic. This transfer must not only occur safely and reliably but also without discomfort to the occupants. A very tall building, 75 floors or more, may be perfectly safe but sway too much (or accelerate too quickly when it sways) for the comfort of those inside. The structure is generally composed of two separate assemblies, the superstructure (above grade) and the foundation (at and below grade). While they are both structural they do contend with fundamentally different performance requirements; the superstructure contends with a wind load and the foundation not. The foundation must resist hydrostatic pressure and the superstructure, hopefully, does not.

Essentially, the vast majority of performance requirements for architectural materials can be divided between load transfer and barrier system requirements. First, load transfer is broadly defined as the ability to sustain the stresses resulting from the transfer of forces through to the ground and the foundations. Elements within the superstructure are required to sustain substantial compressive, tensile, bending, shearing, torsion and bearing stresses depending on the arrangement of forces relative to the geometry of the element. Primary elements of load transfer include columns, beams, trusses, cables and cable nets, shells and other structural elements.

Figure 3.6

Photo showing the more common arrangement between structure and building enclosure. The superstructure, coated in a mineral foam for fire resistance, is kept inside the weather barrier of the envelope assembly. The connection between the envelope and structure is very simple, consisting of aluminum clip angles projecting from the steel angle that forms the edge of slab condition. As a finished building, the columns seen here will be entirely covered by an interior finish material (gypsum board) and will not be a primary expression of the architecture.

University Park Development, MIT and Cambridge.

Figure 3.7

The arrangement of structure and building envelope of the Lloyd's of London building is much less typical than the assembly shown in the image opposite. In this building the superstructure has been placed "outboard" of the building enclosure on the outside of the building. The substantial architectural interest that this creates comes at a cost, not only of more complicated construction procedures but also increased maintenance to the material of the structure because it now has to endure the vicissitudes of the weather.

Lloyd's of London Building, London, UK.
Norman Foster, Architect.

Second, the building must mediate between an unstable exterior climate and the human physiological need for a stable interior environment. This general requirement is addressed by two systems, the exterior envelope and the building services. We will focus on the exterior envelope. This system is composed of several interconnected assemblies, the exterior wall, roof, foundation wall and floor. It includes all glazed openings, including skylights and glazed atrium assemblies and opaque surfaces, horizontal soffit areas, rainwater drainage system, doors and other components. In other words, any assembly that contributes to mediating between the unstable outside and the stable inside.

A barrier system is defined as a set of components that possess the ability to manage flow between two environments. The conditions within each environment may vary with respect to one another. The barrier system acts to control the flux of mass and energy between the two. Air, water vapor, liquid water, particulates, gases, humidity, temperature, radiation, and other factors may be present in either of the two environments. The control of flow from one environment to another is the role of the barrier system. The primary barrier system of contemporary buildings is the exterior envelope assembly. Another common barrier system is an interior partition.

Coupling the requirements of these two types of systems with the properties of materials is a creative technical and design process that can yield surprising architectural results. However, to work in this mode one must have the attributes of a wide range of materials available and an understanding of the performance requirements of architectural systems. This is why we return to the properties of materials and the performance requirements of architectural systems (Doran 1995).

The systems that are most closely examined in this book are the exterior envelope and the structure. Both are materials intensive assemblies, highly dependent

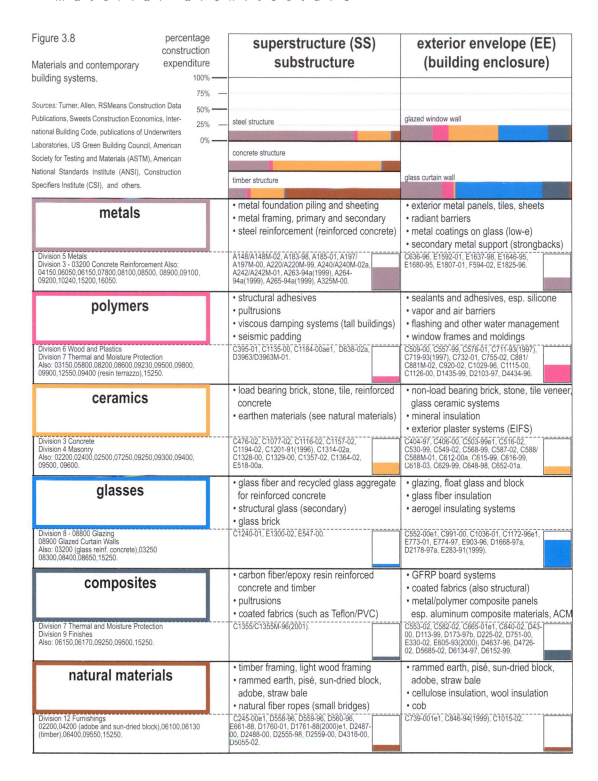

Figure 3.8

Materials and contemporary building systems.

Sources: Turner, Allen, RSMeans Construction Data Publications, Sweets Construction Economics, International Building Code, publications of Underwriters Laboratories, US Green Building Council, American Society for Testing and Materials (ASTM), American National Standards Institute (ANSI), Construction Specifiers Institute (CSI), and others.

percentage construction expenditure

	superstructure (SS) substructure	exterior envelope (EE) (building enclosure)
	steel structure	glazed window wall
	concrete structure	
	timber structure	glass curtain wall

metals

Division 5 Metals
Division 3 - 03200 Concrete Reinforcement Also: 04150,06050,06150,07800,08100,08500, 08900,09100, 09200,10240,15200,16050.

- metal foundation piling and sheeting
- metal framing, primary and secondary
- steel reinforcement (reinforced concrete)

A148/A148M-02, A183-98, A185-01, A197/A197M-00, A220/A220M-99, A240/A240M-02a, A242/A242M-01, A263-94a(1999), A264-94a(1999), A265-94a(1999), A325M-00.

- exterior metal panels, tiles, sheets
- radiant barriers
- metal coatings on glass (low-e)
- secondary metal support (strongbacks)

C636-96, E1592-01, E1637-98, E1646-95, E1680-95, E1807-01, F594-02, E1825-96.

polymers

Division 6 Wood and Plastics
Division 7 Thermal and Moisture Protection
Also: 03150,05800,08200,08600,09230,09500,09800, 09900,12550,09400 (resin terrazzo),15250.

- structural adhesives
- pultrusions
- viscous damping systems (tall buildings)
- seismic padding

C395-01, C1135-00, C1184-00ae1, D638-02a, D3963/D3963M-01.

- sealants and adhesives, esp. silicone
- vapor and air barriers
- flashing and other water management
- window frames and moldings

C509-00, C557-99, C578-01, C711-93(1997), C719-93(1997), C732-01, C755-02, C881/C881M-02, C920-02, C1029-96, C1115-00, C1126-00, D1435-99, D2103-97, D4434-96.

ceramics

Division 3 Concrete
Division 4 Masonry
Also: 02200,02400,02500,07250,09250,09300,09400, 09500, 09600.

- load bearing brick, stone, tile, reinforced concrete
- earthen materials (see natural materials)

C476-02, C1077-02, C1116-02, C1157-02, C1194-02, C1201-91(1996), C1314-02a, C1328-00, C1329-00, C1357-02, C1364-02, E518-00a.

- non-load bearing brick, stone, tile veneer, glass ceramic systems
- mineral insulation
- exterior plaster systems (EIFS)

C404-97, C406-00, C503-99e1, C516-02, C530-99, C549-02, C568-99, C587-02, C588/C588M-01, C612-00a, C615-99, C616-99, C618-03, C629-99, C648-98, C652-01a.

glasses

Division 8 - 08800 Glazing
08900 Glazed Curtain Walls
Also: 03200 (glass reinf. concrete),03250 08300,08400,08650,15250.

- glass fiber and recycled glass aggregate for reinforced concrete
- structural glass (secondary)
- glass brick

C1240-01, E1300-02, E547-00.

- glazing, float glass and block
- glass fiber insulation
- aerogel insulating systems

C552-00e1, C991-00, C1036-01, C1172-96e1, E773-01, E774-97, E903-96, D1668-97a, D2178-97a, E283-91(1999).

composites

Division 7 Thermal and Moisture Protection
Division 9 Finishes
Also: 06150,06170,09250,09500,15250.

- carbon fiber/epoxy resin reinforced concrete and timber
- pultrusions
- coated fabrics (such as Teflon/PVC)

C1355/C1355M-96(2001).

- GFRP board systems
- coated fabrics (also structural)
- metal/polymer composite panels esp. aluminum composite materials, ACM

C553-02, C582-02, C665-01e1, C840-02, D43-00, D113-99, D173-97b, D225-02, D751-00, E330-02, E605-93(2000), D4637-96, D4726-02, D5685-02, D6134-97, D6152-99.

natural materials

Division 12 Furnishings
02200,04200 (adobe and sun-dried block),06100,06130 (timber),06400,09550,15250.

- timber framing, light wood framing
- rammed earth, pisé, sun-dried block, adobe, straw bale
- natural fiber ropes (small bridges)

C245-00e1, D558-96, D559-96, D560-96, E661-88, D1760-01, D1761-88(2000)e1, D2487-00, D2488-00, D2555-98, D2559-00, D4318-00, D5055-02.

- rammed earth, pisé, sun-dried block, adobe, straw bale
- cellulose insulation, wool insulation
- cob

C739-001e1, C846-94(1999), C1015-02.

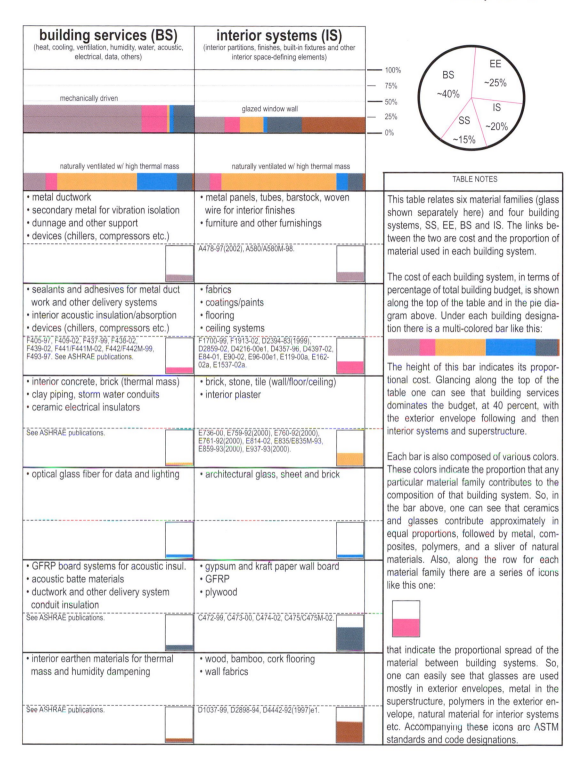

building services (BS) (heat, cooling, ventilation, humidity, water, acoustic, electrical, data, others)	interior systems (IS) (interior partitions, finishes, built-in fixtures and other interior space-defining elements)
mechanically driven	glazed window wall
naturally ventilated w/ high thermal mass	naturally ventilated w/ high thermal mass
• metal ductwork • secondary metal for vibration isolation • dunnage and other support • devices (chillers, compressors etc.)	• metal panels, tubes, barstock, woven wire for interior finishes • furniture and other furnishings
	A478-97(2002), A580/A580M-98.
• sealants and adhesives for metal duct work and other delivery systems • interior acoustic insulation/absorption • devices (chillers, compressors etc.)	• fabrics • coatings/paints • flooring • ceiling systems
F405-97, F409-02, F437-99, F438-02, F439-02, F441/F441M-02, F442/F442M-99, F493-97. See ASHRAE publications.	F1700-99, F1913-02, D2394-83(1999), D2859-02, D4216-00e1, D4357-96, D4397-02, E84-01, E90-02, E96-00e1, E119-00a, E162-02a, E1537-02a.
• interior concrete, brick (thermal mass) • clay piping, storm water conduits • ceramic electrical insulators	• brick, stone, tile (wall/floor/ceiling) • interior plaster
See ASHRAE publications.	E736-00, E759-92(2000), E760-92(2000), E761-92(2000), E814-02, E835/E835M-93, E859-93(2000), E937-93(2000).
• optical glass fiber for data and lighting	• architectural glass, sheet and brick
• GFRP board systems for acoustic insul. • acoustic batte materials • ductwork and other delivery system conduit insulation	• gypsum and kraft paper wall board • GFRP • plywood
See ASHRAE publications.	C472-99, C473-00, C474-02, C475/C475M-02.
• interior earthen materials for thermal mass and humidity dampening	• wood, bamboo, cork flooring • wall fabrics
See ASHRAE publications.	D1037-99, D2898-94, D4442-92(1997)e1.

Pie diagram: EE ~25%, BS ~40%, IS ~20%, SS ~15%

100% — 75% — 50% — 25% — 0%

TABLE NOTES

This table relates six material families (glass shown separately here) and four building systems, SS, EE, BS and IS. The links between the two are cost and the proportion of material used in each building system.

The cost of each building system, in terms of percentage of total building budget, is shown along the top of the table and in the pie diagram above. Under each building designation there is a multi-colored bar like this:

The height of this bar indicates its proportional cost. Glancing along the top of the table one can see that building services dominates the budget, at 40 percent, with the exterior envelope following and then interior systems and superstructure.

Each bar is also composed of various colors. These colors indicate the proportion that any particular material family contributes to the composition of that building system. So, in the bar above, one can see that ceramics and glasses contribute approximately in equal proportions, followed by metal, composites, polymers, and a sliver of natural materials. Also, along the row for each material family there are a series of icons like this one:

that indicate the proportional spread of the material between building systems. So, one can easily see that glasses are used mostly in exterior envelopes, metal in the superstructure, polymers in the exterior envelope, natural material for interior systems etc. Accompanying these icons are ASTM standards and code designations.

on the material properties of their components but also behaving in ways that reflect the systemic nature of their designs. A building that is served by these two systems fulfills the most essential performance requirements of architecture.

By conceiving of the building's requirements in this way it is also clear that the set of properties that are important in each set of systems is quite different. Generally, load transfer and energy absorption are important requirements of structural materials. Of course there are many other properties that are relevant, but essentially the ability to successfully transfer a load is the necessary attribute.

While the necessary set of attributes for materials used in the exterior envelope are properties that contribute to their effectiveness as barrier materials, the ability to manage a flux, energy or mass, is the important attribute of a barrier material. The flux may be measured in terms of heat, or air, or liquid water, solar radiation, visible transmission, and so on. What is important here is the clear distinction with structural materials. Barrier materials control flux, structural materials transfer loads. One may recognize the fact that these are not as distinct as one might believe. They both involve the management of energy, and in the case of barrier materials, mass as well.

Conceptually, a building's structural frame and building enclosure are the two essential features of a viable volume, a habitable shelter. Enclosing volume successfully can be fully achieved with these two systems. Building services are necessary to maintain a comfortable interior environment, including the heating, ventilation and cooling of the space, management of the level of humidity, reasonable light levels, and acoustics. The interior spaces themselves are delineated by assemblies of partitions, finishes and other space-defining components. This system is also materials intensive, especially in certain building types like the modern commercial office interior. Finally, the furnishings inside the building allow for an accommodation of the activities for which the building has been designed (Taylor 2000).

By clearly fulfilling performance requirements, materials can efficiently contribute to a working building by their use within components and assemblies. By not fulfilling performance requirements materials can adversely affect their respective assembly, the building system and the entire building itself. Specifying the correct material by understanding the basis for its performance through a good understanding of mechanical and physical properties is the best way of ensuring a workable materials solution.

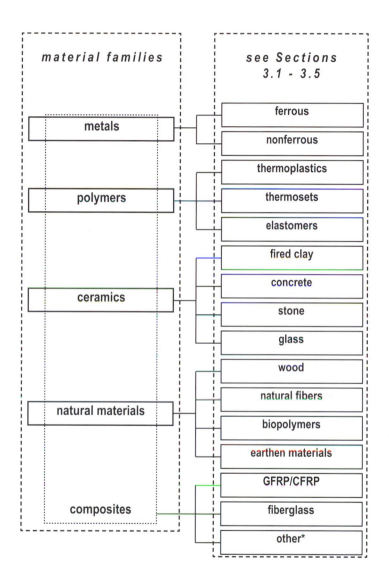

Figure 3.9

Classification of material families and common materials used in building construction.

*Composites include metal/metal, ceramic/ceramic, ceramic/metal, polymer/metal, and many other types. GFRP, CFRP and fiberglass are all examples of fiber reinforced polymers (FRP).

Sources: Ashby and Jones (2001a,b), Walker (2001), Harper (2000), and others.

Material Families and Properties

Material Families

Material families are designations that are useful for discussion of the various properties of a wide range of substances. These designations are generally accepted classifications in materials science and other disciplines. This classification places greater emphasis on the grouping of common properties than on typical applications. These properties are measurable manifestations of the atomic and molecular composition of the materials contained within each class.

Generally aligning along commonalities in their mechanical properties, these five classes encompass all engineering and architectural materials. The addition of natural materials is intended to be inclusive of all biological materials. While some biological materials and structures will have greater similarities to ceramics (seashells, fired clay brick, marble) or composites (bamboo, wood) and other material classes, it is much more useful to consider these materials within a class of their own. A primary reason for this distinction is the chemistry of many of these natural materials, based as it is substantially in organic chemistry.

Material Properties

Material properties are the attributes by which a substance is defined. These attributes are the useful conventions of scientific disciplines, intent on analyzing behavior, formulating theories and synthesizing models that correlate the atomic and molecular composition of materials with the properties that are exhibited. While properties define the behavior of the material, molecular and atomic arrangements determine these properties (Callister 2003).

Like materials themselves, material properties can also be classified into groupings of behavior. The first classification divides material properties into general categories, intrinsic and extrinsic. As the two labels suggest intrinsic properties are particular to the material itself and dependent on its atomic and molecular makeup as mentioned above. Intrinsic properties do not change under steady state environmental conditions. Of course, they may change due to repeated loadings, temperature changes, UV radiation exposure and many other environmental inputs. Extrinsic properties are independent of the material's atomic and molecular properties. These attributes are "outside" of the material itself, often dependent on the context, be it economic, environmental, social or cultural. These properties are also called *attributable* properties; they have been attributed to the material by society's particular economic structures, social needs and tastes. For example, in this book, we are classifying embodied energy as an extrinsic property, highly dependent as it is on external conditions such as regional processing technologies, transportation energies, and local construction practices. It is also dependent on how one defines and weighs the various environmental

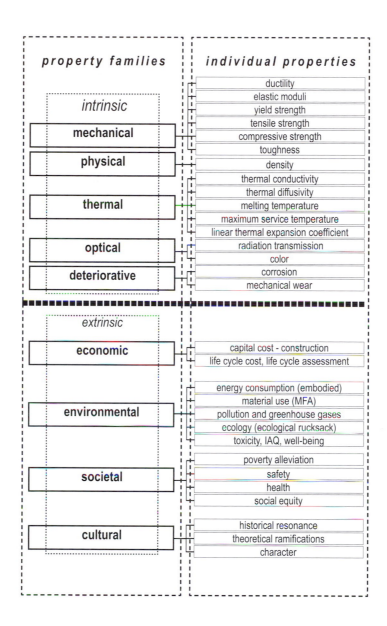

Figure 3.10

Classification of material property families; intrinsic and extrinsic and specific properties belonging to each.

Sources: Ashby and Jones (2001a,b), Walker (2001), Harper (2000), and others.

consequences of the use of a material. There is continuing debate on this issue (Hagan 1998).

A designer will consider both kinds of properties - often simultaneously (Cornish 1987). Architectural design, in particular, is a process in which intrinsic and extrinsic properties are often intertwined quite tightly (Cowan and Smith 1988;Robbin 1996). Reaching an optimal material solution is the subject of Chapter 4.

Mechanical properties generally measure the energy absorption characteristics of a material during many different types of load transfer situations. A column, axially loaded, will be in compression and its compressive strength is a measure of its capacity to transfer that load without undue movement or collapse. Physical properties account for the optical, electrical and thermal properties of materials. These properties are simply measuring other kinds of energy absorption and transfer. Both sets of properties are relevant to architectural applications. For any given design situation, the relevant set is dependent on the building system to which the material is being assigned. Optical properties are obviously important for glazing and thermal resistance for insulation. Additional properties, such as the galvanic potential between metals, will be addressed in the section for which it is relevant.

Material properties are also classified into two scales, the micro and the meso. The macroscopic scale is reserved for the structural, or system behavior of an assembly. The microscale is defined as those phenomena that occur due to elements that exist in sizes between the atomic scale and 100 microns, or the point at which human vision works. The meso relates to the behavior of elements that compose the macroscopic system.

Contemporary designers have been relieved of the perceived burden of understanding the basis for the classification of materials due to their mechanical and physical properties. For many reasons too involved to describe here, the contemporary designer may not understand the most basic attributes of a material and how these attributes determine the behavior and potential use of that substance. As a result, much design is fairly limited in terms of its explorations of the innovative uses of materials.

Finally, architects do not normally employ a systematic method for the selection of materials for particular performance requirements. Often, designers are guided almost exclusively by past practice, experience, codes and generally accepted practice. Not a bad set of criteria. However, value can be gained from a systematic method that both quickly communicates relevant material data and guides the designer toward solutions not immediately obvious, see Chapter 4.

The following chapters intend to map the material classes of metals and alloys, polymers, ceramics and glass, composites and natural materials for use primarily in architectural applications. Building systems are the recipients of these materials, so it is critical that the performance requirements of building systems form the framework within which the search for appropriate materials is accomplished.

Intrinsic Attributes

Because they are physically inherent to the material, intrinsic properties can be measured, using accepted methods and accepted values may be confirmed. Most of the primary intrinsic properties have been established and recorded. It should be emphasized that the definitions given here are general for the purpose of communicating the essential character of the property. Some materials, such as concrete, have very specific metrics for its material properties established by regulatory bodies, such as the ASTM International.

The following is meant as a primer, an introduction for the reader. It places the presentation of material properties for each material family following material chapters in a commonly understood framework. Further reading is highly recommended, especially as it pertains to the highly regulated construction materials, concrete, steel, timber and nonstructural metallic alloys.

Mechanical

Strength

Units: various stress units depending on material family

Strength is defined and measured in many different ways, because diverse materials carry load and deform differently. Its definition, and therefore its measurement, is primarily dependent on two factors; mode of loading (tensile, compressive, bending, torsion etc.) and the character of deformation and failure of the material. Sometimes the setup for the loading also influences the definition of strength. Different issues are examined, for example, whether one is using a three-point bending test setup or a four point test setup. Many variations of these tests exist including the use of a notched beam to measure the opening of an initial crack formation to better assess the composite action of, say, a reinforced concrete specimen. Differences between these variants is not as important as a discussion of the essential differences between the definitions of strength.

Metals exhibit well-defined elastic behavior under loading. The measure of strength for metals is defined as the point at which a 0.2 percent strain has been reached. This proof strength (also called *offset strength* and *offset yield strength*) is the point at which the metal begins to experience internal rearrangement of its structure. Small offsets between crystals occur before this point. The 0.2 percent strain is a good indicator that these offsets have now become quite large. Other materials produce stress-strain curves that indicate an initial yield stress, a period of plastic flow and then a resumption of stress increase.

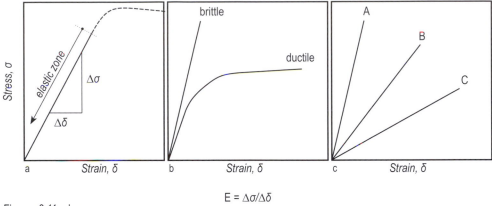

$$E = \Delta\sigma/\Delta\delta$$

Figures 3.11a, b, c

Graph (a) represents the relation between stress and strain (Young's modulus, E), graph (b) illustrates representative curves for a brittle and ductile material and graph (c) relates three separate elastic relations A (highest strength and stiffness), B (middle strength and stiffness) and C (low strength and stiffness).

Tensile strength is commonly used in assessing the ultimate strength of metals because it is an easier value to measure, it is useful as a relative measure of strength across a vast number of materials and it allows the estimation of other properties that are more difficult to measure. Metals handbooks most often reference tensile strength.

Strength in polymers is measured differently, it is simply the point at which the stress-strain curve becomes nonlinear. Materials can exhibit different strength values for tension versus compression. For many polymers compressive strength can be as much as 20 percent larger than tension. Elastomers yield almost immediately upon receiving an applied force. They are the best representatives of viscous flow.

Ceramics and glasses fail suddenly and unpredictably. Their yield points require stochastic analysis, see Figure 3.14. They also behave very differently in tension than compression, often leading to a practical designation of zero tensile strength. Many ceramics are approximately 10 to 15 times stronger in compression than tension.

The strength of composites is again defined as a point in the loading in which nonlinear behavior is recorded. Various percentages for the offset are used. Because fiber reinforced composites depend on their fibers for a significant role in absorbing energy from the applied load, they tend to perform better under tension than compression, up to 30-50 percent better.

Cellular materials can be distinguished immediately by their compressive stress-strain curves. Cellular materials include foams, sandwich materials with honeycomb interlayer structures, and even some low density woods. A description of the mechanism of compression of cellular

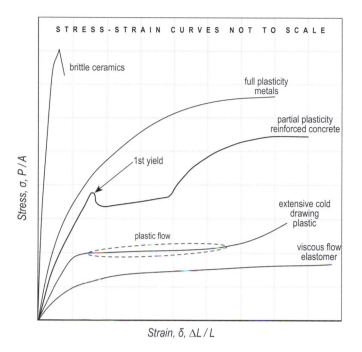

STRESS-STRAIN CURVES NOT TO SCALE

brittle ceramics

full plasticity metals

partial plasticity reinforced concrete

1st yield

extensive cold drawing plastic

plastic flow

viscous flow elastomer

Stress, σ, P / A

Strain, δ, ΔL / L

Figure 3.12

Compilation of diverse stress-strain curves produced by various types of materials.

materials includes three stages. The first stage is a short elastic zone in which the cell walls are compressed but not deformed significantly. This is recorded as a distinct elastic zone with some strain. Stage two occurs when cells walls (or cell struts, depending on the structure of the foam) begin to buckle and compress. This stage results in a great deal of strain. Stage three is the final compression of the material with cell walls fully failed and compressed against one another and the foam fully evacuated of its air pockets, Figure 3.15 (Ashby et al. 2000).

A discussion of the strength of natural materials is difficult to encapsulate in this short section. Earthen materials behave as weak ceramics. Natural fibers carry tension and no significant compression. Wood, being orthotropic, is a complicated material. The full discussion of strength for each is given in Section 3.5.

Elastic limit
Units: same as stress, and again highly dependent on material family
As with many properties, the definition of elastic limit differs among the various material families; however, it generally refers to the stress level at which point a material is permanently deformed. Therefore, units are stress units. Past this limit, a material will cease to behave *elastically* and will not return to its original shape.

For metals, as discussed above, the definition is based on an offset yield of 0.2 percent. For polymers the elastic limit is reached when the material displays a clearly inelastic stress-

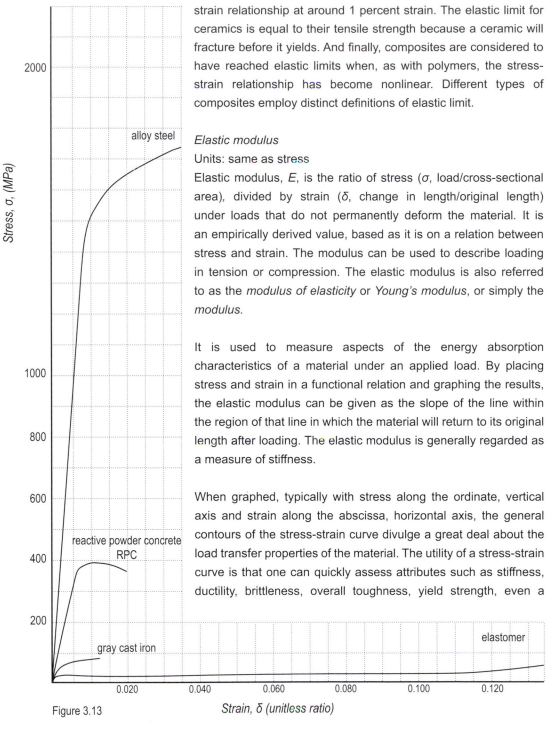

strain relationship at around 1 percent strain. The elastic limit for ceramics is equal to their tensile strength because a ceramic will fracture before it yields. And finally, composites are considered to have reached elastic limits when, as with polymers, the stress-strain relationship has become nonlinear. Different types of composites employ distinct definitions of elastic limit.

Elastic modulus

Units: same as stress

Elastic modulus, E, is the ratio of stress (σ, load/cross-sectional area), divided by strain (δ, change in length/original length) under loads that do not permanently deform the material. It is an empirically derived value, based as it is on a relation between stress and strain. The modulus can be used to describe loading in tension or compression. The elastic modulus is also referred to as the *modulus of elasticity* or *Young's modulus*, or simply the *modulus.*

It is used to measure aspects of the energy absorption characteristics of a material under an applied load. By placing stress and strain in a functional relation and graphing the results, the elastic modulus can be given as the slope of the line within the region of that line in which the material will return to its original length after loading. The elastic modulus is generally regarded as a measure of stiffness.

When graphed, typically with stress along the ordinate, vertical axis and strain along the abscissa, horizontal axis, the general contours of the stress-strain curve divulge a great deal about the load transfer properties of the material. The utility of a stress-strain curve is that one can quickly assess attributes such as stiffness, ductility, brittleness, overall toughness, yield strength, even a

Figure 3.13

Stress-strain relations for a select number of materials now represented at an actual scale illustrating extreme differences.
Source: Ashby and Jones (2001a).

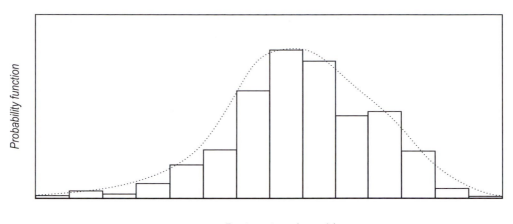

Fracture stress (ceramic)

Figure 3.14

Stochastic failure curve - typical of ceramic materials and other substances substantially lacking in ductility.

Source: Ashby and Jones (2001a).

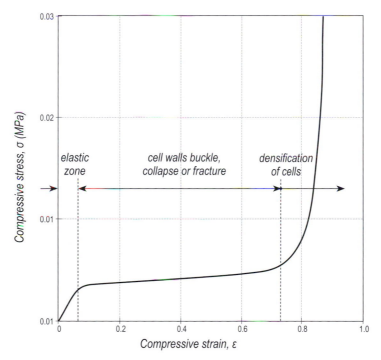

Figure 3.15

The three distinct stages of the compression of cellular materials. Aluminum, ceramic and polymer foams all clearly display this kind of behavior due to the substantial movement of the material as the cells are crushed until fully compacted (densification).

Source: Adapted from Ashby et al. (2000).

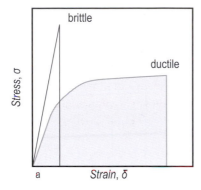 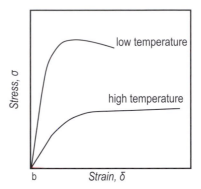

Figure 3.16a, b

Graph (a): the area under the stress-strain curve is representative of the "toughness" of a material.
Graph (b): resistance to mechanical loads is often dramatically affected by temperature.

general sense of the likely micromechanical failure mechanism. In short, the plotting of stress versus strain is one of the most useful diagrams available and will be used extensively in the following sections to make fundamental distinctions between material families and individual materials.

Figure 3.11c shows several stress-strain relations. Lines of a steeper slope, line A, are stiffer materials, they tend to exhibit smaller amounts of strain per unit of stress. Lines B and C exhibit more movement over the same increments of stress than A and are less stiff. These are just the very basics, and much of what has been covered on E should be a review from a structures or materials and methods course. However, it is useful to begin to relate these basic concepts to the distinctions between material families.

In Figure 3.12, several of these relations are shown. Each corresponds to a typical curve from the metals, ceramics, polymer and elastomer material families.

One can see immediately that the separate curves have very distinct characteristics. First, their slopes vary a great deal in overall shape. Ceramics are brittle, stiff and often very strong. Metals, especially ductile metals, are

Material	ϵ_f
concrete, unreinforced (compression)	0
concrete, reinforced	0.02
soda glass	0
low-alloy steel	0.02-0.03
mild steel	0.18-0.25
carbon steel	0.2-0.3
stainless steel, austenitic	0.45-0.65
stainless steel, ferritic	0.15-0.25
cast irons	0-0.18
iron	0.3
aluminum	0.5
copper	0.55
brasses and bronzes	0.01-0.7
natural rubber	5.0

Figure 3.17

Tensile ductility, ϵ_f (except for certain materials such as concrete, unreinforced).

Source: Ashby and Jones (2001a).

also strong, but less stiff and showing a great deal of elongation before breakage. Reinforced concrete, as one example of a composite material, demonstrates the peak at first yield and then a redistribution of load transfer to the reinforcing steel. An elastomeric polymer and wood have similar contours showing a great deal of elongation before breakage. Further details for each material class is given in their respective chapters. Please note that the curves are *not* to the same scale. They are shown together merely for comparison of their shapes, not their absolute values. Figure 3.13 places several representative curves in relation to one another at the same scale.

By glancing at the stress-strain curve and noting several key features it is possible to learn a great deal about the material. For example, does the curve end abruptly, as in ceramics, or after a long drawn-out elongation like ductile metals? A sudden end at a high level of stress usually means a catastrophic failure - violent and dangerous. Does the curve display any intermediate peaks, as in concrete; typical behavior for a composite. A peak and then a resumption of load-carrying capacity demonstrates the ability of the material to redistribute the load to another part of itself, such as from the matrix material to the tensile reinforcing material, like a whisker, woven textile, or other fibrous form. Does the curve possess a well-defined elastic zone? If so, loading within that stress range will most certainly assure the maintenance of the component's shape.

Ductility
Units: unitless
Between yielding and fracture a material will often elongate permanently, or deform. This plastic deformation is an indication of the ability of the material to change its internal structure to accommodate an applied load. A measure of this deformation before fracture is the ductility of a material. A material is deemed brittle, if it exhibits less than about 5 percent strain at fracture. Ductility can be expressed as follows:

$$\% \text{ elongation} = \frac{l_f - l_0}{l_0} \times 100$$

where l_f is the total displaced distance and l_0 is the original length. Ductility is extremely important to architectural materials, especially structural materials. Providing warning before failure is a critical attribute for the safety of occupants of a building. The steel in reinforced concrete grants ductility to the composite and makes it one of the most successful structural materials ever conceived. In some developing regions steel is a relatively expensive material for buildings and contractors have been known to systematically under-reinforce concrete structures. This is a particularly dangerous practice in areas of seismic activity. Under-reinforcing concrete returns the composite to modes of failure more akin to the catastrophic shattering of a ceramic. Several values of ductility, ε_f, are given for common building materials in Figure 3.17.

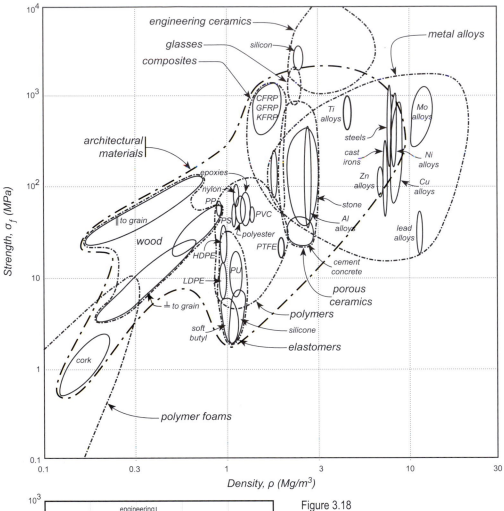

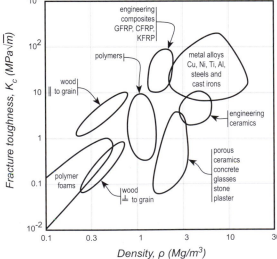

Figure 3.18

Strength as related to density. Definitions of strength range from the point of yielding (inelastic behavior) to actual fracture. For metals and polymers strength is determined by yielding tension, for ceramics, under compression, for elastomers the point of tearing under tension.

Figure 3.19

Resistance to the propagation of a crack (and therefore catastrophic and quick failure) is represented by fracture toughness. Ceramics are found to have very low toughness, while fiber reinforced materials (GFRP, CFRP and KFRP) have good resistance to crack propagation.

Source: Ashby and Jones (2001a,b).

Toughness

Units: various, see Figure 3.20

A useful value to consider here is the area under the stress-strain curve, this is called the toughness of the material. Toughness is essentially a measure of a material's ability to absorb energy and resist the propagation of cracks from an applied load. The actual value of toughness depends on many factors and varies greatly with the material and will not be discussed here. Various standards exist for the determination of toughness for various materials (Barr et al. 1996;Gopalaratnam 1995;ASTM C 1018-97 1998). Another closely related property is the resilience, defined as the area under the elastic portion of the stress-strain curve. Resilience is representative of the stored elastic energy of a strained material. The search for "tougher" and more resilient materials is a search for materials that retain some level of service life after initial failure. While this may seem like a search for a material of last resort, it is simply a search for safer materials. When it comes to building structures, those materials that can survive various stages of damage under loading and still resist some significant fraction of its initial yield strength can act to save occupants from a catastrophic collapse. Two values are often referred to here; the toughness, G_f, and the fracture toughness, K_c. Various values for each are given in Figure 3.20.

Material	G_f (kJ/m^2)	K_c (MN/m$^{3/2}$)
concrete, unreinforced	0.03	0.2
concrete, reinforced	0.2-4	10-15
soda glass	0.01	0.7-0.8
mild steel	100	140
medium carbon steel	13	51
high strength steel	15-118	50-154
cast irons	0.2-3	6-20
aluminum alloys	8-30	23-45
pure ductile metals Cu, Ni, Al	100 -1000	100-350
GFRP	10-100	20-60
CFRP	5-30	32-45
fiberglass	40-100	42-60
common woods ‖ to grain	0.5-2	0.5-1
granite	0.1	3
polypropylene	8	3
polyethylene (low density)	6-7	1
polyethylene (high density)	6-7	2

Figure 3.20

Toughness, G_f, and fracture toughness, K_c, for a variety of materials.

Source: Ashby and Jones (2001a,b).

Shear modulus

Units: stress units

Similar to Young's modulus, the shear modulus is simply the elastic portion of the stress-strain curve for a material in shear.

Hardness

Units: stress units (Brinell, Janka) and other units

An array of tests, and definitions, are used to measure the hardness of a material. The various tests cover a very large range of material reactions to the imposition of an impact (Vickers, Knoop, Rockwell, Shore A, Brinell hardness tests), scratch (pencil hardness, Mohs scale),

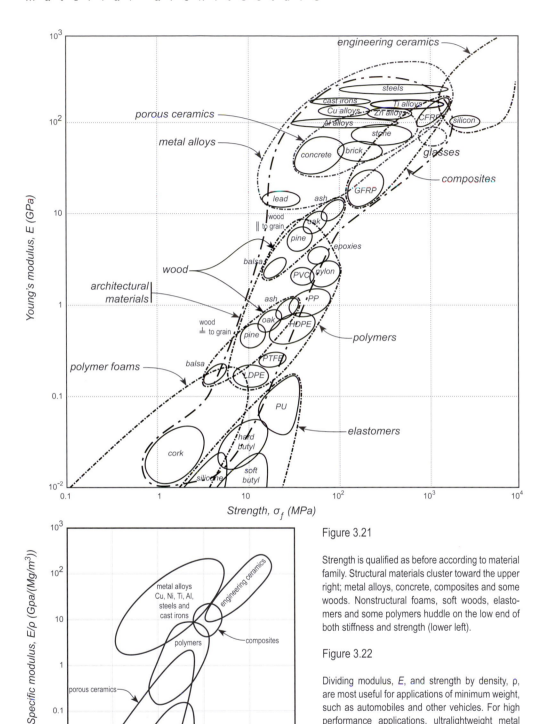

Figure 3.21

Strength is qualified as before according to material family. Structural materials cluster toward the upper right; metal alloys, concrete, composites and some woods. Nonstructural foams, soft woods, elastomers and some polymers huddle on the low end of both stiffness and strength (lower left).

Figure 3.22

Dividing modulus, E, and strength by density, ρ, are most useful for applications of minimum weight, such as automobiles and other vehicles. For high performance applications, ultralightweight metal alloys, engineering ceramics and composites are in direct competition.

Source: Ashby and Jones (2001a,b).

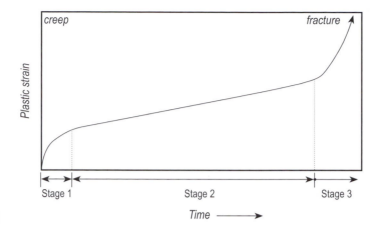

Figure 3.23

The three stages of creep, primary (Stage 1), secondary (Stage 2) and tertiary (Stage 3). Notice there is a resemblance to the behavior of cellular materials under a crushing load, Figure 3.15.

Source: Adapted from Walker (2001).

or other surface applied load. Each test represents the value of hardness with different units. Relating these tests to one another, or other material properties is not a simple task. Therefore, the first step in assessing the hardness of a material is understanding the units and parameters of the test that is being used.

Also, most of these tests are used with respect to characterizing the materials from one or a limited set of material families. For example, the Brinell and Janka hardness tests are used to measure the hardness of wood and wood composites.

Creep

Units: same as strain

When a material is loaded over time, depending on the family to which it belongs, it may display a tendency to deform slightly and even progressively. This deformation will change over time, typically beginning very slowly but then settling into a linear period in which displacement progresses to a hardening, and, if the load is intense enough, fracture. These stages are shown in Figure 3.23. The load, strain, time involved and possibility of fracture are all dependent on the material and the loading configuration.

This kind of deformation may seem a negligible, almost trivial effect of the loading of buildings, but it can sometimes have dire consequences. The creep of structural concrete is an intensely studied phenomenon because of the widespread use of this material as the primary structural frame of countless buildings all over the world. Over the relatively long periods of time that much structural concrete is intended to serve, creep may become an issue that needs to be addressed by initial design and engineering. Situations like long spans, very heavy concentrated loadings and cantilevers are particularly likely to cause some creep effects.

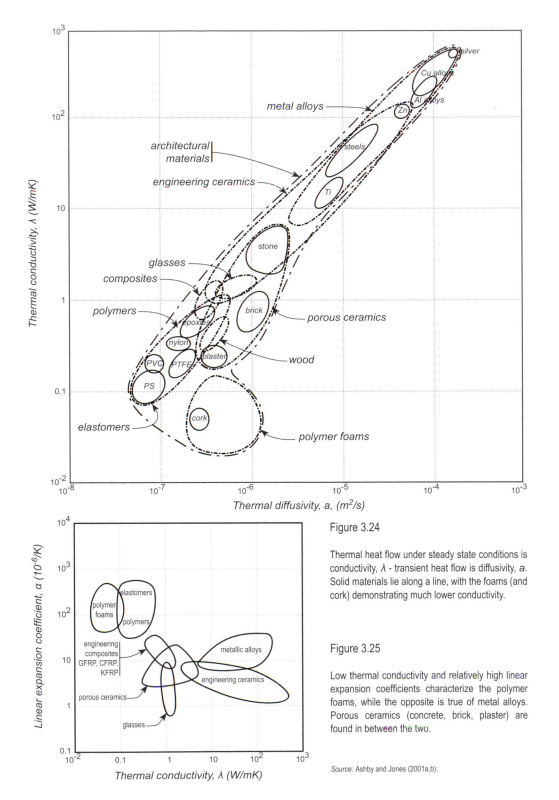

Figure 3.24

Thermal heat flow under steady state conditions is conductivity, λ - transient heat flow is diffusivity, a. Solid materials lie along a line, with the foams (and cork) demonstrating much lower conductivity.

Figure 3.25

Low thermal conductivity and relatively high linear expansion coefficients characterize the polymer foams, while the opposite is true of metal alloys. Porous ceramics (concrete, brick, plaster) are found in between the two.

Source: Ashby and Jones (2001a,b).

Elongation

Units: unitless ratio

Expressed as a percentage of the original length of a specimen loaded in tension, elongation is simply the extension of the length of the specimen at fracture (Ashby and Jones 2001).

Thermal

Temperature changes (a measure of the flow of heat) produces a dramatic effect on the tensile strength, the moduli and the yield strength of many materials (Incropera and DeWitt 2002). In particular, metals, polymers and polymer composites are significantly weakened in high temperatures. Figure 3.16b illustrates these points.

Thermal conductivity

Units: W/m.K

In a steady state condition, the ability of a material to transfer heat is its thermal conductivity, λ. Therefore, when there is a thermal gradient, like a temperature difference, between one side of a material and the other, and each of the two temperatures is constant, then the rate of heat flow per unit area through that material is the measure of its thermal conductivity.

Thermal diffusivity

Units: m^2/s

In a nonsteady state condition, or transient condition, the ability of a material to transfer heat is its thermal diffusivity, *a*. In the case of a heat impulse, a discrete (noncontinuous) influx of heat, the rate of transmission of that heat flow through a material, is a measure of the heat diffusivity. In other words, thermal diffusivity measures how well a material allows heat to "diffuse" through it. Heat diffusivity is defined as the thermal conductivity, λ, divided by the product of the density, ρ, and the specific heat of the material, C_p;

$$a = \frac{\lambda}{\rho C_p}$$

Thermal diffusivity may at first seem an esoteric quality of a material and yet it is a central aspect of the tactile quality of materials and also plays a central role in the determination of viable materials for heat storage for passive heating and cooling through the use of thermal mass. The rate at which heat is distributed through a material affects the "feel" of a material. If a material conducts heat well, it will generally have a high thermal diffusivity. A metal feels cold because it *takes away* heat from your fingertips faster than a material of low thermal diffusivity, such as wood. Figure 3.24 shows a plot of thermal diffusivity versus conductivity for some familiar materials. One can see that the range plotted confirms well to one's intuition regarding the feel of the material. Some metals have a thermal diffusivity 250 times that of the polymer foams.

Linear thermal expansion coefficient

Units: unit strain/unit temperature change

Most materials, in most of their phases, expand with an increase of their internal temperatures. Along with corrosion, this attribute leads to some of the most problematic, and easily avoided, durability issues. Thermal expansion is the measure of strain per unit temperature change. Besides for the thermal expansion of materials, another temperature related set of phenomenon is important to consider. The volume changes that occur in phase change, that is the change from a solid to liquid to gas and back, results in dramatic changes in volume. The most problematic of these phenomena is the expansion of water upon freezing. Liquid water infiltration itself contributes to the degradation of building materials in many ways. However, the additional characteristic of its expansion upon freezing leads to tremendous problems especially during the transitions between the seasons. Water retained within a material, or between materials in an assembly, throughout the warmer seasons only acts as a vice to split open joints and spall concrete.

Specific heat capacity

Units: Joule/kg x Kelvin

The quantity of heat required to raise the temperature of a unit of mass of a material by one degree.

Specific latent heat

Units: Joule/kg

The heat required to change the phase of a unit of mass of a material from solid to liquid or liquid to gas, without a change in temperature.

Melting temperature

Units: temperature units

Intuitively obvious as a concept, it is nevertheless useful to bring a bit more precision to this measure than what is offered by that intuition and real world experience. The need for fire protection of structural materials is based on the well-known relation between strength and temperature. Many metals radically change their ability to sustain an applied load above certain temperatures.

Maximum service temperature

Units: temperature units

Maximum service temperature means many different things for the various material families because loss of service occurs in diverse ways for a metal, polymer, ceramic or composite. Essentially, it is defined as the ceasing of the ability of the material to sustain any reasonable mechanical loading at an elevated temperature.

Hygrothermal properties

Units: various depending on barrier function

A recent addition to an assessment of the behavior of architectural materials, especially those used for the exterior envelope, are hygrothermal properties. The set of hygrothermal properties describe the behavior of materials subjected to temperature, pressure and humidity differentials. Under these conditions heat and air flow, vapor diffusion, moisture absorption and several other processes are coupled together to describe the complex behavior of various materials (Trechsel 2001).

It has been shown that the presence of substantial moisture over long periods of time can lead to real problems including wood rot, excessive expansion, rust, condensation and a variety of material failures. In addition, the growth of molds, mildews and other biological materials within building envelopes and other systems has resulted in problems with indoor air quality. Today, our envelope assemblies are more layered than ever, prompting calls for careful design to avoid trapping moisture and causing conditions that lead to health problems and premature failure (or underperformance) of the system. General system design approaches are often sufficient to address many potential problems that may result from temperature and relative humidity differentials. These include adding vapor and air barriers at appropriate places in the envelope and generally following principles that stress barrier redundancy and water management rather than attempting to perfectly seal a building (Brock 2005). For these properties, space in this text is limited and the reader should refer to the references given here (especially Trechsel 2001). Useful definitions are:

Vapor retarder: a vapor retarder is currently expected to provide a barrier that does not exceed 1 perm or 1 grain H_2O/hr . sft . in. Hg (57.38 ng H_2O/s . m^2 . Pa), the passage of one grain of water vapor per hour through one square foot of material at a pressure gradient of one inch mercury from one side of the material to the other - see ASTM E 96 and ASTM C 755, Practice for Selection of Vapor Retarders for Thermal Insulation.

Air barrier (or retarder): an air barrier is a material that does not allow an air leakage rate that exceeds 0.06 cfm/ft² at 0.3 in. of water ($0.3 \cdot 10^{-3}$/(s $\cdot$ m²) at 75 Pa), according to ASTM E 1677.

It is extremely important to understand that material properties are profoundly affected by factors such as temperature, humidity, light, repeated loading, corrosive agents and many other real world stressors. In essence, the design of viable architectural assemblies is based on understanding the ways in which materials behave in time, under fluctuating conditions. Those fluctuating conditions are around us every day. Diurnal temperature and humidity swings, passing low and high pressure systems, precipitation, seasonal variations in all of the above and time dependent phenomena such as corrosion and material creep act to change the material properties of the substance.

For example, the vapor permeability of some materials varies depending on temperature and humidity. Kraft paper acts as a vapor retarder under relative humidities below 35 percent. Above 50 percent the paper facing becomes semi-vapor permeable with a perm range from 5 to 10. Polyethylene varies in permeance by a factor of 4 between $65°F$ ($18°C$) and $100°F$ ($38°C$).

Therefore, like many material properties, hygrothermal properties vary with time and varying pressures, temperatures and levels of humidity. The developing science of the behavior of materials in exterior envelopes due to their hygrothermal properties takes this variation into account. Failure mechanisms are time dependent and only become a factor for most materials when the surrounding environment sustains a relative of humidity of 90 percent or more for several days.

Extrinsic Attributes

Attributable to the material only with respect to a specific context (a time and a place) and highly dependent on the location of its processing and application, extrinsic attributes are constantly changing and dependent on local, regional and sometimes international factors such as the number of primary manufacturers supplying the material, economic cycles (especially in construction), political conditions and many others. It will not be a surprise that this book cannot offer a comprehensive treatment of extrinsic attributes.

In practice, architects are well aware of some of the actual values of extrinsic attributes, especially cost. Many practicing architects have the cost of most major materials at their fingertips. What is not so readily available are values for environmental, societal and cultural attributes. It is much harder to assign a cultural value to an aluminum extrusion versus bronze castings. And yet there are clear differences based on their previous uses, historical precedents and associations with particular buildings and architects. Titanium is routinely associated with the work of Frank Gehry, concrete with LeCorbusier, and paper tubes with Shigeru Ban. Glass is the expert domain of contemporary designers like James Carpenter and Tim MacFarlane. The associations are undeniable and irresistible.

Economic

Architects and their projects are at the mercy of first cost. Because buildings are expensive and large, the initial construction cost often dominates all other lifetime costs of the building.

Construction cost ("First Cost")
Simply the cost of the construction of the building, sometimes including the fees charged by the design team. These costs are often the result of, essentially, an auction to place a price on the construction cost of the project by bidding contractors.

This is what happens when a project has been submitted for bids ("goes out to bid").

Therefore, there is very little science and very much messy accounting that results in a number that can be applied to the construction cost of a building.

Life cycle cost (LCC) and life cycle assessment (LCA)
These cost and assessment models are one of a number of methods meant to establish the larger cost of the facility, over its service life, to an owner, to society generally or other entity. LCC is a method now routinely used by owner/occupiers such as universities, hospitals, museums and other large institutions. While some office complexes are commissioned by the major (or sole) tenant, with the intent to occupy the facility for the long term, LCC is still rarely used in place of, or to complement, a first cost budget in these kinds of buildings.

LCC, LCA and other lifecycle costing methods are being required more often by public agencies when commissioning buildings for their use. Also, most sustainable design rating methods (such as LEEDS in the United States and BREEAM - British Research Establishment Environmental Assessment Method - in the UK) are requiring the use of lifecycle costing or assessment calculations.

And yet, the simplistic and uninformed application of LCA methods on a broad scale may begin to diffuse the principles that generated interest in an alternative assessment of environmental impact in the first place. It is useful to remember that LCA is just one method that is part of a much larger suite of *physical accounting* strategies that assist in the establishment of the actual use of materials for any particular economic activity. All the methods fall within the category of Material Flow Analysis techniques championed by the industrial ecologists and are intended to uncover the *physical economy* that is often substantially masked by the valuations assigned by the financial, or monetary economy.

This is a cornerstone of industrial ecology and warrants further reading beyond the confines of this book (Baccini 1991).

Ecological

The most commonly applied metrics assigned to the environmental impact of building materials are embodied energy, toxicity and fraction recycled. These three tend to dominate discussions regarding the environmental aspects of materials today.

However, the study of the ecological aspects of materials is entering a new phase, characterized by the difficult acknowledgement that no human activity that uses energy or materials is sustainable, no matter how renewable the material. The fact of entropy is driving a more rigorous study of the issues that need to be considered when faced with the daunting task of aligning an awareness and interest in environmental issues and orchestrating massive material expenditures, dissipation and likely (and sometimes) unavoidable degradation of natural environments. The invocation of ecological perspectives, and analogs, on the use of construction materials within the larger technical cycles of human industry promise an illuminating reconsideration of the challenges to be faced and the opportunities to be gained. Construction ecology, and its cousins in other industries, are making good progress in the delineation of processes that can be directly addressed by the designer. For example, the growing body of knowledge regarding the *rucksack* attached to the use of any material (especially mined minerals and processed ores) is providing a better sense of the total material costs of a particular material selection.

In addition, the complex lifetime structure within which buildings serve society is being examined for characteristics that may better inform the architectural profession of the design opportunities for buildings of smarter design lifetimes. As demonstrated in Chapter 2, already a number of design approaches and industry players are seeking to profit from this complexity. Also, examining the lifetimes of buildings is not a simple task - it inevitably captures topics as ephemeral as aesthetic preferences, changing definitions of obsolescence and shifting working patterns and business models.

It is also well known now that we have entered into an era in which the material store of our cities and buildings has become a significant fraction of all of the processed materials of our human societies. This "ultimate sink" of contemporary materials is not our landfills but the existing stock of materials in daily use - the anthropogenic stock (Brunner 2004;Wolman 1967). Buildings are a portion of this material stock and likely form a substantial component of it - if not the majority share. This is a research topic that deserves concerted effort.

Not much is known of this existing stock, but several researchers have remarked on the need to better outline the true nature of this materials store (Brunner 2004;Ehrenfeld 2004;Lifset 2004). Clearly, at least to this author, maintaining and responsibly regenerating this existing stock will become the design opportunity of this century and beyond. Once ores begin the downward spiral of critically diminishing quality, and all of the world's forests reach a steady state of harvesting and regrowth, the making of buildings will be focused on the extension of the service lives of our most useful buildings and the reclamation of materials from those less critical to meeting the continuing needs of society.

Societal

Society will often take stock of its health by assessing the state of its buildings. There is no more immediate symbol of the disintegration of societal health, of an erosion of the optimism of a society, than deteriorating and abandoned buildings and underutilization of the material wealth of the existing building stock. In fact, this symbol is not only an indicator but also a cause for regarding that society's health is under siege. Buildings are material things, no doubt, and their value as symbols of societal health far transcends their actual material value. But buildings also register a material state that reflects the broader state of society.

This material state can best be characterized as the societal properties that relate the value of place to the material investment that those inhabitants are willing to undertake. A society will be willing to invest in a place if there is considerable optimism about the future. The financial investment that is showered on the real estate of Midtown Manhattan in New York City speaks to a boundless expectation of continued prosperity. This hyper-localized condition has been in stark contrast to regions of the outer burroughs for many decades now. Regional optimism can also be seen as the European Union expands and projects its environmental concerns on a wider area.

But the intransigent and corrosive degradation of entire regions of the midwest United States is an equally singular indication of deep societal mistrust of the prospects for the economic and cultural future of these areas. For example, downtown Detroit is a testament of the extraordinary differential of value between the enormous material expenditures of the past and expectations for the future. Vast hotel and commercial structures are left abandoned, with no real expectation for a renaissance to rival the past, despite the visible reminders of the enormous economic and material investments of just a few decades ago. These expenditures were real - they consumed huge chunks of material resources - and yet their value today approaches nil. Therefore, the extrinsic properties of materials - as defined through the expectations and desires of society - have the power to trump any value based in the intrinsic properties that define the utility of materials themselves. This interplay between the intrinsic and the extrinsic is one of the most consequential processes that leads us to place value and determine utility in the physical artifacts that we make. In Chapter 2, the Seattle Kingdome was used to illustrate the overpowering forces that can be mustered against a building that surely could have continued to serve - with modifications - the desires of a public in need of the luxuries of late 20th century sporting entertainment.

As economies become more intricately intertwined, global concerns are apt to affect the thinking of a broader set of people in a more diverse set of societies. Today the priorities of focusing on responsible approaches to our limited resources is bringing an array of separate disciplines together in assessing the methods by which societal concerns evolve.

Cultural

There is no better indication of the exuberance and optimism of a society than the awareness it possesses and attention it dedicates to the cultural value embodied in its architecture. From the identification of the cultural value of museums, performance halls, civic buildings and historically important architecture to the 20th century drive to formulate the criteria for defining the mandate for preservation, taking care of the existing building stock is one of the responsibilities of a collective sense of good stewardship. It is not surprising that buildings are quickly targeted, destroyed and neglected during times of war and other catastrophic economic and social upheavals. But during times of relative social and political stability, cultural lines of thought have a chance to flourish, evolve and interact across many modes of production. Since the last world war, architectural thought has had a chance to cultivate the discourse that has come to define specific cultural value in individual buildings.

Again, the continuing service that these buildings actually offer and the quantifiable value of the materials that comprise their systems are far surpassed by the intangible value that they represent to societies that increasingly place value on legacies of past cultural production. It is curious that much writing about the deplorable state of the built landscape does not often recognize the healthy regard today for the existing built landscape. In most cities today, new building proposals are met with - sometimes vociferous - local reaction that is ideally focused on emphasizing the value of the existing built fabric. This kind of broad, and public, concern for the heritage of the built landscape is a good indication of the persistence of the cultural value of existing buildings. What the criteria are that determine value, in other words, the actual *cultural properties* that can be cited in determining the cultural utility of buildings, are a complex and highly dynamic discussion. However, one attribute of this set of properties is clearly the tenacity with which cultural properties, and the value derived therein, are an important component of our built world.

These enduring values, societal and cultural, and the emerging values of an ecology of the built world are leading toward a recognition that great value - and design opportunity - rests with the tremendous material legacy of the existing anthropogenic stock of buildings. These ideas are furthered discussed in the Epilogue - Building Ecologies.

Metals

The business of Architecture is to establish emotional relationships by means of raw materials.

LeCorbusier, 1931

Industrial Strength

Metals constitute the backbone of modern industrial capacity. Ductility, high strength, hardness, durability, conductivity and ease of processing are just some of the qualities that make metals a critical material in most industries. Abundance also contributes to the success of this family; most elements of the periodic table are metals and many rocks contain several types of ore. For example, the vast majority of rocks and soil found anywhere contain some amount of aluminum, the third most common element on earth (Zahner 1995;Wilquin 2001). Metals are employed in architecture as an important barrier material in the building enclosure (flashing, window frames, radiative barriers), a primary load transfer material in building structures, and many other applications in all building systems. Even when modern concrete is selected as an alternative to metal, it is the reinforcing steel bars that make the composite viable. Steel frames allowed the American skyscraper to become economically viable. Aluminum extrusions are now the material of choice for large curtainwall assemblies. Copper and zinc have prevailed as important roofing materials and titanium has recently been introduced as an exterior finish metal.

Figure 3.26

The application of titanium sheet metal to this exterior form is the result of both aesthetic interests and the fortuitous temporary drop in price for the metal. The performance potential of this exotic metal extends far beyond its use as the rainscreen for building enclosures.

Guggenheim Bilbao, Bilbao, Spain (2001).

Frank O. Gehry, Architect.

Gehry (1995).

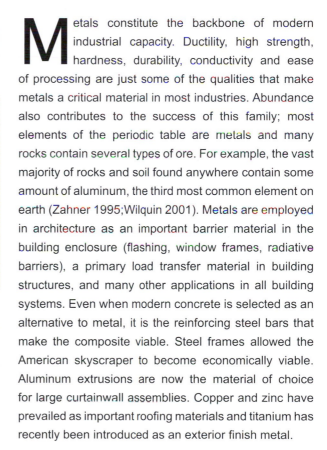

Of course many other metals have been used in buildings through the centuries. Lead, tin, brass and bronze have been used for roofing tiles and ornamental filigree, door handles and doors themselves. Internal reinforcing of stonework and exterior cast facades have been made from number of metallic alloys. Coping and flashing, scuppers and standing seam assemblies have been made from metals for many building types, in many climates.

After the Stone Age and into the middle of the 19th century, the important aspects of technological innovation were based on the development of new metallic alloys and their application in new tools and machines. The Bronze and Iron Ages overlapped by a thousand years as iron, and then steel, were to become the dominant modern materials. Bronze was discovered around 3500BC, iron 1500BC, although these dates vary significantly depending on the region of the world under consideration. For example, because of the higher temperatures that African furnaces reached with the use of tropical hardwoods, most of that continent completely bypassed the Bronze Age and entered straight into the Iron Age. But for much of the rest of the world the use of bronze dominated the making of tools and other implements as the discovery of iron and then steel changed tool-making. Weaponry has always been a great catalyst in the development of materials, as much now as it was in the ancient world.

The seven metals of antiquity were copper, tin, gold, silver, iron, lead and mercury. These were the only known metals until well into the 13th and 14th centuries when antimony, arsenic, bismuth and zinc were discovered. In the centuries since, many more have been added to the list so that now there are 86 known metals. Of these only 10 are regularly used in architectural applications; iron, copper, lead, tin, zinc, nickel, tungsten, titanium, chromium, and aluminum. Other metals are also used in small amounts for various alloys.

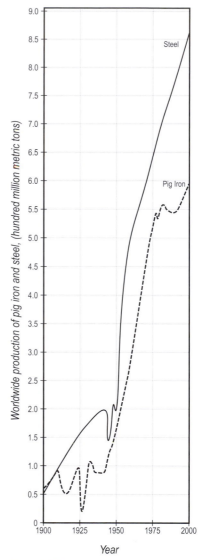

Figure 3.27

Worldwide production of iron and steel during the 20th century.

Sources: US Bureau of Mines, Mineral Resources of the US, 1900-23, US Geological Survey, Mineral Resources of the US, 1924-31, Minerals Yearbook, 1932-94, Commodity Data Summaries, 1962-77, Mineral Commodity Summaries, 1978-95, Mineral Commodity Summaries, 1997-2002, Minerals Yearbook, V.I, 1995-2000.

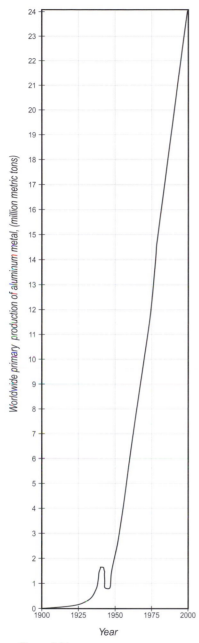

Figure 3.28

Worldwide production of aluminum during the 20th century.

Sources: USGS Minerals Handbooks, and Minerals Yearbook, also US Geological Survey, Mineral Resources of the US, 1924-31.

Beginning in the mid-19th century, developments in alloying, processing and production, and an elementary understanding of metallurgy, quickly accelerated the intensity of research and the quick application of various metals. Innovations, such as the invention of the Bessemer and Kelly processes in the 1850s for removing impurities from steel, quickly made iron the material of choice for industry (Moavenzadeh 1990). Aluminum, having been discovered in 1808 by Sir Humphry Davy, remained an expensive luxury metal for many decades, until consumption dramatically increased with the invention of the electrolytic reduction of cryolite in 1886, simultaneously by Hall in America and Heroult in France. This allowed an economical yield of much greater quantities. First used in construction in the mid-1920s, by 1966 production of aluminum was second only to steel. Stainless steel and ductile tungsten steel were developed at the beginning of the 20th century and have now become standard metals for an array of applications. Alloys of all metals have multiplied rapidly during the 20th century.

After World War II, leading aluminum producers in the United States were suddenly confronted with an excess capacity that had ballooned 500 percent over a 5 year period. They determined that transportation, packaging and construction were industries that could provide the demand for the supply of aluminum that could be supplied. They quickly succeeded in entering these markets and eventually altering the material landscape of these industries. The development of hundreds of aluminum, steel, nickel, chromium, magnesium and other metallic alloys are the lasting legacy of decades of intense research and development. In many ways, the birth of the modern industrial world was midwifed by innovation in the processing and novel application of metallic alloys. Recently though, while the use of metals has not abated, the pace of development has decelerated. Today, other materials - polymers, composites, ceramics and glasses - have taken the spotlight away from metals.

Figure 3.29

Rivaling buildings in scale, complexity, materials intensity of use, and durability, the technology of weapons has always been the most consistent and insistent catalyst for innovations in materials research - as it has been for metallurgy in the 20th century.

British cruiser, London, UK

The smelting of metals contributes about 13 percent of the global emission of sulfur dioxide, the chief component of acid rain. Also, the mining of 900 million tons of metal produced 6 billion tons of waste ore. The majority of this waste comes from the mining of gold, copper and iron ore. The proportion of waste produced to ore extracted has increased with the decrease in the quality of ore grades (Sampat 2003).

Demand for metals was very strong during the 20th century, with a growth rate consistently averaging around 3 percent per year. Recently, however, the demand for metal ore in developed regions has leveled off or actually dropped slightly (van Vuuren et al. 1999). This can be attributed, at least in part, to the continuing "decarbonization" of advanced economies - the metals sector being just one element of this trend (Ruth 1998). As with several large industries, improvements in productivity, the use of lower-carbon fuels, the development of "cleaner" industrial processes and the general dematerialization of society has contributed to this decarbonization. The opposite is true in developing regions where demand is still very strong - averaging 5-8 percent, with greatest demand occurring in Asian countries, especially China. However, there is still a substantial differential between present consumption in developed countries (~275-325 kg/capita) and that of developing regions (~55 kg/capita).

Figure 3.30

Detail of structural "cage" of curved hot-rolled structural sections, hollow steel structural sections (HSS), gusset connector plates and tubular "stub-ups" to receive the sheet metal of the exterior envelope. The geometric complexity of this building was realized using 22 million pounds and 12,500 individual members of structural steel.

Walt Disney Concert Hall, Los Angeles, CA (2003).
Frank O. Gehry, Architect

Recovery of metals and recycling has become a major source for all ferrous and many nonferrous metals. The relationship between the primary market for metals and recycled and scrap metal sources has been shown to be complex and difficult to predict. It seems that the availability of scrap metal is only secondarily related to global metal pricing and primarily influenced by a diverse set of factors including consumption, changes in production technologies and changes in consumer preferences (Tilton 1999). The specific levels of recycling and scrap metal recovery are given for each ferrous and nonferrous material in the next few sections.

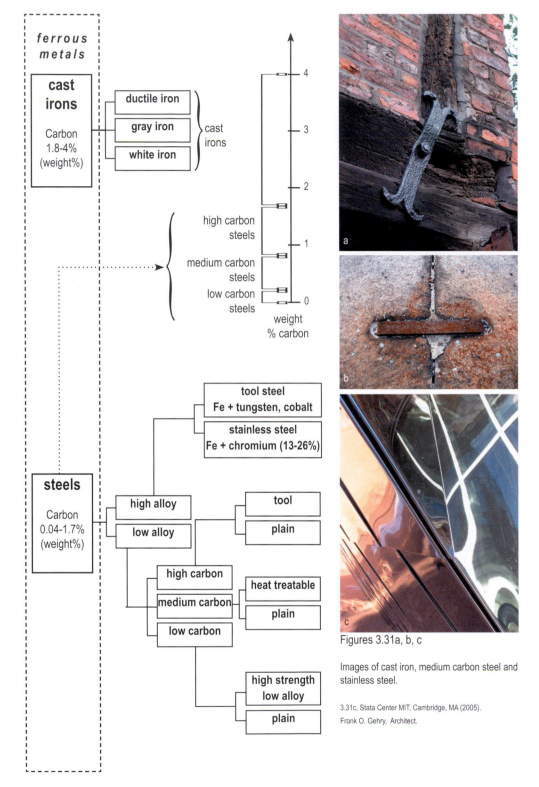

ferrous metals

cast irons
Carbon 1.8-4% (weight%)

ductile iron

gray iron

white iron

} cast irons

4

3

2

1

0

high carbon steels

medium carbon steels

low carbon steels

weight % carbon

tool steel
Fe + tungsten, cobalt

stainless steel
Fe + chromium (13-26%)

steels
Carbon 0.04-1.7% (weight%)

high alloy

low alloy

tool

plain

high carbon

medium carbon

low carbon

heat treatable

plain

high strength low alloy

plain

Figures 3.31a, b, c

Images of cast iron, medium carbon steel and stainless steel.

3.31c, Stata Center MIT, Cambridge, MA (2005).
Frank O. Gehry, Architect.

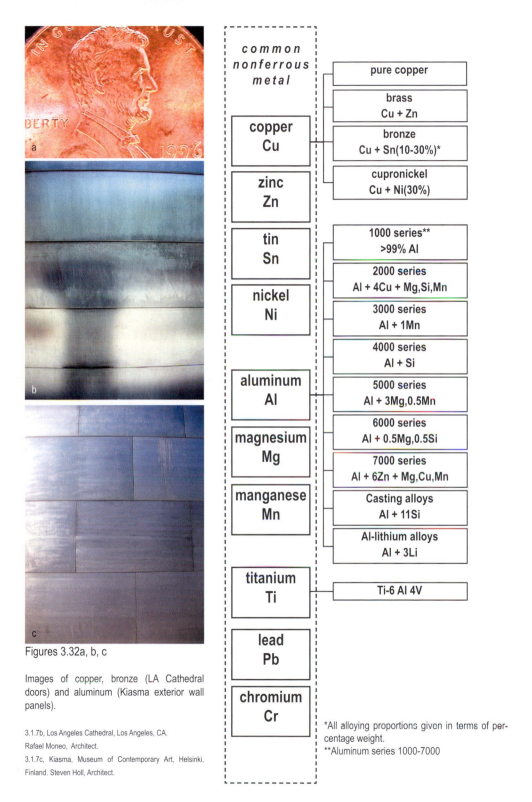

Figures 3.32a, b, c

Images of copper, bronze (LA Cathedral doors) and aluminum (Kiasma exterior wall panels).

3.1.7b, Los Angeles Cathedral, Los Angeles, CA. Rafael Moneo, Architect.

3.1.7c, Kiasma, Museum of Contemporary Art, Helsinki, Finland. Steven Holl, Architect.

common nonferrous metal

copper Cu
- pure copper
- brass Cu + Zn
- bronze Cu + Sn(10-30%)*
- cupronickel Cu + Ni(30%)

zinc Zn

tin Sn

nickel Ni

aluminum Al
- 1000 series** >99% Al
- 2000 series Al + 4Cu + Mg,Si,Mn
- 3000 series Al + 1Mn
- 4000 series Al + Si
- 5000 series Al + 3Mg,0.5Mn
- 6000 series Al + 0.5Mg,0.5Si
- 7000 series Al + 6Zn + Mg,Cu,Mn
- Casting alloys Al + 11Si
- Al-lithium alloys Al + 3Li

magnesium Mg

manganese Mn

titanium Ti
- Ti-6 Al 4V

lead Pb

chromium Cr

*All alloying proportions given in terms of percentage weight.
**Aluminum series 1000-7000

115

Classification and Properties

Classification

Metals are best classified as ferrous, or iron bearing, and nonferrous, lacking iron content. The ferrous metals are those whose primary constituent is iron, such as cast and wrought irons, steels including stainless steels, and many other alloys combining nickel, chromium, carbon and other materials. Ferrous metals account for an overwhelming majority of engineering applications. Over 90 percent of all metals consumed globally are from the ferrous alloy family.

Ferrous alloys (iron-bearing) are very good engineering materials because of the following reasons. First, iron is relatively economical in its extraction, processing, forming, alloying and fabrication. The iron mining and steel production industries are competitive and well-established enterprises. Despite the prevalence of government subsidies and national tariff protections, the global competitive market is still the primary determinant of the steel production business. Second, ferrous alloys are extremely versatile materials, both strong and ductile with good fracture toughness and high moduli. Protected against corrosion, oxidation and galvanic, ferrous alloys exhibit good durability. Processing can be accomplished through cold and hot rolling, extrusion, forging, drawing and casting. Joining is achieved through a variety of methods including welding, intrusive fasteners, mechanical joints and others. Third, variety of surface treatments, both mechanical and chemical are possible making ferrous metals attractive in both challenging environments and aesthetically sensitive installations. This combination makes it the preferred choice for structural engineering applications and an attractive choice for nonstructural architectural metalwork, such as exterior envelope panels, decorative elements and fascias, copings, sidings and many other decorative situations. Fourth, iron is an abundant material in the

Figure 3.33

Complex cast ironwork serving as the physical load path from the horizontal to the vertical.

Smithfield Market, London, England.

Figure 3.34

Tower sheathed in stainless steel "scales".

Stata Center MIT, Cambridge, MA (2005), Frank O. Gehry, Architect.

gold	6000BC
copper	4200BC
silver	4000BC
lead	3500BC
tin	1750BC
iron, smelted	1500BC
mercury	750BC

Figure 3.35

Approximate dates of discovery for the seven metals of antiquity.

Figure 3.36

This bronze sculpture displays the rich coloring of an aged patina.

Earth's crust, readily accessible and easily extracted, relative to other metals (Llewellyn 1994).

The classification of steels is based on the chemical composition of the alloy. Three systems are the most commonly used, the Unified Numbering System (UNS), a classification system developed by the American Iron and Steel Institute (AISI) and another by the Society of Automotive Engineers (SAE). In the United States the most widely used standards for steel products are those of ASTM International. Many other classification systems are in use, most of them regionally based. In Germany, the Deutsches Institut fur Normung produces the DIN numbers, the Japanese Industrial Standards Committee has developed JIS Standards, the United Kingdom uses British Standards (BS), France, AFNOR, Italy, UNI and Sweden adheres to the SS developed by the Swedish Standards Institution (Davis 2001).

The nonferrous metals used in architectural assemblies include aluminum, copper, tin, nickel, zinc, titanium and chromium. This collection of diverse metals possesses a very broad range of properties and is thus used in a great variety of architectural applications. However, it is possible to generalize the distinction between the applications of both ferrous and nonferrous metals. Ferrous metals are used in many structural situations in which the transfer of compressive, tensile, bending, shear and torsional loads is required. Most nonferrous metals are not generally used for load transfer, with the exception of some uses of aluminum in secondary structural assemblies such as strongbacks for curtainwalls. The nonferrous metals are primarily used to provide material for all types of weather barriers, from metal roof construction to building enclosures, seals and other applications. Because of the superior corrosion-management performance of some nonferrous metals (zinc, lead, anodized aluminum) they are often specified to provide the first line of defense against the weather. Their use in rainscreen applications is proven.

Alloys

Metals are almost never used in their pure forms. Not only are these pure forms often difficult and expensive to produce but it has been found that combining metals often results in mixtures that outperform the pure metal elements. Through alloying (sometimes referred to as inoculation) a very large array of useful metals with a wide range of properties has been made available to every industrial sector. The vast majority of these alloys have been classified and entered into various standardized designations defined and controlled by national and international standards organizations. Therefore, alloys for most industrial uses are highly standardized materials with deep information resources readily available to designers, inventors, engineers and architects (Davis 2001).

Because combining metals often results in material property changes, alloying is purposefully done to improve the utility of the host metal. That utility may involve one or several properties including physical, processing or service attributes. Improvements in stiffness, hardness, corrosion resistance, even color can be achieved by alloying one or more metals into another. Often several shifts in property accompany any particular alloying process; however, most alloying is accomplished with one of a very few number of target properties. Architectural applications usually target strength and corrosion issues as the primary benefits that can be gained from alloying two or more metals together.

Two general types of alloying are used today. The first involves the alteration of the chemical composition of the surface of a metal. This can be achieved by using one of several different processes including plating, cladding, nitriding, ion implantation, carburizing, hot dip galvanizing and other processes. This kind of alloying affects only the attributes of the surface of the host metal and is therefore used to improve such properties

A00001 - A99999	Al and Al alloys
A01001 - A63562	Al foundry alloys, ingot or casting
A82014 - A87475	wrought Al clad w/ wrought Al
A91030 - A91450	wrought Al alloys, nonheat treatable
A93002 - A95954	wrought Al alloys, nonheat treatable
A98001 - A98280	wrought Al alloys, nonheat treatable
A92001 - A92618	wrought Al alloys, heat treatable
A96002 - A97472	wrought Al alloys, heat treatable
C00001 - C99999	**Cu and Cu alloys**
wrought alloys	
C10100 - C15760	pure and low alloy Cu
C16200 - C16500	cadmium Cu
C17000 - C17700	Cu-Be alloy
C18000 - C19900	Cu and high Cu alloys
C20500 - C29800	brasses (Cu-Zn)
C31000 - C35600	leaded brasses (Cu-Zn-Pb)
C40400 - C49080	tin brasses (Cu-Zn-Sn-Pb)
C50100 - C52900	phosphor bronzes (Cu-Sn-P)
C53200 - C54800	leaded phosphor bronzes
C55180 - C56000	Cu-Ag-P and Cu-P
C60600 - C64400	Al bronzes
C64700 - C66100	silicon bronzes
C66200 - C66420	Cu alloys
C66700 - C67820	manganese bronzes
C68000 - C69950	silicon brasses, other Cu-Zn alloys
C70100 - C72950	Cu-Ni alloys
C73150 - C79900	Ni-silvers and leaded Ni-silvers
cast alloys	
C80100 - C81200	cast Cu
C81300 - C82800	cast Cr-Cu, Be-Cu alloys

C83300 - C85800	cast red, yellow, leaded brasses
C86100 - C86800	cast Mn bronzes and leaded Mn bronzes
C87300 - C87900	cast Si brasses and bronzes
C89320 - C89940	cast Cu-Sn-Bi alloys
C90200 - C94500	tin, leaded bronzes
C94700 - C94900	cast Ni-tin bronzes
C95200 - C95810	cast Al bronzes
C96200 - C96800	cast Cu-Ni alloys
C97300 - C97800	cast Ni-silver alloys
C98200 - C98840	cast leaded Cu alloys
C99300 - C99750	cast copper alloys
E00001 - E99999	**rare earth alloys**
E00000 - E00999	actinium
E01000 - E20999	cerium
others	
E90000 - E9999	yttrium
L00001 - L99999	**low-melting metals**
L00001 - L00999	bismuth
L01001 - L01999	cadmium
others	
L13001 - L13999	tin
L50001 - L59999	lead
M00001-M99999	**misc. nonferrous metals and alloys**
M00001-M00999	antimony
others	
M10001-M19999	magnesium
M20001-M29999	manganese
M30001-M39999	silicon
P00001-P99999	**precious metals and alloys**
R00001-R99999	**reactive and refractory metals and alloys**
W00001-W99999	**welding filler metals**
Z00001-Z99999	**zinc and zinc alloys**

Figure 3.37

Unified numbering system (UNS) of nonferrous metals and alloys.

as corrosion resistance, hardness, color and other surface-related properties. The second type of alloying involves the inclusion of one kind of metal element into the body of another. This change in the bulk composition of the metal results in an alteration of the host metal's properties throughout its matrix. This kind of alloying is used to affect bulk material properties such as overall stiffness, tensile strength, toughness and many other attributes.

The most common reason for combining metals is the improvement of the strength of the host metal at room temperature. This is achieved by alloying the atoms of one metal into the bulk of the host metal. The atoms of metals are arranged into crystalline structures that are called grains. These grains affect the micromechanical behavior of the metal, for example by altering the actual path of shearing between one part of the metal and another under an applied load. An improvement in strength is often achieved by altering the arrangement of these crystals by the inclusion of the atoms of another element. Many types of dislocations occur as a result of the deformation of a metal under an applied load. Improving a metal's strength usually entails augmenting its ability to resist plastic deformation by better impeding the slip that occurs between adjacent crystal layers. For example, including a smaller metal atom among the larger metal atoms of the host metal produces a longer path for the dislocation. This creates more interference for the formation of a fracture and therefore improves its ability to resist plastic deformation.

The specific processes used in alloying metals, and the properties of the resulting mixture, are highly dependent on the metals involved. Alloying can only occur up to the solid solubility of the host metal. The relative sizes of the alloying metal and the host metal determine the arrangement of these elements with respect to one another in the alloy. The atoms of the alloying metal may be small enough to fit into the structure of the base metal, or they may replace base metal atoms altogether.

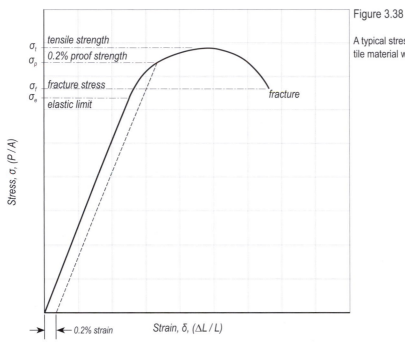

Figure 3.38

A typical stress-strain curve for a ductile material with a clear elastic zone.

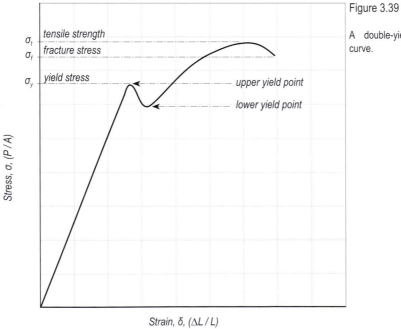

Figure 3.39

A double-yield point stress-strain curve.

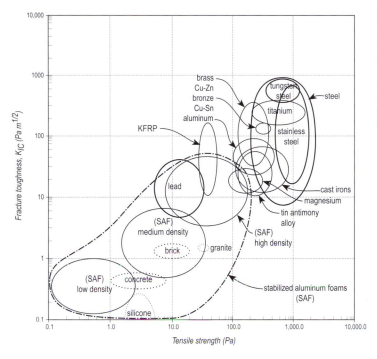

Figure 3.40

Fracture toughness and tensile strengths of selected metals.

Sources: CES software 4.5, ASM International (2002), Dominghaus (1988), Llewellyn (1994), Davis (2001), Wilquin (2001), Zahner (1995).

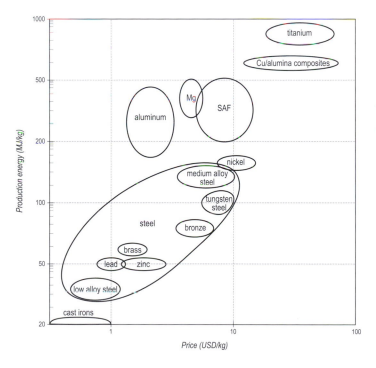

Figure 3.41

Production energy versus cost of selected metals.

Sources: CES software 4.5, ASM International (2002), Dominghaus (1988), Llewellyn (1994), Davis (2001), Wilquin (2001), Zahner (1995).

As an alloy cools from its molten state it may assume a number of stable phases, again depending on the compatibility of the alloying atoms with the structure of the base metal.

Besides improvements in strength, other mechanical properties may be profitably altered through alloying. After strength, the most common include improvements in hardness, fatigue resistance, creep resistance and corrosion resistance. Each of these properties is predictably altered with alloying. Service improvements include improvements in heat and cold resistance, corrosion resistance, greater toughness and better hardness and wear resistance. Improvements in processing include easier castability, weldability, solderability, formability and machinability. Improvements to physical properties include all the major attributes of metals; elastic modulus, density, magnetic and electrical properties, thermal expansion, color and others (Cornish 1987).

Alloying can be accomplished by several melting and casting techniques as well as mechanical surface treatments. Again, these techniques vary greatly depending on the base metal and the alloying metal. Manufacturers of architectural components can obtain most useful alloys in the form of prealloyed ingots that can be used directly in the making of the architectural product (Davis 2001). The highly standardized classification of alloys used for architectural applications assures that architects can obtain all relevant information about their performance from a variety of sources published in manuals and posted on the internet (see the Bibliography for internet sources).

Properties

Elastic Moduli
The elastic moduli of metals varies greatly from 45 GPa for magnesium to 407 GPa for tungsten. Many metals produce stress-strain curves with a well-defined elastic zone and then a plastic zone that demonstrates substantial ductility. This alone distinguishes the metal family from every other material family in a very important way. Metals carry load in very useful ways, demonstrating good resilience and significant ductility. There are a few exceptions. For example, gray cast iron does not produce a well-defined elastic zone and some metal alloys may be made to behave as brittle materials.

Yield Strength
Yield strength in metals is measured in a very particular way because of the difficulty in establishing a clear departure from elastic behavior. For metals that demonstrate an elastic zone the convention adopted is the use of a 0.2 percent strain limit to determine the yield stress. This is determined by using an offset line, parallel to the slope of the elastic portion of the stress-strain curve and noting the stress as it approaches a 0.2 percent strain. When it reaches this strain level, the corresponding stress is recorded as the yield strength of the metal, see Figures 3.38, 3.39.. The yield strength is a measure of the metal's capacity to

resist plastic deformation. Most metals continue to carry increasing loads after the initiation of plasticity. The ultimate load reached for a metal under tension is another measure of its strength.

Ductility

A distinguishing characteristic of metals is that they are generally significantly more ductile than most materials. Ductility, as a measure of the ability to deform a material's shape without producing cracking makes the processing of metals especially attractive. Also, once a metal is stressed beyond it's elastic limit, its ductility allows it to slowly deform without the catastrophic breakage of a ceramic or glass.

Corrosion

Any treatment of the family of metals is not complete without discussion of the effects of corrosion. Along with high temperatures, it is the most critical weakness of metals, limiting its use and requiring maintenance. Corrosion is the scourge of ferrous metals in particular, as these metals do not form stable protective oxidation layers. The structure of iron oxide, or rust, is a thin flaky sheet-like deposit that easily falls away from the metal exposing a fresh layer for attack. Corrosion can be an extraordinarily expensive problem especially when it affects structural steel in large civil structures. It affects the structural assemblies of building frames, the bolted and welded trusses of bridge construction and various other structures that use standardized steel members. It has also become clear that corrosion is a major factor in the durability of reinforced concrete structures. Through micropores and the presence of water in the concrete matrix itself, corrosion attacks the reinforcing rods of the composite and creates intractable maintenance problems. A recent study indicates that, due to corrosion of metals, the yearly loss to the national economies of the UK and the US may be at least 4 percent of their respective gross national products (Kruger 1990).

Corrosion is an electrochemical process that generally attacks the surface of metals. The process involves the passage of electrons from one location to another. The electrons may travel within one metal or be transferred from the surface of one metal to another. Both types will be described below.

Corrosion occurs when an electrochemical cell is produced. This cell is composed of an anode and cathode linked by the transfer of electrons. The anode, or anodic site, is the location where the metal is dissolved into metallic ions or converted into corrosion species such as rust. The cathode, or cathodic site, is the location that receives the electrons shed by the metal at its anodic site. The circuit results in the steady dissolution of the metal and the production of the familiar oxidation products and pitting that signals corrosion.

Corrosion most readily occurs in wet environments in which oxygen and water come together to react with the electrons at the cathode. Corrosion can also occur in relatively

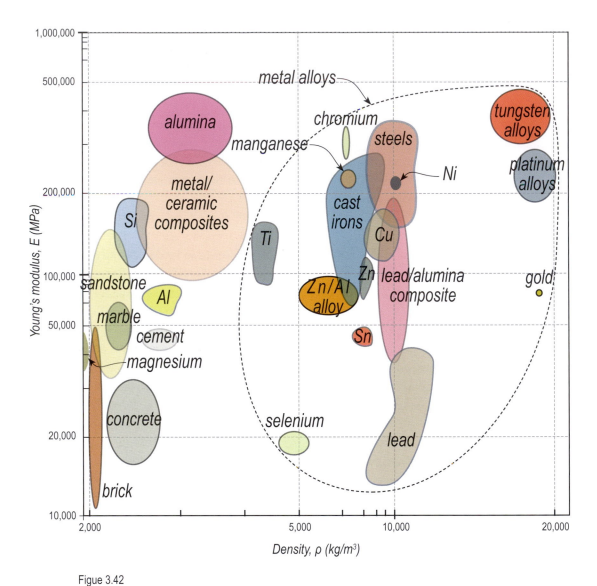

Figue 3.42

Young's modulus versus density for a set of metals.

Sources: CES software 4.5, Ashby et al. (2000), ASM International (2002), Dominghaus (1988), Llewellyn (1994), Davis (2001), Walker (2001), Wilquin (2001), Zahner (1995).

dry environments in which the relative humidity occasionally reaches levels that allow the deposition of moisture into cracks and other imperfections in the metal. These sites can then act as the catalyst for corrosion by producing positively charged ions that result in an acidic micro-environment.

Atmospheric pollution can also produce acidic rain and particulate deposition on the surface of metals that promotes the initiation of the electrochemical transfer that allows corrosion (Mikhailov et al. 1995). In terms of the corrosion to metals, the most damaging atmospheric pollutant is sulfur dioxide, which then reacts with rainwater to produce weak sulfuric acid. Other chemical species found to contribute to metallic corrosion are the chlorides, carbonates and nitrates. Different metals respond very differently to various atmospheric pollutants. This type of pollution has been shown to be a major concern in chronically polluted regions as is found in the less regulated eastern European countries (Uhlig and Revie 1985;Knotkova et al. 1995;Abdul-Wahab et al. 2003). In addition, the deposition of salts on the surface of metals also promotes corrosive processes by creating hydrophilic areas that attract moisture and again begin the process necessary for a working electrochemical cell.

The most important determinant of the rate of corrosion in metals is the nature of the environment. Marine, humid, urban, industrial environments are caustic in ways that promote the initiation and the continuation of severe corrosion. Rural, dry, nonindustrial settings are least problematic. Other determinants include the composition and microstructure of the metal, the position of the surface of the metal with respect to many conditions including its relative exposure, proximity to other surfaces, protection from salts and pollutants, regular wetting and drying and, of course, the level of maintenance. In any situation, with any metal, proper maintenance, such as cleaning or repainting will prevent and solve most corrosion problems.

Corrosion management seeks to avoid the critical failure of metallic components through the use of appropriate materials or types of maintenance required by the materials. The use of sacrificial oxidation, as in Korten steel, other protective oxidation and pre-weathered patinas, organic high performance coatings, application of corrosive resistant metals and cathodic protection are all technologies used to create a manageable situation. Extensive guidelines are available from a variety of leading metal trade groups specializing in the specification and care of architectural metals. Several useful websites are listed in the Bibliography.

Corrosion also occurs between metals. Because of differences in the conducting potential of diverse metals, electrons may be transferred from the surface of one metal to the other. The more reactive metal will act as the anode and corrode, the less reactive metal will act as the cathode and be protected from corrosive action. Therefore, the galvanic series is a relative ranking illustrating the placement of many metals in terms of their reactivity (anodic tendency), Figure 3.44. Coupling together metals that are far removed from one another on this list risks the potential that corrosion will be catalyzed. Typically coupling metals together that are contained within a single set of brackets will not lead to corrosion - roaming outside of the brackets will, most likely, lead to some corrosion, depending on the environmental conditions. The rate of corrosion is typically expressed as a corrosion penetration rate. This is usually expressed as a loss of material thickness over time, most often per year.

Ecological Properties

A good argument can be made for the benefits of using metals in buildings based on their capacities to contribute to an environmentally sound design strategy. This is primarily based on two separate sets of issues; (1) durability and extended-life performance and (2) recycled and recovery rates.

Properly detailed and treated, many metals demonstrate superior durability when compared with most alternative materials. Used for building structures, and therefore typically isolated from the corrosive and mechanically stressful forces of the exterior environment, metals can achieve service lives in the hundreds and thousands of years. Clearly then, the durability of structural steel in buildings usually far outstrips its use in bridges, towers and other "exposed" structures. Used as an exterior wall surface material, metals endure the various caustic elements of the environment reasonably well but require much greater maintenance and repair attention.

As shown below (Figure 3.52), many metals are already recycled and recovered in large quantities. This is especially true in construction because metals comprise the most valuable and most easily recoverable and recyclable material used in building. Doing so reduces both the energy and material wastage of mining extraction and refinement. Because most metals, and steel in particular, can be remelted and formed again, scrap metals are an important source for architectural components. In 2003, flat-rolled aluminum products

Figure 3.43

Surface corrosion of painted steel when exposed to a marine environment.

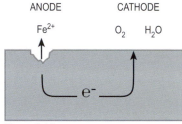

Figure 3.44

The electrochemical cell of corrosion on the surface of a metal. The transfer of electrons in the corrosion of iron occurs as follows:

$$Fe \rightarrow Fe^{2+} + 2e^-$$
$$O_2 + 2H_2O + 4e^- \rightarrow 4OH^-$$

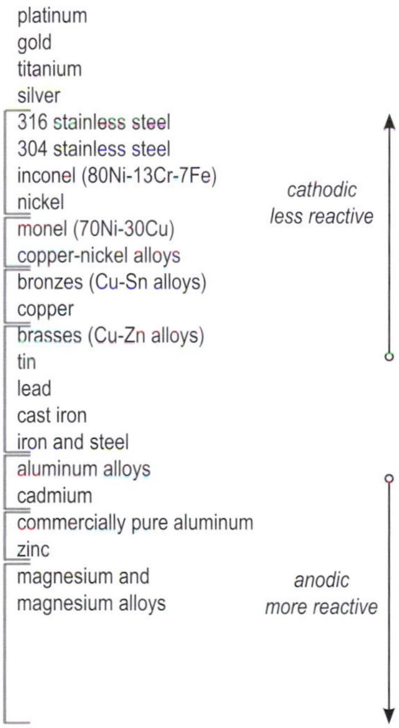

platinum
gold
titanium
silver
316 stainless steel
304 stainless steel
inconel (80Ni-13Cr-7Fe)
nickel
monel (70Ni-30Cu)
copper-nickel alloys
bronzes (Cu-Sn alloys)
copper
brasses (Cu-Zn alloys)
tin
lead
cast iron
iron and steel
aluminum alloys
cadmium
commercially pure aluminum
zinc
magnesium and
magnesium alloys

cathodic
less reactive

anodic
more reactive

Figure 3.45

The galvanic series.

contained 80 percent recycled content, copper (excluding wire) 75 percent, zinc 30 percent, and steel 32 percent for basic oxygen furnaces and 96 percent for electric arc furnaces. All of these claims and many others are made by the various sectors of the metal industry, so it is important to corroborate data across an array of information sources (Kriner 2004).

Processes

Metals are easily processed using heat and mechanical working. Smelting is the original process from which metals were separated from the ore. Heated to high temperatures the metal flows to the bottom of the furnace and other materials are segregated toward the top of the melt. This slag is removed and the metal is recovered in the form of a *bloom*.

Cold hammering can be employed to shape the softer metals like copper and bronze. Hot hammering, or more commonly referred to as forging, is the process of shaping and hardening a metal while it is at an elevated temperature. This process mechanically removes impurities and shapes the metal while it is more malleable. Annealing is the reheating of the metal, often during the process of forging, to reset the crystalline structure and prevent cracking. Quenching, the rapid cooling of a very hot metal, can be used with an iron and carbon alloy to produce much stronger metal. And finally casting is the process of melting a metal until fluid enough to pour into a mold.

Other processes are also commonly use to make metal components; such as extrusion, powder forming, laser welding, stamping and hydroforming. Hydroforming, for example, is the process of hydraulically expanding metal tubes into a form to produce continuous portions of varying section configurations lately used for the making of automobile chassis and frames (Aluminum Now 2005a). However, two methods in particular - one old and one new - have been gaining increased

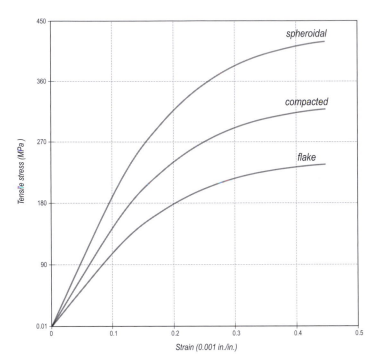

Figure 3.46

Unclassified cast irons showing the influence of graphite morphology on stress-strain curves.

Source: Adapted from ASM International (2002).

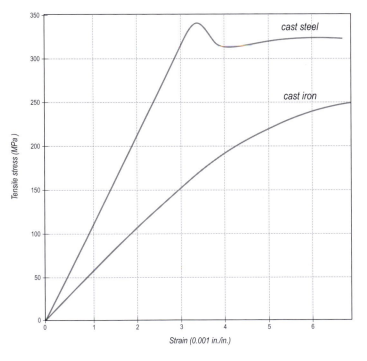

Figure 3.47

Unclassified cast steel and cast iron stress-strain curves.

Notice the fact that cast steel exhibits a distinct yield point.

Source: Adapted from ASM International (2002).

Figure 3.48

High-strength structural steels, typical initial stress-strain curves.

Source: Adapted from ASM International (2002).

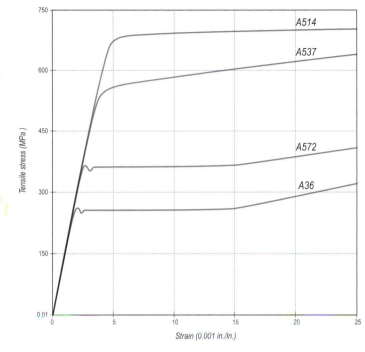

Figure 3.49

Behavior of two common stainless steels.

Source: Adapted from ASM International (2002).

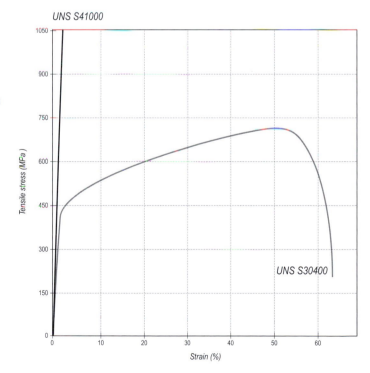

popularity for their economy and productivity benefits; investment casting and powder forming. Investment casting involves the time-honored methods of pouring molten metal into a ceramic mold. Complex and large parts, once assembled from separate machined pieces and welded, are now produced using investment casting (Mueller 2005). Powder forming involves the use of extremely fine metallic powders that are used to make complex parts by filling a mold with the metallic powder and heating and placing under high pressures. Thin-walled parts of complex geometries are economically produced using this forming method (Pease 2005;Sandberg 2003).

Metals

The following sections treat each major ferrous and nonferrous metal in more detail.

Cast Iron and Steel

Carbon content distinguishes cast irons from steels. The addition of carbon greatly alters the material properties of the metal. The addition of carbon strengthens the metal while decreasing its ductility. Various processes of working iron and steel, such as tempering, can reintroduce ductility and increase the toughness of high strength steels.

Cast irons contain a carbon content of between 1.8 and 4 percent (by weight). Steels contain a carbon content of between 0.4 and 1.7 percent. Furthermore steels are classified as low, medium and high carbon, again with respect to the carbon content of the material. In addition, steels are classified according the amounts of other alloying metals included and are called either low or high alloy steels. Low alloy steel contains low levels of chromium and nickel and high alloy steel, known as stainless steel, contains higher levels (18-26 percent chromium and 8 percent nickel). It should be noted that while the small differences in the percentage of carbon greatly affect the properties of the metal, these percentages are always given in terms of weight. However, the carbon atom is roughly one-fifth the weight of the iron atom and therefore five times the number of carbon atoms are needed to amount to one percentage point by weight.

Low carbon steels are used for a variety of low stress applications including construction and miscellaneous structural situations. Medium carbon steels are reserved for a higher level of stress concentrations and therefore are used for bolts and nuts. High carbon steel is used to make springs, cutting tools, machine parts etc. (Honeycombe and Bhadeshia1995).

Pure iron melts at 1,535°C. With the addition of small amounts of carbon, by using charcoal fuels the melting point can be reduced to about 1,150°C. For thousands of years, this temperature was out of the reach of ancient kilns and ovens. During this time, the primary sources of iron were meteors that had been found, collected and scavenged for small items treasured more for their novelty than their utility. Iron could not otherwise be separated and worked into useful implements. Eventually, in many parts of the world, producing temperatures of and beyond 1,150°C became possible and ironmaking developed into a widespread practice. However, the dissemination of this knowledge was slow and the accumulation of material resources necessary for the task of smelting iron was still a substantial commitment for any civilization of the time.

In China cast iron had been discovered by the first century BC. In Europe, the metalsmiths of the middle ages worked out incremental improvements over time through intuition and experimentation buoyed by the belief in the "magic" of the processes that led to an accumulation of basic craft knowledge. Eventually, organized improvements to the furnaces that increased their working temperatures led to the making of pig iron that was then used for cast and wrought iron. Weapons were the first implements to take advantage of the benefits of this new metal. With larger and better controlled furnaces, the production of cast iron increased dramatically.

However, the increases in the use of metals - and the accompanying wood fuel for the furnaces - from the 12th through the 15th centuries contributed to intense environmental pressures on the forests of Europe. Along with ship building, timber housing, and the increasing demands for domestic wood fuel and a general flourishing of economic activities of all types, the new art and craft of metallurgy contributed to the rapid decimation of the forests of Europe, especially those of England and Holland (Bernal 1954). Inevitable scarcities then led to the broad adoption of coal and a renewed search for alternative methods for producing useful alloys from iron ore. It also created the opportunity for Russia, Sweden and America to enter into the race for the production of iron, for these countries still had intact substantial timber resources.

Adopting coal as an alternative fuel source for the making of pig iron and continuing improvements in the iron making processes drove the price of the metal downward. Between the 1730s and 1800, the price of pig iron had been reduced by half. Cast iron was now produced to serve large-scale needs, such as civil structures - bridges, towers and building frames.

During this time, methods for making steel at comparable production scales as cast iron were not as successful, not for want of attention to the problem. Not until the invention of the Bessemer process (in 1854) had a radical new approach been taken in the production of steel. Henry Bessemer proposed and realized a system for injecting hot air through the molten pig iron, burning off some of the carbon while the remaining was left to combine with the iron to make steel. Bessemer both conceived of the process and invented the machines necessary to realize it.

Position		Country	Total for 2004	Compared to 2003
2004	2003		(million metric tonnes)	
1	1	China	272.5	23.2%
2	2	Japan	112.7	2.0%
3	3	United States	98.5	5.2%
4	4	Russia	64.3	2.5%
5	5	South Korea	47.5	2.6%
6	6	Germany	46.4	3.6%
7	7	Ukraine	38.7	4.9%
8	9	Brazil	32.9	5.7%
9	8	India	32.6	2.7%
10	10	Italy	28.3	5.6%

Figure 3.50

In 2004, 1.05 billion metric tonnes of crude steel was produced, an 8.8 percent increase in production over 2003. China accounted for 25.8 percent of all steel production and the Asian region grew its overall production by 13.2 percent.

Source: Adapted from Fewtrell (2005).

Even then, the Bessemer process required high grade ores that were still expensive to acquire. Therefore in 1879, Gilchrist Thomas introduced a new open hearth furnace with a basic liner that absorbed the impurities of the less expensive low grade ores and led to the industrial production of inexpensive steel. It is interesting to note that Thomas, an accomplished metallurgist, made his discovery through sound scientific principles of the time. His is one of the first truly scientific inventions of the industrial revolution.

Cast iron was first used extensively in the making of new bridges during the early to mid-1800s and culminated in the building of the Crystal Palace in 1851. The 100 foot span Coalbrookdale Bridge in Shropshire, England, 1777-81, was the first iron bridge built. Soon afterward, in 1793-96, a bridge at Sunderland was built with a span of 206 feet and the Schuykill Bridge, span 306 feet, was completed in 1809. Between 1818 and 1826, Thomas Telford built the Menai Suspension Bridge connecting North Wales and the Isle of Anglesey. This bridge has a main span of 579 feet (Pevsner 1968).

But what Nikolaus Pevsner calls the "aesthetic character" of iron was not fully expressed in architecture until the building of Henri Labrouste's Bibliothèque Ste-Geneviève in Paris, 1843-50, and J.B. Bunning's Coal Exchange in London, 1846-49 (Pevsner 1968). Train sheds and exhibition halls then adopted the material and it proliferated across Europe and eventually the United States.

Iron, cast and wrought, was the first modern material to have an immediate and radical effect on the form of architecture. The triangulated truss, gusset plates, tensile rods, thin columns and

Aluminum alloy classifications

1XXX	Al of 99% minimum purity
2XXX	Al-copper alloys
3XXX	Al-manganese alloys
4XXX	Al-silicon alloys
5XXX	Al-magnesium alloys
6XXX	Al-magnesium-silicon alloys
7XXX	Al-zinc-magnesium alloys
8XXX	Miscellaneous alloys, e.g. Al-lithium alloys

Figure 3.51

Architectural aluminums come primarily from the 6000 series of Al alloys.

Source:
Zahner, Walker, Davis.

Metal	Recycling percentage
aluminum	42
chromium	24.7
copper	37.2
iron and steel	57
lead	65.7
magnesium	34
nickel	32.7
tin	25
titanium	45
zinc	24.8

Figure 3.52

Recycling percentages of apparent supplies in the United States. Apparent supply is the amount of processed material available plus imports and the amount taken from current supplies. Figures are for the year 1997.

Source: Adapted from Geiser (2001), Smith (2003), and USGS Minerals Reports.

flanged beams crossed paths with the metal filligree of the mid-19th century and produced the iconic structural lattices that indicated something very new. As with any new materials, it did take some time for designers to fully understand the potential and constraints of these ferrous metals, as was demonstrated by the collapse of a portion of the Crystal Palace soon after its construction was completed.

Since the successful production of large quantities of steel, developments have progressed furiously. However, ferrous metals have significant drawbacks that are still the subject of much research (see "Emergent Metals", below).

Stainless steels are iron alloys containing at least 10.5 percent chromium. Other metals used to customize the corrosion resistance, hardness and other properties of stainless steel are copper, nickel, titanium, silicon, molybdenum, aluminum, nitrogen and sulfur. Stainless steels are of five types; martensitic, ferritic, austenitic, duplex (ferritic-austenitic) and precipitation-hardening. They are often employed in challenging environments where corrosion is a critical issue. In such scenarios, the most common stainless steels used are Types 304, 304L, 316 and 316L. Type 430 is sometimes used when particularly caustic environments are to be encountered (NiDI 2002a).

The recycling of steel is a substantial enterprise in many developed regions of the world. It is also clearly a major source of metal in developing regions. Data for recovery and recycling of steel in developing regions is very difficult to obtain. The existence of an array of businesses in countries like India, China, Turkey, several African and Asian nations is good indication that the recovery of steel scrap is accomplished at high levels. Even the difficult recovery of steel reinforcing from concrete is economically viable in many underdeveloped regions. Yet quality problems can result from such reclamation. For example, in Turkey, where the reclamation of steel reinforcing bars from concrete involves a straightening process, the integrity of the material comes into question (Elias-Ozkan 2003). The balance between quality of materials, economic gain and environmental benefits is often a difficult one.

In the United States, the recycling rate for steel scrap has been around 60% for the past two decades and 50% since the end of World War II. The recycling rate for steel scrap is defined as the total scrap recovered versus total raw steel produced. In 1998 an estimated 75 million metric tons (Mt) of scrap was generated and 35Mt of old scrap and 18Mt of new scrap was consumed . The United States produces 10.6 percent of the total world production of steel, 7.3 percent of the pig iron produced globally (Smith 2003).

Nonferrous Alloys

The growth in the production of nonferrous and "light" alloys is approximately 7 percent per year, a healthy pace that reflects the prevalence of a general dematerialization of metals in society and the substitution of highly engineered alloys for an array of heavier (lower performing) materials. The lighter metals (aluminum, magnesium and titanium) are attractive to industry generally because of their low densities, good strength to weight and stiffness to weight ratios and good to excellent corrosion resistance (Polmear 1995). Aluminum is commonly used in many architectural applications and titanium will most likely retain a small market as an exterior finish material. Magnesium has been very useful in small consumer items and may have a place in some high tolerance architectural components (such as pin-through type glass connectors).

Many of the heavier nonferrous alloys - copper, tin, zinc, lead - have been used for architectural applications for millennia because of their ductility, corrosion resistance and wear tolerance. For example, copper is dense and quite ductile, possessing an extremely valuable

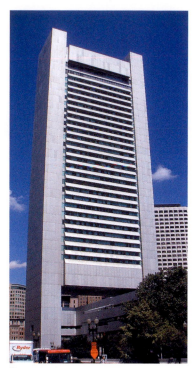

Figure 3.53

A building completely sheathed in aluminum exterior wall panels.
Federal Reserve Building, Boston, Massachusetts, USA.
Hugh Stubbins & Associates, 1974-78.

Figure 3.54

A lead tile roof surface.
King's College, Cambridge, UK.

134

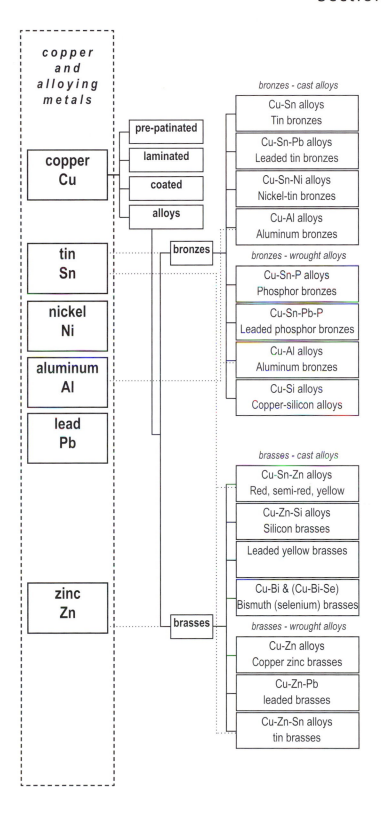

set of properties useful to many purposes in building construction.

Aluminum

Aluminum (or aluminium) is the third most abundant element of the Earth's crust and the second most consumed metal on Earth, behind iron. However, in its refinement and industrial applications it is a late arrival behind all of the major metals known today. Its abundance is challenged by the difficulty of extracting it pure from the ores in which it is found. Bauxite is the primary feedstock for the refining of alumina, the mineral precursor to the metal, aluminum. Bauxite contains 40-60 percent alumina. Other source minerals include alunite, kaolinite and vermiculite.

Aluminum has been known for slightly more than 200 years. Sir Humphry Davy definitively established the existence and also named aluminum in 1808. Soon afterward, P. Berthier discovered the primary feedstock for alumina, near the village of Les Baux in France. Bauxite is still the primary source for aluminum ore. Hans Christian Oersted seems to have been among the first to refine metallic aluminum in 1825. The density of aluminum was calculated by Friedrich Wöhler in 1827, two years after he had also worked out a process for producing very small quantities of the metal. After attempts were made to improve his method by others, with some success by 1885, worldwide production started reaching into the tonnes.

Finally, the modern process of electrolytic refinement that led to the economical separation of aluminum from bauxite was developed in the late 19th century. In 1886, Paul Louis Toussaint Héroult in France and Charles Martin Hall in the United States independently invented almost identical techniques for the electrolytic processing of bauxite to obtain aluminum. Each of these inventors, coincidentally both 22 years old at the time

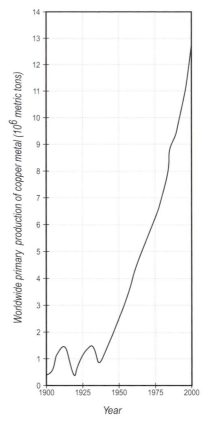

Figure 3.55

Worldwide production of copper metal.
Sources: USGS Minerals Handbooks, other.

Common (or tin) Bronze
(0.9)copper + (0.1)tin

Aluminum Bronze
(0.85)copper + (0.11)aluminum + (0.4)iron

Brass
(0.7)copper + (0.3)zinc

Leaded Yellow Brass
(0.67)copper + (0.29)zinc + (0.03)lead + (0.01)tin

Figure 3.56

Copper alloys and proportional contribution of separate metals.

Sources: USGS Minerals Handbooks, other.

Figure 3.57

The copper-clad dome of the London Planetarium.

London, UK.

Figure 3.58

Detail of the surface of preweathered copper panels.

Figure 3.59

A copper exterior wall surface.

New York, NY, USA.

of their discoveries, went on to apply for patents and initiate the development of what is now the proven modern method for refining aluminum. Today, the essential aspects of what is now called the Hall-Héroult process is still used to refine aluminum at much greater rates and less expense. By passing a high current of approximately 150,000 amperes at a low voltage through a molten electrolytic bath of cryolite (sodium aluminum fluoride) the aluminum is separated and precipitates to the bottom of the container to be siphoned off and cast into large ingots.

Over the intervening decades since Hall and Héroult made their discovery, aluminum production has increased dramatically, making this useful metal available to an array of industries while also straining the energy burden of the production of metals worldwide. In 1900 worldwide production amounted to 6,800 metric tonnes, 20 years later 125,000 metric tonnes and in the year 2000, 24,000,000 metric tonnes.

Today Australia is the world's largest alumina refiner (30 percent) and the United States is the leading producer of aluminum metal at 20 billion pounds annually. US production accounts for 10.8 percent of global production (Smith 2003). Aluminum production has been growing at a steady rate of between 3 and 5 percent per year. In the US today, nearly 15 percent of all aluminum production is consumed by the building and construction industry. The largest increases in construction have been in the residential sector. Aluminum alloys have proliferated and are now organized according to several classification schemes including one that uses a number series from 1000 through 8000.

Series 1000 contains those aluminum alloys used for low stress applications, such as foils. These alloys are also good electrical conductors. Series 2000 is reserved for higher stress situations such as the exterior skins of airplane fuselages, forgings etc. Series 3000 is characterized by aluminums of moderate strength and fairly good ductility and corrosion resistance. Applications include roofing, cooking implements and the ubiquitous soda can container. Series 4000 is used for ornamental work. Series 5000 is used for applications in which greater strength is required including weldable plate, pressure vessels and ship superstructures. Series 6000 contains those alloys most frequently used for architectural applications including mullions, window frames, anodized extrusions and other components. Series 7000 again contains alloys used in aircraft. And finally Series 8000 is characterized by lower densities and good strength again making these alloys useful in aeronautical applications.

The environmental ramifications of aluminum extraction extend well beyond the energy used in its refinement. Chief among these environmental impacts is the local disturbance caused by the mining of alumina bearing minerals. Because typical aluminum ore deposits are located in "blanket-type" deposits, that is, in horizontal layers that necessitate mining of large areas of land, a great deal of the landscape is violently and often permanently disturbed. Regeneration techniques are available to repair this damage but the largest bauxite mines are found in the tropics, the Caribbean and the Mediterranean, areas in which regeneration is not always accomplished. As a result, large tracts of rain forest have been spoiled by the need to completely clear land of its upper layers of soil in the mining process. A recent study has shown that as much as 22 kg of tropical rainforest are destroyed for every ton of bauxite mined (Bargigli et al.2002). At best 1 ton of aluminum can be refined from 2 tons of alumina refined from 4 tons of high grade bauxite ore.

Aluminum is a highly recycled material, currently 60-90 percent of all aluminum produced is reclaimed and recycled into second generation use. Producing secondary aluminum ingot requires 5 percent of the energy of primary aluminum. Also, the German Aerospace Center in Cologne, Germany, has developed

Figure 3.60a, b

A bronze railing detail and door handle.

138

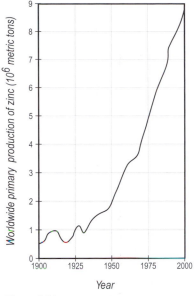

Figure 3.61

Worldwide production of zinc metal.

Sources: USGS Handbooks, other.

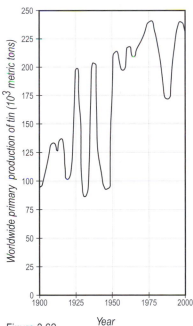

Figure 3.62

Worldwide production of tin metal.

Sources: USGS Minerals, other.

an aluminum recycling process that uses solar radiation as the primary energy source. Testing at a plant built in Almeria, Spain, has demonstrated the potential for using solar radiation in this way.

However, even with recycling, studies show that the substitution of aluminum for steel in typical building superstructures is not an environmentally sound strategy (Bargigli et al. 2003). Currently, it is being used as the superstructure material for the specialized modular building market (Aluminum Now 2004d). The use of aluminum is certainly worthwhile for the superstructure of vehicles, especially automobiles where the weight reduction contributes to significant fuel savings over the lifetime of the automobile (Saito et al. 2000). In addition, the automobile industry recycles aluminum at very high levels, up to 90 percent in northern Europe. This industry can take best advantage of the 95 percent energy savings in the use of secondary rather than primary aluminum.

Copper

Copper is known to have been in use as early as 2200BC, and possibly before, for roofing, scuppers, sinks and other fixtures, various fixtures and implements. seven hundred years later bronze was developed and it is likely that the first bronzes were discovered during the smelting of copper tinged with impurities, including tin. Ancient copper was refined from ore mined in Armenia, Egypt and Cyprus. The Romans developed extensive mines, particularly in Spain, to get at other sources of the metal. As with most useful metallic ores, copper is not found freely available in nature; the primary sources of copper are the minerals cuprite, malachite, azurite, chalcopyrite and bornite.

During the 18th century copper started to be used to sheath the bottoms of boats and ships to protect the oak outer planking. The English adopted this method until about 1832, when it was replaced by less expensive bronze. In fact this is just one example of the more valuable attributes of copper - its ease of combining with a variety of other metals to produce broadly useful alloys. Today copper is alloyed with zinc, tin, aluminum, beryllium, chromium, manganese and others.

In buildings, copper has played an important role analogous to the application to the bottoms of ships in the 18th century. For environmental durability and water management, copper has been used as a flashing material and sheathing on dormers, roofing sheets, gutters, canopies, windows, copings and many other conditions where water needs to be directed away from the building.

Copper, like aluminum, is also a highly recycled material. It is tempting to believe that recycling is a modern idea born of the awareness to be better stewards of the environment. This is true for many materials, but when it comes to metals like copper, recycling and the recovery of scrap metal have been an integral part of its material flow from its first use. The reclamation and recycling of metals for another use avoids the effort, and expense, of extraction and smelting. Copper, in particular, is known to have been reused because of its ease of mechanical workability. The reclamation of hammered sheets of copper was easily achieved without the need for additional chemical or thermal treatment.

Furthermore, the recycling of metals in developing regions is done with an efficiency and urgency born of economic necessity. Some of the most advanced materials reclamation and recycling material flows occur in the urban slums of India, China, Latin America and Africa. Unfortunately, concerns regarding toxicity, pollution from reprocessing, child labor and many other important societal issues are not adequately considered in the informal industries that focus on material recycling in developing regions.

US production of mined copper amounts to 9.8 percent

Figure 3.63a, b, c

Various examples of ceramic coated steel components.

Getty Center, Los Angeles, CA.
Richard Meier, Architect.

Figure 3.64a, b

Titanium was used as the primary cladding
material for much of this building. The sheets
were field applied and act as a typical rainscreen, protecting the various layers of weath-
erproofing materials below. The appearance
of staining was the result of a combination
of factors not including the weathering of the
titanium itself.

Guggenheim Bilbao, Bilbao, Spain.
Frank O. Gehry, Architect.

Figure 3.65

Titanium investment casting part of approximately 2ft L x 1ft W x 4inches D.

Sources: Howmet Casting, USA.

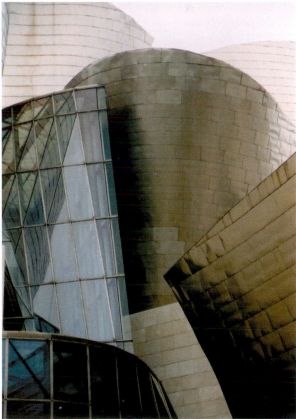

of global production. Today, complete recycling is accomplished with an energy use of 3-25 percent of the energy needed to produce copper from ore. As a result, copper recycling has been at relatively high levels for decades. In the US, already in 1975 fully 40 percent of consumption was dependent on recycling. However, because of adequate current supplies the price of copper has held steady or declined over the past 30 years. Currently, approximately 38 percent of all total global copper production is reclaimed and recycled into second generation use. The United States and Europe are the largest scrap copper consumers at approximately 48 percent and 39 percent respectively, while China leads the world in percentage increase in copper scrap consumption (Jolly 2003). It is worth noting that copper has a fairly well-defined depletion date of less than 70 years, see Figure 3.3. In the intervening years, it is inevitable that recovery and recycling rates will climb dramatically.

Tin, Zinc, Chromium, Nickel and Titanium

Tin became highly useful as one of the components of bronze before it was refined for use as a separate metal. The first implements date from about 2000BC but the smelting of tin wasn't widespread until 500 years later. Confused with lead by the Romans, who called both metals *plumbum*, it was rarely used alone. It is highly malleable and highly resistant to corrosion. Zinc is primarily used for surfacing for improved durability, often laminated with copper. US production of tin (through the smeltering process) is 4.8 of global production. US mined zinc accounts for 9.5 percent of world production (Smith 2003). Chromium and nickel are both important alloy metals for imparting good corrosion resistance to ferrous metals. Titanium is exceptionally corrosion resistant and lightweight. Used in aerospace and other high performance applications in which structural performance at high temperatures is a requirement, titanium has nevertheless seen use in several buildings recently, see Figures 3.64a, b. The best known application has been its use as a cladding material in the Guggenheim Museum in Bilbao, Spain, designed by the Frank O. Gehry. The US contributes 10.2 percent of titanium production through the mining of its concentrates, Ilmenite and leucoxene (Smith 2003).

Metals in Contemporary Architecture

As described above, metals are a primary structural material for buildings and a prime choice for flashing systems and exterior finish materials. Structural steel was the first material that allowed for the development of the pin-connected three dimensional frame, as well as the large-scale tension net, large-scale bridge trusses, and suspension structures among other structural forms. Also, metals have been a critical material for modern rainscreen assemblies, window and curtainwall assemblies and other constructions of the modern building enclosure. Therefore, metals have fundamentally influenced the making of modern architectural form.

As another example, the use of steel studs has increased greatly during the last two decades. As a replacement for wood studs, steel is preferred by some contractors and dismissed by others. The advantages include superior ductility and dimensional stability over wood studs. However, a 20 gauge steel stud will conduct ten times more heat (on average) than a wood stud. Therefore, systems to place the steel stud as far into the insulation as possible are being investigated along with the general study to improve the performance of exterior envelopes (Hart 1999). As a rigid sheet material metal has been used in ductwork and exterior envelope panels. Each has greatly aided in the increasingly distinct separation between the building systems.

Aluminum is now the primary metal for use in curtainwalls, both for mullions restraining glazing and as a surface finish panel. Recently, it has seen a resurgence in this latter use, both for buildings of rather mundane aspirations (rural bus stations, warehouses, industrial buildings) and buildings of very high design aspirations. Aluminum is also being used in numerous products to form structural monocoque assemblies using sheet Al sandwiching an interior honeycomb or folded plate structure. Recently, aluminum has also been used as a flooring material in several buildings, notably the new Seattle Public Library, designed by Rem Koolhaas of OMA. One product (Alumafloor, www.aluminumfloors.com) currently dominates the market and was the supplier of the floor tiles for the project (Aluminum Now 2004b). Also in a rather unusual application, the environmental artist Ned Kahn recently covered the six-story, 260 feet long facade of the largest parking structure in the Carolinas in the US with 160,000 small (3 inches square) aluminum tiles in the making of a permanent sculpture named "Wind Veil". The tiles are allowed to flutter in the wind and register the movement of large gusts of air across the surface - a predominantly aesthetic application for the purpose of taming the massive scale of the structure (Aluminum Now 2005c).

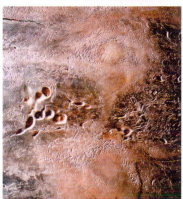

Figure 3.66

Detail and full length of bronze exterior wall finish panels.

American Museum of Folk Art, New York City, USA, 2003. Tod Williams Billie Tsien & Associates.

Figure 3.67

A nickel surface.

Figure 3.68

A block of stabilized aluminum foam (SAF) showing the results of indentations made by steel spheres dropped onto the surface to measure the mehcanical energy absorption of the foam.

Source: CYMAT Allusion® sample, USA.

Emergent Metals

As briefly mentioned in the introduction, the pace of the development of new metallic alloys has been decreasing these past few decades. This follows the immensely productive period between 1850 and 1950, when innovation in metals progressed at a frenetic speed. These hundred years were dominated by the development of dozens of new alloys, both ferrous and nonferrous. However, since the 1950s, polymer and composite science and engineering has overtaken metals in the pace and diversity of the development of its material class. At some point in the future, this pace will slow for polymers as well.

An initial indicator of the loss of prominence of metallurgy has been the renaming of mining and metallurgy departments to departments of materials science and engineering. Where once metals - their extraction, processing and development - were the prime focus of the science of materials, they are now very much in competition with polymers, high performance ceramics, electronic materials of many kinds and the exploding field of nanomaterials. Nevertheless, the slower but steady development of metallic alloys continues along with the discovery of new materials and the invention of new processes. Superplastic alloys, shape memory alloys metal

Figure 3.69

A photomicrograph that clearly shows the thin-walled structure of a stabilized aluminum foam.

Source: CYMAT Alusion® sample, USA.

matrix composites are all recent developments. And in fact, the maturation of the science of metals has only recently been fully realized in architectural assemblies. Metallic alloys once developed for higher performance scenarios, for example high strength aluminum alloys for aeronautical applications, are now available for architectural assemblies. Improved corrosion resistance, better strength with ductility, reliable coatings and other surface treatments and a better understanding of the behavior of metals, especially at high temperatures, have been a benefit to improving the quality of metals used in architecture.

In addition, inventions involving the mechanical lamination of various materials including metals, polymers and glasses have found useful applications in construction and other industries. Polymer-metal composites, a common version being two sheets of aluminum sandwiching a thermoplastic, have found a place as panels for the exterior envelope of buildings. This kind of polymer/metal laminate is also now being used as a resilient and impact worthy material for construction of the next generation of double hulled oil tanker ships. Also, metal-metal composites have been used for many decades as resilient and durable sheet metal for roofing and exterior wall surfaces. A zinc-titanium-copper mechanical composite is but one of a variety of metal/metal laminates available on the market for use on roofs and walls.

The use of metals in textiles has also been a new direction. Ceramic-metal oxide fibers such as Nextel™ (3M Corporation) consisting of alumina/boria/silica fibers (62 percent Al_2O_3, 14 percent B_2O_3, and 24 percent SiO_2) are used in high performance thermal barrier applications. Other metal textiles have been used for a variety of aesthetic and performance applications. Woven steels of many density ranges and configurations have been used in contemporary architecture as space-defining elements. Popularized by Dominique Perrault first in the Grande Bibliothèque Nationale de France in Paris, several manufacturers have made woven stainless steels a part of their architectural metal product lines.

And there is renewed interest in the potential for using more cast irons, especially spheroidal graphite cast iron (SG) - an iron with useful tensile and ductile properties, Figure 3.70 (Fleischman and Sumer 2003). Several buildings of the last couple of decades have taken advantage of the relative ease of producing complex components from cast metals. The Western Morning News Headquarters in Plymouth, UK (completed in 1993), designed by Nicholas Grimshaw and Partners is a prime example of the use of this material in the glazing brackets of the exterior envelope. The continued and possibly increased use of this metal is almost assured.

Innovations in new metals have come from several research and industry development efforts. This section of the chapter highlights several that are most interesting for contemporary architecture:

Ultralight metals
Cellular metals
Composite metals
Metals for long-life structures
High performance steel (HPS)
New fire-resistant steel alloys

Figure 3.70

Cast steel joint intended as a truss connector.

Courtesy of Hitashi Metals.

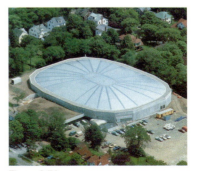

Figure 3.71

Air-supported stainless steel roof using 304 stainless steel sheet.

Dalhousie University, Halifax, Canada.
Sinoski Engineering Ltd.

Ultralight Metals

Most research of low weight metals is focused on developing new materials for the automotive industries. Several avenues of study are under way and while it is neither reasonable nor worthwhile to suggest that these materials can be directly transferred to architectural applications, nevertheless they form an important set of research interests that may be relevant to architectural form.

Several separate efforts currently exist. They are separately treated here because of their rather distinct characteristics.

Very lightweight, thin gauge stainless steels have been used in air-supported or air-inflated roof membranes. The use of the steel extends the lifetime of the roofing and does not require a rigid structure. Stainless steel 304 has been used in this application. At a thickness of 1.6 mm spans of 70-90 meters have been built, Figure 3.71.

Much research is attempting to produce lightweight and ultralightweight metals for industry (Degischer 1997). Alcoa recently achieved new strength to weight ratios for an aluminum alloy developed for Boeing. Other very exotic alloys are receiving research attention such as a titanium aluminide alloy being produced for the high temperature environment of propulsion systems.

In addition, hollow stainless steel assemblies (HSSA) are being developed for use in automobiles. These very thin and lightweight stainless steel composites are intended for use as impact resistant panel materials, Figure 3.72a, b (Jobb 2003a).

Cellular metals

The most innovative form of cellular metals includes the metallic foams, known as metfoams. Metfoams are

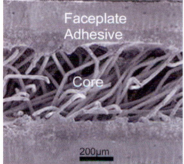

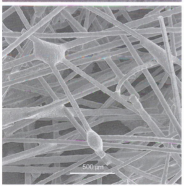

Figures 3.72a, b
Micrographs of HSSA composite showing section through sandwich above and image of steel fibers and droplets of epoxy resin binder.

Photos courtesy of Professor Bill Clyne, Department of Material Science, University of Cambridge, UK, 2003.

cellular materials processed from a solid metal to encapsulate voids within the body of the material. These are very new materials currently being examined by researchers and industry for their novel set of properties (Ashby et al. 2000).

A few metfoams are commercially available, most being either aluminum or nickel (Duocel 2005). Aluminum foams are often referred to as stabilized aluminum foams (SAF), Figures 3.68, 3.69. Other metals have also been made into foams but do not have a wide range commercial uses, at the moment. The cost of metallic foams is fluctuating and difficult to establish with any long-term certainty. At the moment, these materials are rather expensive compared with their solid metal precursors.

The set of novel material properties includes being lightweight and stiff, offering good thermal and acoustic control. Cellular metal foams may very well be useful in roofing applications where weight becomes a critical issue particularly in long span situations. The metal foam interlayer between sheets of aluminum would provide rigidity at a good strength to weight ratio.

Composite Metals

Composite metals are of two general types. The first is a mechanical composite composed of the physical adhesion of a metal component with another material, metallic or nonmetallic. This can be accomplished by using an adhesive to bond two metals together, or one metal may be coated by another etc. The second is a material in which a material, metallic or nonmetallic, has been incorporated into the metal, much as a reinforcing fiber is incorporated into the matrix of a polymer making a fiber reinforced polymer.

The first form, mechanical composites, are the source of a number of architectural products that already exist. Aluminum composite materials (ACM) are sandwiches of two or more aluminum sheets bonded to an interior polymer core (Sullivan 1997). Products with names like Alumicor™ and Alucobond™ are materials in which a metal sheet (aluminum) has been bonded into a sandwich structure with a polymer interlayer. The resulting material has good impact resistance, good stiffness and is relatively lightweight. As a finish material in a rainscreen application for a building enclosure it is a successful composite.

Also, aluminum honeycomb of various geometries and gauges is used as a stiff substrate for a variety of finish materials like wood and marble veneers, metal sheet, fabric wall coverings etc. The aluminum material in this application tends to be thicker than an ACM and cannot be bent in the field. A further refinement of this idea is to be found in current ideas about the use of metal polymer composite panels as part of the safer designs for double-hulled tanker ships. Composite metals composed of several metals bonded together are also a well-known set of materials used in architecture. Terne-coated steels, zinc-coated copper and titanium and zinc-coated aluminum (galvalume) are all materials used primarily in exterior envelope and roofing applications.

Cool roofs are prime users of these kinds of metals. In fact a recent CRCC study points to galvalume as being the best choice for cool roofs.

The second form of metal composites includes recently developed metals for high performance applications. It is difficult to imagine that most of these materials will one day have a use in architecture. The kinds of attributes that they possess are well beyond the needs of even the most intensive performance requirements for metals in buildings. However, predictions of future applications have been incorrect before and some modern materials that were developed for high performance engineering applications, such as carbon fiber, epoxies and aramid fibers, are finding their way into architecture.

Metals for long-life buildings and civil structures

Recently there has been a renewed interest in the attempt to design and construct structures that are able to achieve much longer service lives. This interest has been revived by the wide adoption of lifecycle costing methodologies and the realization that post-war civil infrastructure is becoming dangerously aged. Also, interest in long-life building assemblies is being prompted by long-life initiatives in other industries seeking better ways in which to reduce the consumption of materials (directly and indirectly) as part of the extraction, processing and manufacturing processes (Jobb 2003b;Hoeckman 2001).

Long-life buildings and civil works value durability above many other criteria. A calculation is made that a longer life will return a net benefit to society, therefore the inevitable premium to be paid upfront is amortized over a very long period of time. The new cathedral in Los Angeles, designed by Rafael Moneo, is one example of a long-life building of concrete.

Figure 3.73

Exterior of Guildhall Yard East, a 700 year design life building constructed with the use of stainless steel reinforced concrete.

Guildhall Yard East, London, England, 1998.
W.S. Atkins, Architect.

Figure 3.74

Stainless steel reinforced concrete bridge.

Coos Bay Bridge, 2003.
Oregon, USA.

Civil projects are also considering the benefits of long-life design. The use of reinforced concrete, while initially thought to be a long-life material, has had to be reconsidered under the growing awareness of the complexity of real durability. One solution has been to use stainless steel reinforcing bars as the primary steel reinforcing of these structures (Magee and Schnell 2002). Projects recently completed include the Guildhall Yard East addition to the building that has been the seat of London City government since the 13th century (NiDI 1996). The 90 by 30 meter extension to the Guildhall cost £50 million and adds a building housing four office levels and three basements, built over an old roman amphitheater. The design called for a building that would attain, with normal maintenance, a design life comparable to the buildings around it, in the range of 700 years or more. To satisfy this desire 140 tonnes of S30400 stainless steel bars from 6 to 25mm dia. were used as the primary reinforcing for the concrete of the building, Figure 3.73.

In the state of Oregon, in the United States a $12 million bridge has used 363 tonnes of stainless steel rebar, the largest quantity of stainless steel incorporated into the concrete superstructure for any bridge in North America. The Coos Bay Bridge, situated in an extremely corrosive marine environment, is replacing an aging timber bridge and has been designed to reach 120 years without any significant maintenance, Figure 3.74 (NiDI 2003). The stainless steel used for the project was S32205 alloy (22 percent chromium, 5.5 percent nickel, 3 percent molybdenum), with very good corrosion resistance. The cost of stainless steel rebar represents 13 percent of the bridge budget, not a significant premium above the typical 10 percent dedicated to steel reinforcing. Because stainless steel can achieve high yield strengths of 520 MPa or higher, overall less steel needs to be used. Also using this stainless steel alloy are several bridges linking Brooklyn, New York, to the island of Manhattan. The stainless steel rebar reinforced concrete bridges aspire to a maintenance-free lifetime of 100 years (Materials Progress 2004).

Smaller bridges are also using stainless steel not only for their reinforcing of concrete but for welded box beams and girders and other sheet applications. The Sickla Canal Bridge in Hammarby Sjöstad in the southern part of Stockholm uses a duplex stainless steel S32205, for much of the bridge's post-tensioned central box-girder superstructure and nonstructural components, such as handrails. The designers Erik Andersson, Jelena Mijanovic and Magnus Ståhl chose the material for its long life and low maintenance (NiDI 2003).

Two other reinforcing systems meant to extend the life of buildings are FRP (fiber reinforced polymer) reinforcing and a material called MMFX Microcomposite Steel reinforcing bar.

FRPs are used in a variety of forms as a substitute for steel bar reinforcing in reinforced concrete. More on this material is given in Section 3.3 Ceramics and Glasses.

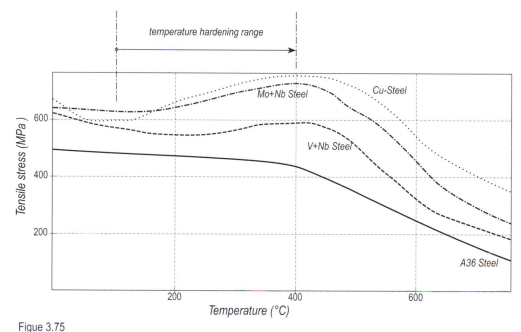

Figue 3.75

Heat-resistant steel alloys: performance under elevated temperatures.

Source: Walp et al. (2004).

High performance steel (HPS)

Two developments deserve treatment here; fire-resistant steel and fracture resistant steel. Both of these use cast steel as the basis for connectors that can resist both higher stresses and elevated temperatures.

First, there has been successful development of fire-resistant cast steel alloys that retain a much greater proportion of their service strength at higher temperatures. These steel alloys retain a little over two-thirds of the service strength at elevated temperatures as high as 600°C (Hitashi 2002). Second, cast steels have been improved to provide metals that are better at resisting the kinds of stresses endured during violent events like earthquakes.

New fire-resistant steel alloys

The search for steels that better resist losses of strength due to higher temperatures has recently yielded some interesting results. While still preliminary, and requiring substantial additional research, it has been found that certain microalloys demonstrate better performance at higher temperatures than any other steel alloys studied (Walp 2004). In fact, several alloys combining steel and various amounts of vanadium (V), molybdenum (Mo), niobium (Nb) and copper (Cu) resulted in alloys that not only demonstrated better performance than A36 steel but actually showed increased strength over the temperature ranges from 250 to 550°C (480-1020°F), a range in which A36 steel begins to display signs of the beginning of substantial weakening, Figure 3.75. This work is extremely important in demonstrating that continued research in the metallurgy of construction metals may yield results that would make our buildings safer from catastrophic fires and other events.

Polymers

So, more than a substance, plastic is the very idea of its infinite transformation; as its everyday name indicates, it is ubiquity made visible. And it is this, in fact, which makes it a miraculous substance: a miracle is always sudden transformation of nature. Plastic remains impregnated throughout with this wonder: It is less a thing than the trace of a movement...

Roland Barthes, 1964

Planet Petroleum

Figure 3.76

Detail of a double layer of ethylene/tetrafluorotheylene (ETFE) film used for "pillows" under positive pressure which form the primary exterior envelope material of this large building. As a result of its good tensile strength, high transparency, resistance to UV radiation and gas impermeability, ETFE is now in widespread use in this kind of application.

Space Centre, Leicester, United Kingdom (2003).
Nicolas Grimshaw, Architect.

The fragment above is one of many observations that attempts to articulate the strange nature of modern synthetic plastics. These materials - mostly originating from the flasks of the corporate research laboratory - have come to be used in buildings in many ways, as substitutes for traditional materials or the missing material link in a new building assembly.

The family of polymers includes an enormous array of materials that have proven extremely useful in practically every modern industrial enterprise. The novel combination of versatile mechanical and physical properties, ease of processing, seemingly endless formulations, competitive pricing and global availability have made polymers a primary source material for all manner of manufacturing enterprise. Per unit volume, more polymer resin is consumed today than steel, aluminum and copper combined and the production of synthetic polymers accounts for 80 percent of the organic chemical industry. The rate of growth in the use of polymers in construction is approaching 10 percent per annum.

The successful development of a dizzying array of polymers is the result of one of the earliest and best organized large-scale partnerships between university-based material science research and commercial product development (Fenichell 1996). Beginning in the early years of this past century and driven by the explosion in the use of petroleum as the primary nonrenewable natural resource of the 20th century, synthetic polymers have come to occupy a dominant place in the making of a vast diversity of contemporary things. The extraordinary success of this partnership has been as momentous in establishing new businesses and shaping the character of modern industry as it has in founding new domains of scientific and engineering specialization (such as polymer and composite science and engineering).

The proliferation of synthetic polymers has been a direct result of the vast extraction, refinement and consumption of crude oil and other hydrocarbon fossil fuels. "Cracking" crude oil into smaller molecules provided the basic molecular building blocks of polymer science. Once these smaller monomers were produced in quantity, the industrial production of synthetic polymers was possible. Currently, the production of plastics accounts for 4 percent of total oil consumption.

While the use of crude oil - petroleum liquid as it is found in sedimentary rocks between 10 and 270 million years old - dates back to caulking and sealing ships in Mesopotamia around 4000BC, embalming in ancient Egypt and oil lamps in Cicero's Rome, its global resource significance began its steady rise during the late industrial revolution with the invention of the combustion engine and the incandescent lamp.

But first, the use of kerosene as a lamp fuel, refined from crude oil, prompted the first real demand for this "black gold". During the first two decades of the 20th century, the increase in the demand for electricity from oil-fueled power plants and gasoline for the newly invented

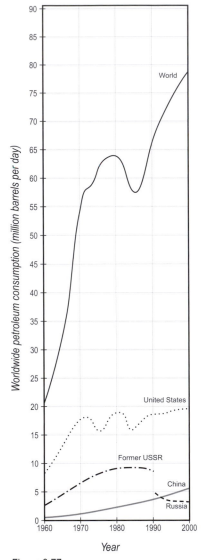

Figure 3.77

Petroleum consumption worldwide and selected countries 1960-2000. There is reliable and diverse evidence to suggest that daily crude oil production will reach a historical peak in the latter half of this decade.

Sources: US Department of Energy, US Geological Survey. International Energy Outlook (2004), EIA.

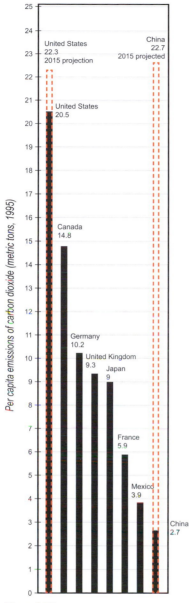

Figure 3.78

International carbon dioxide emissions (a primary greenhouse gas). Note the projected 2015 CO$_2$ emissions for China and the US. China is expected to surpass the US as the largest national source of carbon emissions in 2015.

Sources: World Resources Institute (1999), World Resources 1998-99. International Energy Outlook (2004), EIA.

automobile dramatically increased the value of this natural material and fostered the development of better refining processes and better performing fuels. The 1930s brought about the need for fuels especially for high performance aircraft engines during and after the war and the decades of the 1950s and 1960s witnessed the development of jet fuel induced by the growth in airline travel.

Prospecting, exploration, extraction, refinement, distribution and consumption on an unprecedented scale have driven a petrochemical global economic engine that will most surely continue for some time, despite the current popular excitement about the emergence of hydrogen and renewable energy technologies. During the 20th century global consumption of fossil fuels has accelerated by a multiple of 50. It is now generally accepted that carbon emissions have dramatically increased as a direct result of the refining of petrochemicals and the indirect result of industrial and other economic activities dependent on this fuel resource. Carbon emissions will undoubtedly continue to increase until the major national economies of the globe significantly curb carbon-releasing industrial and transportation activities.

The making of polymers from the petrochemical soup of crude oil originates with several primary compounds including polyethylene (PE), polyvinyl chloride (PVC) and polystyrene (PS). These are derived from ethylene and polypropylene (PP), in turn derived from the monomer propylene. Methane is the simplest hydrocarbon - consisting, as it does, of four hydrogen atoms and one carbon atom (CH$_4$). Synthetic rubbers, or elastomers, are derived from butadiene, ethylene, benzene and propylene. Polyester fibers constitute fully half of the production of synthetic fibers. Nylon and acrylic fibers comprise most of the remaining production of synthetic fibers (Berger and Anderson 1992; Yergin 1991).

Figure 3.79

The massive PTFE poly(tetrafluoroethylene) structural fabric enclosure of the Millenium Dome. Textiles of synthetic polymer fibers have become an important architectural material with a very interesting future.

Millennium Dome, London, UK. Richard Rogers and Partners, 2000.

All of these polymers, and dozens more, are to be found in modern buildings, or used in the making of architectural components (Wilson and Yost 2001;Lefteri 2001)(Dietz 1969;Dominghaus 1988;Makovsky 2000).

The commercial development of new polymers and the maturation of polymer science have also been critical contributors to the evolution of contemporary building systems and the variety of polymer components that constitute a wide range of building assemblies. The novel combination of low densities, broad range of strength and resilience, ease of processing, great variety of carefully tuned chemical formulations and continuing innovation in the science of polymers has made this class indispensable to novel solutions for contemporary architecture. Every contemporary building system and most assemblies are dependent on some kind of synthetic polymer.

However, *synthetic polymers* are only the very latest type of polymer material to be used in the construction of habitable space. In fact, for many thousands and, in some cases, tens of thousands of years, natural polymers have been used as an integral material in the construction of dwellings, communal buildings and other shelters. Straw, wood, grasses, animal skins and bones and other biological polymers have been used for primitive dwellings and continue to be an important source material for advanced modern constructions. These *natural* polymers, derived from the biological processes of animals and plants, have been the renewable resource of choice for societies in the past and currently for those not yet introduced to the particular advantages of synthetic polymers. Note, however, the fundamental distinction between almost all synthetic and natural polymers; natural polymers are generally a renewable resource, synthetic polymers are mostly nonrenewable - obtained as they are from crude oil.

156

Figure 3.80

Primary vapor and liquid water barrier applied to the face and around window openings of a precast structural frame. Notice that this polymer material (with an adhesive backing) is quite malleable and allows for substantial elongation. Also notice the entrapped air.

Simmons Hall, MIT. Steven Holl, Architect.

Along with stone and earth, natural polymers have been the favorite source material for many architectural applications, from the making of weather resistant skins to the binding of structural elements and the waterproofing of construction gaps. These natural polymers are quite different in many ways from synthetic polymers. Due to their particular material properties, regional origins and historical and cultural significance, most natural polymers are addressed in detail in Section 3.5 Biomaterials and Loam.

In addition, natural polymers played an important role in inspiring the formulation of early synthetic polymers. The flood of synthetic polymer development in the 20th century was preceded by a long period of experimentation with the modification of natural polymers in the 19th century. These biologically derived polymers were refined for industrial uses in the middle of the 19th century, with the development of the vulcanization of natural rubber in 1844 and the development of cellulose-based materials beginning in 1862. Vulcanization is the process of cross-linking, or chemically bonding, the separate chains of a base elastomer. This process was used by Charles Goodyear in 1839 to produce a much more resilient and industrially viable polymer from natural rubber. The vulcanization of natural rubber is a process still used today. In 2000, worldwide consumption of natural rubber exceeded 7 million metric tons with principal applications in automobile tires.

Much of this innovation started when the European explorers of the Americas brought back samples of tree sap that could be formed into resilient objects. Waterproofing fabrics were one the first applications that the indigenous peoples of Mexico and South America taught to their European conquerors. The French nobleman Charles Marie de La Condamine brought back to France natural rubber from Peru in 1735. This material was used to create waterproof boots and fabrics. Experimentation with the waterproofing of fabrics in the 1820s eventually led Charles MacKintosh to develop a process of curing rubber to produce a waterproof fabric composite. The result was the invention of the English "Macks", the first commercially produced natural rubber raincoats (Fenichell 1996).

In the United States and Europe, the commercialization of chemically modified natural polymers and their products came quickly on the heels of several key discoveries. First, in 1840s Massachusetts, Charles Goodyear successfully synthesized a polymer by treating natural rubber with sulfur, the previously mentioned process of vulcanization. In Germany, Christian Friedrich Schönbein produced a better process for producing volatile guncotton in 1846, derived of a method to nitrate cellulose. The first polymer fibers, acetate and rayon, were both derived of cellulose during the final quarter of the 19th century and are known as "cellulosic" fibers. During the following decades, a variety of cellulose and natural rubber-based polymers were developed with names like collodion, collodion lacquer, Parkesine, India rubber, Gutta-Percha, celluloid, xylonite, pyroxylin, cellophane, rayon and many others (Harper 200;Domininghaus 1988).

Truly synthetic materials, on the other hand, are a relatively new development. The first synthetic polymers were not only novel materials but became commercial successes very quickly. After reaping the rewards of a windfall for the invention of a novel photographic paper, Leonard H. Baekeland of New York State set about experimenting with polymers, eventually developing the first synthetic polymer, Bakelite, in 1908. Baekeland's research had convinced him that a synthetic shellac was a much needed material bypassing the necessity for natural sources of the base polymer. He was seeking a substitute for celluloid and natural rubber, the two primary sources of modified polymers up to that point. After successfully controlling the chemical process of synthesis, and producing the first synthetic thermoset, the commercial production of this phenol-formaldehyde

1866	-	Celluloid
1867	-	Xylonite
1891	-	Rayon
1911	-	Bakelite
1918	-	Cellulose acetate
1920	-	Urea-formaldehyde
1924	-	Acetate
1927	-	vinyl resins, PVCs
1929	-	SBR
1930	-	Rubber
1931	-	Polychloroprene
1934	-	Acrylic
1934	-	Nitrile rubber
1938	-	Polystyrene
1939	-	Nylon fiber
1939	-	Polyethylene
1939	-	Vinyon
1941	-	Polyurethane
1941	-	Saran
1943	-	Silicone
1946	-	Epoxy resins
1946	-	Metallic
1949	-	Acrylic
1949	-	Olefin
1950	-	Acrylic fibers
1953	-	Polyester
1954	-	PET
1954	-	ABS
1957	-	Polypropylene
1958	-	Polycarbonate
1959	-	Spandex
1960	-	PTFE
1961	-	Aramid (Nomex)
1968	-	LLDPE
1971	-	Aramid (Kevlar)
1983	-	PBI
1983	-	Sulfar

Figure 3.81

Chronology for commercial introduction of select polymers.

Beginning in the late 1920s, almost all of these polymers originated with work accomplished by scientists in corporate research and development laboratories. Consequently, the material family of synthetic polymers was the first substantially protected by intellectual property rights as an essential aspect of its origin. A curious by-product of this has been the explosive proliferation of proprietary trade names for many new polymers challenging the non-specialist to distinguish between scientific and non-scientific labels.

Polymers (homopolymers)

ABA	acrylonitrile-butadiene-acrylate
ACM	acrylic acid ester rubber
AN	acrylonitrile
AZ(O)	azodicarbonamide
BR	butadiene rubber
BS	butadiene styrene rubber
CA	cellulose acetate
CN	cellulose nitrate
CSF	casein-formaldehyde
EP	epoxy resin
EPS	expandable polystyrene
ETFE	ethylenetetrafluoroethylene
PA	polyamide
PA66	polyamide 66
PAN	poly(acrylonitrile)
PBA	poly(butylacrylate)
PC	polycarbonate
PCTFE	poly(chlorotrifluoroethylene)
PE	polyethylene
PE-HD	high density polyethylene
PE-LD	low density polyethylene
PEEK	poly(etheretherketone)
PET	poly(ethyleneterephthalate)
PF	phenol-formaldehyde
PI	polyimide
PIB	polyisobutylene
PIR	polyisocyanurate
PMMA	poly(methylmethacrylate)
PP	polypropylene
PS	polystyrene
PSU	polysulfone
PTFE	poly(tetrafluoroethylene)
PU	polyurethane
PVB	poly(vinylbutyral)
PVC	poly(vinylchloride)
PVC-P	plasticized poly(vinylchloride)
PVC-U	unplasticized poly(vinylchloride)
SI	silicone
SP	saturated polyester
UF	urea-formaldehyde
UP	unsaturated polyester
VF	vulcanized rubber

Copolymers

ABS	acrylonitrile/butadiene/styrene
EPDM	ethylene-propylenediene
ETFE	ethylene/tetrafluoroethylene
SB	styrene butadiene

Figure 3.82

Common abbreviations of selected synthetic polymers.

(PF) resin began in 1909 and signalled the beginning of the rapid development and commercialization of dozens of synthetic polymers during the 20th century. Afterwords, urea-formaldehyde resins (UF) were developed in the 1930s and the more robust melamine-formaldehyde resins in the 1940s. Applications of PF and UF were immediately exploited in articles as diverse as appliances, radios, utensils, secondary building elements, such as door knobs and other fittings, electrical insulation, kitchen and bathroom components and many other items in which a durable, moldable material could offer an easy substitute.

The prevalence of synthetic polymers took another great leap with the emulsion of chloroprene into a rubbery mass in 1930. Dupont eventually named this material Neoprene®. This discovery was the first of several important landmarks in polymer science that came out of the research labs of Dupont, directed at the time by Wallace Carothers. Having left a faculty position at Harvard in 1927, to become the head of Dupont's newly established pure science division, Carothers oversaw the birth of the large-scale industrial, commercial research enterprise - an organ of scientific investigation married to the priorities of commerce. As described in Chapter 1 of this book, the ramifications for the construction industry have been enormous.

During the 1930s, Carothers' team continued to produce synthetic polymers whose molecular weights dramatically exceeded previous polymers by many thousands of monomers. Within just a couple of decades, a number of useful new polymers had been synthesized and commercially produced in large quantities, including Nylon 66 (polyamide 66), Teflon (polytetrafluoro-ethylene), Lucite (polymethyl methacrylate), Butacite (polyvinyl butyryl), Dacron (polyester fiber), and many others. As a commercially important part of this activity, synthetic fibers became a research and development field in its own right. By the end of the 20th century and in the United States, synthetic fibers accounted for 70 percent of all fibers produced industrially; a dramatic increase from 1 percent in 1924. Again, another instance of the shift from renewable to nonrenewable materials - natural to synthetic fibers (see Chapter 2, Figure 2.9).

Development of synthetic polymers has continued unabated for the last 160 years. From the structural silicone sealant in curtainwalls to the high density polymer, PTFE, and metal pads used for seismic isolation of entire buildings, polymers have become an integral material of contemporary buildings faster and more deeply than any other material class. Polycarbonate, discovered in 1956 and commercially produced by GE Plastics under the Lexan® brand starting in 1973, is now widely used for glass substitution in building applications. Neoprene® is commonly used for gasketing and load transfer conditions in exterior envelope assemblies. Polyethylene is an important barrier material. PVB is the leading interlayer material for laminated glass assemblies. These and other synthetic polymers are now fully accepted in construction and future substitution opportunities will surely continue as long as the development of new polymers is sustained and the polymers and chemicals industries continue to search for new markets to satisfy their production capacities.

Polymers, more than any other material class, have sprung from materials science research and developed alongside the maturation of materials science and engineering in the 20th century. The world wars were instrumental in catalyzing the search for new polymers and expanding the production of known synthetics. However, the sustained drive for new materials during the last 100 years is indisputable evidence of the irreversible symbiosis between scientific research and modern commercial enterprise. The story of the development of synthetic polymers during the 20th century is one of the clearest examples of the maturation of this scientific, technical and commercial partnership.

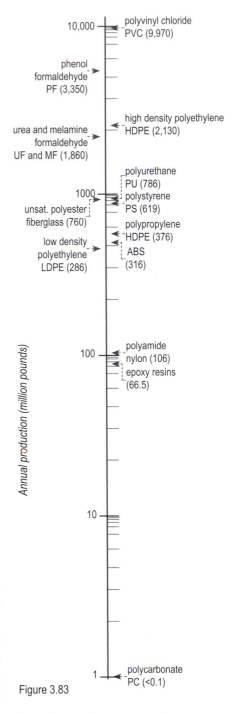

Figure 3.83

Production levels for some typical polymers used in construction (2001).

Sources: Wilson and Yost (2001) and various others.

Today, the success of the industry is clear. In fact, Ben (Dustin Hoffman's character in the movie *The Graduate*) would have fared quite well had he decided to go into "plastics". In the US today 225 billion pounds of synthetic organic chemicals are produced compared to a mere trickle in 1900. In 1999, production of plastics had reached 85 billion pounds (38.5 million tonnes) from 15 billion pounds (6.8 million tonnes) in 1967 (American Plastics Council). Today more than 60,000 distinct compounds are commercially produced. More are added every year. Plastics in construction accounts for 22 percent of resin sales, close behind packaging - the leading consumer (Wilson and Yost 2001).

Plastics have deeply infiltrated almost every industry. As a result, modern societies consume and discard tremendous amounts of polymers. Generally, polymers are durable materials. This is useful for product lifetimes and reliability and problematic for end-of-life disposal. In the US, approximately 20 million tons (17 million tonnes) of polymers are disposed of every year amounting to just over 9 percent of the national total solid waste stream. Relatively small amounts of construction polymers are recycled. Estimates based on very small data samples range from about 3 percent to 5 percent (Selke 2000;Vest 2001).

And while it would seem that polymers discarded in landfills are prevented from dissipating into the environment, recently it has been shown that a substantial percentage of all known production of polymers is eventually dispersed widely into the environment.

A recent study has found that the accepted schematic polymer material flow through contemporary society does not fully account for all wastes without proposing that great amounts are lost to the environment every year. The study found, surprisingly, that a great volume of plastics may persist in the Earth's oceans as microscopic particles that have resulted from the degradation of larger pieces of various polymers (Thompson et al. 2004;Revkin 2004). Concentrations of this kind of pollution have dramatically increased over the past two decades. The long-term effects of widespread, global contamination of the environment by small particles of every synthetic polymer are yet to be established. However, one can reliably predict that this dispersion will only increase with the increase in the use of plastics worldwide and the pressures to discard ever-increasing volumes of used plastic items.

For example, in Africa, very thin-walled plastic bags for everyday consumption are discarded anywhere and everywhere and spawned an environmental problem of vast landscapes covered in the synthetic remains. In Kenya alone, 100 million light polyethylene bags are used every year. Durable and lightweight, these bags will endure and travel with the wind for a thousand years leaving vast parts of urban Africa covered in the ugly bloom now known as the "African flower" (Lacey 2005).

Unanticipated environmental impacts are also a result of the rapid infiltration into all aspects of building construction; the inevitable consequence of quickly developed and commercialized new materials. Issues of indoor air quality (IAQ), chemical toxicity in processing and new waste streams, uncertain environmental durability and the misuse (sometimes for lack of information or reliable data) of polymers by the design community, have been landmarks along a steep but necessary learning curve (Hagighat and De Bellis1998;Fenichell 1996;Tenner 1997).

For example, the complex issue of sick building syndrome has focused attention on the contribution of polymers and volatile organic compounds - adhesives in particular - to the off-gassing of building assemblies, especially interior finish products and sheathing materials (Hagighat and De Bellis 1998). Furthermore, questions have been raised about the real lifetime durability of some polymers used in applications that encounter challenging environmental conditions. The novel material properties of synthetic polymers led to their early use in curtainwalls designed and built in the late 1940s and 1950s. Many of these early applications have experienced quick degradation that has led to premature system-wide failures. It was understood that improvements in elastomeric sealants were clearly needed to achieve economically reasonable durability and lifetime reliability. Similarly, early protective coatings on metal and solar barrier films applied to glass have also experienced failures due to rapid degradation under environmental stresses like UV radiation, diurnal temperature swings and humidity levels. And finally, large-scale building applications in which polymers were used as the primary enclosure material for the building volume were early experiments that never led to significant market acceptance (Dietz 1969).

Since these early applications, many improvements have been made. The silicone class of elastomers has been improved dramatically in durability and performance reliability. The use of polychloroprene (Neoprene®) has been perfected in sealing applications and mild load transfer in metal and glass curtainwalls. Polymeric organic coatings on metal panels for the

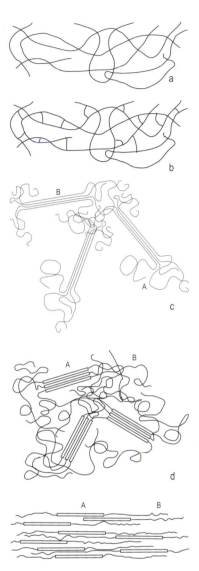

Figure 3.84a, b, c, d

A series of graphics showing various aspects of synthetic polymers:
a: macromolecules, not cross-linked
b: macromolecules, cross-linked
c: amorphous (A) and crystalline (B) polymers forms
d: liquid crystal polymer: (A) linear unit, (B) flexible unit. In figure above the molecules are not aligned (translucent), below the molecules are aligned (transparent).

Sources: Walker (2001), Domininghaus (1988), Doran (1995), Harper (2000).

building enclosure have demonstrated very good service lives, routinely exceeding warranty limits.

As a result, the use of polymers in construction continues to be a growing sector of the building materials market. For example, the use of metal flashing has been under tremendous competitive pressure from the flurry of polymer barrier materials on the market. The lighter weight, ease of handling, very competitive pricing and lower skill levels required to apply these materials makes it the obvious choice for most any building type. Any number of polymer products are available but the "peel and stick" products - which do not use independent fasteners and can be molded to the opening geometry - are gaining market share quickly.

The use of polymers in the exterior envelope is a good example of the prevalence of this material class in contemporary building materials. Composite board systems using thermoset resins and synthetic fibers, rigid and nonrigid polymers insulation, sheet roofing membranes, foundation waterproofing and many other products are either substantially or entirely composed of synthetic polymers. In fact, the spatial volumes enclosed by many contemporary buildings are entirely sheathed with a continuous surface of one kind of synthetic polymer or another.

The growth of the use of polymers, in the exterior envelope in particular, deserves consideration for durability issues. As with many new materials, the property attributes of synthetic polymers are well known through precise laboratory testing. However, the behavior of these materials over long periods of time and in close proximity with other materials belies infallible prediction of lifetime durability and performance. The uncertainties arising from idiosyncratic building conditions, exposures and design considerations will always lead to variations in the lifetime durability of materials. It is only with time that the full range of synthetic polymers and their actual behavior in an architectural context can be assessed with any great level of confidence.

As with any material used in construction, the assembly's performance should not be entirely based on a material's properties, however reliable its performance. The system design, that is the relationship between various portions of the system's components, must also be taken into consideration. In an exterior envelope assembly, redundancy of barrier systems should always be the primary strategy for achieving the necessary level of performance. Therefore, while one would never count on metal flashing to take complete command of the prevention of liquid water intrusion in the building, the same should apply to the use of polymers in the exterior envelope. Clearly, as with any other material family, the use of polymers in construction will continue to develop. And yet, despite the technical challenges and environmental ramifications, polymers have continued to serve persistent aesthetic aspirations of translucency, lightness, plasticity and a unique concordance with the mutability of modernist forms (Antonelli 1995;Kahn 2005;Kaltenbach 2001;Lefteri 2001).

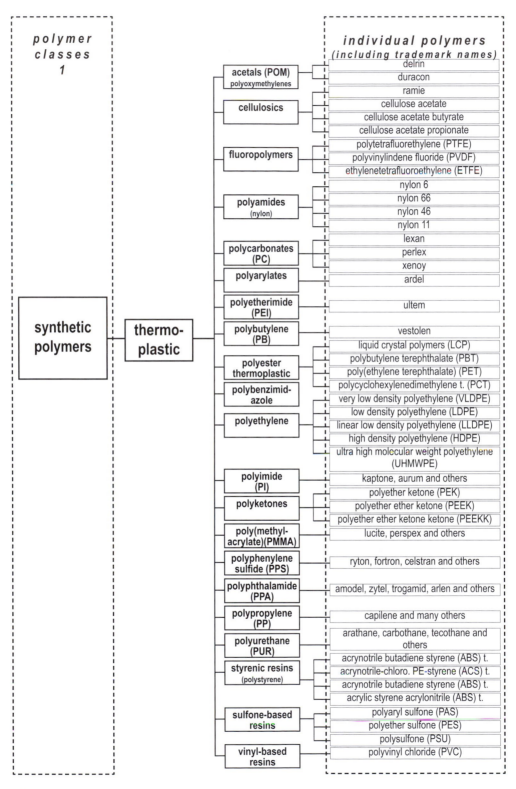

polymer classes 1

synthetic polymers → **thermo-plastic**

individual polymers
(including trademark names)

class	individual polymers
acetals (POM) polyoxymethylenes	delrin
	duracon
cellulosics	ramie
	cellulose acetate
	cellulose acetate butyrate
	cellulose acetate propionate
fluoropolymers	polytetrafluorethylene (PTFE)
	polyvinylindene fluoride (PVDF)
	ethylenetetrafluoroethylene (ETFE)
polyamides (nylon)	nylon 6
	nylon 66
	nylon 46
	nylon 11
polycarbonates (PC)	lexan
	perlex
	xenoy
polyarylates	ardel
polyetherimide (PEI)	ultem
polybutylene (PB)	vestolen
polyester thermoplastic	liquid crystal polymers (LCP)
	polybutylene terephthalate (PBT)
	poly(ethylene terephthalate) (PET)
polybenzimid-azole	polycyclohexylenedimethylene t. (PCT)
polyethylene	very low density polyethylene (VLDPE)
	low density polyethylene (LDPE)
	linear low density polyethylene (LLDPE)
	high density polyethylene (HDPE)
	ultra high molecular weight polyethylene (UHMWPE)
polyimide (PI)	kaptone, aurum and others
polyketones	polyether ketone (PEK)
	polyether ether ketone (PEEK)
	polyether ether ketone ketone (PEEKK)
poly(methyl-acrylate)(PMMA)	lucite, perspex and others
polyphenylene sulfide (PPS)	ryton, fortron, celstran and others
polyphthalamide (PPA)	amodel, zytel, trogamid, arlen and others
polypropylene (PP)	capilene and many others
polyurethane (PUR)	arathane, carbothane, tecothane and others
styrenic resins (polystyrene)	acrynotrile butadiene styrene (ABS) t.
	acrynotrile-chloro. PE-styrene (ACS) t.
	acrynotrile butadiene styrene (ABS) t.
	acrylic styrene acrylonitrile (ABS) t.
sulfone-based resins	polyaryl sulfone (PAS)
	polyether sulfone (PES)
	polysulfone (PSU)
vinyl-based resins	polyvinyl chloride (PVC)

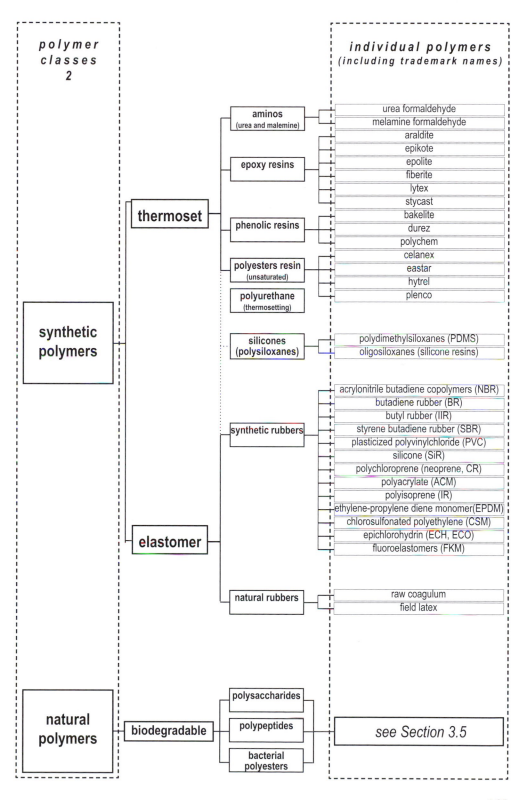

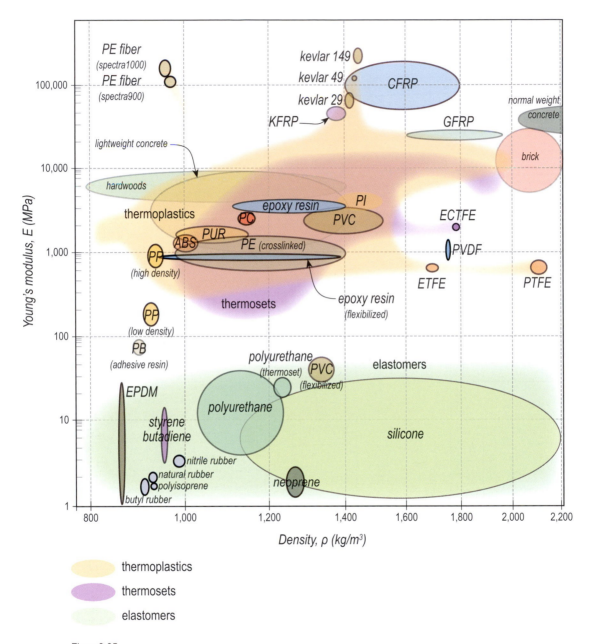

Figue 3.85

Young's modulus against density showing thermoplastics, thermosets and elastomers.

Sources: Produced with CES 4.1: Granta Design Ltd., Walker (2001), Dominghaus (1988), Doran (1995), Harper (2000).

Classification and Properties

Early in the development of polymers, it was understood that one attribute substantially defines the unique properties of the material class - high molecular weights. That is, polymers are characterized by many small molecules (monomers) stitched together to form long, sometimes unruly, macromolecules of unprecedented sizes.

These chains distinguish polymers from other much smaller molecules because of three factors:

1. chain entanglement,
2. intermolecular forces,
3. motion speed.

As these long chains are formed, processed and poured, extruded and cast, en masse under a variety of conditions, the chains may fold in on themselves many hundreds of times and thus become "entangled". Polymer chains were also found to possess very large intermolecular forces - a result of the extremely large size of the molecules. This property makes many polymers quite strong. And finally, these very long chains of molecules naturally move - pour, creep, stretch - more slowly than smaller molecules, again because of their sheer size (Harper 2000;Domininghaus 1988).

Because so much of the novel properties of polymers rests on the length of the molecular chain, early work focused on the goal to dramatically increase the maximum number of monomers that were pieced together to form ultrahigh molecular weight materials. Since that time, many other considerations have been research goals in the now sophisticated and rather distinct science of polymers.

Polymers chains number in the several thousand monomer units long, bound in essentially two ways. First, these chains are bound together with the attractive forces between individual atoms in the chain. These intra-chain forces are the stronger of the two forces, by a factor of up to 100. Second, the chains themselves are sometimes bound to one another. The type, and therefore strength, of these inter-chain bonds substantially determines the typology of the polymer and its primary material properties. The complete morphology of these atomic and molecular links and the composition of the monomer units determine the classification of individual polymers into three distinct types; thermoplastics, thermosets and elastomers. While this classification does segregate most polymers into one subfamily or another, certain polymers can have attributes that allow it to belong to more than one of these groups. However, for the vast majority of polymeric materials these distinctions are the most useful method of classification.

Figure 3.86

Fracture toughness and tensile strengths of selected polymers.

Sources: CES software 4.5, Domininghaus (1988), Harper (2000), Davis (2001).

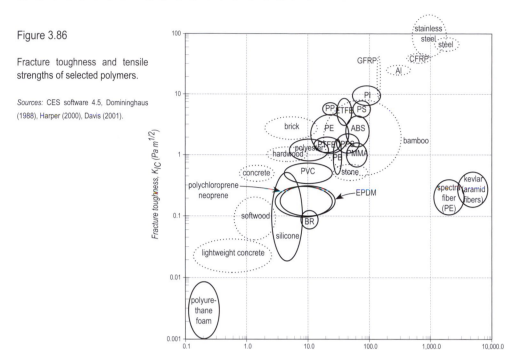

Figure 3.87

Thermal conductivity and diffusivity of selected polymers.

Sources: CES software 4.5, Domininghaus (1988), Harper (2000), Davis (2001).

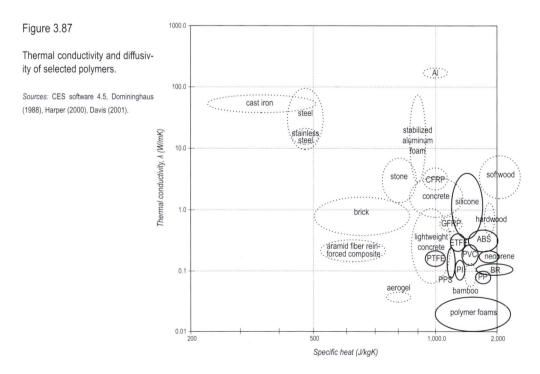

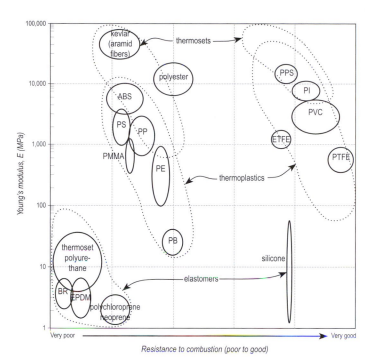

Figure 3.88

Flammability of selected polymers.

The graph shows a comparison between polymers in terms of both their stiffness (E) and their resistance to combustion.

Sources: CES software 4.5, Dominghaus (1988), Harper (2000), Davis (2001).

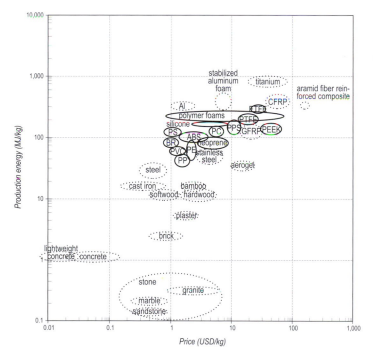

Figure 3.89

Production energy versus cost of selected polymers.

Sources: CES software 4.5, Dominghaus (1988), Harper (2000), Davis (2001).

Changing any number of variables - degree of cross-linking, chain length, monomer and copolymer composition - all make it possible to precisely customize the properties of polymer materials. Also, by varying the number of monomers per chain, the atomic structure of the monomer, the molecular weight and weight distribution along the chains, the degree of crystallinity and many other attributes, the polymer can be precisely engineered for specific purposes. These variables are too numerous to fully address in this book and delve into technical issues not useful here. However, the consequences of such variation are important, for example the range for modulus (E) is very great, from under 1 MN/m^2 to 50 GN/m^2 - a multiple of 50,000. Most polymers are, however, lower in moduli than most metals. The variables that contribute to this range are the topic of polymer science books several of which are listed in the Bibliography (see especially Domininghaus 1988, Doran 1995 and Harper 2000).

Also, the forms and processes in which polymers are manufactured vary greatly between the various general types and particular formulations. Polymers of many kinds can be extruded and cast into sheets and structural sections, pulled into fibers, formed into nonwoven composites, molded and cast to make stable solids. The form and the process are highly dependent on the molecular composition of the polymer (Domininghaus 1988).

Classification

The three subfamilies, thermoplastics, thermosets and elastomers, can be easily distinguished from one another.

Generally, thermoplastics are distinguishable by their ability to return the solid polymer to a liquid state by heating it to the appropriate temperature. Thus, with heat (thermo) becoming plastic. For many thermoplastics it seems this process is theoretically

Polymer	Embodied energy (feedstock energy) megajoules/kg
low-density polyethylene LDPE	80.5 (51.5)
high-density polyethylene HDPE	79.9 (48.5)
expandable polystyrene, PS	83.7 (47.8)
polyvinyl chloride, PVC	65.2 (23.5)
acrylonitrile butadiene styrene ABS	95.0 (45.8)
polycarbonate PC	116.8 (38.0)
epoxy resins	140.7 (42.6)

Figure 3.90

Embodied energies of important construction polymers including feedstock energies in parentheses.

Source: Wilson and Yost (2001)

1	PETE: poly-ethylene terephthalate
2	HDPE: high-density polyethylenes
3	V: vinyl/polyvinyl chlorides
4	LDPE: low-density polyethylenes
5	PP: polypropylene
6	PS: polystyrene
7	Other: all other resins

Figure 3.91

Recycling codes for synthetic polymers.

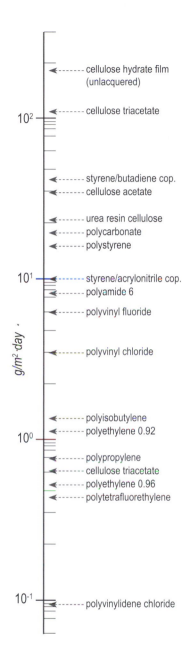

Figure 3.92

Water permeability of plastic films under 25°C/
77°F temperature gradient, humidity gradient
90% to 0% rel. humidity. Films of 110µm/3.94
mils.

possible many dozens of times without appreciable depreciation of its properties. Just as thermoplastics are able to be reheated into a liquid form, thermosets are not. Elastomers are distinguished in a different way. Elastomers are materials that exhibit highly elastic properties - to an extent that any significant load transfer is precluded by elongation or compressive strain. Clearly, these distinctions are not entirely exclusive from one another. Some elastomers may exhibit properties that would also characterize them as either a thermoplastic or a thermoset. Some polymers are easily converted from a thermoplastic to a thermoset by the addition of copolymers. Therefore, distinctions between these three subfamilies are useful but not always easily applied to all polymers.

Thermoplastics

Thermoplastics are primarily characterized by the fact that the long polymer chains of these materials are not chemically bonded, or cross-linked. Lacking these macromolecular bonds allows the chains to slide with respect to one another, the direct consequence being an easy return to a viscous state when heated. Therefore, thermoplastics can be reprocessed by reheating, liquefying and reforming through casting, molding or other processes. This makes thermoplastics the most easily recycled polymers. Given the fact that polymers now comprise 9.2 percent of the total municipal solid waste (MSW) produced in the United States - an increase of just under one million tons in 1960 to 20 million tons today - the potential recyclability of individual polymers is a property that any designer should be aware of (Selke 2000).

Even though fossil fuel materials are the primary feedstock of almost all synthetic polymers, the energy of production for polymers is still quite low. The production of an object in synthetic polymer, such as polyethylene, uses approximately 30 times less energy than the same item in aluminum, a metal with a comparable strength

Figure 3.93a, b

Detail of the pneumatic "pillow" assembly of EFTE film spanning the curved tubular hollow steel sections (HSS) of the exterior envelope. A constant positive pressure is required to counter any incidental loss of air from within the pillows. The detail on the left shows the flexible tubing system for maintaining a positive pressure within the ETFE pillows and the on the right, the heat welded seams that hold the ETFE sheets together.

Space Centre, Leicester, United Kingdom (2003).
Nicolas Grimshaw, Architect.

to weight ratio. This alone has continued to make polymers the most economic choice in the manufacture of a wide array of consumer products and building components. Development of inexpensive additives, such as fillers and extenders, has also aided in the economy and minimization of polymer energy content.

The subfamily of thermoplastics is comprised of a huge number of polymers including the cellulose polymers, vinyl polymers, polystyrenes, polyamides, and acrylic polymers. ETFE, PTFE, PVC, polyurethanes, styrenic resins, polycarbonates, PP and PE, among many others, are thermoplastic polymers that are extremely important in building systems.

The following are brief descriptions of a select number of thermoplastics important to architecture.

Polycarbonate (PC)
Currently PC has become one of the most important glass replacements available to the construction industry. Along with ETFE, PC has emerged as a viable candidate for performing close to the level of glass for glazing systems because of its exceptional transparency, high strength, resistance to degradation caused by UV radiation, acceptance of a wide range of coloring, and high dimensional tolerances even at high temperatures. These properties also

Property	Kevlar 29	Kevlar 49	Kevlar 149
density (g/cm^3)	1.44	1.44	1.47
tensile modulus (Gpa)	83	131	186
tensile strength (Gpa)	3.6	3.6 - 4.1	3.4
tensile elongation (%)	4.0	2.8	2.0

Figure 3.94

Comparative values of the three types of crystalline aromatic polyamide (aramid) fibers available today. Known as Kevlar® fibers, these materials have become important additions to the set of fibers used in composite materials.

Sources: Harper (2000), Dominghaus (1988).

Fiber	Ultimate tensile strength (N/mm^2)	Specific strength tensile strength/ density
polyester	1,120	0.81
e-glass	2,500	0.96
s-glass	4,600	1.84
aramide Kevlar 49	2,900	1.92
nylon	990	0.87
carbon fiber	2,200-5,400	1.13-3.00
mild steel	300	0.03
prestressing steel	1,700	0.22

Figure 3.95

Reinforcing fiber materials.

Sources: Harper (2000), Dominghaus (1988).

make PC one of the most popular engineering plastics - used in applications as diverse as consumer appliances, power tool housings, safety helmets, motorcycle wind shields, CDs and DVDs, prescription and safety glasses, cell phones, canopy applications and many others. Global consumption of PC in 2000 was in excess of 1.8 million tonnes, from 600,000 tonnes in 1990, and the yearly growth hovers around 8-10percent. Discovered in 1898, PC was not introduced into large-scale industrial production until 1958 (simultaneously by Bayer of Germany and General Electric of the US). Today most major chemical companies produce products made of PC. Polycarbonate consumption is divided among a variety of final uses with the top three applications garnering the majority of the material; 32 percent glazing and sheet products, 22 percent electronics and 18 percent optical. The remainder is split between automotive, appliances, recreational, packaging, medical and others.

While PC is known to scratch and lose some transparency when used for architectural glazing, architects are not commonly aware of the real cause. Some of the loss in transparency may be caused by the grinding action of dirt when the surface is cleaned. Soot, wind-blown dust, and other particles can easily indent and scratch the surface during cleaning. Also, PC can absorb significant amounts of water at sustained higher temperatures and relative humidities (33°C and 65 percent RH). When this happens streaking and blistering may result.

Ethylenetetrafluoroethylene (ETFE)

As mentioned above ETFE represents the other widely considered alternative to silica-lime glass for architectural applications. Its application to buildings is much more limited because of the fact that ETFE is usually applied as a nonrigid film and therefore requires some method for placing the material in tension. The most common technique is using ETFE in a pneumatically controlled "pillow" configuration. By creating positive pressure between two sheets of ETFE and sealing the edges, the material can be used for skylights and, on occasion, vertical glazing.

Aromatic polyamides (Kevlar)

Aromatic polyamides can be classified into three groups: crystalline polymers in the form of fibers (aramid fibers such as Kevlar - a trademark name originally applied to this aramid developed by DuPont), crystalline thermoplastics, and amorphous copolymers. Aramid fibers and textiles have been of greatest interest for architectural applications both as reinforcing in composites and as a blast-resistant interlayer in an exterior wall.

In fact, this latter use of blast protection with Kevlar fabric has been applied to a substantial portion of the Pentagon Building in Washington DC for blast resistance. Beginning in 1993 and prompted by the Oklahoma City bombing, the building enclosure of the Pentagon was reinforced with a continuous Kevlar fabric inserted between structural columns and held in place with an intermediate grid of hollow steel structural sections. The assembly proved quite effective in limiting the ballistic effect of dislodged materials from the building's wall. Along with the laminated safety glass used in the openings, the reinforced section of the building saved dozens of lives (Novitski 2000).

Three types of Kevlar are available; Kevlar 29, Kevlar 49 and Kevlar 149, in ascending order of tensile modulus and strength and descending order of elongation. Kevlar 49 is the most widely used fiber for high strength fabrics used as reinforcing for composite materials. Kevlar 29 is comparable in tensile strength to e-glass fibers and is therefore an easy substitution for weight savings. A major application of K49 fabric is personal armor composites; very high impact and abrasion resistance makes this fiber an ideal choice for military and security personnel body armor. Combined with other fibers, such as graphite, Kevlar composites have become a significant addition to high performance composites.

Figure 3.96

The application of a polymer nonwoven barrier material to a light wood frame building.

Northern Virginia, USA (2005).

Figure 3.97

The application of a self-adhered polymer flashing material.

Cambridge, UK (2004).

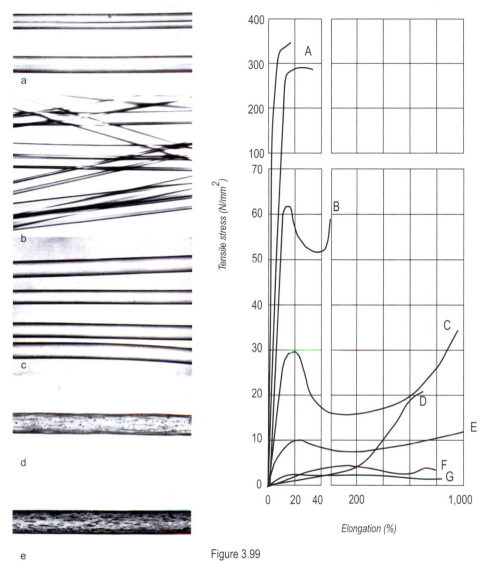

a

b

c

d

e

Figure 3.98a, b, c, d, e

Fiber photomicrographs

a. rayon
b. nylon
c. polyethylene
d. acrylic
e. polyvinyl chloride

Figure 3.99

Comparison of tensile stress versus elongation for some polymers and metals

A. Steel
B. Copper
C. Polycarbonate
D. Natural rubber
E. Polyethylene-high density
F. PVC - plasticized
G. Silicone - elastomer

Source: Adapted from Domininghaus (1988).

Kevlar is quite hydrophilic - absorbing environmental moisture quite readily and losing strength and lifetime durability in the process. Also aramid fibers generally do not resist degradation due to UV radiation very well. Applications of Kevlar to the exterior envelope of a building thus require some protection from moisture and solar radiation.

Polytetrafluorethylene (PTFE)

Known popularly as Teflon®, PTFE is used in buildings as a coating for structural fabrics, plumbing components, electrical wiring and a variety of fixtures, as a surface material for high stress load situations such as the bearing pads for bridges and seismic isolation systems for buildings, for paints and finish coatings, for interior wall coverings and for a variety of tapes, adhesives and sealants. Developed at Dupont's Jackson Laboratory in 1938, Teflon® has come to be known as a superior low friction material, important to applications in which the adhesion of dirt and other particles is detrimental to performance. Thus its importance as a nonstick and self-cleaning surface for architectural assemblies - especially structural fabrics and structural bearing surfaces.

Polyethylene (PE)

More polyethylene is produced globally than any other synthetic polymer. Available in grades of varying density from very low density PE (VLDPE) to ultrahigh molecular weight PE (UHMWPE) polyethylene has enormous range of thermal and mechanical properties. PE also allows a wide range of copolymer possibilities. As such PE serves as the precursor for a vast array of more complex polymers. Polyethylene, as a sheet material, is most widely used as a very good vapor barrier in exterior envelopes, especially for residential construction. It is also available to be used as a reinforcing fiber in certain types of concrete (Soroushian et al. 1993).

Polypropylene (PP)

The polymer repeating unit that comprises polypropylene comes directly from the products that result from the "cracking" of petroleum. Polypropylene's properties are similar to PE but it is slightly stiffer and has a higher melting temperature. The largest proportion of production is for fibers used in innumerable consumer and household items. Some of these fibers are used for geotextiles applied to ground stabilization purposes. Until recently polypropylene has not been used in any great quantity for apparel items. With the introduction of PP (known sometimes as capilene) for insulating wear, its production for apparel has increased significantly.

Commercial production of PP began in 1957 by Montecanini, Hercules Incorporated and Farbwerke Hoechst AG. The polymer was originally discovered in 1954 by the Italian chemist Giulio Natta and his assistant Paolo Chini. For a part of this work Natta was awarded the Nobel Prize in 1963.

Poly(methylmethylacrylate) (PMMA)

Also known as acrylic, PMMA is used in applications in which a clear and very hard material is necessary. It is found in coatings, caulks, paints and other media, and is best known by its trade names Lucite, Plexiglas and Acrylite. Polymerized from methyl methylacrylate, acrylic has been used as a glass replacement for interior and exterior glazing conditions.

Polyurethane (PUR)

See thermosets.

Styrenic resins

Polystyrene (PS) is produced from the repeating unit known as styrene (phenylethylene) that results from a reaction of ethylene and benzene. Because PS retains a large ring-shaped phenyl group (C_6H_5) the molecule is not able to be compacted. This results in the material being both transparent and relatively rigid. Today the material is extremely useful as a packing and insulation product, but its introduction to market took many decades to secure. PS was discovered in 1839 by the German physicist Eduard Simon but it took almost 100 years for purification of the monomer and improvements in the process engineering by Robert Dreisbach of Dow Chemical to make a commercially viable polymer. Due to its very good vapor and gas permeability, transparency and rigidity, PS is used extensively in packaging both for perishable items and nonperishable products like CDs. It is also an important construction material with 10 percent of total global production diverted to construction applications - as insulation, compressible fillers, and other purposes.

Vinyl-based resins

The most important architectural material of all plastic resins is PVC. It has been used extensively since the commencement of industrial production in 1927 and - in its unplasticized form - is now used in building products such as pipe, especially drain pipes, window and door frames, siding, resilient flooring and many other assemblies and products. While PVC is the most heavily used plastic in contemporary buildings, it is also used in an enormous array of consumer and industrial products. Every year, more than 10 billion pounds (4.5 million tonnes) is consumed in the US alone and 60 percent of total PVC production is devoted to construction products. Its worldwide production is second only to PE, because of its very high rigidity, low cost, range of properties, flame resistance, and ease of combining with other polymers to produce a wide array of useful materials. However, significant questions regarding the environmental and health impacts of PVC have been raised (Altschuler 2004). Not only has its use in buildings been questioned, but the entire chlorine-based industry has come under attack from various environmental organizations (Tukker and Kleijn 1999).

The primary reason for this concern is the use of carcinogenic chlorine as a major constituent of the process of PVC production. The chlorine industry devotes 30 percent of its production to the manufacturing of PVC. The final PVC resin is 57 percent chlorine (by weight). The argument that, in light of this carcinogen, PVC and other chlorine-based materials should be phased out of building materials is understandable and, ideally, the best solution. However, the situation is more complex than ideal. In fact, recently the United States Green Building Council released a draft report that clearly states that the organization does not believe that "PVC is consistently worse than alternative materials on a life-cycle environmental and health basis" (EBN 2005). Not unexpectedly, the vinyl industry agrees with this conclusion (Burnett 1993).

The sources of concern over PVC in buildings includes all phases of the manufacture, use and discard of the material. In manufacture, the use and transport of large quantities of chlorine and vinyl chloride, the production of dioxins, furans and polychlorinated biphenyls (PCBs) - all highly toxic substances to both humans and a variety of wildlife species - pose serious threats to maintaining a safe environment. At least in one known case, an entire town in Lousiana was relocated due to very high indoor concentrations of vinyl chloride. Lawsuits and subsequent settlements resulted in sealed records, but it is generally known that the contamination of ground water was due to spillage from a nearby Georgia Gulf PVC factory (Malin and Wilson 1994).

In addition, substantial objections to the use of PVC in buildings has noted the danger of environmental contamination from the burning of PVC. Hydrochloric acid and many caustic and toxic substances are produced when PVC burns and the danger of environmental contamination exists both from accidental building fires and the intentional burning of construction and demolition waste (Kelley 2001).

And finally, at the end of life, PVC products pose a real challenge in both landfilling and recycling. Because the polymer melts (and then burns) at a much lower temperature than PET - another common plastic used in containers and other consumer items - PVC makes the

Figure 3.100

A temporary polymer weather barrier for the party wall of a building under repair.

London, UK (2003).

Figure 3.101

Polymer water barrier applied as part of the exterior envelope system.

Folk Art Museum, New York, NY, USA (2002).
Billie Tsien, Tod Williams, Architects.

178

process of recycling very difficult. Any PVC that is mistaken for PET and left in the recycling batch will burn, produce hydrochloric acid and other toxic gases and pose a substantial corrosion risk for the machinery. Even landfilling, though much less of an issue than recycling, may result in a slow decomposition that also releases an array of unhealthy chemicals. Debate continues on this, and most, topics regarding PVC (Wilson and Yost 2001).

Intense discussion was recently prompted by a proposal for granting LEED® credit to excluding the use of PVC products in buildings (Altschuler 2004). While concern regarding the health effects of processes used in the manufacture of PVC have been circulating among various building-related stakeholders for some time, only recently has there been an organized effort to establish the science and reach an informed conclusion (EBN 1993, EBN 2005). Preliminary results indicate that a simple recommendation to eliminate the use of PVC products in buildings based primarily on process-related environmental issues ignores the fact that alternatives do not significantly improve the situation. There is some debate regarding this conclusion (Finaldi 1993). Clearly some alternative materials, such as fiber reinforced cement products used for siding, do not engender the use of chlorine, their overall lifecycle impact may not be any better than PVC in most situations (Altschuler et al. 2004).

PVC was first developed by German scientist Eugen Baumann in 1872 but commercial production did not begin until 1930 with the marketing of the Union Carbide polymer Vinylite, used as the substrate for long-playing (LP) records. Since then, many varieties of the polymer, plasticized and copolymerized, have been introduced by a dozen separate companies.

Thermosets

Thermosets are a distinct grouping of polymers primarily based on the fact that their polymer chains have been irreversibly cross-linked, rendering the material incapable of returning to a liquid state. The initial cross linking can be accomplished through an application of heat, chemical catalysts, ultraviolet radiation, or other agents (Walker 2001);Davis 2001). The state that results is an infusible one, barring easy subsequent processing. Therefore, the best use of thermosets should be targeted toward long-life situations in which the value of recycling is substantially exceeded by the value of another important performance parameter or the thermoset can be usefully downcycled.

Thermosets include phenolics (including Bakelite), aminoplastics, epoxies, polyesters, polyimides and some polyurethanes. These kinds of polymers are normally used in conditions in which severe temperatures or other environmental stresses would cause a thermoplastic to degrade. The following are brief descriptions of a select number of thermosets important to architecture and industry generally.

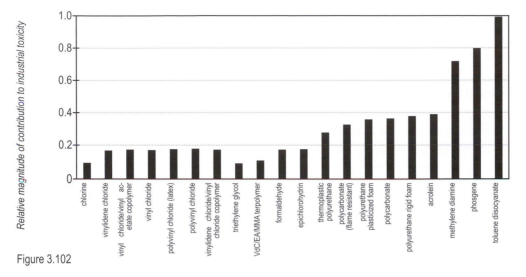

Figure 3.102

These polymeric compounds are primary constituents in the toxicity of industrial processes.

Sources: Adapted from Graedel and Allenby (2003), Domininghaus (1988).

Aminos

Produced with amino groups and combined with urea or melamine, these thermosets are cured at high temperatures to produce durable solids. Used extensively for bathroom and kitchen fixtures, these thermosets were discovered in the 1930s and became one of the first competitors of Bakelite (phenolic resin). Also used in the repair of damaged wood (from insect damage or rot) urea formaldehyde and melamine formaldehyde resins are able to penetrate small cavities and fill cell volumes.

Epoxy resins

Epoxy resins were formulated beginning in the 1930s in Switzerland at Ciba A.G. (now known as Ciba-Geigy) under the trademark name Araldite and further commercialized by Shell Chemicals in the 1950s. This class of thermoset resins has become one of the major polymer materials used in applications as a pure resin product applied to surfaces and as a composite with fillers and fiber reinforcing. Most liquid epoxy resins are derived from epichlorohydrin, a product of phenol and acetone or formaldehyde (Doran 1995). The epoxy system may be provided with a curing agent (hardener, crosslinker, activator) that initiates the solidification of the resin at ambient temperatures or may be cured using heat or UV radiation. Many varieties of epoxy resins and hundreds of curing agents supply the construction industry globally. Applications include adhesives, paints and coatings, the matrix material for composites and many other high performance scenarios. Several varieties are also used for repair and fillers in historic wood and concrete (Reinprecht 2000). Epoxy resins originate as viscous liquids that, upon curing, form tough and rigid solids that possess very good adhesion properties and generally good durability. They can be made incombustible and resistant to many caustic chemicals with additives. Applications for buildings have included adhesives, primers and coatings, mortars and grouts, sealants, pastes and as a matrix for encapsulating fibers or other inclusions. From large-scale structural repair of concrete bridges and buildings using carbon fiber and epoxy resin textiles to the renovation of historic wood detailing, epoxies are an ideal thermoset (Doran 1995;Harper 2000;Davis 2001). Epoxy resins are also used extensively for flooring finishing systems for both interior and exterior applications.

Epoxy resins are also extensively used as the matrix polymer for several kinds of architecturally important composite materials, such as glass fiber reinforced polymers (GFRP), carbon fiber reinforced polymers (CFRP) and pultrusions (Hashem and Yuan 2001). For ease of processing and excellent bond to a variety of reinforcing fibers, epoxy resins are often the best material choice (see Section 3.4 for more on composites).

Phenolic resins

Low cost, good durability, heat and chemical resistant, this type of resin spawned the well-known Bakelite material of the early 20th century. These resins are most often compression molded into diverse shapes that serve many industries. In construction, PF resins are used extensively as the binding agent in exterior grade engineered wood products including oriented strand boards, plywood and other composites.

Polyester resins

Used for large-scale building panels, boat hulls and other vehicles, this resin is high strength, chemically resistant, rigid, transparent and inexpensive.

Polyurethane

Developed by Otto Bayer in the late 1930s, polyurethanes are produced en masse principally for insulating foams. Varieties are easily produced yielding a wide range of chemical resistance, flexibility, and mechanical properties. These polymers contain repeating molecular units that include both oxygen and carbon bonded to nitrogen. Polyurethanes can be both thermosets and thermoplastics depending on the degree of crosslinking. In buildings, thermoset polyurethanes are most common and used for carpets, upholstery and insulation materials.

Thermoset silicone

Silicone can be formulated as a thermoset or an elastomer. See silicone under elastomers, below.

Elastomers

Elastomers, or rubbers, are characterized by their mechanically elastic attributes; greatly beyond either thermoplastics or thermosets. One qualitative definition stipulates that an elastomer has the ability to return to its original shape after it has been stretched to twice its original length at room temperature. Elastomers are also essentially incapable of transferring any significant loads in compression. Deformation of the mass of the elastomer prevents significant energy absorption. Natural rubber (NR) was the first elastomer to be extensively used by modern industry. Ethylene propylene diene copolymers, EPDMs, are a large class of polymers used extensively in roofing applications and other barrier products.

Plasticized polyvinylchloride (PVC)
See PVC in thermoplastics.

Silicone (SiR) - polysiloxanes, oligosiloxanes
Silicones are a major group of *inorganic polymers* - that is, silicones do not have a carbon atom backbone but rather consist of monomers of silicon and oxygen atoms. These repeating inorganic monomers receive side groups of atoms and molecules - including organic molecules - attached to the silicon atom. As with organic polymers, the various properties of silicone can be modified by varying the number and type of side groups, crosslinking and overall chain lengths. The two primary groups of silicones are polydimethylsiloxanes (PDMS) and oligosiloxanes (silicone resins).

Silicone has many industrial uses as a high performance sealant and gasketing material, adhesive and lubricant. Also, silicone is being used more and more for a vast array of consumer, medical, recreational and safety products. Silicones are chemical and oxidation resistant, stable at very higher temperatures, water resistant, nonconductive and highly elastic. Many silicones produced for sealant purposes can easily achieve an elongation of 800 percent over a service lifetime of several hundred thousand cycles making this group of inorganic polymers an ideal substitute for natural and synthetic rubbers.

Silicone's main uses in buildings include sealants for glazed curtainwalls and stone veneer assemblies, window frame assemblies, adhesives for a broad range of components including roofing materials, flashing materials, tiles, finish materials and many other items. In structural glazing, silicone acts as both a seal and a load transfer material. Improvements in its development have resulted in a broad range of silicone products used in the building enclosure both for new buildings and major upgrades and refurbishments. For example, the European Union Berlaymont Headquarters in Brussels was recently renovated with the addition of a large double-layered glass facade using structural silicone as the primary sealant material (CES 2004). In fact, in the past two decades innumerable modern facades have been repaired and upgraded using silicone materials for much better performance and durability.

Polychloroprene (neoprene, CR)

Known most commonly as neoprene, its initial commercial trademark, this polymer is used extensively in sealants, gaskets and other joining applications. The material is often manufactured as a cellular material, making it compressible.

Ethylene propylene diene monomer (EPDM)

Used as a major roofing membrane material, EPDM sheeting is joined together with heat to make a multi-layered weather barrier.

Properties

See individual polymers for property descriptions.

Polymers in Contemporary Architecture

The bulk of synthetic polymers in architecture is used in nonstructural applications as part of the building enclosure assemblies, interior finish and space-defining assemblies and various components and devices of the building services systems, such as insulation on electrical wiring, silicone sealants, polymer foam insulation materials and numerous woven and non-woven textiles (Brookes 1998). Polymers used as part of the superstructure are quite limited because of their lower moduli (with the exception of the use of PTFE (Teflon®) for bearing surface applications). However, several new high density polymers may be on the cusp of application to structural systems, see "Emergent Polymers", below.

Polymers in buildings are routinely used for the following applications:

1. barrier systems,
2. sealants,
3. adhesives,
4. fabrics, textiles, foils and other sheet materials (nonrigid), and
5. composite materials (boards, FRPs, composite textiles).

The industrial production of organic materials was initially restricted to coal-tar dyes and pharmaceuticals. These were obtained from by-products associated with the coking of coal. As described at the beginning of this chapter, fossil fuels - oil and gas - are the primary source materials for polymers in the US and worldwide. Earlier, Europe relied on calcium carbide obtained from coal to produce acetylene as a primary intermediary for much of their polymer production until the early 1950s.

Figure 3.103

This bus station in Holland is constructed of polystyrene blocks held together and covered by a polyester surface. The building's designers satisfied a tight budget and challenging durability requirements in the making of the largest completely synthetic structure standing today.

Building, Hoofddorp, Country (2005).
Nio ArchitectenPhoto courtesy of Maurice Nio. Photographer Hans Pattist.

Barriers, Sealants and Adhesives

Many of the polymer descriptions given above demonstrate the widespread use of these materials in three very important applications; barriers systems, sealants and joint systems and adhesive systems. Barrier systems have been discussed at length and include the use of EPDM as a roofing material, ETFE as a glazing substitute, PU and expanded PS as insulation materials, PE and nylon sheeting as vapor and air barrier materials and many other polymers in the service of controlling heat and mass flux. Sealants and adhesives are also well served by a variety of polymers, notably the epoxies (one and two part), the silicones, polychloroprene and several other compressible polymers and a rich variety of tenacious industrial glues.

Textiles, Films and Foils

In addition, an important subset of synthetic polymers are textiles, films and foils (Braddock and Maloney 1998). In building construction, these nonrigid materials have been used for essentially two very different applications. First, they have been exploited for their extremely useful properties as barrier systems in orthogonal nonstructural exterior envelope applications. Many polymers are used in this capacity including polyethylene, nylons, polyurethane,

Figure 3.104

Detail of the tensile restraint of a coated structural fabric assembly.

Space Centre, Leicester, United Kingdom (2003),
Nicolas Grimshaw, Architect.

polyesters etc. The latest material to be introduced in this way are the ETFE foils used as a glass substitute in large transparent surfaces (Gayle et al. 2001;Willmert 2002). However, most applications of textiles and foils to the exterior envelope are not visible elements of a building, yet still important improvements to the continuous planar barrier systems required of contemporary multi-layered exterior wall assemblies. Vapor, air and radiant barriers as well as insulation materials, flashing systems, sealant joints, expansion and construction joint systems and roofing systems have all been substantially improved by the introduction of ever more varieties of nonrigid sheet materials (AFMA 1988).

The second important use of polymer sheet materials in architecture is structural fabrics - the result of extraordinary design and structural work investigating viable building volumes and lightweight shelters through tensile geometries (Berger 1985,1999;Kronenburg 1997;Davey 2000;Otto and Rasch 2001;Mollaert 2002;Rein and Willhelm 2000;Robbin 1996;Talarico 2000). Coated and composite fabrics and foils have been the primary material for load transfer and form definition for these types of structures. The most commonly used materials

Figure 3.105a, b, c

Construction fabrics are now commonly used to prevent debris from falling onto surrounding sidewalks and also to establish a moderately protected interior construction environment. The size of textile pieces and the speed with which enormous expanses of building are covered prompt the examination of opportunities for permanent textile facades for rectilinear frame buildings (see Chapter 5).

Various locations (2005).

for structural fabrics structures are PVC-coated polyester fabrics and PTFE-coated glass fiber fabrics. Cable stay tents, tensile curvatures and pneumatic structures are all dependent on the ability of these materials to safely transfer loads associated with the exterior shell of the building as well as satisfy the performance requirements of the exterior envelope and protect the inhabitants from the elements (Topham 2002;Mollaert 2002;Blum 2002). While these fabric forms have been a fruitful and exciting subset of the use of sheet materials in architecture, it has remained a specialized type of form for a very small set of building types (airports, stadia, warehouses and other long-span spaces).

These applications share the requirements of acting as a mediating surface between the fluctuating unstable exterior environment and either a sheltered area, in the case of a canopy

Figure 3.106

Another example of the coverage potential of today's fabrics.

Kendall Square,Cambridge, MA (2005).

or other limited shelter, or a stable interior environment. The material continuity of nonrigid sheet materials lends itself well to these needs.

Textile, film and foil materials are used to fulfill the various performance requirements of an exterior envelope. Textiles are formed through the interplay of fibers; woven, braided, knitted etc. Foils and films are extruded, cast or otherwise formed into a continuous material not composed of fibers. The advantages of using a nonrigid material in establishing a continuous barrier plane between the exterior and interior are numerous; the ability to overlap the material, conform to complex geometries and spatial conditions, join it to other barrier systems, cover large areas quickly and generally verify that the entire surface area of the volume of the building has been adequately covered. In addition, most textiles and foils are lightweight, durable and manufactured under high quality control conditions (AFMA 1988).

Barrier system requirements have been separated into distinct performance needs and often distinct material layers. The need to control air infiltration, vapor intrusion, radiant heat loss or gain and other issues of energy and mass flow are often satisfied with the use of separately applied material layers.

There is good science and construction practice in this separation. First, each material designated to control a specific kind of flux can be placed within the envelope in the location that allows it to perform as desired. A vapor barrier placed in an insulated wall needs to be located on the warm side of the insulation, a radiant barrier needs to be placed against a layer of air etc. Second, each material can be engineered to serve its specific function efficiently and reliably. A vapor retarder material may not satisfy air barrier requirements and vice versa. Third, the separation of materials allows for the design of exterior envelopes that have good "drying potential" - the ability to dry themselves periodically and maintain a durable assembly.

Many of the materials used for these barrier systems are polymers. Polyethylene film is the common material used along with aluminum foils and asphalt and felt for roofs for providing good vapor retarding systems. Perm ratings close to zero can be achieved; 0.08 perms for a 0.004-inch thick film of polyethylene. Air barrier materials include closed cell foams, foils, painted interior kraft paper and gypsum board, liquid and sheet applied rubberized membranes, "housewrap" materials such as Tyvek® and many other products. Among these products, polymers are well represented.

Most buildings that use tensile fabric forms do so to provisionally shelter and sometimes weather-enclose space. The anticlastic geometry of tensile fabric surfaces lends itself best to a delineation of the overall volume of a building or the making of a sheltering canopy. The two opposing curves work together to resist vertical downward loads from rain and snow and uplift from wind pressures. And whether the fabric is a canopy or defines the enclosure of a building, it is both transferring structural loads and resisting environmental forces. Therefore, tensile fabric structures require sheet materials that can both transfer large tensile loads, often over substantial spans, and resist the diurnal and seasonal changes in environmental forces and the resulting degradation offered by the climate.

As a result, all fabrics used for these purposes have come to contain at least two separate components; a fiber for tensile load transfer and a coating (or additional fiber network) for resisting the various forces of the environment, protecting the fiber and acting as the primary barrier surface for the assembly. The two components work together to fulfill the requirements of the membrane. Therefore, they need to be chemically and thermally compatible, easily processed into a composite and fulfill reasonable service lifetimes. Additionally, other components may need to be included for a fully viable material such as an insulating fill and

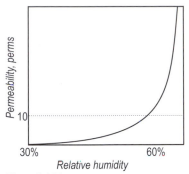

Figure 3.107

Permeability of a "smart" vapor barrier showing the capacity of the material (nylon) to "open" up allowing vapor to pass at higher humidities. The utility of this property in exterior envelopes is valuable when moisture is trapped inside an assembly causing the relative humidity *within* the wall to increase dramatically. At higher humidities the vapor barrier becomes much more gas permeable allowing the wall to "dry out" and not retain moisture.

Source: Trechsel (2001).

fabric, fire-resistant coatings or fibers, acoustical absorbing material, additional UV radiation protection and anything else needed for safety or required by the particular needs of the project. In order to accomplish all of this, the materials of choice are coated fabrics.

To accomplish load transfer, only a few fibers have the capacity to resist the stress levels normally encountered in building-sized surfaces. The fibers most commonly used are polyester threads (PET), glass and aramid (commonly known by its Dupont trade name, Kevlar).

Polyester is one of the primary industrial fibers used today. It combines very high strength and superior shear resistance, but is susceptible to degradation from UV radiation over time. PVC is most commonly used in coating polyester fabrics; however, it also suffers from long exposure to UV radiation and eventually becomes brittle. The solution for this problem is the addition of softeners (Blum 2002). Glass fibers are used with either a silicone or PTFE coating. For the purpose of resisting the typical forces that are part of the daily environment, one of three coating types are normally chosen.

In addition to anticlastic tensile fabric structures, pneumatic buildings have also explored the use of high strength nonrigid sheet materials for "permanent" buildings, canopies, temporary shelters, civil structures and other building types. The materials used for this application are the foils made of PVC, ET and THV (tetrafluoroethylene, hexafluoropropylene and vinylidene fluoride).

Recently "smart" materials have been identified to fulfill barrier needs dynamically. Motivated by computational simulation demonstrating the value of a variable gas permeable film for buildings, one product currently available on the market uses a film of nylon 6 (polyamide-6 and 99 percent by weight) and caprolactum (1 percent by weight) for a smart vapor barrier system that allows for a range of permeability depending on environmental conditions. At relative humidities of less than 40 percent the film works as a vapor retarder of under 1 perm, at 60 percent RH it allows vapor movement across its thickness at rates approaching 10 perms. This is an extremely useful property that allows a wall assembly to increase its drying potential and therefore its overall lifetime durability. Hygrothermal research indicates that many materials begin to deteriorate under extended periods of more than 70-90 percent relative humidity (Trechsel 2001). Most porous building materials do not absorb enough water to sustain organic growth below these very high relative humidities. Decay fungi and bacteria require in excess of 95 percent RH, mold fungi 75 percent. By reacting to high RH values, the vapor retarding film allows the wall to dry before any significant moisture accumulates and irreversible damage occurs.

Composite Matrix Materials
Polymers have proven to be the most versatile matrix material for embedding high performance fibers. Fiber reinforced polymers (FRP) now include glass-fiber reinforced polymers (GFRP),

carbon reinforced polymers (CFRP), Kevlar and other polymer fiber reinforced polymers (KFRP) and steel fiber reinforced polymers. The most commonly used polymer matrix materials for composites are epoxy resins, polyesters, nylon 6.6, polypropylene and PEEK (polyether ether ketone). These materials are discussed at length in Section 3.4 Composites.

Emergent Polymers

It can be expected that polymers will continue their prodigious industrial expansion of the last few decades with the development of more versatile, less expensive and environmentally robust materials incorporated more deeply and integrated better into various architectural assemblies. This is a welcome possibility, as there are significant performance improvements that polymers may be able to address. Of course, it will be equally important to address issues of resource use and waste management as the volume of polymers increases and the technologies of reclamation, recycling and biodegradation improve (Stevens 2002;Satkofsky 2002).

Useful application possibilities continue to abound for synthetic polymers. For example, barrier systems for buildings can be greatly improved with polymers that can carefully modulate their properties to strategically control the flow of mass (air and water) and energy (heat). The recent work to produce "smart" vapor barriers is one example of this. Smart vapor barriers that vary their permeability by a factor of ten are already on the market (MemBrain™ produced by CertainTeed Corp.). As discussed above, this attribute is simply a material property of the nylon 6 (polyamide) used for the product. Next generation composite sheets, films and fabrics promise an emerging field of polyvalent nonrigid materials ideal for application to the building enclosure of contemporary buildings. Another emerging use of textiles in architecture is the development of multi-layered assemblies, either as part of a laminate rigid board or as part of a nonrigid sandwich. Most of these systems are being developed to target one performance aspect of the exterior envelope.

Polymer textiles and extruded sheet materials have also played an important role in blast and fire protection. As discussed above with Kevlar fibers and fabrics, polymer fibers have great potential in addressing life safety issues in buildings by applying known thermally resistant polymeric materials. For example, Nomex® (another registered brand from Dupont for an aromatic polyamide, or aramid fiber) is used extensively in clothing and other products to protect people from intense heat in industrial and emergency situations. Sometimes referred to as "advanced thermal technologies" this textile (and others) have the great potential of advancing fire protection systems for buildings. One can envision the application of thermal "blankets" made of thermally resistant textiles as an alternative method for the protection of structural steel frames.

Performance issues	Cyano-acrylates	Epoxies	Silicones	Urethanes	Two-part acrylics
Positive	excellent with rubber and polymers	diverse formulations	very wide service temperature range	excellent toughness and ductility	good impact resistance and ductility
Negative	low solvent resistance	2 part requires mixing	low strength	moisture sensitive	mixing required
Service temperature range (°F)	-65 +190	-65 +400	-65 +600	-65 +300	-65 +400
Environmental resistance	poor	very good	good	good	good
Adhesion to substrates					
metals	very good	excellent	good	good	excellent
polymers	excellent	fair	fair	very good	excellent
glass	poor	excellent	very good	good	good
rubber	very good	fair	good	good	poor
wood	good	very good	fair	fair	good

Figure 3.108

Industrial polymer adhesives and their properties.

Sources: Small and Courtney(2005), Domininghaus (1988).

In addition to these textiles, a number of polymers are poised to be introduced into architectural applications for interior and exterior applications. The refinement of polymer blends developed for their abilities to impart better flame resistance, decreased smoke density upon combustion and improved environmental durability will bring a variety of polymer materials into construction over the coming decades. For example, an interesting polymer is polyetherimide; the material recently chosen for use in the construction of the cockpit structure and interior walls of the new Boeing C17 jetliner (Materials Progress 2004). Polyetherimide does not produce toxic fumes, very little smoke and will self-extinguish when exposed to flames - a useful set of attributes for airplanes and buildings.

These, and many other polymer materials will continue to change the material composition of our building systems. This section will focus on just a few materials.

High strength polymer structural adhesives
High density structural polymers
Next generation polymer fibers and textiles (including smart polymer fibers)

High Strength Polymer Structural Adhesives

The search for higher performing polymer adhesives has been an important research priority for polymer science and engineering. As a result, industrial adhesives have been vastly improved during the past two decades. Applications include every major industry in the bonding of materials in every material family to one another. The typical reasons for this interest include the ability to bond dissimilar materials, sealing continuously against the environment, avoiding intrusive and stress-inducing mechanical fasteners and - as with any emerging technology - reducing the overall cost of the application. Eight major varieties of structural adhesives are most commonly used; anaerobics, cyanoacrylates, hot-melt adhesives, epoxies, polyurethanes, light-cure acrylics, silicones and two-part acrylics. For our purposes here, we will focus on epoxies, acrylics and urethane adhesives.

The latest array of epoxy adhesives achieve high strengths at both room and elevated temperatures. Epoxies can be composed of more than one resin and a hardener, cross-linker, or activator-primer. One-part epoxies are generally cured using heat (but can also be cured using UV radiation) and two- and three-part epoxies cure with complete mixture of the resins and the hardener. Epoxies can bond a diverse variety of materials together and can fill large volumes with very little to no shrinkage. Widely used in many industrial and construction applications, epoxies are relatively slow to cure, requiring setting times between 15 minutes and several hours. Complete curing may require 24 hours or more (Small and Courtney 2005).

A good deal of research has been focused on improving epoxies of all kinds. The 3M Company (www.3M.com/adhesives) has been a leader in this area and currently offers several high strength and fast-curing epoxy adhesives for use in a variety of applications (Driscoll and Campagna 2003). Major industrial epoxy-makers include Henkel (www.henkel.com), Dupont (www.dupont.com), BASF (www.basf.com), Epoxy Systems, Inc. (www.epoxy.com), Dow Plastics (www.dow.com/plastics), Epoxy Technology (www.epotek.com) and others. Because of the very broad use of these materials, most large chemical, and some polymer composite corporations have an epoxy adhesives division.

Epoxies have seen real improvements in performance resulting in the latest developments of "toughened" epoxies of 4,500 psi strength in overlap shear. Also, recently epoxy films have been developed (www.3M.com/adhesives). These heat-cured films allow one to cut out precise shapes to be used in bonding two surfaces together.

Acrylic adhesives are best used for applying to a very broad diversity of bonding surfaces. Somewhat less strong (4,200 psi overlap shear) than the strongest epoxies, acrylics are generally less costly. Current applications include bonding metal hinges to metal door frames and many other secondary structural conditions. Urethanes (polyurethanes) are reserved for applications that require highly elastic connections that are meant to absorb mechanical energy. The least expensive of the three, urethanes, provide good durability and service at room temperatures but lose strength at elevated temperatures (Driscoll and Campagna 2003).

High Density Structural Polymers

High density plastics have been applied to a number of challenging infrastructure applications, including as a load transfer component of a light rail transit system. In addition, high density plastics have been used in high performance environments including aerospace applications and nautical applications. The use of Teflon as a bearing surface for bridges has already been mentioned and epoxy resin matrices for use with reinforcing fibers are being used for transmission towers and lightweight bridges.

Many diverse types of polymers can be classified as high density. The most useful materials are those that are also fire resistant and environmentally benign.

Next Generation Polymer Fibers and Textiles (Including Smart Polymer Fibers)

From time to time aesthetic interests and technology research seem to converge on a material or system. This has been the case with contemporary fabrics; emerging aesthetic interests seem to correlate closely with the priorities of highly specialized and technical research focused on high-performance fibers and fabrics. Designers of many kinds - architects, industrial, fashion and others - have decided that new fabrics deserve a great deal of attention for both their visual and tactile attributes and their performance capabilities. The interest has originated from many sources: academic, industry, government (primarily military) and specialty consumers.

A sampling of the research project published by the National Textile Center (NTC 2004) illustrates the breadth and depth of current interest in developing smart and high performance textiles. Included in the portfolio of research for 2004 are projects that demonstrate a dizzying array of textile materials developed from fibers that behave in ways far beyond traditional woven materials.

For example, one project examines the potential for the development of fluoropolymer-based plastic fibers (POFs) for communication using smart textiles. These fibers could be embedded in composites, drawn through very small conduits or applied to surfaces to provide communication potential for spatially smart environments. Another project seeks to develop fibers that experience dramatic changes in color under the influence of varying external electrical fields. These fibers would be woven into a textile that could then respond to a variety of external stimuli. Another avenue of research involves biomimetic manufacturing based on the processes that spiders use to draw ultrahigh strength fibers derived of biological materials at room temperature. Development of fibers are also addressing issues of thermal resistance through new materials. A recent NTC project undertook the investigation of fire-resistant fibers using Nylon 6 and nanoparticles (see http://www.ntcresearch.org/).

The aesthetic interest in emerging materials for novel fibers and textiles has been rising and falling over the past two decades. Various design projects have experimented with textiles, films and fibers not normally used in architecture and exhibits have focused on polymer textiles and other nonrigid materials. The recent exhibit of textiles, *Extreme Textiles,* at the Copper-Hewitt National Design Museum in New York City is an example of this interest. Other exhibits of the recent past include *2010: Textiles and New Technology* (Crafts Council, London, 1994), *Mutant Materials in Contemporary Design* (Museum of Modern Art, New York, 1995), *Skin: Surface Substance + Design* (Cooper-Hewitt, 2002) and *Technology as Catalyst: Textile Artists on the Cutting Edge* (Textile Museum, Washington, D.C., 2002) (Kahn 2005).

Clearly this convergence of technical advances and aesthetic interest calls for sustained attention from both research and design circles (see Chapter 5).

Ceramics

Reinforced concrete is the best structural material yet devised by mankind. Almost by magic, we have been able to create "melted" stones of any desired shape, structurally superior, because of their tensile strength, to natural stone.

Pier Luigi Nervi, 1956

Figure 3.109

Cavernous, massive and luminous, York Minster, in the north of England represents the artistic and technical height of "ceramic" architecture.

South Transept, York Minster, York, UK.

Brittle Space

In northern England, massive Gothic minsters and cathedrals occupy the old centers of many towns and cities. Their towers, visible for miles around, evoke a lost landscape, tempered by the banality of the contemporary buildings that surround them today. Inside, the massive vaults and arches capture acres of some of the most solemn space in the world. In York, the Minster dates back a thousand years to the reign of William the Conqueror, crowned by the Archbishop of York, Ealdred in 1066 at Westminster Abbey. At that time the stone church occupied a site that had first been built upon by Edwin, the pagan king of Northumbria. He had built a wood church, but by the time he died, in 632, work had begun on a larger stone building.

Today, after several fires, sackings, periods of rebuilding and finally political and religious stability, the Minster at York is carefully looked after. Walking into the building, the sheer size is overwhelming in a way that is still breathtaking even to those who have been to a number of Gothic cathedrals. The solemnity is only partially the effect of physical scale. The cavernous acoustics, pervasive absence of heat, and cool flames of refracted light passing through the enormous expanses of "grisaille" glass mark the territory of the cathedral as emphatically as the delineation of the stone walls.

These cathedrals are some of the most comprehensive ceramic environments ever built. Their materials - stone and glass - not only completely orchestrate the phenomenological aspects of the space, but also determine the physical form, the transfer of structural load and the maintenance of an interior environment. The arches, flying buttresses, piers, vaults, domes, spires and colonnades maximize the capture of volume while minimizing internal stresses in the stone. In these buildings, an eminently informed geometry is the primary determinant of form.

In York Minster one is surrounded by the hard brittle materials of the family of ceramics (along with the timber roof). These materials are united by their singular lack of ductility. Ceramics are those materials that are held together with nonmetallic or inorganic bonds. Ceramics used in construction typically contain silica (SiO_2) as a prime component. Defined in this way, the material family of ceramics includes fired brick and tile, limestone and granite and other stone, cement and concretes, plasters and even glass.

In this chapter, four different kinds of ceramics are given special attention because of their primary importance in buildings; fired clays, stone, concrete and glass. Each belongs to this group and yet, more than any other material family, they represent a great diversity of properties and individual materials.

The long history of ceramics can only be hinted at here because of the diversity of materials and their prevalence in buildings since the beginning of civilization. Bricks reinforced with straw from the most ancient cities, gypsum and lime mortars, ancient concrete using volcanic ash and other pozzolanic materials of Roman buildings, and glass dating back to the Pharaonic Egyptians demonstrate the great age

Figure 3.110

Cracks not only develop within individual stone units, but traverse mortar joints to continue through the masonry system.

York, UK.

and diversity of ceramics materials. This deep history and ubiquitous use are clear indications of the enduring utility of ceramics in construction. Widely available materials, and easy processing in the making of small, discrete pieces of useful building components have made this material family very popular. There has been no more expedient way to form building blocks than the hand-shaping and sun-baking of mud bricks.

And yet despite their historically deep and widespread use, some ceramics are challenging materials to use in contemporary design. Their high strength but low ductility necessitates careful attention to loading conditions and detail interfaces with other materials, particularly other ceramics. The lack of useful ductility means that ceramics do not distribute internal stresses as well as metals, composites or polymers. Through deformation, ductile materials, like metals, can redistribute applied forces and adapt without sudden failure. Ceramics tend to concentrate stresses for lack of a mechanism to redistribute these forces.

In addition, crack propagation in ceramics is a complex problem that also leads to sudden failure. The combination of the lack of ductility and susceptibility to crack propagation makes ceramics a material for which the risk of failure is particularly difficult to assess. For buildings, this mode of failure, even it if occurs at very high stress levels, is to be avoided at all costs because of the lack of warning for catastrophic failure and the subsequent danger of the loss of life. Unfortunately, this has led to a steady erosion in the making of load-bearing masonry structures, once the most common structural system.

These issues span the family of ceramic materials from structural clays to concrete to glass. Problems arise from specifying mortars that are much stronger than the brick it supports, to improperly padded glazing beds and brittle sealant materials, to spalling of concrete and brick due to freeze-thaw cycles. The lack of ductility

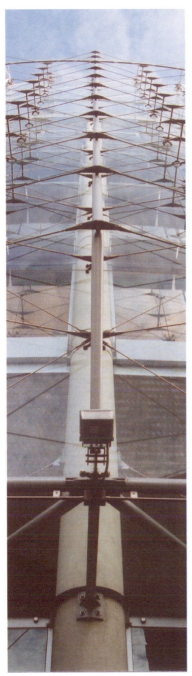

Figure 3.111

Glass, unpredictable in tension - as are all ceramics - must be accompanied in this instance by a metallic webbing that acts to transfer all tensile loads.

London, UK.

197

Figure 3.112

The complexity of the figure belies the segmented construction of the masonry elements of this terracotta frieze.

Sevilla, Spain.

has caused countless problems for modern architecture in particular. This can be attributed, to some extent, to the progressive loss of the craft of ceramics, and masonry construction generally. Without an equally deep set of skills to match the history of the material, inevitable problems have surfaced. Some architects and engineers are well aware of these issues and recently, interest has been revived for the use of lime-based mortars (as opposed to cement-based) in the making of modern masonry walls (Cardwell et al. 1997).

However, one must remember that buildings are complex assemblies of diverse materials brought together into systems. Even though ceramics are brittle materials, the systems in which they have been employed can accommodate weaknesses of the material while taking full advantage of its strengths. And even despite the brittle failure mode of ceramic materials, structures of brick and stone have been shown to possess substantial ability to accommodate changing environmental loads over very long periods of time. Masonry structures hundreds of years old are the best examples of this durability and "system ductility". Recent work with historical masonry structures demonstrates the depth of this accommodation and shows that masonry can achieve a high level of adaptability to changing conditions (Heyman 1995;Ochsendorf 2002).

One result of this erosion of skill has been the decrease in the use of brick materials for building enclosures. It is true that there are now numerous competing systems from all material families that can substitute the use of brick in building enclosures. Many of these competing materials are nonstructural and thus more specifically aimed at providing only the necessary components for a reliable barrier system for the building. This also defines the limited role of contemporary brick in most masonry buildings in the developed west. The brick simply acts as a nonstructural screen, often a rainscreen, set apart from the structural

Figure 3.113

Cleaving stone reveals the brittle nature of this natural ceramic.

Maine.

frame of the building. But due to its greater weight, higher skill demands in construction and a much greater number of individual pieces to be assembled on site (as opposed to, say, metal panels) brick materials have been under competitive pressures like never before. And yet, the continued use of structural tiles in the Mediterranean region and throughout South and Central America is still very strong. Structural tile infill for partitions and concrete frame buildings are used all over the world - requiring only moderate levels of skill and employing the least costly of materials.

The ceramics included in this section all generally possess the distinctive combination of brittleness and low cost (with some exceptions) despite their diversity. However, one of the reasons that the naming of this section specifies glass separately from other materials classified under ceramics is the very particular properties of glass under various loading conditions (Behling 1999;ISE 1999;Rice 1995). In addition, it is a material used in ways unlike any other ceramic material because of its transparency. The ability to admit light makes it unique among all other materials in this family. The particular properties of glass, and the other ceramics addressed here, are treated next.

Classification and Properties

Classification for this material family is complicated by the fact that it is useful to emphasize the subfamilies of glass, concrete, fire-clay ceramics and stone - as they each play a fundamental role in the making of contemporary buildings. Therefore, the following sections treat each subfamily separately.

Classification

Five material trees follow. One each for fired clays, stone, concretes, glasses and high performance ceramics.

Fired Clays

Fired clays are among the oldest of building materials, having been used steadily for one hundred thousand years. The primary use of fired clays throughout history has been as a masonry unit in a structural wall. Vernacular architecture is rich with the application of bricks and tiles.

In modern architecture, structural clay materials were an integral component of very new architecture of the early 20th century.

Despite this integration into frame structures, masonry, and brick materials in particular, were identified by the leaders of post-war modernist ideals, as truly regressive materials. The brick itself was attacked as an anti-modern construction material, subjecting workers to unnecessary toil and resulting in architectural nostalgia. The effect on building in brick as a whole was not truly devastating, but the removal of this material from the center of architectural discourse was critically effective. Even today, brick materials and masonry in general are out of place from the leading edge of architectural aesthetic, for better or worse.

Figure 3.114

West window, built by master mason Ivo de Raghtan and glazed by Master Robert in the years 1338-39.

York Minster, York, England.

Figure 3.115

Brick corner showing the texture of the brick.

British Library, London, UK.

Figure 3.116

Window wall of a large contemporary commercial office building.

333 Wacker Drive, Chicago, Illinois, USA.
Kohn Pedersen Fox, Architects.

Figure 3.117a, b

Stone details.

University of Cambridge, Cambridge, UK.

However, today, fired clay masonry materials are still widely used in developing regions of the world. The huge number of people, on the order of 1-2 billion, live in masonry buildings whose primary material is clay.

In addition, in the explosive urban growth of megacities around the world clay products acting as a structural partition in concert with concrete frames are the material of choice in Mediterranean, South and Central American countries.

Essentially three types of materials are present in almost all clay products; hydrated clays which are composed of silicates and alumina (30-55 percent), a fluxing material which can be a feldspar or other material (25-55 percent), and an inert filler like quartz (25-45 percent). The three are mixed in a variety of proportions to vary the performance attributes of the material and its aesthetic qualities. Because fired clay products are often used as a surface material for buildings their aesthetic qualities are important components of the making of the product.

The word "clay" is used both in reference to mineral materials that have a particle size not exceeding 2 micrometers and to the family of materials composed of silicates and alumina, as described above (Velde 1995). This latter designation allows for particle sizes from angstroms to millimeters. Clays are often mixtures of smaller sized particles and larger crystals of quartz, carbonates and metal oxides and are generally found as part of the natural surface or just below the surface of the Earth (Foley 1999).

The six primary clays mined and used in the United States are ball clay, bentonite, common clay, fire clay, fuller's earth and kaolin. Ball clays, common clay and shales, fire clays and kaolin are the primary contributors to building materials including bricks, firebricks, structural tile, terracotta and regular tile. Fuller's earth is used in the production of Portland cement. Of all clays used in the United States, 64 percent are used

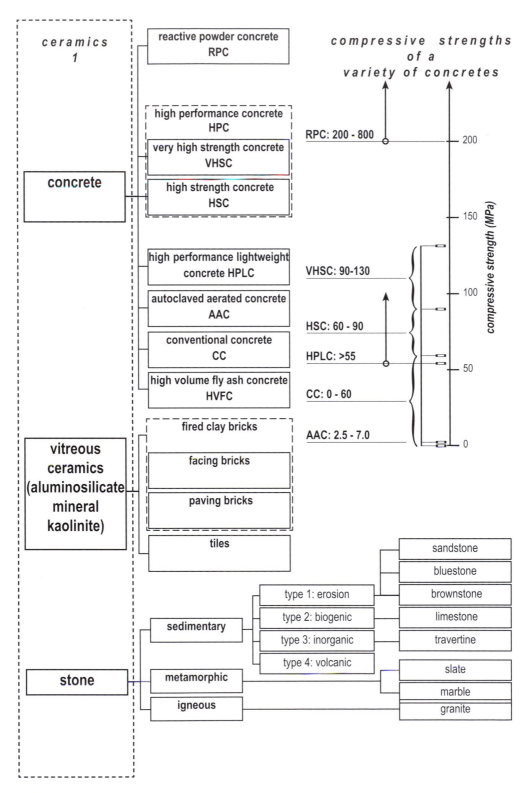

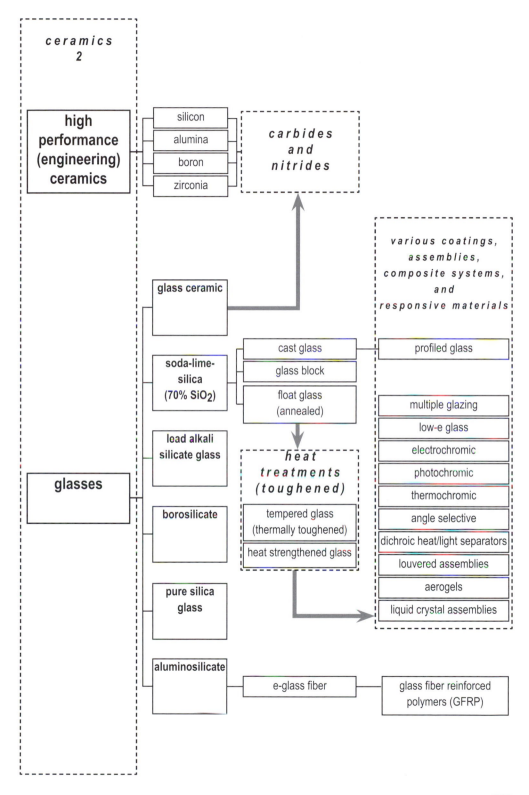

in construction (Virta 2001). Papermaking, fertilizer, industrial absorbents, and other industrial uses and an array of consumer products consume the remaining clays.

Clays are often used as found in nature with very little processing before firing. For products with more stringent requirements, such as flooring and wall tiles, the constituent materials may be processed before inclusion in the mix.

Clays tend to be very hydrophilic, absorbing great quantities of water and expanding accordingly. Some clays can expand by 100 percent of their dry volume when saturated causing problems for buildings built on some kinds of clay deposits.

The making of structural clay products is energy intensive because of the high temperatures needed for proper bonding of the constituent materials. Temperatures in the range of 980°C to 1260°C are typical for producing fired clays.

Stone

Natural stone in architecture is used in two general forms; dimension stone and crushed stone. Dimension stone includes all rock that has been sawn, split, shaped or otherwise prepared for use in the building fabric itself. The second kind consists of crushed, pulverized, ground or broken stone that is used in great volume for any number of applications including drainage, concrete aggregate, soil stabilization, road bedding and many other large-scale civil engineering applications as well as a multitude of industrial uses. The volume of crushed stone consumed annually overwhelms that of dimension stone.

It would not be useful here to outline the history of stone in architecture. Stone has been used for making buildings in every period of time and every civilization.

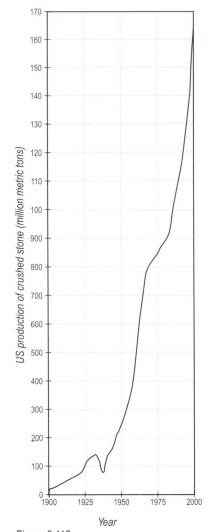

Figure 3.118

The use of crushed stone has greatly increased over the past 100 years.

Source: US Bureau of Mines, Mineral Resources of the US, 1900-23, US Geological Survey, Mineral Resources of the US, 1924-31, Minerals Yearbook, 1932-94, Commodity Data Summaries, 1962-77, Mineral Commodity Summaries, 1978-95, Mineral Commodity Summaries, 1997-2002, Minerals Yearbook, V.I, 1995-2000.

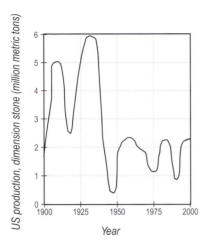

Figure 3.119
While the amount of dimension has decreased over time. This is partly due to the substantial dematerialization accomplished through refined sawing and finishing techniques.

Source: US Bureau of Mines, Mineral Resources of the US, 1900-23, US Geological Survey, Mineral Resources of the US, 1924-31, Minerals Yearbook, 1932-94, Commodity Data Summaries, 1962-77, Mineral Commodity Summaries, 1978-95, Mineral Commodity Summaries, 1997-2002, Minerals Yearbook, V.I, 1995-2000.

Figure 3.120

Stone quarry.

Detailing, or even outlining this history will take this section far beyond its mandate and deep into topics not necessary here.

Traditionally, stone has been a material of low cost and local availability. Every region of the world possesses some useful stone of some variety, although only a small minority of available stone has ever been useful as a structural material. Assessing the structural viability of stone can be a tricky proposition because the material is a natural resource of great diversity in consistency, composition and quantity. While this lends certain distinctive qualities to the material, it introduces risk. As a result, today stone is primarily used for nonstructural purposes, having been soundly (and irreversibly) replaced by steel and concrete. The overwhelmingly nonstructural use of stone today has essentially transformed the material into a surface treatment. In fact, some of the latest technological developments have been focused on producing ever-thinner slices of the material, sometimes reinforced with textiles or light metals (see "Emergent Ceramics and Glass", below).

Dimension stone has been made from all three of the general geological types of rock; igneous, sedimentary and metamorphic. The three kinds of stone are easily distinguished from one another by process of origin. Igneous rock is created from geological processes that involve heat and sometimes pressure. This kind of rock is the result of the cooling, and crystallization, of molten rock. Silicate minerals are most common and form crystals, the sizes of which are dependent on speed of cooling and depth of formation. Sedimentary rock is the result of geological forces of erosion and transport in which smaller particles are often carried and deposited by wind and water. Metamorphic rock results from the application of transformative forces, heat sometimes combined with pressures at depth, on a combination of igneous and sedimentary deposits (Patton 1990).

These designations are useful to distinguish generic

205

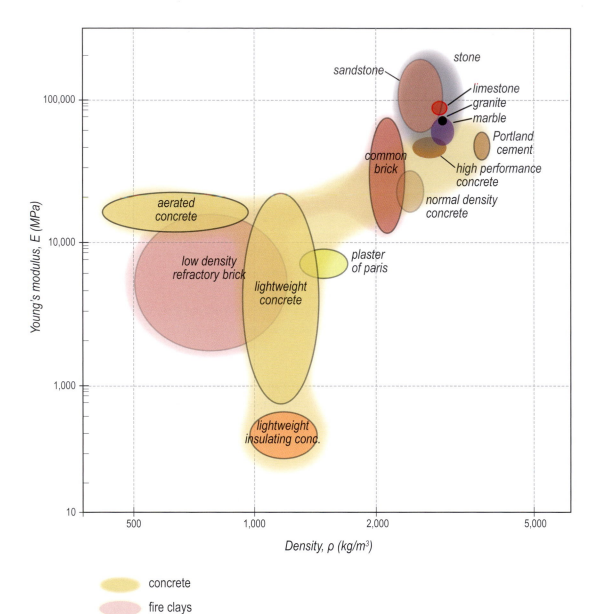

concrete

fire clays

stone

Figure 3.121

Young's modulus against density.

Sources: Produced with CES 4.1: Granta Design Ltd.

types of rock but the architectural application of stone is often discussed mainly in reference to granite, limestone, marble, sandstone and slate. These materials have been the primary stone sources for architectural applications both structural and nonstructural in premodern and modern architecture. Granite is the only igneous rock of the five, limestone are sandstone are sedimentary and marble and slate are metamorphic. Their properties vary widely primarily due to their very distinct origins.

Concrete

Concrete is a well-known and well-used material having had a history of extraordinary early achievement, subsequent neglect and loss of knowledge and skills to the flux of European history and modern revival and development. By one estimate it has been a material of construction for nine millennia (Bentur 2002). Today, the material science of concrete is a specialty unto itself with standards, testing procedures, nomenclature and a variety of analysis methods solely devoted to its various forms. This book will not delve into a comprehensive rendering of the field. That would be unreasonable. The intention here, as with all of the materials covered, is a discussion of the leading edge of material innovation for architectural assemblies. It is assumed that the reader, if interested, will pursue other sources for a comprehensive knowledge of concrete.

It is useful here, though, to offer an outline of its history, its most common constituent materials, production and current research domains as they pertain to architectural form and building construction.

Cement, the primary binding component of concrete, was used in wall plasters in Babylonia and Egypt but the first structural concrete was developed by the Romans around the 3rd century BC. It is well known that the material technology and many of the techniques of construction for concrete were lost for centuries and partially recovered in the mid-18th century, when Joseph Aspedin received a patent for Portland cement in 1824. The introduction of steel reinforcing by J.L. Lambot in 1848 heralded the beginning of 150 years of development, application, global proliferation and design using modern reinforced concrete.

Modern concrete is a composite consisting of cement, water, aggregates small and large, various admixtures from superplasticizers, other polymers, pozzolans and other materials. Reinforced concrete has the added component of some kind of tensile reinforcing that increases its flexural, shear, tensile and other mechanical properties. Reinforcement is typically accomplished using steel bars anchored together and placed in the volume of the concrete formwork. It may also be achieved using very small fibers called "whiskers" made of glass, synthetic polymers or steel.

Concretes are often manufactured locally, or regionally at least, as the constituent materials are

Figure 3.122

View of the underside of concrete slabs in construction.

Stata Center, MIT (2004), Frank O. Gehry, Architect.

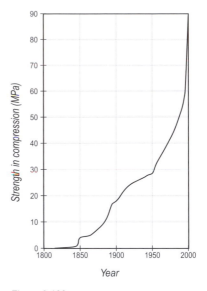

Figure 3.123

Improvement in concrete compressive strength over time

Source: Adapted from Bentur (2002).

widespread. The energy necessary for the manufacture of cement is quite high; however, it constitutes a small percentage of the total material used in concrete. Portland cement production requires approximately 3,000 kJ/kg. This value has decreased significantly from the 5,000-6,000 of a few decades back, through better kilns. It is theoretically possible to lower this to less than 2,000 kJ/kg with even more efficient kilns. It is also possible to increase the amount of combustible waste, industrial and municipal, used as fuel for cement kilns (Lawrence 2004).

Most concretes, or *cementitious* materials, are composed of three components; calcium, silicas and aluminates.

Concrete exhibits the typical lack of ductility of a ceramic. It fails catastrophically under an applied tension or compression. Reinforcing is used to temper this behavior and imbue the material with a ductile capacity. Therefore, it is reasonable to suggest that reinforced concrete should be included not here with other ceramics but in Section 3.4 Composites. The reasons for including it here are that its properties as a ceramic dominate its use in architecture and these same properties are quite different from those of composites (composites being defined primarily as fiber reinforced polymers).

As a general rule, higher strength concretes tend to be more brittle than lower strength varieties. The aggregates in a lower strength concrete tend to arrest the propagation of cracks leading to multi-cracking, a common attribute of a composite. Various distinct formulations of concrete have been developed in the last several decades. The following lists and briefly describes some important types.

Aerated autoclaved concrete (AAC)

Aerated autoclaved concrete (AAC) is a cellular cementitious material, generally not including reinforcement within the matrix of the concrete, but often used such that it can be grouted and reinforced on site. It is produced in the form of a block or slab and mortared in place with either a typical cementitious mortar, or a proprietary mortar provided by the manufacturer. The concrete is made of the same typical components of any concrete product - cement, lime, sand, gypsum, water - with the addition of an expanding agent that produces a gas that acts to create the cellular structure of the material. The greatest advantages of the block system are its much lower weight per block and the ability to cut it with a typical band saw, making the working of the block on site much easier.

Even though the material has been used in Europe and Asia for more than 50 years, it was only introduced in the United States in the early 1990s by two companies, Hebel and YTong. Worldwide production at that time exceeded 31 million cubic meters produced in over 50 factories worldwide (ECT 2003). Entire building volumes can be made from AAC using the various forms of block slab and wall panels. Issues regarding the porosity of the material still need to be resolved and studies are under way to determine a useful measure of its absorption

Figure 3.124

Exterior view of one of the cast in place concrete piers.

Unity Temple, Oak Park, Illinois, USA, 1908.
Frank Lloyd Wright.

Figure 3.125

Interior view of the concrete skylight coffers.

Unity Temple, Oak Park, Illinois, USA, 1908.
Frank Lloyd Wright.

Figure 3.126

The use of concrete, as a structural and non-structural material is pervasive across the globe. As an industry, the production of cement contributes just under 10 percent of the total CO_2 emissions globally.

Rio de Janeiro, Brazil (2000).

and retention of moisture. Because the material is often used as en exterior wall material, this is an important issue to resolve. AAC has been widely adopted for a variety of building types, from small residential to schools, warehouses, and other building types (Jardine and Cameron1999). A variant of AAC is fiber reinforced AAC - a synthetic fiber product that boasts better toughness and resilience while still remaining a lightweight material.

High volume fly ash concrete (HVFC)

HVFC concrete is closer to ancient concrete than any other type. The concrete used in ancient Roman buildings contained a very high content of pozzolanic volcanic ash. The very fine powder of the ash provides an excellent compacting material for low, or even no, cement content concrete. It is clear, given the longevity of some Roman buildings, that the durability of such a material is very good - under the right conditions. The analog of this material today is the ash recovered from the burning of coal primarily in electrical power plants. This material is 60-90 percent extremely fine silica (glass) beads that are ideal for high compacting and producing a good substitute for some of the Portland cement content of modern concrete. In fact studies show that the composite may be more durable because it is less permeable and therefore less susceptible to attack from water (Parsons 2000).

HVFC is receiving a good bit of interest from both research and industry sectors and several buildings in the United States, Europe and other regions of the world have had good success with the material. Some longer periods of setting times, limitations of pouring in cold weather, occasional need for superplasticizers for better workability and variations in color characterize the major drawbacks to the material. In invoking the use of HVFCs, architects, contractors and some researchers regularly state that the reduction of the use of cement is an important way for construction to contribute to the reduction in global CO_2 emissions. It has been accepted by some in the professions and research that between 6 and 8 percent of all global CO_2 emissions can be traced to the production of cement for the making of concrete for construction (Wilson 1993). What percentage of these emissions is unavoidable is not clear. Replacing concrete with other materials may not improve environmental impacts. The fact is, some type of material needs to be used for the vast global construction that is needed for housing the world's increasing population. Concrete's widespread availability makes it an attractive material with regard to emissions that result from transportation. The issue deserves greater study (van Oss and Padovani 2002).

All useful properties of modern concrete have been vastly improved over the last 150 years. All of the primary mechanical properties have seen dramatic improvements primarily through experimentation with its constituent materials. As mentioned above the science of concrete is a very specialized field in which the micromechanical behavior has been very well outlined.

Glass

The primary distinction between glass and all other ceramics is that it is noncrystalline. Its defining properties are a result of a lack of crystallization during its cooling. This makes it an amorphous solid that does not readily yield to applied forces but rather fails catastrophically as a result of the rapid propagation of microcracks. Its noncrystallinity is also the reason why glass is transparent, making it the primary material for building apertures that architects make into windows and other openings. No other material, aside from some polymers like polycarbonate, can substitute for its clarity in light transmission.

The attributes that are less well known are its strength, stiffness, dimensional stability and relative lack of thermal distortion. These properties make it a useful material for all kinds of loading situations in which precise fit and minimal distortion are required. It is obvious why glass is the material of choice for optical applications, its optical qualities are superior to any other material. However, just as important in these applications is its strength and dimensional stability.

It is possible that the discovery of glass, as a recognizably new material of uncommon strength, surface smoothness and translucency, was made when the silica and other impurities in fired clay liquefied and formed glazes. This would be analogous to the discovery of copper that had formed 'blooms' of metal from ores also from fired clays. It has been established that glazes date back to Egyptian faïence of 10,000-7,000BC. Glass is, for the most part, a manufactured material. Because it is the result of the liquefaction and rapid cooling of silica and other materials, it is not found in any quantity in nature. Natural glass has been found in places where very high temperatures can yield to rapid cooling, like the active zones of volcanoes, where small pieces of natural glass are found.

Once the material was discovered, the history of glass in architecture is primarily the evolution of processing techniques brought about by the demand for larger panes of the material for buildings (Elliot 1992;Fierro 2003). This is particularly evident during the period from 1850 to the present. From crown glass to the modern float glass method developed by William Pilkington in the 1950s, the history of the material is really a history of the development of an industry.

As in concrete, the Romans were the first to focus on the development of glass for the making of small vessels and other glassware. Over the centuries the Syrians, Venetians, Germans, English and French were also involved in bringing the material into its present form. The Americans also made contributions in the early 20th century.

The processes that were developed started with the first standardized method for the making of relatively flat panes of glass for buildings, the crown method. This involved the use of the centrifugal force from spinning a blown bubble of molten glass into a flat disk and then resting it in a bed of sand to cool. It was then cut into rectangular, diamond or other shapes for use in windows. The cylinder process also started with the blowing of a molten glass bubble and its elongation by swinging it in deep troughs dug into the floor of the glassmaker's workshop to produce long cylinders that could then be cut and flattened into sheets (ISE 1999).

Both of these methods were manual, highly skilled activities that were not well positioned to produce the enormous quantities of glass that would soon be demanded for cast iron buildings beginning early in the 19th century. Of course, at this time cast iron was beginning to spawn a new architecture; light, airy and consisting of nothing more than beams, slender columns and ribs to both delineate the volume of the building and transfer all of the necessary loads of the structure. The high strength of this new metal allowed for much larger expanses of glass for its openings. It also allowed for the easy insertion of a simple pane of glass. Dimensional regularity and geometric consistency became important qualities.

However, the cast iron buildings of the industrial revolution were not the first buildings that required large expanses of glass. The cathedrals and minsters of medieval Europe had progressed in the technology of shaping stone so that the first large-scale superstructural skeletons were actually these Gothic stone buildings (Heyman 1995;Mark 1993). Within the stone framework, vast areas of wall envelope were sheathed in small pieces of glass held within a metal framework. The York Minster in northern England is an exceptional example of these metal and glass infill walls. Using 'grisaille' glass, mostly white of milky cast glass pieces, set in a lead latticework, the Minster foreshadows the use of plate glass set within cast iron that was still 500 years in the future.

From hand methods it was inevitable that automation was a likely solution to some of the issues that glassmaking was contending with during the early 19th century. The process of automation using a glass cylinder machine that increased the speed of production and quality of the sheets obtained from large glass cylinders was inaugurated into commercial production in 1910. But the real breakthrough came with the development of the various techniques for producing flat sheets directly from the molten glass material.

The first methods involved drawing out or rolling out molten glass directly from the furnace. These methods also required grinding and polishing and led to very large losses through breakage and inconsistency of surface quality. Finally, it was not until 1952, that the first modern "float" glass process was proposed by Alastair Pilkington of the British glass company Pilkington Brothers Ltd. Even though perfection of the process was to take seven years, it proved to be a breakthrough both for the dramatic increase in the speed of production and the decrease in the proportion of breakage (Elliot 1992;Amstock 1997).

These processes have led to an industry that is extremely good at producing huge expanses of flat sheets of glass for buildings. In fact, the recent growth of the global glass industry has been on the order of 13percent per year. An astounding figure for manufacturing. The production of flat glass for buildings and automobiles is now more than 2 billion meters^2 per year. The major producers of glass worldwide now number only in the dozens. During the past several decades there has been a vast consolidation in the industry that has led to extremely large producers in Europe, the United States and Asia.

Strengthened glass, heat tempered, and annealed, and composites such as laminated glass and fire-insulated glass, are an important part of the architectural glass market (Schittich et al. 1999;Wigginton 1996). Coatings on glass and the development of assemblies such as double and triple insulated glass products using polymer film interlayers and noble gases have brought significant improvements to the thermal and transparency properties of window assemblies (Schwartz 2003). Today, double skin glass facades for buildings that are passively serviced are prompting a great deal of interest from both technologists and designers (Oesterle et al. 2001).

Properties

It is important to distinguish the type and character of the material properties useful in considering ceramics from all other materials primarily because of the singular lack of ductility. For example, ceramics exhibit very large spreads when trying to establish yield strengths. It is very difficult to establish a well-defined failure load because of the unpredictably of the material.

In addition, while fired clays, stone, concrete and glass exhibit many important similarities, they also describe an extremely wide range of strengths, thermal conductivities, moduli, and many other properties. Beginning with the fact that these are both natural materials of minimal processing (stone) and highly synthetic composites (reinforced concrete), it is not useful to compare all of them in the same way. This is why careful consideration has been given to offering the limited comparisons that follow.

Ceramics and Glass in Contemporary Architecture

Glass, fired clays, concrete and other architectural ceramics are most often considered separately because of their very different applications; structural, nonstructural, weather barrier, and other situations.

All of the ceramics considered here were introduced into architecture at an early point in history. If one includes the glazings of tiles, glass in buildings goes back to the ancient world.

With the exception of reinforced concrete, ceramics are employed in buildings in relatively small, discrete pieces. Glass panes can be made large, but do not approach the sizes of reinforced structural concrete or structural steel members. The steel reinforcing of concrete allows the individual components of the material to be made at a much larger scale.

Load-bearing masonry construction is a particularly interesting use of ceramic materials in architecture. Given the fact that ceramics fail stochastically, and by definition there is a much greater uncertainty about the yield point of the material under loading, why would an architect decide to assume this kind of risk? Is this why contemporary load-bearing structures are so rare? The question is worthwhile pursuing in more detail here because it reveals the relationship between material properties and the properties of a building system, in this case a structural system.

The stress levels in masonry are typically much lower than other structural materials. This has been well established (Heyman 1995). Part of the reason this is so, is because of the processing requirements of the material itself. A unit of sandstone is simply difficult to produce in thin sheets because it cleaves and falls apart. Stone has a "grain" and, as such, is prone to

Figure 3.127

The City of London building.

City of London Building, London, UK.
Norman Foster, Architect.

Figure 3.128

A double skin facade assembly.

Helsinki, Finland (2003).

cleaving but because this is the case, and the material is delivered at larger sizes, essentially to keep it together at some acceptable rate, then the stress levels that it resists are much lower simply because the area that is presented for load transfer is much greater. Therefore, the material never comes close to experiencing levels of material failure and the governing attribute is geometry, not material properties.

Therefore, this leads to the idea of a certain "flexibility" in load-bearing masonry structures. They do not collapse easily because the masonry adjusts itself to changing load conditions, such as experienced during settlement of foundations. The system is flexible. And it is self-adjusting because of the gaps between masonry units, not because of any "give" contributed by the units themselves. In fact, we've seen that the masonry materials do not possess any useful levels of ductility. The gaps, the mortar joints, may open up and take up changes in the relative position of individual masonry units. In this way the wall has a certain flexibility that is in marked contrast to the lack of ductility of the material itself.

Of course, the development of stress concentrations is a risk that is posed when masonry settles into new positions. This is especially true when the amount of cross-sectional area is significantly reduced by the opening of cracks between masonry units that do not allow transfer of load. As a result, the load seeks an alternative path. This path may pass through less cross-sectional area than the original position allowed. Clearly, it is possible to fill in these cracks and reestablish a load path through the new mortar. In any case, repair can address this issue.

So, it is not enough to consider simply the material properties of the components used in a building system; it is necessary considering the behavior of the system as a whole with due attention given to the contribution of each component in the behavior of the whole.

215

Emergent Ceramics and Glass

The Holy Grail of structural ceramics is achieving substantial ductility and high strength at a cost competitive with other structural materials. The ability of a ceramic to deform to an appreciable degree under varying loading while not losing the substantial strengths of this family of materials is a much sought-after set of properties. Applications would include cost- effective structural glass, a new generation of masonry, and concrete with a tensile strength that does not develop microcracks when it creeps over time. Of course each one of these materials calls for a unique solution to the challenge. And, as discussed shortly, certain aspects of load transfer, damage control and resistance to fracture may be inherent attributes of the system, and therefore need not be a necessary attribute of the material. It is important to keep this in mind in seeking out solutions for acquiring valuable properties - should it be an attribute of the material, or the system?

For example, let's consider the issue of ductility. Most ceramics clearly lack this property to any appreciable extent and yet systems that use ceramic materials can be made to behave such that the material can accept varying loading over time, even under very stressful events like an earthquake. The ability of the system to adapt to varying and sometimes dynamic loading conditions is an attribute of the system of discrete masonry units and mortar joints and therefore need not be a property of the material. For example, masonry "gives" a little under varying loading because of the gaps between masonry units - the mortar joints take up some movement. They may crack and even dislodge in doing so but the resultant movement protects the integrity of the system as a whole.

Similarly, reinforced concrete is a system that allows for movement and can sustain substantial bending and tensile loads due to the reinforcing steel. But this movement may lead to cracks forming in the concrete.

Figure 3.129

View of glass block exterior walls of the Hermès Building in Tokyo.

Maison Hermès, Tokyo, Japan. 1998-2001.
Renzo Piano Building Workshop, Genoa, Italy.
Photo courtesy Renzo Piano Building Workshop, Genoa, Italy
and photographer Michel Denancé.

Property \ Material	Macor*	Steel	Cast iron
Density lbs/ft³	157	490	432
Fracture toughness ksi	1.4	40	39
Young's modulus psi	10×10^6	30×10^6	24×10^6
Modulus of rupture ksi	15	40	42
Compressive strength ksi	50	40	50
Coefficient of thermal expansion $\mu\varepsilon/°F$	7.2×10^{-7}	6.5×10^{-6}	7.0×10^{-6}
Operating temp. limit °F	1832	650	660
Poisson's ratio	0.29	0.29	0.26
Radio freq. transparency	yes	no	no

Figure 3.130

Typical properties for a machinable glass ceramic (Macor®), steel and cast iron.

Macor® is a registered product of Dupont.

These cracks, in turn, may compromise the durability of the system by allowing water deep into the composite. While the system can accommodate various loads, the ceramic characteristics of the concrete itself do not allow for movement, without some kind of cracking.

Therefore, even though the system may be protected because of aspects of its own components, the material itself may be compromised - decreased durability due to cracks formed, water incursion, freeze and thaw effects and other deteriorating processes.

However, developing a new generation of structural ceramic materials of low cost, high ductility and high compressive strengths, which can be used in masonry walls or as part of a structural frame, will have an immediate impact on the safety of buildings around the world. Especially in seismic zones that span developing regions, a low cost but ductile masonry would benefit the millions that currently suffer the ravages of regular earthquakes.

Therefore, the reinforcement of ceramics is an important avenue of research for a range of architectural applications both high performance and exotic and low-tech and inexpensive. Many diverse research efforts are addressing just this goal - as an example, the fiber reinforcement of concrete has occupied countless research and industry personnel working on a wide variety of fibers and inclusion morphologies.

Concrete is one of the topics of emergent ceramics addressed here. While concrete research has been concentrated on many fronts, only a very select few topics can be described here; that of ductile concrete, reactive powder concrete and smart concrete. In addition to these topics several others are treated in greater detail in the final pages of this section.

Emerging Concrete

       High Performance and Ductile concrete

       Reactive powder concrete

       Smart concrete

Emerging fire clays

Stone

       Fiber reinforced stone

       Laminated stone

Insulating and reflecting ceramics

       Paints and coatings

       Ceramic Foams

Emerging Glass

       Glass ceramics

       Foamed silicates

       Responsive glasses

       New glass laminates

Emerging concrete

The ubiquity of concrete as a primary construction material globally poses both challenges and opportunities to the development of new concretes for useful purposes. Because it is used so widely, managing the quality of the materials and assuring the making of safe concrete structures have been met with mixed results and some catastrophic consequences. Major building collapse during earthquakes in Turkey and Taiwan indicate that the standards for safe structures are not well enforced. As the global population grows and urban environments become increasingly dense, the need for better construction supervision will become an important public health issue.

Equally, the opportunities for effecting widespread improvements in the quality and safety of buildings of all types is certainly a set of issues that could be addressed through better concrete materials. By developing higher strength, better quality, ductile and more durable concrete, vast material and energy savings can be gained rather quickly. Also by using better the components of concrete as it is formulated today and seeking alternative materials, concrete can be made to be a less disruptive and ecologically problematic material. These comments are rather general, based as they are on projections of future conditions. However, several specific issues come to the fore when considering the possibilities for future concretes.

Ecologically improved and sustainable materials for concrete are an important part of the research effort now and will surely be ever more important as stresses on material resources and energy increase. The topic is a multi-faceted one because it involves the impact of processing, construction, demolition and the waste produced from the use of concrete in

Figure 3.131

Precast RPC bridge section being prepared for placement.

Sherbrooke, Quebec, Canada. 1998-2001, 1997.
Le Groupe Teknika and Bouyges S.A.

Source: Photo courtesy of city of Sherbrooke.

buildings. The use of materials and the emissions associated with these processes should be examined individually and opportunities for improvements should be sought.

For example, it has been suggested that the future of concrete includes the evolution of the material from one based primarily in Portland cement to a material more generally based on a range of fine particulate materials acting together as both binders and fillers. In this sense, the cement of concrete will cease to be the only binding component in an array of fine powders, pozzolanic materials, industrial by-products, and other 'high-tech' and specialty binder materials (Bentur 2002). This "evolution" means that the field of concrete technologies will expand enormously encompassing the study of the binding and compaction capabilities of all manner of materials (Aitcin 1998, 2000).

These kinds of concretes may be able to contribute to an overall reduction in the use of Portland cement globally. In fact, many new concrete products, from HPC to ductile concrete to low cement earthen materials to alternative binder concretes, all result in the possibility of the reduction in the overall use of concrete. This diversity of paths for better concrete - seemingly all resulting in lower Portland cement use - is a reason for optimism in the future of concrete technology.

The topics that find themselves under the headings of "sustainable" or "green" concrete are also diverse. Alternative materials, cleaner and more efficient processing, CO_2 emission suppression and sequestration, greatly improved durability for long-life structures and the recovery of demolition waste for reuse as aggregate are all meant to fulfill the goals of dematerialization over time and lowering energy consumption. The best path here is the coordination of these various efforts toward an integrated solution for the question of sustainable intent in the use of concrete in buildings and civil structures. One of the most promising avenues for this coordination is in the consideration of the service lives of buildings and civil structures. Critical to this work are definitive explanations for the mechanisms that determine the durability of the material itself. Much work has been accomplished in this area and it has been determined that transport mechanisms, the surface characteristics of the material, and the composition of the composite are the key elements of a complete understanding (Schiessel 1996).

Of course, besides these technical issues, it will be important to take a holistic approach in the use of concrete for the making and operation of buildings, including issues of uncertainty and change in the lives of buildings (see Chapter 2, Time and Materials), but in doing so, the material of concrete can be made to positively contribute to a societal goal. While some researchers and practitioners are working toward this goal, the obstacles - across the globe and including thousands of research and industrial entities - will necessitate much time and probably necessitate the intervention and regulation of a coordinated set of governmental bodies for real progress to be made (Bentur 2002;Hoff 1996;Rostam 1996;Sakai 1996).

In the service of this effort the materials most likely to achieve the best results, at least in the short term, are alternative pozzolanic materials engineered to increase the strength and toughness of the material while contributing significantly to its durability through better resistance to water infiltration (Glavind and Munch-Petersen2000;Damtoft 1998).

High Performance and Ductile Concrete

High performance concrete (HPC) is generally characterized by the following properties; ease of placement, compaction without segregation, early age strength, long-term mechanical properties, permeability, high density, toughness, volume stability and long-life in severe environments generally due to the lack of connecting capillary pores. To achieve these properties the formulation of HPC is carefully regulated to maximize compaction and homogeneous distribution of all constituent materials in the mix. High performance concrete has generally replaced high strength concrete as the designation of the array of concrete mixes that achieve performance well beyond that of normal concrete.

Ductile concrete is now a reality. Recently, successes in developing a ductile concrete have led to entry into the marketplace (Ductal 2005). Ductile concrete is a material for which the inherent improved fracture toughness of the concrete results in a material that does not necessarily require steel reinforcement. This is a huge breakthrough. The concrete developed has greatly improved strength (compressive strengths up to 200 MPa, flexural tensile strength beyond 40 MPa), is self-compacting, and demonstrates a mode of failure that rivals ductile structural materials such as steel and timber. The ramifications of this development will most likely be very substantial because it begins to answer the desire for a ductile ceramic material. Already many projects are under way, some completed, and many more planned.

Currently the only drawback is the cost, substantially more than regular concrete.

Reactive Powder Concrete

Reactive powder concrete (RPC) is an extremely high strength concrete material. Boasting compressive strength of 200 to 800 MPa, these concretes reach performance levels far beyond conventional, and even most high performance concretes. RPCs are also extremely ductile, more than 250 times that of normal concrete and possess extremely good flexural strength of around 50 MPa (Dowd and O'Neill 1996;O'Neill 1995;O'Neill and Dowd 1995;O'Neill et al. 1995;Richard and Cheyvezy 1994, 1995). How is this accomplished?

The careful grading of particulates such that maximum compaction is achieved along with the addition of very fine whiskers of steel wire result in a material that defies the normal behavior of concrete. Large aggregate is not used and the fine sand, Portland cement and the addition of silica fume are carefully proportioned such that their interaction maximizes bonding. As a result of this mix of materials, this kind of concrete is much more expensive than even HPCs, by approximately 5-8 times. Therefore, this material will not, at least in the short term, serve as a significant substitution material for normal concrete. It has been used on several structures, most notably a pedestrian bridge in the city of Sherbrooke, Quebec, Canada.

Smart Concrete

A novel use of carbon fibers has resulted in a concrete material that can be monitored for its structural integrity. This "smart" concrete is a normal mixture with added short carbon fibers that both increase its toughness and allow for the measurement of an electrical resistance through the cured structural member. As a load is applied and the concrete absorbs energy the electrical current that passes through the medium varies with the changing contact between fibers and matrix and the production of microcracks (Chen and Chung 1996).

The carbon fibers add approximately 30 percent to the material cost of the system. This is a substantial increase that makes it likely that the scenario for the application of this kind of concrete will be for structures of particularly sensitive functions. Certain key members of a bridge structure can be made with a smart concrete thus allowing a limited but important "snapshot" of the health of the structure.

This type of smart concrete has not been tested for application in structures at the time of writing this book. Most concrete monitoring involves the use of individual sensors placed on the surface or within the matrix of the concrete. Additional work in this field promises to bring interesting and ultimately useful capabilities to concrete mixtures that can be monitored for the structural health of individual members.

Finally, it is worthwhile commenting here on the fact that modern reinforced concrete has always been the subject of much passionate discussion regarding the appropriate forms that should be produced from its rich potential as a fundamentally plastic material (plastic in the sense of fluid). Even today, decades after the work of Nervi, Torroja, Candela, and others including the true original structural pioneer, Robert Maillart - do engineers and architects write and speak passionately about the wealth of form possible with the material (Schlaich 2001)?

Emerging Fired Clays

Reinforced ceramics have been developed for industries that require very high performance. These ceramics are reinforced through the same principles as any fiber reinforced materials - within a ceramic matrix, ceramic or metal fibers are introduced for the purpose of enhancing its energy absorption characteristics.

Figure 3.132

A sample of machinable glass ceramic shown above and in detail below.

Fiber Reinforced Stone

Stone, as a processed natural material, has continued the path from a structural material transferring low levels of stress to a purely nonstructural material layer valued primarily for its visual and tactile qualities. These nonstructural applications are being achieved with stone layers of ever-decreasing thicknesses. Recently, several composites using stone as one of many layers have been developed. These composites are strengthened in various ways and typically use either fiber reinforcing or metal substrates in sheet form or lighter more rigid honeycomb backing.

Despite the notable use of stone as a structural material in several recent signature buildings (such as the Padre Pio Chapel of Renzo Piano), technological developments in the processing of all types will continue to sponsor its incorporation into the widening array of

Figure 3.133

A sample of fiber-reinforced stone veneer.

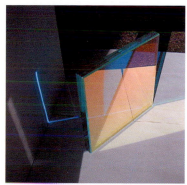

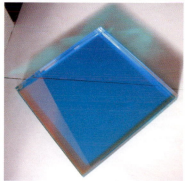

Figure 3.134a, b

Two images of dichroic glass.

composite products. E-glass and carbon fibers have been used to endow the stone composite with greater flexural and tensile strength. It has been shown that carbon fiber reinforcing can increase the general load capacity of stone by a factor of ten (Kurtis and Dhoran 1997). It has also been shown that increased layers of composite fibers yield stone composites that are much stiffer than the unreinforced material.

Reinforcing stone with high strength fibers is currently done primarily to limit damage from cracking and the fracturing of pieces from the composite panel. However, there is remaining potential to apply fibers and structural fabrics in laminations such that the stone can be used to transfer greater loads than is possible through the unreinforced material itself. It is possible that such composites will regain some structural capabilities for stone.

Laminated Stone

In addition, stone is also being laminated to diverse substrate materials for the purpose of achieving composites that are more robust in a variety of applications than the natural stone itself. Laminations of stone on glass, rigid sheet polymers, metal and various kinds of particleboard and plywoods are now commonly seen in interior applications and some exterior envelope assemblies. In the latter, thin sheets of stone are protected by the glass layer from the effects of humidity and liquid water when used as an exterior envelope material.

Insulating and Reflecting Ceramics

Ceramics can be formulated for valuable attributes as an insulator of heat transfer and reflector of radiation. Two very different forms of ceramic materials have taken advantage of these capabilities; paints and coatings, and ceramic foams.

Paints and Coatings

Ceramics, in particulate form, may be used as a constituent in paints and coatings that have diverse reflective and insulating properties. Several of these materials are currently used for improving the barrier qualities of the exterior surfaces of buildings, and many more promise to be developed with an ever-increasing range of properties.

Currently, several products that contain a mixture of a variety of ceramic particles and resin binders are being used as reflective and thermal resistance paints for the exterior of buildings. These products are best at reflecting infrared radiation and increasing the durability of the substrate.

Ceramic Foams

As with the development of metallic foams, ceramic foams provide a surprising and alluring set of materials that may have a role in architectural assemblies. These fiber-free materials are formed from technical ceramics through several different methods.

In addition, carbon foams are also receiving a good deal of attention for their good insulating, low coefficient of thermal expansion, high strength and energy absorbing properties (Spradling and Guth 2003). Made from petroleum, coal tar and synthetic pitches (graphitic foams) or from less expensive materials like coal (nongraphitic), carbon foams are used for speciality heat exchangers and thermal management components. Applications for buildings are, at the moment, limited.

Emerging Glass

The two areas in which there is concentrated research effort at the moment are the making of exotic forms of aerated silica materials and other foamed glass materials and the technology of responsive thin films.

Figure 3.135

Two examples of stone "laminates":

(top) a stone and aluminum honeycomb core composite for use as an interior finish material and (below), a lamination of stone, a PVB interlayer and glass for use as an exterior envelope system.

In addition, there is interest in continuing to develop glass ceramics as machinable, high strength materials for small-scale industrial components. Of course, these are not the only developments in glass technologies. The work in new laminated glass assemblies continues and has proven to be one of the most fruitful areas of research and product development. Chapter 5 describes the development of a textile reinforced laminated glass developed in the Department of Architecture at MIT. In addition, the search for a solution to the nickel sulfide impurity continues with, as of yet, no definitive results.

Glass Ceramics

Glass ceramics are dense materials that are of high strength, moderate fracture toughness, excellent durability, nonporosity, and low thermal expansion. Many types of glass ceramics have been developed since introduction of the first; Pyroceram by the Corning Glass Works. These materials are also very good electrical insulators and are transparent to radiation at various frequencies. These materials can be cast or easily machined using typical metalworking tools and thus allow for the making of complex forms quickly and economically. Several types of glass ceramics offer excellent sealing, joining and metallizing performance. Recent increases in production volumes have reduced the overall cost and increased the likelihood of their selection for metal substitution in high performance engineering applications.

Glass ceramics are materials that are made to crystallize after they have reached their final form in a glassy state. Introducing a dense crystalline structure into the glass produces materials of high density. As such these materials retain the attributes of glasses while possessing improved mechanical and thermal properties beyond those of their constituent components.

Foamed Silicates

Also known as aerogels, these materials are superinsulators of very high thermal resistance. Much has been written about aerogels and little applied to buildings but this may begin to change as the price continues to slowly decrease.

Responsive Glasses

Glass substrates that are augmented with a variety of coatings have been made to respond to environmental conditions of various kinds (Bauer 1995;Fischer-Cripps and Collins1995;Lefteri 2002). In addition, various glass assemblies using additional materials that can be caused to change their properties induced by an electrical charge, solar radiation or other energy sources, are becoming more diverse and commonly used in buildings. These "switchable" glasses are too numerous to individually describe here, but a general outline of advances is useful with a particular emphasis on the leading edge of research in emerging responsive glass (Compagno 1999). The field of large-scale switchable glasses is called chromogenics (Lampert 1999).

The application of an electric current that induces a change in the optics of the glazing is called electrochromics and is now the most widely applied technology for responsive glass. Phase dispersed liquid crystals (PDLC) and suspended particle devices (SPD) are two types of electrochromics.

The primary strategy for achieving responsive glass materials has been the making of assemblies that contain two or more reactive agents. These agents are either liquid or solid, most often polymeric or metallic formulations that are typically quite costly. Much effort is being made to discover economic thin films and other coatings that, when applied to the glass substrate, can achieve similar changes in optical qualities. Research at the Lawrence Berkeley Laboratory in the US has yielded some intriguing results with the development of switchable thin films.

New Glass Laminates

Glass, as a nonporous durable and strong substrate, is an ideal material for combining with various other materials in the making of high performance assemblies. The explosive growth of the laminated glass industry is a testament to the diverse utility of these combinations.

The polyvinylbutyral interlayer polymer used with most glass laminations is an inert polymer capable of receiving many types of materials including metals, organic material, textiles and stone. Other polymers are also used as a laminating material, but to date PVB continues to dominate the laminated glass market.

Composites

The North American value of fabricated FRP composite structures for emerging infrastructure applications is estimated... [to grow by 750 percent by 2010].

Composites Worldwide, 2001

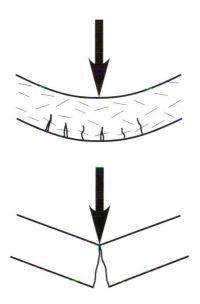

Figure 3.136

Diagram showing failure mode of unreinforced solid and fiber reinforced solid due to bending. The upper fiber reinforced beam exhibits multi-cracking and the lower unreinforced beam fails through the initiation and rapid propagation of a single crack. The simple idea of embedding fibers in a solid matrix is as old as mud bricks and straw, but the invention of new composites continues unabated today.

Source: Adapted from Moavenzadeh (1990).

Ancient and Novel

Composite materials, as an idea of distinct functional elements merged and resulting in a novel and more useful whole, has its origins in the nascent biological sciences of the 17th century. Today it is closely associated with a time in the 1950 and 1960s when a new family of high performance criteria led to the development of complex, and often unpredictable materials. Modern composites are very much an invention of engineering. These exotic materials, more than any other, marked the beginning of a new era in materials development and assembly engineering for high performance situations. Polymer and ceramic composites were the first high performance fiber reinforced materials and were born of the needs of an industry that required ever-greater strengths under strict weight limitations - that of the aeronautical industry of the mid 20th century.

And yet, composite building materials have been a part of architectural assemblies for millennia. The straw in sun-dried bricks has limited shrinkage and strengthened the dried blocks from splitting apart easily. Other ancient combinations of natural fibers and mud have been used in most every climate and culture. The value of combining materials into symbiotic assemblies has not been lost on the vernacular builder. This section addresses those materials for which the word composite refers to a highly engineered, carefully manufactured material of unusual properties, well beyond the typical materials used in architectural applications.

Composites, at their most essential, are simply combinations of separate materials, usually for the purpose of capturing a novel set of properties not possible with the use of one material alone (Hull and Clyne 1996). For example, combining a good thermal insulating material that may be porous with a waterproof sheet, of no significant thermal resistance capabilities, produces a composite that can be used as a good thermal barrier with good moisture resistance. Making a composite amounts to assembling two or more materials.

As such, composites are not a separate family of materials in the same way that ceramics, polymers and metals are. A broad definition of the material family of composites correctly designates it as existing at the intersection between all other material families. As a result, every other material family contributes to the making of various composites. By combining at least two of any metal, ceramic, glass, elastomer or polymer, one can produce a composite that may prove useful.

For our purposes here, most of these combinations are treated in the sections devoted to the constituent materials themselves. Therefore, metal-polymer materials are situated in Section 3.1 Metals, reinforced concrete and laminated glass in Section 3.3 Ceramics and Glass. This section addresses the large grouping of materials referred to commonly simply as *composites*. These are materials characterized by fiber reinforcing of a matrix material. Commonly known as engineering composites, these materials have very distinct properties that deserve separate treatment.

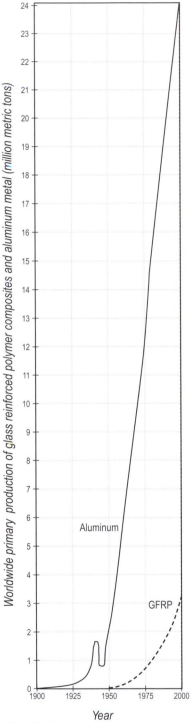

Figure 3.137

Aluminum and GFRP production comparison.

Also, latterly this section emphasizes the fact that the development of composites is now reaching a mature stage in which major past obstacles have recently been overcome. The issues of flammability, off-gassing, excessive creep over time, degradation from UV radiation and other topics have received substantial research attention and progress has been made (Bakis et al. 2002). Remaining issues abound, especially with regard to standards, but breakthroughs have been made. The era of the composite building is within reach.

In fact, many uses are now becoming industry standard or will be soon. The use of woven carbon and glass textile adhered to concrete structure with epoxies is now in full use especially for the purpose of refurbishment and repair (Mouritz et al. 1999,Mouritz and Cox 2000;Pochiraju and Chou 1999). These materials not only stiffen the structural element but also act to protect concrete from the weather, especially ambient liquid water and vapor, and add to its lifetime durability. Also, polymer, glass and carbon reinforcing is being used as a substitute for steel as internal reinforcement in concrete. Many positive aspects of this replacement (such as higher strength to weight ratios, lighter and thinner sections etc.) must be balanced by the fact that the resulting FRP-reinforced concrete design exhibits less ductility than the normal steel reinforced concrete (Bakis et al. 2002).

Composite (FRP) bridge decks are now being tested and installed in locations as diverse as Virginia, Kentucky, Georgia and other locations in the United States, Japan, the United Kingdom, Denmark and Switzerland (Bannister et al. 1998;Callus et al. 1999). The latest round of projects, begun in the mid-1990s, offers very good prospects for the standardization of the use of these materials in construction. Pedestrian bridge spans of 113 meters have been achieved using structural composites. Vehicular spans have been built that are now on the order of 10-15 meters (Keller 2003;Hooks and Siebels 1997).

Pultruded standard structural shapes have been used in building design and construction. Many towers and transmission buildings in the US, Europe and Asia have used glass reinforced polymers for their superstructures. In Avon, in the UK, Maunsell Structural Plastics provided the materials for a two-story building using a proprietary pultruded interlocking panel system (Raasch 1998). Also, in Basel, Switzerland, a series of large triangulated moment frames constructed of pultrusions formed the superstructure for a demonstration building of five floors (15 meters tall). The "Eyecatcher Building", as it is known, was made using Fiberline standardized structural sections of I-beams, C-channels, T-sections and other sections.

In addition, there is evidence that the market for fiber reinforced structural members and nonstructural panels, sheets and other forms of the material is a stable and growing one. Several companies in Europe, Japan and the United States now offer substantial product lines that serve the building construction industry, as well as civil construction. These companies are at the cutting edge of what will surely be a growing market in the coming decades.

Figure 3.138

Frank Lloyd Wright used translucent fiberglass panels (GFRP) to diffuse light in the main living room of his Taliesen West.

Taliesen West, Scottsdale, AZ (1937).
Frank Lloyd Wright, Architect

The most common form of composite is comprised of two elements; a fibrous material and a surrounding matrix. The fibrous material is chosen to contribute a select set of properties that the matrix does not possess. Likewise, the matrix is selected for its own set of useful attributes that the fiber does not possess. Many composites use the fiber for load transfer, particularly in tension, and the matrix for load transfer in compression. The combination has higher energy absorption than the components individually.

These materials are often referred to by their acronyms, FRP, CFRP, GFRP, KFRP (fiber, carbon fiber, glass fiber and Kevlar fiber reinforced polymers, respectively). CFRP and GFRP are the two most common composites used in buildings. The introduction of FRP into construction has been predicated as much on the benefits to the process of construction as it has been on the material properties of the composite itself. Simplicity of connections, ease of transportation, successful incorporation into the unforgiving context of the construction site have all contributed to the successful introduction of FRPs. Presumably further improvements will continue to enhance the competitive advantage of these materials.

In construction GFRP are the more common composite for load transfer applications. Since their development, the consumption of glass reinforced polymers has grown enormously. Acting primarily as a substitute for lightweight metals, especially aluminum, global GRP consumption continues to grow at the steady rate of about 10-20 percent annually. Compared to the growth of aluminum, a well-established material, it is rather slow; however, GRPs were only introduced in the 1950s and the early rate of growth of this new material rivals any new industrial material of the past.

Various fibers are used to improve the tensile, bending and torsional characteristics of the matrix material and various matrix materials are good candidates for the energy transfer necessary. The fibers most often used are polymers, metals or glass. The emphasis in this section will be on polymer matrices; however, metal matrix and ceramic matrix composites will also be described briefly.

Composites have become an important high performance engineering material because they allow careful customization of functional properties. The most important characteristics of composites are lightness, strength, stiffness and fracture toughness (limiting crack propagation). The most common forms are a material composed of a matrix within which a particulate or fiber is embedded. The combination lends to the material advantages of energy absorption that other materials cannot match. As a natural outgrowth of the chemical industry and the development of polymers and synthetic fibers, composite materials are riddled by a proliferation of trademark names, copyrighted brands and product labels of all sorts. Names like Superdeck™, Duraspan™, Hardcore™ and others are used in the literature simply because these products are made available for research applications. Furthermore, a good deal of the research occurring now is focused on bringing to market systems that will fulfill the requirements of evolving codes. The products themselves are in the process of being certified for an ever-widening scope of uses.

Composites as a distinct material class is a bit misleading. In fact, a composite is simply the combination of a number of materials, of like or different material classes into an *assembly*. However, the properties of composites and their prominence in an array of important design situations make it reasonable to address these *material assemblies* separately.

The history of composite materials is short, dominated by private corporations and therefore seeking quick release into the marketplace. The petrochemical industry and the needs of the automobile industry and national defense spurred growth and innovation with new materials and novel assembly morphologies. Composites were first developed in the 1940s and 1950s. The first composites to be developed used high strength, high stiffness fibers, such as glass, in low-cost and relatively low weight polymers. The next generation, developed during the 1960s and 1970s, used higher strength and stiffness fibers of lower densities such as carbon, aramid and boron. At this time, the applications were exclusively related to defense, commercial aviation and the space industry. As such, these new composites were high performing but very expensive, well outside of the economics of civil or building projects. During the next two decades the price of composites decreased rapidly and the needs of an aging infrastructure in the US and Europe prompted greater interest in the opportunities for these materials in large-scale structural situations (Kelly 1989).

The development of composites has continued on a number of fronts. The development of new materials has clearly driven interest and real-world application. Fiber development alone has brought an array of new materials, with their respective novel properties, to the making of composite materials. Kevlar, Teflon and others have driven the specific strength higher than ever before. The use of Kevlar, in particular, for personal body armor and other protective applications is a direct result of these improvements (Shaker et al. 1999).

Used in military aircraft during the 1960s, composites have always had a significant presence in aviation. Composites can comprise 40-50 of the structural mass of a contemporary aircraft (Kelly 1989). Despite this deep ubiquity in aeronautical systems, there continue to be issues regarding its performance in real world situations. Issues of long-term fatigue, delaminations under a variety of environmental conditions, the proper assessment of damage both minor and major and continuing maintenance issues are reminders of the relative youth of the material in large-scale and challenging engineering applications.

The future is open for composites. The fact that composites are assemblies, rather than molecularly distinct materials, means that the search for productive combinations of materials from all classes is a process that will continue indefinitely. Combining two or more materials together is the wave of the future for many material families promising ever higher performing materials for every conceivable use.

Classification and Properties

In the classification of composites it is best to begin by considering separately the individual components of a composite; namely the matrix and the reinforcing agent, typically a fiber. The combination of these materials leads to the various types of composites that exist today. Therefore, two distinct types of classification

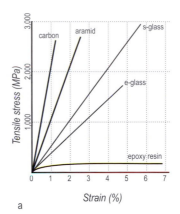

a

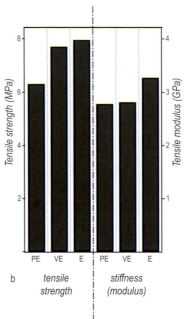

b   *tensile*   *stiffness*
       strength   *(modulus)*

PE   polyester matrix

VE   vinylester matrix

E   epoxy matrix

Figures 3.139a, b

Comparison of reinforcing fiber and matrix material strengths and stiffness. Diagram (a) shows the relative brittleness of carbon and the higher strengths of aramid and glass fibers, diagram (b) shows the higher strength and stiffness of epoxy matrices - together they demonstrate the advantages of glass reinforced polymers over other types.

Source: Adapted from SP (2003).

trees are shown here. The first outlines the types of composites that exist based on the various combinations of materials families possible. The second includes three material trees in which the most common matrix materials and reinforcing fibers are classified according to their material families.

The classification of polymer composites can be accomplished in several ways, but it is important to acknowledge the fact that these materials are composed separately of a polymer matrix and reinforcing fibers derived from several material families. For more detail regarding the types of polymers used in composites the material tree shown in Section 3.2 should provide a starting point. There are also several composites for which architectural applications seem highly unlikely. However, brief description here will complete the discussion of composite types and allow us to continue to material properties. These particular composites use metals and ceramics as the matrix material. Both metal-matrix composites (MMCs) and ceramic-matrix composites (CMCs) also use metal and ceramic fiber reinforcing.

Classification

As described above, classification has been presented on the following pages in two separate ways. First, a number of combinations between metals, polymers, glasses and ceramics are shown. Examples include standard building materials like steel reinforced concrete as well as specialized composites like ceramic-ceramic and metal-ceramic composites. All forms of composites are represented here including particulate inclusions (the aggregates in reinforced concrete), layered or laminated (such as laminated glass and plywood), random fibers or whiskers (e.g. UHPC) and others, see Figure 3.140.

Second, three typical material trees are shown illustrating the array of matrix materials and synthetic and natural fiber materials used in composites. The matrix materials shown, cementitious and polymer, both originate as liquids that are then made to harden through the application of heat or a chemical process (hydration of concrete, for example). An example of a laminate that uses a solid matrix material is plywood; formed through the adhesion of several solid layers of material.

Properties

Composites behave very differently from any other material primarily because they are an *assembly* of material components. Because the internal stresses of the material are not just a consequence of the atomic and molecular forces of the individual materials but also involve the interaction between the two distinct components, their behavior under all kinds of loads can be very complex. As with many of the other material families, the properties that are most relevant in assessing the performance of the material and the definition of those properties are particular to composites.

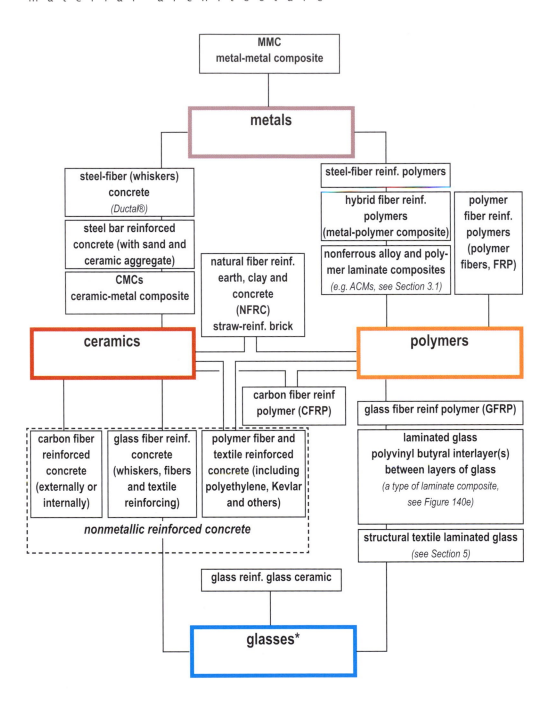

MMC
metal-metal composite

metals

steel-fiber (whiskers)
concrete
(Ductal®)

steel bar reinforced
concrete (with sand and
ceramic aggregate)

CMCs
ceramic-metal composite

natural fiber reinf.
earth, clay and
concrete
(NFRC)
straw-reinf. brick

steel-fiber reinf. polymers

hybrid fiber reinf.
polymers
(metal-polymer composite)

nonferrous alloy and polymer laminate composites
(e.g. ACMs, see Section 3.1)

polymer
fiber reinf.
polymers
(polymer
fibers, FRP)

ceramics

polymers

carbon fiber reinf
polymer (CFRP)

glass fiber reinf polymer (GFRP)

carbon fiber
reinforced
concrete
(externally or
internally)

glass fiber reinf.
concrete
(whiskers, fibers
and textile
reinforcing)

polymer fiber and
textile reinforced
concrete (including
polyethylene, Kevlar
and others)

laminated glass
polyvinyl butyral interlayer(s)
between layers of glass
*(a type of laminate composite,
see Figure 140e)*

nonmetallic reinforced concrete

structural textile laminated glass
(see Section 5)

glass reinf. glass ceramic

glasses*

*Glasses are shown separately here because of the importance of glass whiskers, fibers and textiles in the reinforcement of various types of composites.

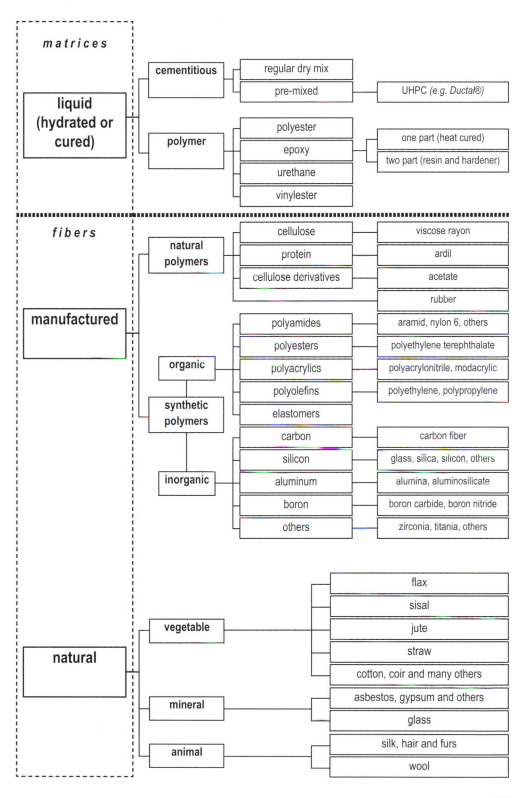

For example, the arrangement of the constituent elements within the matrix substantially affects the behavior of the composite. The orientation of the reinforcing fiber alone can dramatically affect the tensile strength of the composite, Figure 3.143. Therefore, composites are generally highly *anisotropic* - demonstrating dramatically different material properties when measured along different axes.

The matrix material is the host whose energy absorbing properties will be enhanced by the inclusion of fiber reinforcing. As stated above the matrix acts to transfer energy, protect the fibers, and resist certain loads that the fibers cannot, such as compression. The fibers act to enhance the energy absorption of the material through high moduli. The performance of the fibers is enhanced by their protection in a matrix that distributes forces along its lengths. The two acting together prove an effective system for load transfer of various kinds, but for FRPs, their behavior in tension is most impressive.

The interaction between the two components is a mechanical interface. This is where energy is transferred between the matrix and the fiber. A great deal of the overall behavior of the composite is determined by the characteristics of this interfacial zone (Jones 1975). Enhancing the bond at this interface often substantially improves the behavior of the material. Disengagement of the fiber from the matrix constitutes failure of the energy transfer mechanism. So, a reliable and strong bond is absolutely critical to the composite. This is the reason that reinforcing steel has a textured "ribbing" that enhances its mechanical bond to the surrounding concrete.

The materials used for GFRP, CFRP, KFRP and other composites have to fulfill a reliable bonding between the fiber and matrix both chemically and mechanically. Mechanically, the bond needs to be continuous and reliable, offering the greatest surface area for

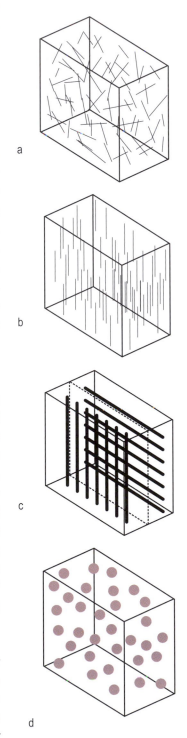

a

b

c

d

236

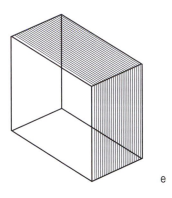

e

Figure 3.140a, b, c, d, e

The various types of possible composite morphologies are shown. Among these are many variations and combinations including braided textiles within a pultrusion, tapes of various widths and compositions, woven fabrics and others.

a: Random fibers or "whiskers"
b: Oriented fibers
c: Oriented fiber reinforced laminations
d: Particulate inclusion
e: Layered (or laminated)

Fiber form	Length (µm)	Diameter (µm)
monofilament	∞	100-150
multifilament	∞	7-30
short fibers	50 -5000	1-10
whiskers	5-100	0.1-1
particulate	5-20	5-20

Figure 3.141

Types and representative sizes of fiber and particulate reinforcement for composite materials.

Source: Adapted from Clyne and Withers (1993).

transferring the energy of the internal stress. Chemically, the bond needs to survive any required processing and serve over the life of the material without debonding or otherwise degrading.

The basic morphology of composites, embedding one material into another, is the most important problem facing the economical recycling of these materials. Success in doing so has been accomplished and it's almost assured that improved methods are on their way. However, the development of new composites should keep in mind the coming difficulties in separation for useful recycling.

Composite Materials

Here again it is generally useful to introduce the variety of composite materials in terms of their distinct matrix materials. There are as many matrix materials as there are material families; i.e. metal, polymer, ceramic matrices are all used extensively. The overwhelming use of concrete in architecture makes the ceramic matrix of cement, sand and aggregate the most common building composite. Polymer matrices, used in vastly smaller quantities are also present in most buildings but most often as a nonstructural material (such as fiber reinforced bituminous roofing composites, asphalt shingles, cellulose fiber cement siding and many other materials).

Polymer matrix composites (PMC)
Glass fiber reinforced polymer (GFRP)
Carbon fiber reinforced polymer (CFRP)
Pultrusions
Metal matrix composites (MMC)
Ceramic matrix composites (CMC)
Carbon-carbon composite (CCC)

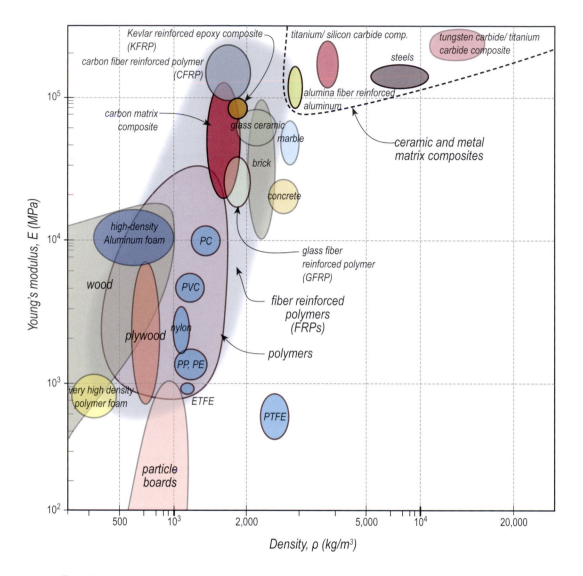

Figure 3.142

GFRP, KFRP and CFRP are grouped together toward the stiffer end of the fiber reinforced polymer (FRP) envelope. To the right with higher moduli are the metal-ceramic composites and the metal-metal composites. Below the FRPs are woods, polymers themselves and lower performance composites such as particle boards and plywood. The two kinds of foam shown here are the high density aluminum foams (stabilized aluminum foams, SAF) and high density polymer foams. Some individual polymers are also shown.

The FRPs sit squarely between the woods and metal alloys and adjacent to concrete and stones.

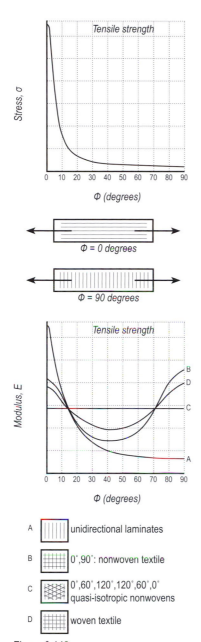

Figure 3.143

Diagrams showing the relationship between fiber orientation and tensile stress and textile type and modulus, *E*. Common sense is confirmed by the fact that higher tensile strength is achieved when the stress is applied parallel to the fibrous orientation and a multi-directional textile demonstrates a higher modulus over a greater range of load angles. *Source:Keller (2003).*

Polymer Matrix Composites (PMC)

PMCs are most commonly reinforced using carbon, glass or aramid fibers. These types of composites are most common, least expensive and routinely used in construction. The most common resins used are unsaturated polyesters, epoxies and vinyl esters, see Section 3.2. Both thermosets and thermoplastics are used - thermosets being more brittle while thermoplastics exhibit useful plastic deformation. Generally, the thermoset epoxy is tougher than unsaturated polyesters and vinyl esters. Common thermoplastic matrix materials are nylon, polypropylene and PEEK (polyether ether ketone) (Clyne and Withers 1993).

Other matrix materials (metal, ceramic) are reinforced with metal, carbon, glass, and other ceramics, but these composites are used in very specialized applications. Reinforcing may be included within a matrix in a variety of forms including long strand monofilaments, multifilaments, short fibers, whiskers and particulates.

Glass Fiber Reinforced Polymers (GFRP)

E-glass is used in a variety of polymer matrices. These moderate strength composites are commonly used for large-scale panels and dense structural elements.

Carbon Fiber Reinforced Polymers (CFRP)

Weaves and bundles of carbon fibers have now found a place in construction technologies and design interest (DelMonte 1981). From the new product for a carbon fiber reinforcing grid for concrete (CarbonCast®) to provocative and preposterous design speculations advocating wholly replacing steel and concrete with a carbon composite superstructure, carbon fibers have engaged engineers and designers alike (Moeller 2001;Hawthorne 2003). The high strength of carbon make it an attractive material for these kinds of applications. Carbon is now also routinely used with epoxy resin as a surface treatment on concrete structures. Both for repair and simple augmentation of the strength of the structure, woven carbon textiles or

239

fiber bundles are adhered to the surface of the structure using a polymeric epoxy adhesive. The CFRP strips (typically on the order of 1.5 mm thick by 150 mm wide) are manufactured using a pultrusion process that allows for the bundling of thousands of individual fibers into a heat-cured linear mass with a tensile strength of 3,000 MPa (Chajes et al. 1994).

Pultrusions

Pultrusions are products of a process in which fibers are drawn through a resin bath and then "pulled" through a sectional die that shapes the impregnated fiber composite into a standard structural shape (Keller 2003). Many kinds of fibers may be used but glass is most common. Several companies have been producing pultruded structural shapes for many years now (see Creative Pultrusions and Strongwell under websites in the Bibliography). The pultrusion market has defined several distinct product lines can be used for building primary and secondary structures:

> a. fiber-reinforced polymer decks,
> b. fiber-reinforced standard structural shapes and sections,
> c. fiber-reinforced grating and corrugated pedestrian traffic products,
> d. braided and woven cables and ropes,
> e. internal reinforcement products (for concrete) (Bakis et al. 2002).

All of these products can be readily found (accompanied by performance specifications and application brochures) on the websites of the major manufacturers of fiber reinforcement and pultrusion products (Creative Pultrusions, Strongwell, Fiberline, Glasforms and others), see the Bibliography.

Metal Matrix Composites (MMC)

The purpose of a composite metal, as with all types of composites, is the improvement of the operating properties of the metal matrix through the inclusion of a useful fiber or particulate. Higher operating temperatures, greater wear, abrasion and fatigue resistance, lessened lifetime creep and customized thermal properties have been achieved by including ceramic or metal fibers and particulates into a metal matrix. Aluminum is a common matrix material in which stainless steel wire, silicon carbide and titanium whiskers have been used to improve its properties. While much research is focused on these types of materials, commercial applications have been slow to materialize (Clyne and Withers 1993). Some automobile engine applications have been proposed and realized and aeronautical applications are also under investigation, in particular in the development of ultralight metal composites. However, the scope of their application is limited to highly specialized, high performance scenarios in which cost does not significantly affect the use of small quantities for improved performance. Therefore, application of MMCs to architectural assemblies may be possible, for better durability for example, but will be limited to small components in critical applications, such as connectors for a structural glass curtainwall (Bowen 1989).

Ceramic Matrix Composites (CMC)

Ceramic matrix composites use materials such as carbon, glass, glass-ceramic, and other ceramic materials as the matrix reinforced by metal and ceramic fibers and whiskers. The search for viable CMCs is focused on high temperature applications in which the relatively low thermal conductivity and expansion of the ceramic material is augmented by higher strength contributed by the inclusion reinforcement.The limitations to finding better CMCs have been the temperature limitations on the fibers themselves. Application for operating temperatures are in excess of 1000-1200°C. Again, the use of CMCs in architectural applications is extremely limited, if of use at all. Even more so than MMCs, the engineering and performance of CMCs has been concerned with conditions that exist far outside the performance of architectural applications.

However, it must be stressed that, with further development, lowering prices, deeper entry into industry in general and the familiarization of these materials, there may arise a time when the application of MMCs and CMCs is a viable and useful step to take. For example, in the search for high operating temperatures, the effort to produce these materials may result in interesting thermal insulation for critical components in a fire. The higher operating temperatures may make these materials attractive to particularly sensitive structural connections.

Composites in Contemporary Architecture

The use of composites as a structural material has been under way in significant research and several important applications during the last few decades. Recently, several projects have used various materials and combination of assemblies in the making of small bridges, structural floor slabs, wall construction, columns and beams and other structural elements (Keller 2003;Hayes et al. 2000). The introduction of composites into construction has been very rapid and as a result, several outstanding issues still need to be addressed and several need to be resolved for the materials to progress much further. The two most pressing issues are the need for standards, in both the characterization of the material and tests designed to standardize the assessment of its behavior under various kinds of loading (Cosenza and Manfredi 2002). The second area of concern is characterization of aging and its effects on durability. These materials are relatively new and comprehensive tests characterizing all durability issues have not been completed (Keller 2003).

Emergent Composites

New composites are arising constantly. In fact, because many composites are manufactured with some component of customization, new composites are relatively easy to make, especially those that involve hand layup or other nonmechanized preparations (SEI 1999). This innovation has also been driven by the emerging durability issues of both steel and especially concrete. In fact, only recently has the scope of critical concrete repair of the huge highway infrastructure of the US become apparent. It is estimated that 40 percent, or more, of the highway bridges in the US need some substantial level of material repair or replacement. FRPs have been cited as one component of the solution to this problem (ECT 2005).

There are three ways in which a new composite can be made. Changes can be made to the fibers, to the matrix, or the relationship between the two can be fundamentally altered. For example, the fibers can be braided instead of stitched and placed in a novel orientation within the matrix. Also, they may be treated before placing them in the matrix as many natural fibers need to be before being placed in polymer or cementitious matrices. As we've seen, the orientation of the fibers dramatically affects the properties of the composite, Figure 3.143.

The fact that composites can be functionally customized and made highly anisotropic allows the designer to specify materials that are meant to serve in highly focused applications. In buildings, the necessity for applying such narrowly defined performance criteria is rather rare in comparison to the more generalized performance of much of the volume of a building's material. However, in light of the coming resource pressures, such as the depletion of primary minerals and the limits to useful recovery and recycling of materials, the capacity to improve the functionality of building materials through the design of highly performance-focused composites will be become increasingly important. Only a very limited number of composite materials are highlighted here. They are:

Smart fiber reinforced polymers
Next generation fiber reinforced composites
Snap joint technology for composite structures
Nanomaterials and biomimetic materials

Smart Fiber Reinforced Polymers

A variety of smart fibers are being developed for use in composites (Ruan et al. 1999)(Kiesling et al. 1996). Health monitoring of structures, luminescence, embedded sensors are a sampling of the applications that are being considered, see Section 3.2 "Polymer Fibers and Textiles Including Smart Polymer Fibers".

Next Generation Fiber Reinforced Composites

Numerous products are emerging on the market as a result of inventions that combine fibers and a matrix for producing a useful composite. For example, three-dimensional carbon and synthetic fiber reinforcing "cages" are being sold as a premanufactured reinforcing system for structural concrete or structural polymers and fiber reinforced plastics (FRP). These products are made from a variety of fibers (polyethylene, polypropylene, aramid (AFRP), e-glass (GFRP), carbon (CFRP) and others) and specified according to the required loads to be transferred. 3D meshes of this kind have been used in Japan by Kajima corporation and others in the reinforcing of both concrete and plastics.

Snap Joint Technology for Composite Structures

The technology of joining is receiving some renewed attention. Two fronts have been challenging the dominance of intrusive fasteners; adhesives (see Section 3.2) and snap joint technologies. Snap joint fastening grows out of the technology as developed for some polymeric components. Shaping two components, one with a "male" and the other a "female" part, allows for a mechanical joining between the two. These kinds of joints are ubiquitous in small plastic objects, from radio, DVD and computer housings to sophisticated medical, electronic and aeronautical assemblies. The size of snap joints has steadily increased as casting and molding of polymeric and composite materials has progressed.

Today, it is possible to construct rather large structures using snap joints. Several demonstration projects have been completed including three transmission towers in Los Angeles using a system developed by W. Brandt Goldsworthy and Associates (Goldsworthy and Hiel 1998). Several large buildings are being proposed in the United States and Europe.

Nanomaterials and Biomimetic Materials

Deriving inspiration from natural forms and materials has always been a preoccupation of human inventors. Nanomaterials and biomimetic materials are included here because a substantial number are composites by definition, combining two or more (and often many more) materials into a material "system". Also, it is increasingly understood that the marvels of some biomaterials is a direct result of their nano-scales - particles, fibers, sheets and other structures that exist at the scale of a nanometer (one billionth of a meter: 10^{-9} meters). Therefore, there is substantial common ground between these very small structures, biomaterials and composite materials.

Nanomaterials are, therefore, materials or structures that are on the order of several to several hundred billionths of a meter in size. The US Patent Office requires that at least one dimension of a "nano-invention" be less than 100 nanometers (labeled Class 977 inventions). However, it is generally understood that a nanomaterial essentially derives its novel properties from its extreme smallness (Feder 2004). The class of materials that fulfill these definitions are already contributing substantially to the developed economies of the world as sunscreen, paint additives, printing inks, new electronic storage media etc.; the National Science Foundation has estimated that nanomaterials now generate roughly 1 billion USD in gross revenue.

Carbon nanotube reinforced aluminum (Kuzumaki et al. 1998) is just one of a number of new composites using a new form of carbon, the spherical or cylindrical arrangement of carbon atoms (bucky balls and tubes). It has been known for some time now that his new form displays extremely high elastic moduli and very good plasticity (Overney et al. 1993;Kuzumaki et al. 1996, 1998). Therefore, it has been examined for use as a reinforcing inclusion in composite materials. Applications in buildings now include uses such as fibrous reinforcing in concrete and composites, high performance insulation, high performance thin films on glass (including conductive, self-cleaning, biodeterrant and responsive), structural adhesives, and a number of sealant materials. Future products for buildings and civil structures include embedded sensors for monitoring structural health or detecting bioagents traveling through a building's air supply ducts.

There is no question that applications for nanomaterials abound and will only continue to proliferate. The major challenges facing the use of nanomaterials have both been long anticipated and only recently understood. First, it has been clear that the processing, material handling, storage and general throughput of the material in an industrial setting requires particularly sophisticated technologies and protocols. Working with very small particles can pose expensive processing issues. Also, the expense of deriving these very small scales is a challenge being met in many diverse ways depending on the form of the nanomaterial (sphere, fiber, sheet, film etc.). An unanticipated but potentially critical challenge facing the use of nanomaterials are the array of health hazards and environmental issues that have been noted as possible by scientists and industry people (Chang 2005). The fact of the extreme smallness of these particles makes their human ingestion very easy, undetectable and prone to cause all manner of health problems; from breathing impairment to acting as carcinogens. Much more work needs to be focused on these issues before nanomaterials are taken en masse by modern industry.

Also, the dispersion of super-small particles does seem to be a negative environmental impact in waiting. While we now know that the dispersion of polymers in the Earth's oceans by very small pieces of synthetic plastics is a global phenomenon, we can't readily predict what the possible dispersion scope will be for even smaller particles as they are used in a greater diversity of production processes. We can only suppose that it is possible that nanomaterials may be the next form of human pollution.

And yet, the future will also likely reveal environmental benefits of nanomaterials. For example, it has been found that iron nanoparticles are particularly good at breaking down known carcinogens by rusting and bombarding the toxin with loose electrons and rendering it less harmful. Infiltrating soils and bodies of water and cleaning up persistent toxic quagmires may be an application ideally suited to the very small (Chang 2005).

Biomaterials and Loam

Extensive deforestation has been a problem for a number of societies throughout history. A larger human population put an increasing strain on local environments generally and in particular supplies of wood – the one readily available resource for heating, cooking and in many cases construction... No one generation would have been conscious of making dramatic changes.

Clive Ponting, 1991

Figure 3.144

A bale of processed cotton, a natural fiber that prompted processing advances ushering forth the industrial revolution. Plant and animal fibers are under considerable reexamination as useful materials for Industry, including buildings and construction.

Lowell, Massachusetts.

Nature's bounty fully exploited

Along with fresh air and clean water, the phrase "natural materials" elicits health, environmental responsibility and thoughtful resource management. It is irresistible to believe that it is fundamentally correct, morally and environmentally, to espouse the responsible benefits of using natural materials in our built environment. How could it be otherwise? Wood is the most useful renewable resource requiring only land and solar radiation and rain. It forms the structure and infill for so many kinds of buildings all over the world. This use continues to compete with its use as a primary fuel (Férnandez-Galiano and Cariño 2000).

Earthen materials - soils and clays - can be gathered from the abundance all around us, molded by hand, dried in the sun and used as bricks. Or placed within the confines of large formwork and compressed to form massive walls. Also, thousands of plant species including bamboo, jute and sisal, flax, kenaf, coir and others grow prolifically across vast regions of the world, yielding useful cellulose fibers for woven walls, thatched roofs, and structural reinforcing. All of these materials are benign, pose no threat to human health, and are easily transformed into pieces of architecture.

245

Advocating their responsible use is simple - but the actual character of our consumption of natural resources has always been more exploitation than stewardship.

Unfortunately, the history of the use of natural materials in architecture (and generally) is characterized by desperate campaigns of unchecked exploitation that have led to massive deforestation and the resultant erosion, catastrophic loss of valuable top soil and desert expansion, irreversible damage to the rich and fragile biodiversity of ecosystems and the spoiling of the ancestral lands of indigenous peoples on every continent.

For the most part the exploitation of our natural resources has lacked any semblance of responsibility and rather strikes one as singularly chilling evidence of the tendency not to respect resource limits. Many civilizations have come to their knees and ended, sometimes devastatingly quickly, in part through a blind plundering of the life-sustaining resources of their immediate natural worlds (Diamond 2004;Ponting 1991). While using natural materials has always entailed some form of unsustainable exploitation, it has only recently become apparent to scientists, historians, politicians and others that we are capable, in fact *we are likely* to tap into our most valuable resources at a rate that will make recovery and adaptation very difficult and often lead to catastrophic social upheaval. The history of the use of natural resources in buildings closely reflects our troubled use of all of our natural resources.

Forests have been the source of materials for every facet of human survival during every period in human history - including providing one of the critical elements for the founding and sustenance of organized civilizations and their physical manifestations - encampments, settlements, cities and regional protectorates and governments. Along with water, and the various animal and plant food sources, wood has been the fuel and structural material of human life.

Figure 3.145a, b

Wood species, both soft and hard, are used in an array of building elements and assemblies. These materials are probably the most familiar building material to most people because of the versatility of its use for structural frames, siding, interior surfaces, furniture, paneling, and many other components of buildings new and old. The warmth and strength of the material make it equally valuable as a finish or structural material.

Figure 3.146

Example of a once common system of heavy wood facade construction from a building in Halifax, Nova Scotia. Called *carré de bois*, this system illustrates the tendency for materials use to be most intense in an area in which particular materials are readily and easily available, locally harvested and serving many other needs, such as boatbuilding and infrastructure (bridges, for example).

Halifax, Nova Scotia, Canada.

And yet, the rampant plundering of this resource has taken place on every continent and characterized every organized city-state and nation's management of their forests until very recently. Ancient forests were initially cleared to gather wood for early settlements and provide land for agriculture and the grazing of domesticated animals. By 6000BC the pattern for civilization's movement throughout the world had been set - agricultural communities cleared land, cultivated crops until the inevitable decrease in soil nutrients and crop productivity prompted the search for alternative land. Clearing once again, cultivation and soil degradation characterized this cycle throughout the ancient world until large-scale cities began to take root.

As a result, the current physical and ecological state of our landscape is substantially due to massive and global deforestation from China and the Indus valley to Europe, Africa, the Americas and Oceania. Ninety-five percent of all of Europe was originally covered in forests - today it stands at 20 percent. China once had forests that covered 75 percent of its land

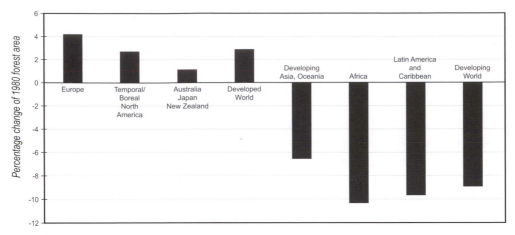

Figure 3.147

The graph illustrates the change in forest areas for developed and developing regions of the world in the 15 years between 1980 and 1995. The contrast between the two regions is sobering and indicative of the continued export of wood out of developing regions as well as the intense use of wood as a fuel in these less fortunate countries.

Source: Adapted from Mathews and Hammond (1999).

mass - today, only 5 percent remain. In the Indus valley, once home to a thriving civilization, the clearing of the forests for construction and fuel for the kilns to dry mud bricks led directly to a weakening of the overall resource base and eventually its demise around 1900BC. In Ethiopia, around 1000AD, the Christian kingdom was forced to move its capital from the north to the south because of the crippling deforestation that had resulted from the development of the city. Within 20 years of moving, the same problem faced the new capital - a 100 mile radius of deforestation had been wrought on the landscape from the incessant clearing of trees for the city's insatiable appetite of charcoal fuel (Ponting 1991;Hughes 1975). And the Mediterranean, once a rich forest of cedar, beech, pine and oak forests, is now arguably no less visually beautiful but nonetheless forever altered into a deforested landscape of shrub and small orchard trees. This massive removal of significant plant biomass has affected the fragile top soil layers of all of these areas and rendered arid, dusty and eroded lands.

Around the world and for much of history, this kind of forest loss was primarily due to the localized fuel and material needs of communities seeking to support critical agricultural and construction activities. The rate at which forests were cut back and their soils degraded overwhelmed their ability to regenerate and thus transformed a naturally renewable resource into a dwindling and ultimately nonrenewable asset. Forests have only recently been managed, but they have always been mined to extinction.

Today, forest loss is no longer a one-dimensional regional condition or a well-defined national issue limited to the geographic or economic extent of any single country. Due to substantial

Figure 3.148

Laminated wood struts held at their ends with cast aluminum joints, all supporting the polycarbonate exterior skin.

IBM Traveling Pavilion, 1983-86.

Renzo Piano Building Workshop, Genoa, Italy.

Photograph courtesy of Renzo Piano Building Workshop, Genoa, Italy and photographer Gianni Berengo Gardin.

global economic pressures to tap their larger, more diverse forests for valuable lumber, developing nations are suffering an overall decline of forest cover, while developed nations have stabilized or augmented theirs, Figure 3.147.

Again, as civilizations have done in the past, the same frenetic exploitation that inevitably leads to critically compromising the very resource that sustains them is driving these developing nations to exploit their forests unsustainably. Coupled with the continuing primacy of wood as a fuel, these countries will need to address this situation before their own most valuable renewable resource reaches an irreversibly compromised state and becomes, essentially, a rapidly diminishing nonrenewable resource.

In addition, the set of resource issues and ecological concerns of importance to forest management and wood use are coincident with those of soils and earthen materials. Actually, the combined set of topics define a significant segment of environmental land use issues, and figure prominently in regional management of ecologies and material flows. Both wood and soil issues involve consideration of the state of the land which supports trees and is partly composed of useful clays, sands and aggregates. Mismanagement of one of these resources will inevitable compromise the other - as just described.

However, the parallels do not end there. Just as wood has been and continues to be a primary construction material, so too are earthen materials. Today, half of the population of developing countries, and almost one third of the world, lives in earthen structures. Buildings of earth have been constructed on most continents and examples have been found that date back to 8000BC (in Russian Turkistan).

The largest buildings and structures ever achieved have been made substantially of earth including the structural cores of the Great Wall of China, the Sun Pyramid at Teotihuacan, Mexico and several tomb and pyramid structures from ancient Egypt.

The relationship between wood and soils is rich and complex. On the one hand, earthen buildings are a direct result of deforestation, as wood became scarce and societies had a need for another readily available and easily worked material. In this sense, the adaptability of civilizations is impressive. On the other hand, earthen buildings are a consequence of naturally arid, barren environments - some of which came about as a result of earlier deforestation. This progression has also played a role in the development of composites that use both woods and other natural fibers and soils, such as wattle and daub construction.

And despite the intensity with which both wood and soils are used for construction and the well-known ecological and environmental issues, the global use of these materials illustrates the prevailing pressures of desperate societal needs. Natural materials are readily available and inexpensive, thus useful to the vast majority of the world's population. These materials are also suited to self-build construction, a process in which community-building ideals can be used for positive results, but in reality is a necessary burden for many of the poorest. In any case, both wood and soils can be obtained without mechanized equipment and special tools and easily maintained without significant expense.

Global agricultural waste material - a prime source of structurally useful cellulose fiber - has been cited as the largest underutilized resource in the world today. A great number of the applications to which natural materials are put in architecture are not necessarily safe or environmentally beneficial, but they do fulfill a critical need for building materials. They are simply the most expedient solutions to issues of dire needs for housing or other basic shelter.

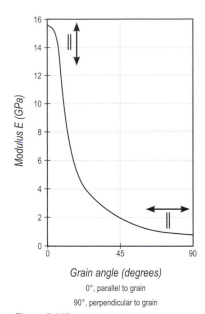

Figure 3.149

Modulus versus grain angle for representative hardwood.

Sources: Adapted from Schniewind (1990) and Hearmon (1948)

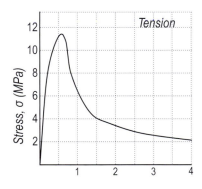

Figure 3.150

Stress versus strain for representative hardwood.

Sources: Adapted from Schniewind (1990) and Hearmon (1948).

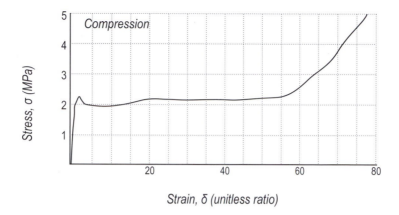

Figure 3.151

Compressive stress-strain curve for a "typical" wood material.

Sources: Adapted from Schniewind (1990) and Hearmon (1948).

It is the dilemma of modernity to advance the use of low embodied energy, inexpensive and readily available natural materials for humane buildings that enhance and support health and well-being, reliably and safely, to its inhabitants. Today the choices to be made in the use of renewable materials are no less difficult and the consequences no less significant than at any other time in the past. Because of the increased use of nonrenewables in society generally, it is reasonable to suggest that the choices today may be more pressing than ever before.

To these ends, a new generation of natural materials is a critical component of introducing the benefits of a less caustic set of modern processes and standardized building products. The economics of natural materials ensure that their uses will continue. The question is, will their use improve the lives of the vast legions of people that need, and can only afford, basic shelter? In addition, how will new uses of natural materials affect the environment?

As with composites, the grouping of natural materials is, not strictly speaking, a distinct and exclusive family but a grouping of various substances united by a set of similar origins in natural processes. These materials also share similar compositions inevitably with overlapping histories and uses. A reasonable way to classify this group is materials that arise from natural processes, biological and mineral, and are used rather directly, with little processing, in an assembly or composite.

For example, wood is a natural composite made of water, cellulose, hemicellulose, lignin and other molecules in varying ratios depending on the species. It behaves as a composite with constituent materials acting together in a symbiosis that results in complex and highly specialized structural behavior achieved through the combination of complementary material properties. As an assembly of more than one material, it is the combined action of their

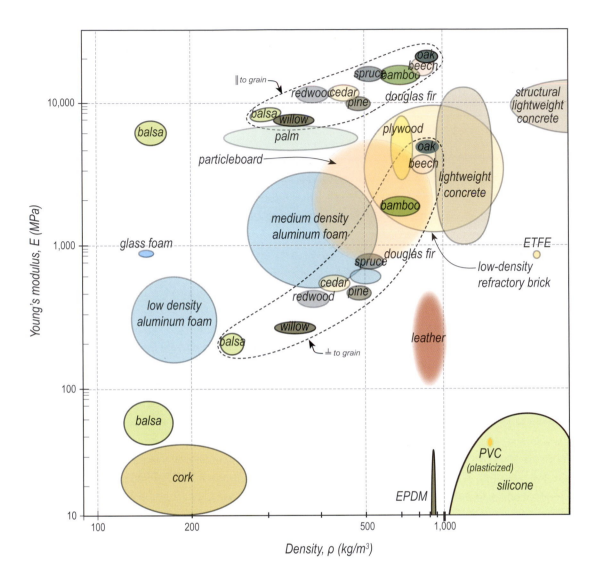

Figure 3.152

Young's modulus for a selection of soft and hard woods.

Sources: Adapted from Schniewind (1990) and Hearmon (1948).
Also using CES 4.5: Granta Design Ltd.

properties that lend the composite its particular characteristics. Wood is also anisotropic, having a grain and exhibiting vastly different properties depending on the axis with which the measurement is taken. For example, balsa wood is anisotropic to a factor of 40. Wood can be broken down both mechanically and chemically into subsets of constituent materials both on molecular and micro-structural levels. Cellulose itself or fiber bundles can be derived from wood.

But as a material produced in nature, it is quite distinct from any other composite. It is used rather directly without a great deal of processing (in comparison to the very extensive and sophisticated biochemical processes necessary to produce it in the first place) and it shares common constituent materials with other natural materials. Its primary structural components are cellulose and lignin, two molecules that also combine to produce the nonwoody natural fibers. And finally, wood is an exceedingly complex material, much more so than any synthetic composite. Besides the structural behavior that is required, it also serves as the primary vascular system for a living organism. No other synthetic composite approaches this level of complexity.

Both renewable and nonrenewable materials, mineral and biological, are included here. Unfortunately, a comprehensive set of natural materials used in construction today and in the past would overwhelm this section and would include thousands of materials produced by biological and mineral processes. These would include material produced by animals, such as chitin from insects, spider silk, the hides and fur of animals, shells, bone, oils etc. It would also include all stones and other minerals including natural fuels such as gas and oil. Some of these materials are still quite relevant to architecture and others such as the coquina limestone of southern Florida are no longer commonly used in buildings. Made of the compressed natural shell deposits of the Atlantic, St. Augustine, the oldest city in the United States, was built of coquina limestone blocks.

The criteria used to dramatically reduce the number of natural materials covered here include research and design relevance to contemporary architecture, potential for technology transfer to future architectural assemblies and the emerging potential to support growing responsible uses in the built environment. Therefore, three large groups have been chosen; wood and wood composites, natural fibers and biopolymers and earthen materials. These three groups include materials as diverse as textile reinforced wood composites, sisal, jute, natural fiber reinforced composites and concrete, bamboo, rammed earth, pisé, adobe and several others. Natural materials are also similar in that they often possess a significant uncertainty in the actual values of their material properties, depending on species, age, environmental conditions and other factors that result in great variability. This partly accounts for their limited use in high performance engineering applications. Obtaining reliable information regarding their properties can be challenging.

The focus here is again on an identifiable set of research trends that are supporting the emergence of new materials for use in architecture. Particularly interesting in this group is the relationship between traditional methods and forms of these materials and emerging contemporary forms. In some cases, the transfer from a traditional use is small and relatively incremental such as in the use of flax and jute fibers in interior finishes for buildings. In others, it involves the combination of the very new and the very old such as in flax-fiber reinforced epoxy composites.

These materials, more than any other family, elicit issues of sustainable development, local materials use and traditional methods alongside high performance and sophisticated processing. Those materials with an agricultural origin bring with them processes and skill sets honed over centuries of cultivation and processing. Those of a mineral origin are linked with craftsmanship and local materials handling that extend back to ancient settlements.

Finally, a reiteration of some essential points. First, these materials are products of the biological and mineral cycles that exist outside of industrial processes. That is, these materials were produced either from geological or biochemical processes. Second, these materials are gathered through extraction or cultivation. Minerals are extracted. Animal and plant materials are cultivated. When biological resources are exploited without cultivation and management, problems arise. Deforestation, destruction of biological and habitat diversity and extinction of flora and fauna are all critical indicators of irresponsible and unsustainable extraction strategies. And third, while the individual materials may have undergone radically different processes in a variety of places on the globe, the list of the primary materials that constitute natural resources is fairly limited. For example, cellulose is the principal structural molecule in all plants. For our purposes here, the primary materials are the focus of this section.

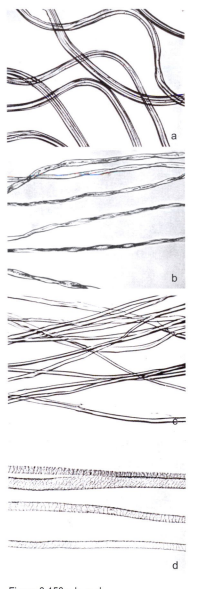

Figure 3.153a, b, c, d

Fiber photomicrographs.

a. cellulose
b. cotton
c. silk
d. wool

Figure 3.154

Compressive stresses versus strain of several wood species. Notice the obvious cellular behavior displayed by each one of the woods (see Chapter 3).

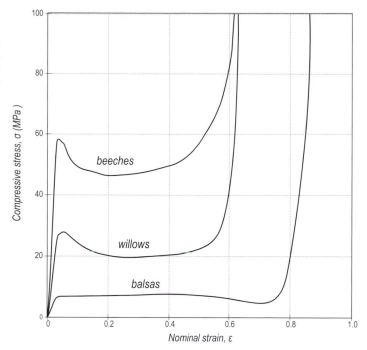

Classification and Properties

Classification

Wood

Is it better to use wood as fuel or as a building material? Throughout the ages, this has been a balance that has rarely found an easy equilibrium. It illustrates the value that wood represents to buildings, both in construction and during their operation. In fact the question is still relevant in many parts of the world in which wood is a leading fuel source. In 1997, 3.4 billion cubic meters of wood was consumed of which 1.9 billion cubic meters was burned as fuel (more than half) (Mathews and Hammond 1999). The combined value of this consumption reached 400 billion USD in the 1990s, about 2 percent of global GDP (Solberg et al. 1996).

Yet even with over half being consumed for fuel wood, more wood (by weight) is consumed in construction than either steel or concrete (LeVan 1998). Global trade in woods has tripled in the last three decades, now accounting for 3 percent of total international trade. Also, North America alone accounts for 40 percent of global production and consumption (Mathews and Hammond 1999). These figures clearly illustrate the place of wood in our modern societies, it still ranks among the most intensely cultivated and consumed materials available.

Not surprisingly, the production of fuel wood and charcoal is concentrated in the developing world (United Nations 1997). The rural poor are the greatest consumers of wood for fuel. Current estimates place the growth in wood fuel consumption between 1961 and 1997 approaching 80 percent (FAOSTAT). This indicates steadily growing pressures from growing rural poor populations for mostly unmanaged unsustainable sources of wood fuel. While it is not clear at what levels these consumption numbers will reach a "critical" point, surely the past is full of the misery of uncertain futures made unsustainable by rampant natural resource abuse.

Clearly, wood is now and continues to be the most important biomaterial used in architecture. From the earliest structures, the use of wood has been a fundamental component of the structural frame. From Laugier's famous icon of the origins of construction and the generation of the pediment from the making of the primitive wood hut to the proliferation of a multitude of modern wood composite materials, it is a material of uncommon utility. The use of wood through the ages has not only shaped entire cultures but also determined the economic basis and social structure of many of the world's societies.

In the developed world, especially the United States, wood is used for light framing of small to mid-sized residential and commercial buildings. This type of construction utilizes small pieces in the making of structurally redundant but resilient buildings. Developed in the United States, light wood framing and the balloon, and then the platform frame method of construction have been exported to parts of the world with ready supplies of lumber. Wood has also, on occasion, been used as a tensile reinforcing material in masonry structures, most notably in the Duomo of Florence and some other large buildings.

Woods used in contemporary buildings are classified into one of two broad categories; softwoods and hardwoods. Most but not all softwoods are conifers. Likewise, most but not all hardwoods are broad-leaved deciduous tress.

Much of the research with wood composites is aimed at reducing the problems associated with the anisotropy of wood, that is reducing the directionality of wood by producing laminates containing layers with grain in different directions, and other materials. Reducing anisotropic qualities has the positive benefit of making the material more versatile in the field and during the manufacture of composite assemblies, like engineered wood box beams and I-beams.

Natural Fibers and Biopolymers

It has been convincingly shown that the production of biopolymers to substitute for synthetic polymers, such as polyethylene or polystyrene, does not confer clear benefits in terms of the overall impact on the environment (Gerngross 1999;Kurdikar et al. 2001). The only clear way in which to take advantage of the renewable resource of polymers derived from plants is the simultaneous use of biomass fuels for an energy source serving the production of these polymers. However, the resource potential of biopolymers and natural fibers is intriguing. Further discussion of these materials is given in "Bioploymers and Biocomposites, Including Natural Fibers", below.

Earthen Materials

Underestimating the importance of earthen materials is easy for those in the industrialized regions of the world. For many western developed countries, the use of earth as a primary structural material has receded into the forgotten past. However, it is again useful to repeat that one third to one half of the world's population still lives in houses built of earthen materials. No construction material has successfully replaced earth in its availability, ease of construction and low cost.

Earthen structures are made of the useful clays that are the result of the erosion of the mineral feldspar and others, containing aluminum oxide, silicon dioxide, iron oxide and other compounds and elements. The clays that result, primarily kaolinite (with trace of illite and others) can be molded, compacted and formed into sun-dried bricks, rammed-earth walls and other earthen systems. Loam is a combination of these binding clays, water and other materials, such as sands, silt and gravel, derived from soils and other terrestrial resources. These other materials do not contribute to the binding of the material but add volume to the finished component - be it a block or a wall. Often earth recovered just below the surface (up to a depth of about 40 cm or so) will also contain substantial amounts of plant matter. These organic materials are not desirable and should be eliminated or avoided (Minke 2000).

Loam can be applied in various ways for construction. Essentially, two main products are possible: blocks, such as adobe, sundried bricks, wet loam clods, earth bags or other relatively small and discrete elements meant as a masonry or paving unit; or in situ agglomerations of loam and various aggregates, such as rammed-earth walls, cast earth, pisé (terre pisé), various composites such as wattle and daub, cob, and earth ball finishing and other earthen plastering systems. Whether cast or molded, hand formed or bagged, rammed or applied to a straw or timber substrate, the use of loam is only appropriate in low stress situations.

The making of loam useful in construction is a very refined science and subtle art. Few reliable sources are available to the architect interested in this kind of material system. Currently several standards and codes do exist - notably in New Zealand - and many more are being developed (NZS 1998a, b, c). Because of the very large mass involved in most loam constructions, the environmental ramifications of recovering kaolinite and other clays, the great variability in the clays themselves and many other issues, building with loam should be undertaken with very great care.

Natural Materials in Contemporary Architecture

The convergence of issues that advocate a more responsible architecture, and the pressing needs of development, poverty alleviation and a resurgence of interest in appropriate technologies for architecture, has prompted a diverse set of initiatives that use natural and "lightly" processed materials. The following highlights some of these while acknowledging the incompleteness of this listing.

Emergent Natural Materials

Hybrid wood composites
Biopolymers and biocomposites, including natural fibers
Animal and plant fiber insulation

Hybrid Wood Composites

Research in wood composites, which include noncellulose materials, especially synthetic fibers, is a growing area. The primary focus of much of this work has been the augmentation of the structural capacity of elements like beams and columns by using high strength fibers and textiles. This type of hybrid wood composite follows closely the work done with carbon and e-glass fiber reinforced concrete.

Especially receptive to this kind of reinforcing are the laminated woods. These engineered woods are easily strengthened by laminating an additional layer of synthetic textile to the bottom face of the beam.

Biopolymers and Biocomposites, including Natural Fibers
(co-author for this section: Harn Wei Kua, PhD candidate, MIT)

Biopolymers, biocomposites and natural fibers are too numerous to treat here in any great detail. However, a very brief outline of origins, composition and current applications is given here.

Biopolymers
Biopolymers are biodegradable plastics whose components are derived entirely or in part from renewable raw materials. That is, bioplastics contain one or more biopolymers as essential ingredients. Although in nature biopolymers are plasticized by native plasticizing agents, in the commercial processes of extraction and purification, "foreign" plasticizing agents may be added to control the physical properties of the bioplastics. In other words, bioplastics can be schematically defined as the addition of biopolymers, plasticizers and other essential additives. The resins used to make bioplastics fall into two broad categories: natural

and synthetic. Natural resins (biopolymers) are largely based on renewable resources such as starch and cellulose, and microbial products. Other polymers such as proteins and pectins may also be used for biodegradable plastics and polymers.

Biocomposites are those composites in which one of the primary components is a material of biological origins. This may be a natural fiber reinforcing of a synthetic matrix material or a bioplastic reinforced with a synthetic fiber, for example.

Synthetic polymers are made of petroleum-based and other feedstocks and include polyester and polyethylene polymers. An example of a biodegradable synthetic polymer is polycaprolactone (PCL), a thermoplastic polyester resin. One has to note that physical or chemical modification of a natural biopolymer may result in a loss of its biodegradability. Conventional, petrochemical-based plastic materials are not easily degraded in the environment because of their high molecular weight and hydrophobic character. Disposal of plastics therefore has become a major environmental concern, resulting in a program to recycle, incinerate or compost these wastes.

Starch is a natural polymer. It is a white, granular carbohydrate produced by plants during photosynthesis and it serves as the plant's energy store. Starch can be processed directly into a bioplastic but, because it is soluble in water, articles made from starch will swell and deform when exposed to moisture, limiting its use. This problem can be overcome by modifying the starch into a different polymer. First, starch is harvested from corn, wheat or potatoes, and then microorganisms transform it into lactic acid. Finally, the lactic acid is chemically treated to cause the molecules of lactic acid to link up into long chains or polymers, which bond together to form a plastic.

Polyhydroxyalkanoates (PHAs) are a family of microbial energy reserve materials that accumulate as granules within the cytoplasm of cells. They are polyester thermoplastics with properties similar to petrol-derived polymers. In fact, their mechanical properties can be tailored to resemble elastic rubber or hard crystalline plastic. The prototype of this family is actually polyhydroxybutyrate (PHB), which is too brittle to be of any extensive use. However, by combining polyhydroxyvalerate (PHV) with PHB, a non-brittle copolymer polyhydroxybutyrate-polyhydroxyvalerate (PHBV) - can be produced. An example of PHBV is BIOPOL, marketed by Zeneca. PHBV has properties very close to polypropylene and polyethylene exceptional flexibility and toughness.

In general, four basic polymers are of interest PLA, PHA, PCL and PGA (polyglycolic acid or polyglycolide). Except PCL, all of the rest are polyesters, with PGA being the simplest kind. PLA contains asymmetrical carbon atoms in its structural unit that enable it to become optically active (Van de Velde 2002). As a result, one obtains the isotactic copolymers of L-PLA and D-PLA. A syndiotactically alternating D,L-copolymer is also obtained. As mentioned, to overcome the weakness of PHB, PHBV (also called the PHB-PHV copolymer) is produced. Another candidate worth mentioning is the random copolymer of 3-hydroxybutyrate and 4-hydroxybutyrate (P(3HB-co-4HB)).

Natural Fibers

Sisal

Though native to tropical and subtropical North and South America, sisal is now widely grown in tropical countries of Africa, the West Indies and the Far East (Bisanda 1992). Sisal is the coarsest vegetable "hard" fibre. There are many varieties of the plant spread throughout the tropical and subtropical world, especially in Central America, but the most important on a commercial basis are AGAVE SISALANA (and its hybrids, the most common of which is known as 11648) and AGAVE FOURCROYDES (better known as henequen).

The East African sisal plant originated in the Yucatan, Mexico (and received its common name from the first port of export) and arrived in what is now Tanzania via Hamburg in 1893. A little later sisal bulbs sent from Kew Gardens were planted in Kenya. Production in East Africa has contracted materially over the past three decades in response to the continuing movement of end products away from the low value agricultural twine market into considerably higher value more specialized end products, such as carpets, wire rope cores, dartboards, specialty pulps, plaster reinforcement and handicrafts. Production is now approximately 20,000 tons per annum in Tanzania, 20,000 tons in Kenya and 12,000 tons in Madagascar. There is also production in Southern China of around 40,000 tons (very largely for domestic consumption) and smaller quantities in South Africa, Mozambique, Haiti, Venezuela and Cuba.

In Mexico henequen production (largely in the Yucatan peninsula) has fallen from a peak of about 160,000 tons in the 1960s to about 15,000 tons today, all of which is converted into product locally. The first commercial plantings in Brazil were not made until the late 1930s and the first sisal fiber exports from there were made in 1948. It was not, however, until the 1960s that Brazilian production really accelerated and the first of many spinning mills, largely devoted to the manufacture of agricultural twines, were established. Today Brazil is the leading world producer of sisal at some 125,000 tons per annum.

Jute

Almost all of the world production of jute and jute products come from developing countries in the Far East. In particular, four countries are the main producers of jute – Bangladesh, India, Myanmar and Nepal. In order to obtain jute fibers from the plant the stems have to be steeped in water (a process known as retting) at an optimum water temperature of 80°F. Microorganisms are also added into the mixture to decompose the gums and soften the

Figure 3.155

Sheep fleece insulation blanket produced by Second Nature Ltd of the UK.

Photograph courtesy of Second Nature Ltd, UK.

tissues in anywhere between 5 and 30 days. The retting process is also found to influence the strength, color and luster of the ensued jute fibers. There are two main types of retting: manual and mechanical.

During manual retting, the fibers are freed from the stalk by light tapping with a mallet and then lashing the stems in water. In mechanical retting, a mechanical decorticator frees the fibers from the stalk, greatly reducing the time of retting and quantity of water needed. After retting, the fibers are collected and laid out on bamboo racks to dry for 2-3 days.

Flax
See Chapter 5 for a discussion of flax fibers.

Animal and Plant Fiber Insulation

Animal and plant fibers have recently been reintroduced into the insulation systems for buildings. These products are generally in the form of pressed mats of fibers held together primarily by the entanglement of the fibers themselves. Various products use fungal inhibitors as well as additives that retard full combustion and reduce smoke generation - usually a low toxic boric acid. And while there is controversy about the use of boric acid as a flame retardant, these products do not use any polymeric binders that may pose off-gassing potential. As with many lightly treated natural materials, the advantages here include the lack of synthetic, caustic, irritating or highly toxic materials in the final product or the processing. Also, some of these products tap into the waste products generated by agriculture or other industries. For example, Eco-Products® insulation uses the cotton fiber recycled trimmings from the denim industry to produce insulation blankets that achieve R values of 13 for 4 inch thick and 19 for 6 inch thick products. Another company, Bonded Logic®, produces a similar product that has also been approved as a Class A building material. Animal fibers (hair or fur) are also used in insulation products for buildings. Thermafleece™ is a product manufactured by Second Nature Ltd of the UK that uses sheep's wool as the primary insulating fiber. Again, the fibers are held in place primarily through entanglement (with the addition of a lofting agent to maintain fiber stability). Also treated with a fire retardant, the wool is inherently less capable of sustaining a flame than cellulose fibers (see www.secondnatureuk.com).

The greatest advantage of these materials is the low thermal conductivity of the fibers themselves; 0.039 W/m.k for wool and 0.2 W/m.k for cellulose, compared with 0.7-1.3 W/m.k for glass fiber. Whether synthetic or natural fiber, if the material becomes wet the thermal conductivity will be compromised.

The disadvantages include the suite of resources issues detailed above, including the management of the renewable resource, associated effects of the processing (such as fuel use, overgrazing, compromised biodiversity etc.). Insulation materials should be tested using the latest ASTM standards including (but not limited to) ASTM C665, ASTM C518, ASTM E96, ASTM E84, ASTM E970, ASTM 379.

Material Selection

...the architect must again begin at the very beginning...architects must exercise well trained imagination to see in each material, either natural or compounded plastics, their own inherent style. All materials may be beautiful, their beauty much or entirely depending upon how well they are used by the Architect.

Frank Lloyd Wright, 1943

Figure 4.1

Industry innovation has presented the designer with a virtually endless array of materials for every application. Far from lacking in choices, the opposite is now true; the designer has been inundated with such a rich selection and so much material property data that management of the knowledge is a challenge in itself. How does the contemporary designer make selections between materials?

Prompting Function, Making Choices

In 1943, Frank Lloyd Wright was well aware of the impending flood of new materials - "compounded plastics" and others. Whether he, or any other architect of the time, could have envisioned the explosive diversity of new materials brought on by polymer science, composite science and engineering, or nanomaterials is unclear. As Mowery and Rosenberg write in *Paths of Innovation, Technological Change in 20th Century America*,

> The last decade of the 20th century differs from the last decade of the 19th, not primarily in terms of larger quantities of goods that already existed in the 1890s; rather, the distinctive differences consist in the present availability of goods for which there was no close equivalent a century ago.

Mowery & Rosenberg, 1998

Availability of goods, "for which there was no close equivalent a century ago", has prompted a proliferation of choices in many things. Nowhere is this more apparent than in disciplines involved in design of all kinds. An increasing diversity has been brought to the processes, possible configurations and materials available for the objects that designers make.

So if, as Mr Wright states, beauty in the use of materials is dependent on the creativity and wisdom of their use, how well do we use contemporary materials in buildings? This chapter addresses this question by suggesting that renewed attention to the methods of material selection may lead to inventive design.

When building in timber, the selection of structural wood members is critical to the character and aesthetics of the frame, its load transfer characteristics and its performance over time. In the making of a stone building, the block from which the cut stone originates must be examined and evaluated before production proceeds. Ideally, these selections are accomplished in a continuous act of formulating design concepts, specifying materials and organizing construction logistics. Yet today, the use of even these kinds of "natural" materials is accomplished within a process of the selection of a standardized system, a timber frame system, a veneer stone rainscreen system or other assembly. The generalized characteristics of the system dominate the specification process. As such, the contemporary architect acts primarily to procure fabricated assemblies of standardized performance attributes. If design is essentially characterized by a selection of systems, then there is little need for the development of material selection methodologies. A designer could simply choose among well known alternatives and work through a set of rules to arrive at a viable solution.

Design has always involved seeking better solutions to satisfy changing needs. But limiting the assembly of buildings to the specification of systems impedes the discovery of design opportunities inherent in materials themselves. Material selection plays an important role by facilitating an all-inclusive scan of the material world. By widening the range of selection to an expansive set of materials, besides those used in standardized systems, the search maximizes the possibility that an unforeseen solution might yield unexpected potential (Cornish 1987).

Of course, it is worth noting that there are very good reasons why buildings continue to be made of the same materials used by Vitruvius, Brunelleschi and Palladio. Concrete, timber and masonry have all been improved in one way or another, but their use in buildings persists because they are inexpensive relative to their unit of service (be it compressive, tensile, bending strength etc.) (Ashby 1999). With the introduction of steel and reinforced concrete, allowable stresses increased dramatically and expanded enormously the formal possibilities for architectural form (Elliot 1992). LeCorbusier, Frank Lloyd Wright, Mies Van der Rohe and others took advantage of this new capacity. But the best materials for structural purposes remain few and a simple graph of cost versus stiffness illustrates why. The relative cost of stiffness (an important structural attribute) shows that traditional structural materials continue to be the best choice, Figure 4.2.

High stiffness and low cost materials are to be found in the upper left-hand corner of the graph. This area contains many of these materials, concrete, steel and iron, stone and brick. They

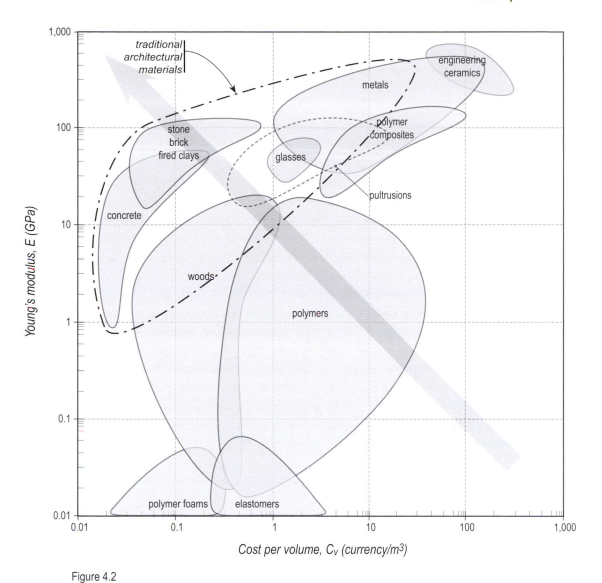

Figure 4.2

Young's modulus against cost per volume.

deliver good stiffness and value. Clearly, advocating more rigorous search methodologies will not necessarily lead to "new" materials being chosen for many architectural applications. For example, synthetic polymers do not exhibit adequate stiffness for most load transfer applications.

But this analysis also shows that a number of new materials are edging themselves higher into the left quadrant. For example, fiber reinforced resin pultrusions for use in structural applications have been developed at ever-lower costs and higher stiffness. Advances in the weaving of the reinforcing fibers, the bond between the fibers and the resin matrix, and improvements to both the fiber and matrix materials, have resulted in a competitive structural material. Assessing its relative structural worth is easily done by placing the material on the graph. Other materials include synthetic fiber reinforced engineered woods and high performance concrete.

However, for the most part high performance fibers, many metal alloys and other attractive materials are still too costly for application in the quantities necessary for structural applications in buildings. Nevertheless, there are other building systems that demand reconsideration where the cost, especially lifecycle cost, of new materials need not preclude their consideration. Generally, the lifecycle cost of a building is dominated by energy expenditures during operation. Using new, higher performing materials in the creation of better performing exterior envelopes is certainly well worth the effort of seeking out these new, better materials. In addition, seeking healthier and less energy intensive interior finish materials is also worth an ongoing material search.

Selection Strategies: Some Accepted Methods

Every material selection process is employed to fulfill a simple need, identifying the best material for a particular application. This section generally describes various methods for material selection and serves as an introduction to multi-objective optimization for architectural material selection, the method identified as holding the best prospect for use in architecture.

A material exhibits behavior as a result of combinations of mechanical, physical, thermal, electrical and magnetic properties, and characteristics such as cost and availability, processing and finishing. Extrinsic properties can, and often do, change with time. The selection of a material based on the optimization of a single property, regardless of all other attributes, is the simplest possible selection process. This is rarely possible or desirable. Material selection usually involves a complicated multivariable process augmented by a number of qualitative considerations in which subjective judgment is indispensable.

For any type of design scenario two sets of entities need to be defined, the first - a set of values, the second - things. The first set describes the goals, or performance criteria, that the design must fulfill. The performance criteria may be any number of goal-oriented values, such as maximum insulation per unit thickness, stiffness per unit weight, fracture strength per density, embodied energy per unit tensile strength etc. A complete set of criteria is often a complex mix of diverse values, including thermal, mechanical, aesthetic, cost and other needs. This set defines the functional domain.

The second set defines the set of physical entities that will satisfy the needs of the functional domain. This set is composed of real things - building products. The materials, components and assemblies of this set can be successfully applied to the design scenario when their particular mix of attributes fulfills the needs of the functional domain. This set is called the physical domain.

The link between the functional and physical domains can be made in many ways, depending on the opportunities and the constraints. For example, if the design scenario limits selection to a particular material, then a materials selection process is not necessary. However, in most situations, the selection of appropriate materials is necessary and forms one of the critical links between these two domains.

As a result, materials selection methodologies have been employed in engineering design for many decades. Their use, as a fundamental link between functional and physical domains, is accomplished in two general phases; Phase 1 organizing huge amounts of material property data and Phase 2 formulating ranking criteria for making useful comparisons between materials.

Phase 1 is data intensive; sometimes involving as many as 80,000 engineering materials, each of which contains data points for 10-12 separate relevant properties. This phase consists in organizing data for the purpose of applying ranking criteria in the next phase. Phase 2 involves formulating a relevant comparative measure with which to rank materials. The measure can be a particular value, such as cost, or may be a complicated formula consisting of many values, ultimately resulting in a numerical ranking. Various approaches have been designed and used, primarily in the automobile, nautical and aeronautical industries.

Carbon fibers and epoxy composites are an example of a successful introduction aided by powerful analytical tools, empirical and theoretical - including material selection methods. With the increasing specialization of individual disciplines, it is becoming more critical for each discipline to be attentive to the development of useful tools that apply to its particular mode of working and set of interests. The engineering disciplines have made this a critical component of their evolving research and development efforts. Architects, advocating for a rich relationship between technology and design, need to assume the challenge of acquiring tools of their own.

The various material selection methods developed for engineering are not easily applied to architectural situations. It is for this reason that the method of multi-objective optimization using material indices is introduced here.

Material Indices and Multi-Objective Optimization

First, before beginning a detailed examination of the method, a simple example will illustrate its immediate utility in a design scenario.

Aside from the properties that characterize much materials selection, such as strength, stiffness, thermal conductivity and other performance-based attributes, architects are often interested in the phenomenological, the experience of spaces and constructed environments. The tactile, the "feel" of materials, is a fundamental aspect of this experience. This example proposes that a designer may wish to provide materials that are warm and soft to the touch. We all have an intuitive sense of these attributes, but is it possible to be more precise about these qualities, and to do it in a comparative way? Can we map these tactile properties?

Limiting ourselves to the softness and warmth of a material, we can do just that. A soft material possesses a combination of low hardness (resistance to indentation and scratching, Vickers hardness scale) and low stiffness (again, as measured by Young's modulus, E). A warm material is slightly more complicated. Materials that feel warm to the touch are both good insulators (low thermal conductivity, rate of heat transfer in steady state) and have low thermal diffusivity (heat transfer in a transient state). In other words, a warm material will tend to transport and disperse the heat from your fingertips and into the material at a relatively slow rate. Therefore, note that in defining a warm and soft material we need to invoke both mechanical and thermal material properties (Ashby and Johnson 2002).

Figure 4.3 shows a graph of these values. We will not derive the individual values that determine the scales of warmth and softness as that would involve more detail than is necessary at this point. Both are graphed such that the tactile sense of each increases toward the origin. Examining the graph is an easy way to quickly grasp the relative positions of a great many potential candidates for the design proposal. Two sets of information can be gathered immediately; the relative positions of many material families and individual materials themselves, and the magnitude of the difference between them.

For example, it can be seen that the materials warmest to the touch are polymers and the softwoods. The next grouping of materials includes kaolin, polymers, Kevlar reinforced composites, hardwoods, fiberglass and brick, a diverse set of materials indeed. Beyond those, aluminum foams, concrete, stone, carbon fiber epoxy composites, and titanium are similar in feel in terms of temperature. It is therefore useful to know that, in terms of the warmth of a material, hardwoods and brick are similar, likewise stone and aluminum foams

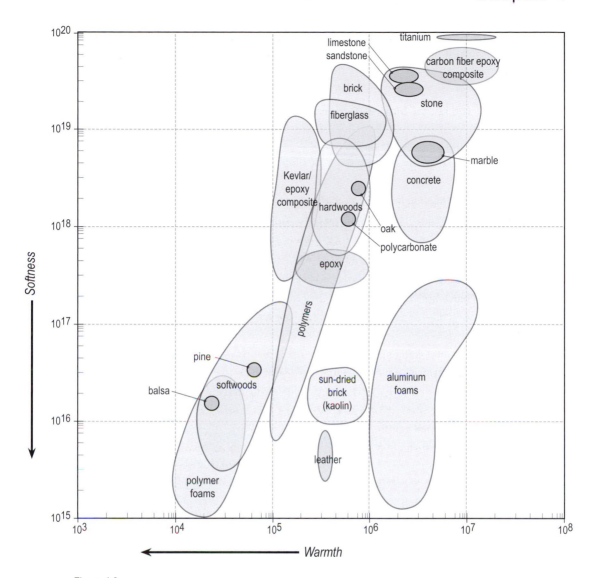

Figure 4.3

Tactile attributes – softness against warmth.

and so forth. The ultimate result is that associations between materials and between intuitive knowledge and the properties of unfamiliar materials can now be made with some authority. These associations can be made independent of aesthetic preferences, ideological intent and even the expectation of "traditional" design solutions. The example can be put to use in the selection of materials for an interior in which the feel of the space is integral with its design. In addition to the comparisons straight from the graph, ratios can be derived that define the best position of a combination of softness and warmth. These ratios are called materials indices, and their use will be demonstrated with examples that follow.

Now it is possible to describe in detail the basis for multi-objective optimization. The method is, in principle, quite simple. In multi-objective optimization, there is again a functional domain and a physical domain. The functional domain for any particular component in an architectural assembly is described by a relationship between the geometry (shape and size), the functional attributes (what the thing does) and the material properties (stiffness, cost, thermal expansion), necessary to fulfill the design needs. In other words, the object to be designed does something, is shaped in a certain way and is made of a particular material. The physical domain is the full specification of the component; that is, the designed thing itself.

The key to the application of multi-objective optimization to architectural scenarios is the simple fact that, in most situations, we know what the object needs to do, we generally know what the geometry needs to be but we do not yet know which material best satisfies the set of requirements. In these cases, multi-objective optimization becomes a powerful way to select materials. For example, in a typical commercial office building design, structural bay sizes are often known early in the design process (and therefore so are effective column heights and beam spans), and the function of any particular thing in the building is usually obvious, a beam is transversely loaded, a column axially etc. Therefore, the only unknown aspect of the relation between function, form and material properties is the material itself.

In light of this, it is possible to derive a series of material indices that directly indicate the best material for the purpose. These material indices are often simple ratios that relate the relevant properties for the purpose that the object is being subjected to. Figure 4.4 shows again the graph of Young's modulus, E, against relative cost, C_v, now with a series of superimposed design guidelines. These guidelines are plots of individual material indices. The three describe distinct functions; Line A stiff plates and slabs, Line B stiff beams and columns and Line C stiff tie rods. Each guideline describes a distinct slope. Remember that the most attractive materials are located to the upper left-hand corner of the graph. In displacing each design guideline to the left it is possible to begin to carefully eliminate candidate materials by selecting only those that are remaining to the upper left of the design guideline. As one slides the guideline to the left more materials are eliminated. The differing slopes mean that the cutoff for various materials will occur at slightly different places and therefore the set of materials that are equally viable at any single position of that particular guideline will also differ.

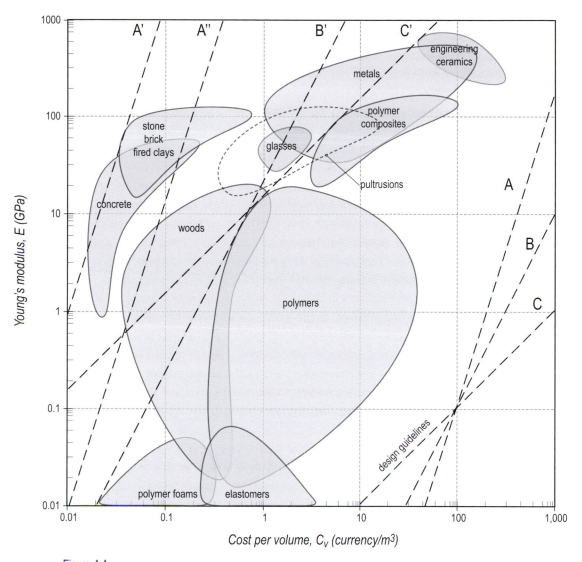

Figure 4.4

Young's modulus against cost per volume, material indices plotted as design guidelines.

Take, for example, the movement of design guideline A from the bottom right to the left, in position A'. This design guideline locates the best materials for use in making stiff planes - plates or slabs. The optimization is the transfer of maximum load, transversely loaded over an area, with minimum deflection and material weight. The slope of the line is 3 because the relation (the material index) itself is $E^{1/3}/C_v$, where E is Young's modulus and C_v is the relative cost per unit volume. Therefore, in placing the line anywhere on the graph, the materials that it crosses have the same value for this index with the line, in that location. Of course, moving along the line will change the actual values for E and C_v for any particular material. Placing Line A (position A') on the left hand of the graph shows that the best material (highest stiffness for least cost) for this purpose is concrete. It is the only material remaining to the left of design guideline A'. Certainly concrete is a primary material in the making of structural slabs. However, in the making of a small plate, for example a table top, the use of wood is a more sensible choice and may be preferred to stone, and fired clays (position A''). And in the making of very small plates, say individual tiles, fired clays are the best materials. As can be seen here, processing, overall weight and other considerations temper this selection method.

Lines B and C are two additional material indices, each derived from an analysis of the statics that govern the function specified. Line B optimizes materials for minimum cost design for stiff beams and columns (material index, $E^{1/2}/C_v$). Position B' shows woods, metals and pultrusions to be viable competitive choices for this purpose. Line C optimizes materials for minimum cost design for stiff tensile rods (materials index, E/C_v). The C' position tells a similar story as B', except that it favors a larger set of metals, a reasonable conclusion for tensile members.

The use of these indices is a powerful method for implementing a structured selection methodology for particular functions; be it structural, thermal, optical or otherwise. Governing material indices for a vast array of functions have been derived and are available for use in this way. Many of the functions that architectural assemblies need to satisfy have been defined and expressed using simple material indices, Figure 4.5.

Also, it is important to stress that the use of material indices, for any particular function, is a comprehensive process of material selection. In other words, in the previous example the selection of materials for a stiff beam (Figure 4.3, design guideline B) is optimized for the materials selected for any beam geometry! Therefore, once a set of materials has been identified, it is no longer necessary to go through the process again. Only when new materials need to be assessed is it necessary to run the analysis again.

Finally, such a method would be difficult without the aid of data management. Fortunately, software has been designed to employ the method of multi-objective optimization using material indices. Currently, the software is being adapted for use in architectural design by the author and Granta Design, the software developers. A version for use by educators and practicing architects alike will be available in the fall of 2005.

Figure 4.5

Function	Material Index	Legend
Stiffness limited design		
tensile rod	E/ρ	E = Young's modulus
column (compression)	$E^{1/2}/\rho$	ρ = density
slab (loaded in bending)	$E^{1/3}/\rho$	
Strength limited design		
tensile rod	σ_f/ρ	σ_f = failure strength
column (compression)	σ_f/ρ	Variously defined depending on the material family.
slab (loaded in bending)	$\sigma_f^{1/2}/\rho$	
Thermal design		
thermal insulation	$1/\lambda$	λ = thermal conductivity
thermal storage (maximum energy stored/unit material cost)	C_p/C_m	C_p = specific heat capacity C_m = material cost/kg
thermal storage (maximize energy stored for given temperature rise and time)	$\lambda/\sqrt{a}$	a = thermal diffusivity

Table of selected material indices.

Source: Ashby (1999).

Assisting Design through Computation and Database Management

Generally, contemporary architects are very good at assessing the extrinsic aspects of potential material selections. For example, practicing architects are well aware of the cost of thousands of products, material systems, strategies and construction methods, and realize projects based on a great variety of extrinsic variables. They are also well versed in the historical significance, cultural import, regional meaning and other intangible and evolving aspects of material systems. Often the value of the art of architecture resides in the architect's ability to construct an integrated whole out of an array of disparate and sometimes conflicting variables. This ability is immensely valuable not only in realizing projects but also in the service of the greater goal to produce buildings that are not simply the sum of their analyzed parts.

The method introduced here assists with the comparison of both intrinsic and extrinsic attributes. However, its great value for architects resides in assisting with the organization of a multitude of intrinsic material property data points. Because extrinsic data changes over time and varies with region (for example, embodied energy) this type of data is less critical to the working of a tool that is meant to assist in only one aspect of materials selection. Once a set of materials has been identified through the use of the appropriate materials index, the designer is still left with the selection of the best material, taking into account aspects that cannot easily be modeled, such as regional significance, the intention to support a local industry, or all of those issues lumped under the unwieldy moniker of aesthetics.

As pointed out by Alan Colquhoun many years ago, the search for a purely deterministic design process through the use of computational tools is a goal not worth pursuing because it is philosophically bankrupt, and logically impossible. This errant pursuit is a symptom of the tension between "biotechnical determinism on the one hand and free expression on the other", which characterizes so much of technical development and creative pursuits in the modern era. This is certainly not what this chapter advocates. However, computational tools have been extremely valuable in the limited and focused application to situations in which a great deal of information is available. While depending solely on computational analysis to deliver fully formed solutions to the architectural quest for form is fundamentally flawed, using computational tools for data analysis is an absolute necessity for material selection. The information era has empowered the architect to access deep data resources in the quest to invent better performing and more engaging form. Therefore, while it is important to integrate both qualitative and quantitative selection methods in any design effort, attempting to do so without the proper tools is an effort doomed to failure, or at least frustration.

Visualizing Inventive Potential

While understanding the mechanics of using a materials selection tool is critical to its success, relating its use to pedagogical goals and professional development is another question altogether. Education should be vigilant not to serve conservative professional models and risk matriculating students pessimistically contemptuous of convention and regulated processes of design. Introducing better methods for particular aspects of the design process is an integral part of actively evolving the profession. It is more productive, and interesting, to continue serving the academy and the profession by identifying pathways that creatively integrate technology and the search for new, more relevant, architectural expression, than it is to serve the convention of the day.

Currently, several schools of architecture offer seminars, design research studios, workshops and other curricular vehicles that teach about nontraditional materials. This is especially critical as it relates to several other emerging technologies of contemporary design including advanced production using CAD/CAM methods and rapid prototyping, computational simulation and visualization and innovative assemblies including exterior envelopes and structural morphologies. The materials selection software used in this seminar provides a database linked to a powerful interface appropriate for use by both design students and professionals. Its implementation in the workshop served to provide quick comparative analysis for many applications and catalyze thinking about potential functionality that had not been previously considered such as producing energy from the wind's pressure on a film membrane, for example.

Integration and Communication

The desire for engaging the potential of new technologies requires an understanding of their potential to serve architectural interests. We know that it is not enough to be fascinated with the miracles of science and engineering. It is also not enough to advocate better design with technologies, without a strategy for doing so. The strategy proposed here is one of communication and integration.

Communication of the potential of new materials can be achieved through the use of tools that precisely delineate needs and potentials. Understanding what architectural systems need is the first step in deciding what aspects of the science of materials are useful to designers. In many schools of architecture, the materials of architecture have traditionally been examined through the filter of the construction trades. This was a valid pedagogical structure when the materials of architecture were substantially controlled by a culture of craft. Typical Construction Materials and Methods courses retain the outlines of this structure. With the introduction of materials that have had their origins not in a workshop or the construction site, but a modern research lab, is it still viable not to be informed by the knowledge of scientific disciplines, and material science and engineering in particular? Rigorous methods for materials selection are one way in which to communicate the various potentials that can be tapped. Computation supports this effort and reveals opportunities for design. It is useful to remember "the purpose of computation is insight, not numbers".

Integrating these tools into the design process requires that designers decide that this kind of knowledge is supportive of their own design process. Tools that do not preference a particular design perspective or position can best be employed to support the intellectual quality of design decisions. Predictably, this kind of integration works best when initiated in the academy, with students who simply adopt its methods as normal convention.

To this end, we need to adopt a highly integrated mode of teaching design and technology. In a 1997 paper, Professor Donald Watson argues that architectural education does not "keep up with technology innovations" and that design and technology issues are trivialized by their segregation from one another. He proposes that technology and design can be linked best through three initiatives; (1) gaining knowledge in the making, that is, accomplishing learning through empirical experience, (2) integrating technological knowledge into the design process, and (3) integrating design and technology issues rather than segregating them from one another (Watson 1997). If this experiment is to bear the fruit of inventive design then it is necessary that a shift take place, from reliance on edited information to an understanding of the basic principles that determine how materials can best be brought to serve architectural needs.

Material Assemblies

The concept of the membrane goes back to the Latin word "membrana", meaning parchment or skin.

Karsten Moritz, 1994

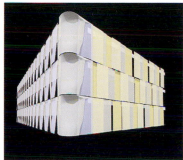

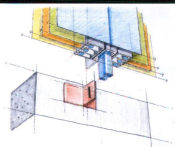

Figure 5.1a, b

The development of high performance fabrics have brought viable materials to the idea of a fabric material exterior envelope. The images above are design proposals for engaging these nonrigid materials into the orthogonal structure of a building.

Multi-Layered Composite Fabrics Research Project
MIT, Department of Architecture (2004).
Fernandez, Principal Investigator.
5.1a: Nat Skerry

New Skin and Bones

Material and form, technique and design - merging these pairs through research is the subject of this chapter. Three studies illustrate the synthesis of technical works and design intent by exploring the application potential of some relatively new materials to contemporary building systems. The first two projects consider the use of new textile materials (and composite fabrics) for the contemporary building enclosure as a multi-layered environmental barrier. The third project investigates the inclusion of natural fibers - specifically flax fibers - as a tensile reinforcing material for a new type of affordable concrete.

Today, the science and engineering, manufacturing, design and construction of high performing nonstructural glass and metal exterior envelopes has been well developed and embodied within a complex building industry and design culture. The first two studies of this chapter attempt to establish a new frontier in the development of nonstructural skins for contemporary buildings through the use of high performance textiles that have been shown to have significant potential in catalyzing the next wave of innovation for the contemporary wall. Two building enclosure projects are

277

described here; (1) a multi-layered high performance textile exterior envelope and (2) a structural textile and laminated glass curtainwall restraint system. In addition to the particular technical issues that arise in each project, the two attempt to define a distinct architectural character (an aesthetic) and range of potential applications for textiles in the next generation contemporary exterior envelope.

In the third project, the global availability of natural fibers and the ubiquity of concrete are brought together in the search for environmentally sound and appropriate construction technologies for the developing world. By recognizing the resource opportunities of finding new applications for the tremendous mass of natural fibers and agricultural waste products and linking it to the need to improve the safety of concrete structures, the final study outlines possible paths toward a humane and sustainable modernity in the least developed regions of the world. All of these projects are meant to elicit the idea that designers can innovate with new materials - or with very old materials in new ways - to effectively address some of the most pressing issues of our day.

Textile Skins

The contemporary curtainwall has generally been assembled of discrete, rigid components. These assemblies are modular, substantially premanufactured, and highly tested systems meant to fully address the needs of a separation between the unstable exterior climate and the need for a stable interior environment. Recently, the contemporary exterior envelope has been the subject of research that seeks to extend the performance of the system as an effective barrier for sustainable architecture (Daniels 1997,2000;Brock 2005). This research includes various efforts to develop responsive assemblies with the capacity to sense environmental forces and act to optimize performance(Compagno 1999;Wigginton 2002).

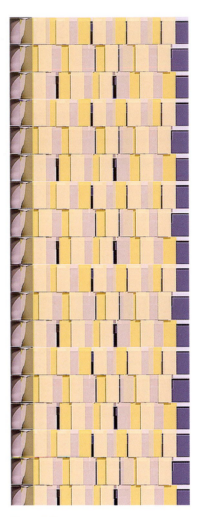

Figure 5.2

A design of multi-layered fabrics on the exterior envelope of a building facade.

Multi-Layered Composite Fabrics Research Project
MIT, Department of Architecture (2004).
Fernandez, Principal Investigator.

In addition, much design thought has recently been focused on the possibilities for a contemporary expression of translucency and lightness based on a minimal material tectonic and analogies to the epidermal structures of living organisms (Riley 1995;Lupton 2002). All of these themes, and others, have placed a great deal of value on the prospects for new material assemblies for the exterior envelope. Textiles are a prime candidate for further study (Gregory et al. 2000;Mills et al. 2000;Walsh et al. 2000;Foulger and Gregory 2000).

Project I: A Multi-layered High Performance Textile Exterior Envelope

The history of the use of fabrics in architecture, particularly as a primary component of the exterior wall, is rich and widespread over time, geography and climate. Recently, with the invention of high performance, polyvalent fabrics composed of newly engineered fibers new opportunities have appeared for lateral technology transfer to architectural applications (HPF 1994), Figure 5.3. These new fibers and fabrics offer useful properties for exterior envelopes that extend the realistic and innovative use of textiles as a primary boundary material between the exterior climate and the interior environment. Multi-layered, insulated, lightweight and durable fabric exterior envelopes are now a reasonable proposal.

Two obstacles currently exist for the application of high performance fabrics in an orthogonal architecture. First, the performance attributes of a multi-layered fabric system have not been adequately investigated. Second, the detailing necessary for the successful restraint and assembly of an exterior envelope require both technical expertise and design vision.

The first envelope project shows an insulated rainscreen exterior envelope composed of a planar arrangement of multiple layers of various fabrics, Figure 5.4. The rainscreen is accomplished by placing an air barrier at layer B. Therefore the pressure equalization chamber is the air space between A and B. Layer A serves to allow a certain amount of air through its surface at a rate that accomplishes the pressure equalization necessary for the successful behavior of the rainscreen.

There has been substantial progress in the use of fabric membranes for several contemporary building types, especially as tensile fabric structures; however, the development of architectural applications has not reflected the enormous innovations in fiber and textile science (see Section 3.2). The modern material science of fibers, primarily synthetic polymers, has yielded dozens of important textile materials and coatings that have come to dominate the primary textile market; namely, the consumer apparel market (Topham 2002;Mollerup 2001;Wigginton and Harris 2002;Braddock and O'Mahony 1998). Only a fraction of these new materials has come to find viable applications in the contemporary exterior envelope.

Trade name	Company	Substrate fabric Weight Weave style Yarn count (warp fill)	Coating Weight (top, bottom) UV topcoat material UV topcoat weight	Finished fabric Thickness Weight
Air Tite® 1532	Erez Thermoplastic	Polyester 270 g/m² weft insertion 19, 18 tpi	PVC 385 g/m², 330 g/m² PVC 295 g/m²	0.8 mm 970 g/m²
Archifab®	Fabrimax	Fiberglass 624 g/m² modified plain 15, 13 tpi	Silicone	0.88 mm 1101 g/m²
Duraskin® B 18089	Verseidag Indutex	Glass fiber-EC3/EC4 180 g/m² L l/l 2040, 2040 dtex	PTFE 355, 355 g/m²	na
Precontraint® 1202 Fluotop T®	Astrup	Polyester HT 1,100/ 1,670 dtex	Plasticized PVC	0.80 mm 1050 g/m²
Sheerfill® I	Saint-Gobain Performance Plastics Corp.	Glass fiber 18 oz/yd² Plain 18, 19 tpi	PTFE 13.5, 13.5 oz/yd²	0.036 in. 45.5 oz/yd²
Shelter-Rite® 8028	Seaman Corp.	Polyester 254 g/m² weft-inserted, warp knitting	PVC Tedlar	950 g/m²
Solus® 1100 HT	Taconic	Glass fiber Plain	PTFE laminate Equal	0.80 mm 1100 g/m²
Solus® 1200B	Taconic	Glass fiber-EC3 Plain	PTFE Equal	0.65 mm 1200 g/m²
Vinagard® 253-25	Vintex Inc.	Polyester 2-ply polyester weft- inserted	PVC Fluorofinish	NA 874 g/m²

Figure 5.3

Table of select composite and high performance fabrics used in building applications.

Figure 5.4

The diagram shows a schematic arrangement in multiple layers of composite fabrics and the corresponding performance attribute that each contributes. Coupling the performance requirements of building enclosures with the useful attributes of new textiles will yield a set of rich research and design projects.

A: exterior finish material
B: air barrier
C: vapor barrier
D: structural fabric
E: foam insulation capsules
F: radiant barrier
G: additional air barrier
H: interior structural fabric
I: interior finish surface

Multi-Layered Fabrics Research Project
MIT, Department of Architecture (2004).
Fernandez, Principal Investigator.

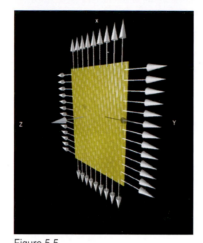

Figure 5.5

Applied force schematic diagram.

Multi-Layered Composite Fabrics Research Project
MIT, Department of Architecture (2004)
Fernandez, Principal Investigator

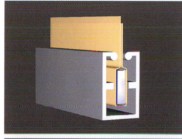

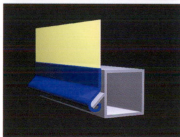

Figure 5.6

Two schematic details showing the need to continuously restrain the fabric material to avoid stress concentrations and unnecessary intrusive fasteners.

Multi-Layered Composite Fabrics Research Project
MIT, Department of Architecture (2004).
Fernandez, Principal Investigator.

Detail Morphology and Assembly Characteristics

A typical curtainwall assembly is accomplished through the application of appropriate materials joined together with a set of carefully considered details serving the performance requirements of the system (McEvoy 1999). Textile materials require a reconsideration of the morphology of details necessary for a successful wall because they are nonrigid materials, strong in tension but ineffective in compression and bending. The edges required the adaptation and invention of details that would continuously and efficiently restrain the end of the sheet material. The details for the condition require the transfer of a coplanar tensile load to the frame on all four sides. For relatively small areas, this tensile stress will be approximately equal on each of the four sides with the exception that the material weight of the sheet would be carried substantially by the upper horizontal. In addition, details are required that allow for the development of some rigidity normal to the surface of the sheet material. This restraint is particularly important to restrict the movement of the fabric due to both sustained positive and negative wind pressure and surface turbulence.

Project II: A Laminated Glass and High Performance Textile Composite

Glass curtainwalls are assemblies of glass, aluminum, steel, insulation materials, vapor retarders, air barriers, sealants and other materials meant to form a consistent barrier between a stable interior and unstable exterior environment. Currently two methods are employed to support and restrain the glass pane within the curtainwall assembly. First, the most common method involves restraining the glass pane within a continuous frame. The glass is mechanically held on all of its edges and its material weight is transferred to the metal mullion frame. The lateral load is also transferred through the glass material and into the metal frame through to the slab edge. This kind of restraint employs mullions as the primary load transfer component.

The second method employs the technique of suspending a pane of glass from the structural frame of the building. This method has been referred to as the suspended glazing and point-fixing method (Schittich et al. 1999). Two methods have been devised to transfer the load of the suspended glass panes to the frame. First, small clamps have been used to attach a pane to its neighbor and transfer the load to the frame. These "patch" fittings were first used on the curtainwall of the Willis, Faber & Dumas offices designed by Norman Foster. Other clamps have been devised and now a great variety of examples exist for this kind of restraint detail. The other method involves drilling a hole through the glass pane and transferring all loads to a metal hanger. The most widely used system is the Pilkington Planar system. Through-glass connections possess the disadvantage of creating moment forces at some point between the glass pane and the structural frame.

This project has been investigating a third method for restraining a glass pane within a curtainwall. With the use of laminated glass there is the potential of using the interlayer material to suspend the pane within a curtainwall assembly. Advantages to this system include the elimination of bending forces within the glass pane or the support component as the transfer of all loads occurs coplanar to the laminar composite. In addition, the interlayer material may be used as an impermeable material eliminating discontinuities in the air barrier system of the curtainwall. These discontinuities, occurring primarily around window assemblies, may be eliminated through the continuation of the interlayer material. Furthermore, it is possible to consider continuous interlayer materials from one pane to the next, insuring no gaps between panes.

The second fabric research project describes experimental and design work for a new type of glass curtainwall, Figures 5.6, 5.8. Using laminated glass and high strength fibers and textiles, the assemblies use a textile reinforced interlayer as the primary structural material for vertical support and horizontal restraint of the glazing to the building structure. With the load testing of a series of samples, first results indicate good potential for further development of this type of assembly. The advantages of such a system include:

1. lighter curtainwall assemblies, requiring less structural support and simpler architectural details,
2. continuous structural restraint of a series of glazing panes, allowing for greater speed and ease of construction,
3. better protection against overall curtainwall failure from earthquake, blast and other catastrophic events, and
4. minimizing air infiltration by using the textile interlayer to better seal areas between glass panes.

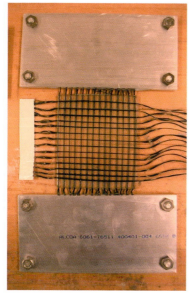

Figure 5.7a, b
Laminated glass test samples.

Structural Fabrics Laminated Glass Research Project
MIT, Department of Architecture (2004).
Fernandez, Principal Investigator.

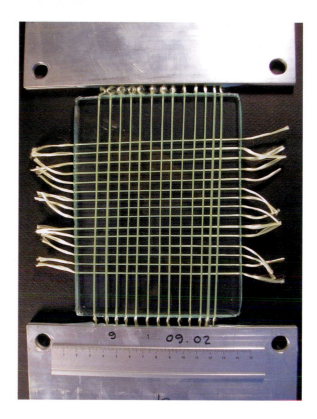

Test Results

Several specimens were subjected to a direct tensile test for the purpose of determining the general behavior of failure for glass laminated structural textiles of e-glass, carbon and aramid fibers (Kevlar® 49). The textiles were laminated to glass using polyvinylbutyral film and then attached to aluminum plates that transferred the load from the load frame. The three types of fibers provided a range of tensile strengths. In addition, two kinds of weave were also tested; a loose 'grid' of individual bundles of fibers and a tightly woven fabric, Figures 5.7, 5.8.

Load testing results revealed that the aramid fibers performed the best overall, both for ultimate strength and a useful load/strain curve. The load/strain curve shows an initial yield point that leads to secondary yield points before complete failure of the laminate. This indicates a complex failure mechanism in which catastrophic failure is supplanted by a phased failure; first some textile elongation and tearing followed by partial delamination of the glass and finally glass breakage.While a thinner, more easily constrained glass wall is certainly an alluring design attribute, the real value lies in the fact that large areas of building wall can be covered using a continuous material system of structural textile and separate laminated glass panes - reducing the number of joints and improving the barrier system.

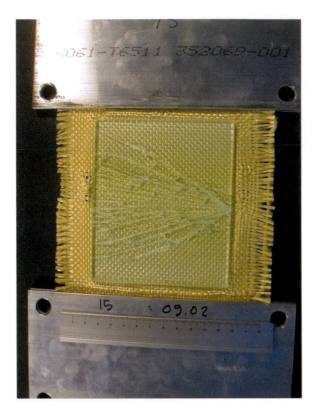

Figure 5.8a, b

Laminated glass test samples and a ruptured sample just after maximum loading.

Structural Fabrics Laminated Glass Research Project
MIT, Department of Architecture (2004).
Fernandez, Principal Investigator.

Project III: Natural Fiber Reinforced Concrete

Worldwide production of all natural fibers eclipses the production of many industrial materials. It has been estimated that 280 million tons of waste biomass are generated each year in the United States alone (Arntzen et al. 2000). Cultivation of the primary natural fibers amounts to 5 million tons globally (2001). There exists a critical need to provide materials that provide safer residential construction especially in areas that suffer the onslaught of natural disasters. The concrete developed here is intended for application in situations in which the quality and quality control of concrete construction produces buildings that do not perform well under seismic loading.

In many regions of the world steel reinforced concrete is the most common construction material. However, the reinforcing steel of the composite is a relatively expensive component. Recent concrete building collapses from earthquakes in Turkey, Taiwan and Afghanistan have highlighted the problem of substandard construction from under-reinforced concrete buildings. While the safe amount of adequate reinforcing steel is relatively small for short span structures, its high expense contributes substantially to the overall cost of the composite. Contractors in these countries and others are tempted to limit or entirely eliminate reinforcing steel in concrete construction. This is a major safety concern especially in areas where the

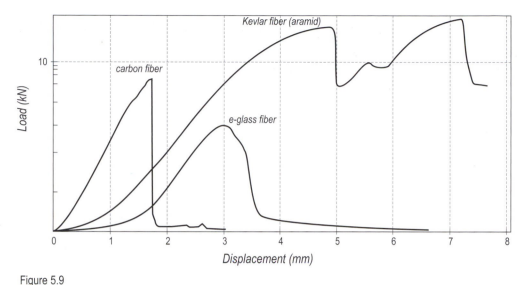

Figure 5.9

Load and displacement curves for e-glass, kevlar and carbon textile/laminated glass samples.

Structural Fabrics Laminated Glass Research Project
MIT, Department of Architecture (2004).
Fernandez, Principal Investigator.

resistance to dynamic loading from earthquakes is critical to the safe occupation of concrete buildings. The augmentation, or partial substitution, of steel with natural fibers in reinforced concrete may be an economical way to offer an alternative method for achieving greater safety in concrete structures around the world.

Specialty products have been formulated from materials derived of plant biomass such as starch-derived plastics, biopolymers for secondary oil-recovery, paper and fabric coatings, not to mention ethanol as a petroleum fuel substitute. While the types and extent of applications of biomass materials to building construction has varied widely, the primary focus of research has been the use of natural fibers derived from plant material for tensile reinforcing in earthen, cementitious and polymeric composites. These composites are generally low strength materials in which the fiber reinforcing serves to aid in the overall strength and toughness of the final mix. Most applications using natural fibers require only very simple and low energy processing. Most natural fibers cannot sustain elevated temperatures and caustic chemical environments and this limitation precludes a broad range of industrial processes.

This study focuses on the mechanical behavior of flax fiber used as a tensile reinforcing and energy-absorbing agent in concrete. The work intends to contribute to the substantial research literature regarding the use of biomass as a source of raw materials for building components. The use of biologically derived materials in components for buildings has been an ongoing project for many decades. Most of the work in this area has been accomplished at research centers and universities in developing regions of the world, sometimes with European and American academic collaborators. Renewable materials that are nontoxic and require low processing energies have become important components of the larger goal to develop environmentally responsible buildings for application to both developing and industrially mature regions.

Furthermore, research has shown the value of carefully targeting appropriate techniques of technology transfer for the particular social, cultural and economic context for which it is intended. The use of natural materials, especially those derived of agricultural practices of a particular location, bring with it a local knowledge base that can be used to develop appropriate processing technologies. With successful development of appropriate building materials come opportunities for catalyzing sustainable and regionally effective economic growth without creating environmental problems. These technologies have the potential of assisting development strategies that are focused on capacity building and poverty alleviation.

Natural Fibers: Mechanical Properties and other Characteristics

Despite the fact that composites such as GFRPs and CFRPs are now used widely in construction, architectural and civil, the use of natural fibers in composite materials has lagged behind.

It is clear from an examination of Young's modulus that a number of natural fibers possess reasonably good mechanical properties for use as structural reinforcement in an architectural composite. Flax rates highest among natural fibers in terms of tensile strength, a property critical to the behavior of a crack inhibitor in a cementitious composite. These mechanical properties, along with relatively low cost, simple processing and

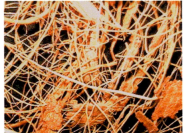

Figure 5.10a, b, c, d, e

Images of natural fibers (top to bottom):
a, b: sisal fiber
c: coir fiber
d: flax fiber

Natural fiber reinforced concrete project.
Fernandez, Principal Investigator.

Figure 5.11

The flax plant species, *Linum usitatissimum*, used to derive fibers for this study.

Natural Fiber Reinforced Concrete Research Project
MIT, Department of Architecture (2002).
Fernandez, Principal Investigator.

ease of handling, offer good possibilities for their use in composites. Natural fibers are composed of a complex combination of cellulose, hemi-cellulose, pectin, lignin, and other materials. The relative proportions of these substances vary markedly between species.

Cellulose can perform the structural function of the plant because it is a linear condensation polymer of anhydroglucose units. The degree of polymerization, P_n, is an important aspect of the morphology of cellulose in the fiber and a primary determinant of the mechanical behavior of the material. The level of polymerization determines the supramolecular structure of the fiber. In addition, this supramolecular structure is the determination of most mechanical and physical properties of the fiber itself. Another important characteristic is the type of cellulose, Type I or II, that is contained within the fiber. The type of cellulose also determines such aspects as the angle of orientation of the cellulose molecules in relation to the direction of the fiber and this affects the mechanical behavior of the fiber.

In terms of cost, flax fiber rates among the more expensive of the natural fibers, often exceeding that of e-glass; with substantial variations among regions. However, this fact alone should not affect consideration of the overall importance of the fiber as a tensile reinforcing agent. Changes in scale of production, distribution and the possibility of a new market will most certainly change the factors under which cost is calculated. The various positive attributes that stand to temper the economic costs associated are as follows:

1. Natural fibers are found globally and often commonly harvested as either a primary material or secondary by-product of well-established agricultural processes. Natural fibers from plant material are the primary source for new biocomposite material

technologies in several industries including building materials, automotive and consumer products.

2. Natural fibers, as the product of natural processes, are renewable and often biodegradable. The environmental impact during seeding, growing and maturation of the plant is restricted to the soil in which it is planted. Taking greatest advantage of the benign quality of the material will require developing industries within the regions with greatest potential to develop natural fibers for construction.

3. Natural fibers fix and retain carbon. The CO_2 released during combustion or decomposition is returned to the environment from which it was originally fixed thereby contributing a net zero sum gain to the overall amount of carbon in the atmosphere.

4. Natural fibers are a group of materials with a long economic, technological and social history within developing and predominantly agricultural regions. This widespread familiarity in cultivation, harvesting, processing and manipulation of natural fibers is an important component in the formulation of sustainable production processes. Certain fibers have been in use for thousands of years. Any development of contemporary technologies utilizing natural fibers can build upon this existing knowledge and vernacular expertise.

5. Natural fibers are much less abrasive than synthetic fibers such as glass and carbon. This lower abrasiveness aids in the various processing steps.

6. Natural fibers generally possess high strength to weight ratios.

7. Natural fibers are nontoxic in most conditions of normal exposure.

The most important negative characteristics are as follows:

1. Natural fibers are strongly hydrophilic. This property is primarily due to the bonding of hydrogen to the hydroxyl groups of the cellulose molecule. This is a problem in both polymer and cementitious matrices. Water absorption before, during and after casting and curing may affect both the durability of the fibers as well as the integrity of the interfacial bond between matrix and fiber.

2. The cellulose molecule, the structural backbone of all plant fibers, is sensitive to attack in an alkaline environment. Careful consideration needs to be taken of the pH level of any matrix material.

3. Most natural fibers begin to disintegrate above 150°C.

4. Mechanical and physical properties of natural fibers vary widely between species and even among fiber bundles of the same species. Natural fibers are a complex mixture of cellulose, hemi-cellulose, lignin, pectin, waxes and water-soluble substances. The proportion of these materials and their arrangement within the fibers is dependent on the particular species. Therefore, the behavior of natural fibers varies widely. Currently the data on the material properties of natural fibers is incomplete. Standardizing the use of natural fibers will require a better data set of mechanical and physical properties than is currently available.

5. The micro mechanical behavior of natural fibers, especially within a matrix, has not been adequately described. Advancing the use of natural fibers reliably and safely will require a concreted effort composed of both theoretical analysis and empirical data.

Materials: Concrete

The work described here uses concrete as the matrix material and flax fibers as the reinforcing element for a biocomposite meant to be employed in structural members for short span buildings. This application has been chosen because it conforms to the requirements of housing; the most common building type using reinforced concrete worldwide. Again, while a great deal of work has been accomplished with regard to the use of natural fibers within a cementitious matrix, there is a need for research investigating natural fibers in concrete. The combination of the sheer number of candidate plant species with the potential to contribute useful fibers for a composite, and the inconsistencies of previous research on the use of natural fibers in concrete and other matrices makes this a fruitful area of research for building construction.

Reinforced concrete dominates the construction industry in much of the developing world today. It is also a primary structural material, along with steel, in much of the developed world. Reinforced concrete serves as the predominate material for the structural frame and, to a lesser extent, the infill material that acts as the exterior envelope of a variety of buildings of all types and scales. Reinforced concrete is particularly prevalent in developing regions for a number of reasons; the relative low cost and good availability of the constituent materials, the use of low skilled labor both in the making of the cement and the forming of the concrete, the ease and low-tech quality of the construction process and the ability to use the material for any number of building components; the roof, floor, wall, columns, piers, foundations and other primary elements of the building.

Flax Fiber

Flax has been used continuously for roughly 10,000 years. Evidence of the use of flax for food as well as textiles has been uncovered from a number of archeological sites dating back to the time of the earliest agricultural settlements in th e Near East. It is clear, from a very early date that a substantial amount of attention was devoted to the cultivation of flax. This crop was one of the earliest sources of a variety of important products, including linseed oil, linen fiber for fabrics and food grain. *Linum usitatissimum*, the most important and useful of flax varieties, found its way around the Near East and was an important crop throughout Mesopotamia and Egypt. The crop then spread to the Middle East, Europe and eventually to the Americas.

Flax belongs to the family of bast plants. Hemp, kenaf, sun-hemp, ramie and jute are also members of this group known for their long and tough fibers. Bast plants are characterized by an outer stem layer that contains 10-40 percent of the stronger fibrous mass of the stem in fiber bundles surrounding a less strong inner fibrous material. Global production exceeds 12 million acres of which Europe and Russia are the primary producers.

The useful fiber is separated mechanically using a variety of techniques. Unprocessed fibers used in this research ranged between 10 and 17 cm. Flax fiber is composed of fiber bundles of approximately 100 microns in diameter. Each fiber bundle contains between 20 and 50 fibrils of 20 microns in diameter each. The fibril is more or less cylindrical in section with a very fine lumen and relatively thick cell walls. Historically, retting (a process of rotting the stems and running them through compressive rollers) has been the method of choice for liberating the useful fiber of the plant. Flax is cultivated to obtain three distinct agricultural products; the seed, linseed oil and fiber. However, these three products cannot be optimally obtained from the same cultivating process or harvesting schedule. The fiber is best obtained from a plant that is immature and not producing seeds at the time of cultivation. These immature plants produce the longest and strongest fibers of the species. In contrast, the fiber obtained from plants cultivated for seeds is of a significantly decreased tensile strength. However, fiber may be obtained in this way and currently forms an underutilized by-product of seed cultivation.

Researchers have identified flax, along with hemp, kenaf, jute and coir, as holding great promise for use in composites for construction materials and other applications. In addition to cellulose produced from the pulp of wood species, the cellulose produced by natural fibers is one of the best naturally produced sources of mechanically interesting natural polymers.

Experimental Program

The following tests were conducted:
Concrete reinforced with flax
1. tensile splitting test: 100 dia. x 200 mm cylinder
2. uniaxial compression test: 100 dia. x 200 mm cylinder
3. 3-point bending test: 100 x 100 x 350 mm beam
Fiber alone
4. Direct tensile test

These tests were considered to be the appropriate number and type required to establish the overall load transfer characteristics of the FFRC. For all tests the mixing proportion of the various concrete components was held constant while the length of the fibers tested varied as 1, 3, 5, 7.5 and 10 cms. The mixing proportions and actual materials used were as follows:

The specimens tested were composed of flax fiber of various lengths randomly distributed within the concrete and additives mix. The fibers were not treated. While there is good

Figure 5.12

Three uniaxial compression test samples of flax fiber reinforced concrete.

Natural Fiber Reinforced Concrete Research Project
MIT, Department of Architecture (2002).
Fernandez, Principal Investigator.

evidence that various treatments of the fibers may increase their longevity in the concrete matrix, as well as contribute to an incremental increase in tensile strength, the study chose not to use any treatments because of the inevitable additional costs that would be incurred. Additional processing costs pose the risk of rendering the material economically untenable as an alternative to typical reinforced concrete, especially in developing regions.

For this series of tests no aggregate was used because of the damaging effect these relatively large elements would have on the flax fiber. Also, it was determined that these aggregates hindered the random and uniform distribution of fibers in the concrete mix. The superplasticizer was kept at a minimum and used only to ease the mixing and casting of the various components. Elimination of the superplasticizer is a future goal of the research.

The hydrophilic quality of most natural fibers makes it somewhat difficult to manipulate the concrete mix due to the substantial water absorption and rough surface of the fiber bundles. This effect tends to compromise a homogeneous distribution of fibers in the concrete mix. Silica fume was used based on studies that have identified pozzolans as substantially contributing to reduced moisture sensitivity of cellulose fiber reinforced cement composites. In addition to these properties, the silica was used to provide a denser filling between all hydration particles and the natural fiber. Substituting the silica fume with a flyash or other industrial by-product is another future goal of the research.

Test Results and Discussion: Toughness

The tests yielded data that were most productive in determining:

1. ultimate strength, and
2. toughness.

By determining these two values, a useful understanding of the energy absorption of the material was made possible. Hannant and Piggott stress the importance of evaluating the contribution of the fiber and matrix separately. The ultimate strength is the easier value to define as it is simply the highest load carried by the specimen, whether in compression, bending or tensile splitting. The value of toughness, while empirically derived in a more complex way, is an important property for fiber reinforced composites. The determination of toughness is guided by numerous international standards. As described by Barr toughness is defined as the energy absorption capacity of the material as determined by the area under the load-displacement curve as obtained by experimental measurement (Barr 1996). This is also the definition given under ASTM C 1018, 3. Terminology, 3.1.5. Additionally, Gopalaratnam lists the standards issued by ACI Committee 544, the JCI SF4, and Belgian, Dutch, German, RILEM and Spanish standards (Gopalaratnam 1995). Generally, all agree that the value of toughness is defined as the area under the load-displacement curves. For this chapter, it is not necessary to calculate a toughness value, rather it is sufficient to use a comparative analysis between load-deflection curves to arrive at useful conclusions for optimization.

Compression Test
Compression tests indicate relatively little benefit in the inclusion of 1 and 5 cm (1-A, 1-B, 5-A) flax fibers in comparison with the unreinforced samples (FC-A, FC-B). Even though there is an increase in the ultimate load for these samples, the failure mechanisms for all of these specimens was relatively catastrophic (that is, the drop-off from the yield load is steep). However, the 10 cm fiber FFRC specimen demonstrates a somewhat better response, resisting a more significant fraction of the load through a much greater displacement and therefore having a larger toughness value. However, when results from fibers of 2.5 and 3.0 cm in length are superimposed over the previous graph, it is clear that this range of fiber lengths performs significantly better than 1, 5 or 10 cm lengths. Both the yield loads and toughness values are greater with the use of 2.5 and 3 cm fiber lengths.

Three-point Bending Test
The bending test is a more complicated test and warrants certain descriptive detail at this point. First, we decided to use a notched beam under 3-point bending instead of the more commonly used unnotched beam under 4-point bending. For brittle materials, such as concrete and mortars, the notched beam test clearly illustrates the mechanical behavior of the composite material, fiber and matrix, at the initiation of the first crack. Therefore, the

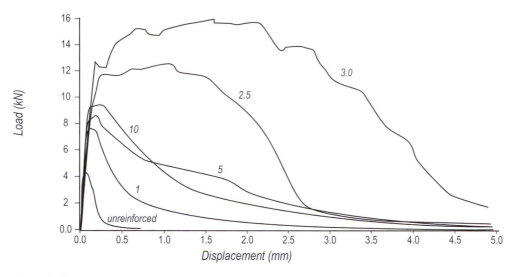

Figure 5.13

Load and displacement curves for a 4-point bending test setup using various flax fiber reinforced concrete mixtures. The labels refer to the length (cm) of the flax fiber as it is randomly dispersed within the concrete matrix. Clearly, the 3 cm fiber reinforcement is superior in strength and overall toughness and shows good multi-cracking behavior.

Natural Fiber Reinforced Concrete Research Project
MIT, Department of Architecture (2002).
Fernandez, Principal Investigator.

notched beam better represents the behavior of the material at the crack surface and also allows a better assessment of the contribution of the embedded fiber on the resistance of the composite with further loading. As a result, the notched beam test is a better test in which to evaluate the behavior of the FFRC composite. At failure, the maximum bending stress is considered to be the flexural strength of the material. For the incorporation of natural fibers within a cement matrix the notched beam loaded in 3-point bending is particularly useful for assessing the actual behavior of the fiber reinforcement. In addition, due to the overestimation of the net deflection of the loaded specimen from measurements obtained through the load frame, it was decided to measure deflection, with respect to its neutral axis, directly from the test specimen.

We also obtained values for deflection from measuring the crack mouth opening displacement (CMOD) directly from the specimen. CMOD is easier to measure than deflection; it is a direct measure of the displacement across the crack opening, and the increase in CMOD is much larger than deflection, therefore making it more sensitive to the failure mechanism. We also determined the toughness through a measurement of the net central displacement as stipulated in ASTM C 1018. The bending test revealed a similar, yet less dramatic, result. The drop-off from ultimate strength is relatively steep indicating that the fiber is not greatly assisting with energy absorption or crack arrest. Tests also confirm the superior performance of the 2.5 and 3 cm fiber reinforced samples. Not only are strength and toughness values greater than 1, 5 and 10 cm specimens but both the 2.5 and 3 cm samples show indications of multi-cracking; a good indicator of energy absorption from the fiber reinforcement.

After reviewing the results of these and other tests, Several more rounds of testing were carried out to arrive at a clear conclusion regarding the optimal length of flax fiber in concrete. From these tests it was determined that a length of 3 cm was the experimentally derived optimal length. In addition, the 3 cm fiber produced a mix that was very workable with no apparent clumping of the natural fibers.

Scanning Electron Microscope (SEM) Analysis
The distribution and characterization of the fiber bundles and the interfacial bond at the fracture surface were investigated using a scanning electron microscope, Figure 5.14a, b, c, d, e. An unpolished specimen was used as the primary method for analyzing the character of bonding between fiber and matrix at the fracture surface. Three general conclusions were reached by studying the microscopic character of the distribution and morphology of the fiber bundles within the cementitious matrix at the fracture surface. The SEM analysis was conducted on all specimen types; concrete with fiber lengths of 1, 2.5, 3, 5, 7.5 and 10 cm. However, the following observations primarily pertain to the 2.5 and 3 cm samples as they were superior in performance to the other fiber lengths.

First, the fiber bundles were found to be both intact and separated into individual fibrils in the hydrated and cured concrete. There was no clear preponderance of one condition over another and both situations were found evenly distributed within the matrix, as far as could be determined.

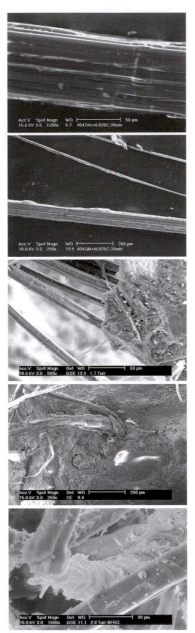

Figure 5.14a, b, c, d, e

SEM micrographs showing flax, loose (top two) and embedded in a concrete matrix.

Natural Fiber Reinforced Concrete Research Project
MIT, Department of Architecture (2004)
Fernandez, Principal Investigator

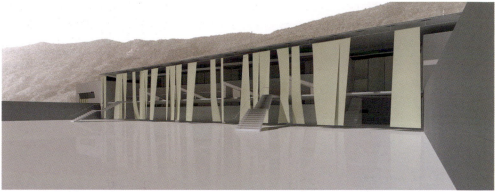

Figure 5.15

A view of a proposed design for a school using various forms of natural fiber reinforced concrete.

Natural Fiber Reinforced Concrete Research Project
MIT, Department of Architecture (2004).
Fernandez, Principal Investigator.

Figure 5.16

Schematic design for a multi-floor NFRC frame for short span buildings. The steel reinforcing necessary is primarily due to shear stresses at the column/beam juncture. While more concrete is required, the overall safety of the structure has been improved.

Natural Fiber Reinforced Concrete Research Project
MIT, Department of Architecture (2004).
Fernandez, Principal Investigator.

Second, as a result of the relative ease of separation into fibrils during casting, there was a concern that cement paste may not have penetrated into the spaces between bundles and fibrils. However, it was found that cement paste had infiltrated into these spaces and had fully surrounded both fibrils and fiber bundles. No areas between individual fibrils or fiber bundles were found void of cement paste. In addition, many fibers that were left exposed at the fracture surface were well covered with cement paste. Also, the SEM images show the formation of large crystals of portlandite in the transition zone interior. The high porosity of the natural fibers induces the formation of these crystals as described by Savastano.

Third, from the examination of at least 56 tested specimens, it seems clear that a variety of failure modes are contributing to the fracture mechanism of the composite. Fiber rupture, debonding, friction, slippage and pull-out all seem to have occurred in failed specimens, indicating that a substantial number of fibers, in a variety of failure modes, are contributing to the increase of toughness through tensile reinforcement at crack formation, propagation and widening. These results indicate that there is evidence for good interfacial bond between the concrete matrix and the untreated flax fibers. Various interfacial bond conditions may be seen. SEM images a, b, c, d, e all show a good interaction between hydrated concrete and the surface of the flax fibers, bundles and fibrils alike, in addition the random distribution of fibers is clearly visible in the images. In addition, the fibers are all seen to be closely bonded to the matrix as well as retaining areas of cement paste on their surfaces even after pull-out from the matrix. Therefore, the images show that the cement and flax fibers are clearly establishing a working mechanical interfacial bond.

Conclusions

Natural fibers take advantage of good strength to weight ratios, wide availability, low cost, ease of processing, ease of recycling and good biodegradation properties. Particular fibers include the most widely available agriculturally important sources of cellulose and lignin. Sisal, straw, flax, hemp, jute, sun-hemp and other tropical and temperate climate natural fibers are examples that have been shown to have good potential for use as tensile reinforcing for composites. Applications for this research are primarily focused on low cost alternative materials for construction in developing regions. Results of the testing and SEM analysis also indicate that:

1. flax fiber contributes well to both the strength and toughness of concrete,
2. flax fiber in concrete is optimized at a length of approximately 3 cm,
3. an effective inclusion morphology of the fibers in concrete is possible with a proper mixing protocol that avoids fiber clumping,
4. flax fibers contribute to the augmentation of the mechanical properties of the concrete composite through a complex combination of fiber/matrix failure mechanisms,
5. FFRC approaches to within reasonable expectations of overall streng and toughness for a viable structural material for buildings of short to moderate spans.

However, flax fibers demonstrate the typical negative characteristics of most natural fibers. One of the most important is that natural fibers are relatively difficult to handle as part of any wet process such as the casting of concrete into molds and forms. The variable surface of the fibers and their varying lengths and grades lead to the fibers forming unmanageable clumps when handling. In this study it was found that the successful handling of the fibers required familiarity with the particular viscosity and overall texture of the concrete and natural fiber mix.

Building Ecologies

The average American born last year will have a life span of 77.3 years and will need the mining of nearly 3.6 million pounds of minerals and metals to sustain their standard of living during their lifetime... Every year 46,414 pounds of new materials must be provided for every person in the United States to make the things we use every day.

Mineral Information Institute, 2005

Figure 5.1

Construction produces large, material-intensive artifacts that, typically, are not easily dismantled for recovery of materials to reinsert into technical cycles.

Design Materials

Individual beliefs, ideologies and philosophies about architecture can be evanescent, ethereal, immaterial - concurrently fleeting and consequential. Carried through the medium of the spoken and written word, these ideals do not require a location, materials or energy - only the ability to foster and contain catalytic ideas that prompt the acts necessary for design.

The design process, employing a suite of techniques for synthesizing these ideas into building proposals, is also minimally material - requiring only pencil and paper and often modeling materials and computational hardware and software.

In contrast, the actual making of buildings - from material extraction, processing and manufacturing to construction - is enormously material intensive, requiring huge quantities of both energy and renewable and non-renewable materials. For example, today the average sized new single-family house in the United States (2,200 square feet) requires more than a quarter of a million pounds of minerals and metals (MII 2005;USGS 2004).

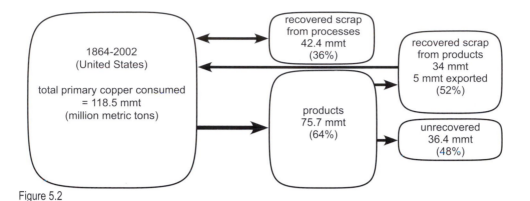

Figure 5.2

The well-developed reuse of copper in the US is shown here. Since 1864 and until 2002, a total of 118.5 mmt were extracted for use in industry; 64 percent was placed in products, 36 percent was consumed in processes and recovered. Of the 64 percent in products, 52 percent has been recovered and reused (or exported). As the mineralogical barrier approaches, the rate of recovery from products will increase dramatically, see Figure 5.3.

Sources: Jolly (2003), USGS (2004).

Essentially, the making of design proposals requires very little in terms of real resources, but consummating those proposals requires enormous material and energy investment.

Today, architects still control the battery of decisions that lead to the material specification and consumption necessary for the successful construction of buildings. Also, designers, through a series of the most fundamental decisions about the building form, are most influential in determining the energy and material consumption of a building over its multi-generational service life. This continuing control over the physical specification of some of the largest and most complex artifacts that contemporary society produces has promoted a growing awareness of the influence designers retain for determining future energy and material consumption. Today, the existing building stock is responsible for one third of our total energy consumption and construction accounts for a majority of the national waste stream. Designers are ideally situated to alter these unfortunate facts. Driving this growing awareness is the now clear evidence of the damaging environmental effects from human industrial activities. This Epilogue introduces concepts that are shaping the study of the effects of human activities on the environment, especially through the lens of industrial ecology.

Building Metabolism - Construction Ecology

Ecology, as the *science of the physical economy of the natural world*, is useful for us to consider as an analogue to human activities. That is, the conditions that characterize the transfers and stores of material and energy in the natural world are representative of similar transfers in the industrial world. Three separate components characterize these similarities.

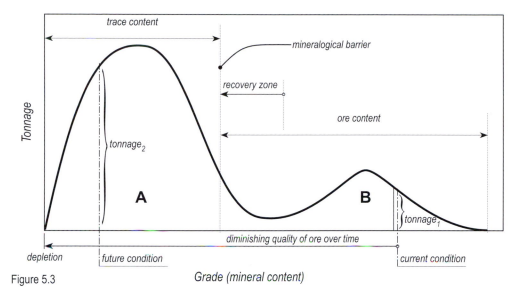

Figure 5.3   *Grade (mineral content)*

Typical curve representing the diminishing quality, over time, of a nonrenewable mineral from the Earth's crust. This bimodal profile clearly shows that the availability of the majority of ore exists as trace amounts in area A. However, much of current mining occurs in area B at relatively easily accessible ore content levels. Many metals and minerals currently mined at ore content (tonnage$_1$) will reach the mineralogical barrier within the next 50-75 years and further mining (tonnage$_2$) will require more energy per unit extracted. Therefore, as mining approaches the mineralogical barrier, the recovery rate will begin to approach 100 percent.

Source: Adapted from Gordon (1987), Graedel (2003).

First, the elements transferred and stored are materials and energy; therefore this is a *physical*, not monetary, economy. In the natural world, only these transfers - of water, mineral and organic nutrients etc. - contain value for the individual actors. Second, the transfers are conducted through a network of linked conduits of exchange, that is, particular pathways serve to facilitate the flow and exchange of certain materials and energy. When an animal consumes prey, digestive processes enable the recovery of proteins, sugars, fats and other materials useful for metabolism. These pathways are often very sophisticated (such as energy harvesting through photosynthesis). Third, individual actors are members of larger groups of like-members, *species*, that may or may not act to optimize conditions favorable for the continued survival of the group as a whole. Each of these components of an ecology are useful for us to transfer to the industry of architecture - the construction of buildings.

First - reflecting the elements above - buildings, while valued in the monetary economy, are essentially physical things requiring substantial material and energy inputs in construction as well as during operation, maintenance, repair and even demolition. This is simply a central premise of Industrial ecology - that the measures used to assess contemporary industries are usually economic, not physical. Construction, like many industries, benefits from a physical accounting distinct from standard economic metrics. As we begin to trace the outline of an ecology of construction, it is clear that these physical resource expenditures directly affect

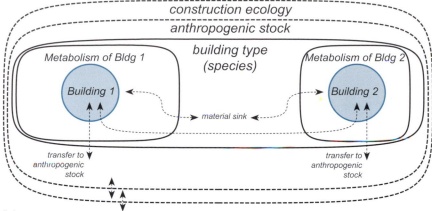

Figure 5.4

The metabolism of individual buildings occurs within the population of the species to which that building belongs. Therefore, Buildings 1 and 2 both belong to a distinct user occupancy type (such as commercial office, residential etc.) that is situated within the anthropogenic stock of all existing buildings. Material and energy transfers between the anthropogenic stock and all other building types and all material sinks and cycles (landfills, ocean dumping, reclamation, recycling, downcycling, incineration etc.) constitutes the network of industrial linkages that defines construction ecology.

the larger context of the environment. In a physical economy assets are limited, for example, the overall store of materials is a limited, finite resource. In a monetary economy, total asset values - as manifestations of market consensus - is unlimited. This is the same for natural ecologies in which the only unlimited resource is solar radiation. Second, the pathways for the transfer of materials and energy in buildings is highly regulated - even in situations in which construction is poorly accomplished and building systems are primitive, Figure 5.4. The most unsophisticated building enterprises are still dependent on the essential physical characteristics of building materials and the realities of industrial processing. Finally, as described in Chapter 2, human activities - and thus the buildings that are designed to accommodate these actions - can be classified in terms of occupancy types. These types can be thought of as characterizing building species - populations of like types that share similar lifetime attributes, Figure 5.5.

Also, in Chapter 2 "Industrial Ecology of Buildings", the metaphor of the ecology of living systems is introduced as a relatively new mode for the study of human industrial activity. In that chapter, the lives of buildings, their design lives and the determination of obsolescence are emphasized as critical characteristics of the ramifications of our design work. The anthropogenic building stock is shown to be a huge physical remainder of the actions of previous generations in the making of the buildings and cities that served their needs and now serve ours.

A serious, and multi-disciplinary reconsideration of the appropriate design lives for buildings of

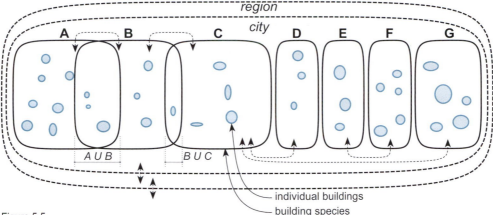

Figure 5.5

Distinct occupancies (such as commercial, residential, institutional, theater etc.) can be used to segregate build-ings into separate populations **A-G** (or species) that transfer materials and energy between each other and the larger environment. The metabolism of individual buildings can be characterized as part of the typical attributes of its species, while the total transfer of materials and energy between the collection of species (A-G) and the larger environments (city and region) defines the ecological burden (or the industrial ecology) of the built world. Note again here, as in Chapter 2, there is an emphasis on the role of the substantial anthropogenic stock of buildings as a fundamental, and growing, material resource. The densification of cities and urban/suburban sprawl are both evidence of the retention of a substantial mass of materials within the anthropogenic stock of existing buildings. Additions to this anthropogenic stock are illustrated as new members of the population of each species (the shaded ellipses). Overlaps in building types, such as commercial office space and institutional office space are represented as the union between sets of distinct species (such as $A \cup B$ and $B \cup C$).

all types is acting to prompt designers to specify more focused building lifetimes; very long-life buildings, or very short-life buildings, or moveable buildings and others focused on hedging the risk of misutilizing material resources in the making of architecture.

All of these issues, and the parallels between natural ecologies and industrial networks of material and energy exchanges, can be used to study the necessary attributes of a construction ecology able to produce, maintain and decommission buildings while directing physical resources responsibly and economically. The study of industrial ecology addresses these issues from a point of view that specifies the individual actors that inhabit a complex system of linked material and energy flows.

At the inception, during the mid-1980s, of the study of human industrial activity from the point of view of linked material and energy pathways, a discussion ensued about which of two phrases best characterized the aspirations of the emerging discipline; *industrial metabolism* or *industrial ecology* (Lifset 2004;Ayres 1989;Ayres and Ayres 1996). Originally proposed by Robert Ayres, the phrase *industrial metabolism* has been largely replaced by *industrial ecology*. While it has been useful to prefer one phrase over another in advancing the field, there are opportunities that arise from making clear distinctions between the two and placing them in a complementary relationship in the discussion of buildings.

For example, metabolism may be utilized best as a way of investigating the actual consumption of materials and energy by *autonomous actors* (individual buildings) that inhabit the larger spatial and temporal context of an ecological system. These individual actors compete for and trade necessary materials and energy as they live out their lives within the system boundaries of a larger set of linked resource flows (ecology). Their overall lives are determined by their "fitness" to serve as productive members of their species (building type), and society as a whole.

Applying this to architecture provides a useful means with which to link individual buildings within the complex system of energy and material flows within cities, regions and national borders driven by the activities of construction, operation, maintenance, repair, adaptive reuse and demolition (Chapter 2, Figures 2.13-2.17). In other words, *metabolism* is a useful analogy for the material and energy flows of the organisms of individual buildings through their service lives while *ecology* is a useful term that defines the flows that result from the interaction between the collection of these buildings and the larger physical context. Using the metabolism analogy, we can propose that the application of industrial ecology to architecture can be achieved productively if we distinguish the resource consumption of the artifact of the building (a complex system in itself) from that of collections of like buildings (species) within the spatial, temporal and organizational contexts that regulate material and energy flows.

As shown in "Industrial Ecology of Buildings", Chapter 2, building use occupancies are an attribute of architecture that generates a classification that parallels the grouping of like entities into evolving populations, or *species*. Each species in turn, characterizes a typical lifetime *envelope* in which size and lifetime are correlated. These species, and their populations of individual buildings, inhabit the environment that allows for ecological structures to flourish, see Figure 5.4.

Therefore, a useful definition of the ecology of construction is the study of the metabolism of building species within the regulating networks of social, economic, political and physical boundaries (city and region) that influence the flow of materials and energy, Figure 5.5. This definition maintains that the fundamental contribution of the notion of *metabolism* is measured and characterized as an attribute of the building itself.

Also, the fundamental contribution of construction ecology is accomplished by studying the behavior of these building species through appropriately formulated measures of material transfers and stores. A hallmark of industrial ecology has been the development of techniques for the measurement and accounting of the actual flows of material and energy through contemporary society. Life Cycle Assessment (LCA), Material Flow Analysis (MFA), Material Intensity Per Unit Service (MIPS), Total Material Requirement and Output (TMRO) and other methods currently exist for the purpose of accounting for transfers of the physical economy (Daniels 2002a, b). There is continuing debate about these techniques, the relationship between the set and the most effective application of each (Brunner 2002a, b;Lifset 2001, 2004). Therefore, further work is required to fully assess the most appropriate methods to apply to the various scales of material flows in construction.

Adaptive Capacity and Sustainable Design

Recently, within several engineering and design disciplines, two separate discussions have been flowing past one another, occasionally mixing and spawning new and useful perspectives regarding the role of design in altering the way we use our material and energy resources. The first discussion has been outlined above - that of industrial ecology and the study of material and energy flows.

The second discussion addresses the challenges of becoming more engaged in an assessment of future needs for the purpose of planning for the most effective distribution of resources. This discussion primarily arises out of the academic community serving business and financial theory and the development of techniques for improved decision-making for policy analysts (Black and Scholes 1973;Trigeorgis 2002;Bell et al. 1988;Morgan and Henrion 1990). This discussion raises the challenge of improving the ways in which any discipline can better assess the uncertainties inherent in dynamic situations and identify the upside potential for carefully managing decisions about the allocation of all kinds of resources. Both decision-making theories and financial valuation models that tackle the various idiosyncrasies of working in the present for gain in the future have contributed to this discussion.

For example, the development of the theory of financial options in the 1970s has led to an explosion of ideas to develop options for real assets - that is, physical assets, such as mining assets (oil, coal and other minerals), manufacturing resources, design options etc. This study of *Real Options* is essentially another way of designing for the future - an activity particularly relevant to architecture.

It is evident that there is a productive link between issues of material and energy flows and studies in uncertainty because both domains are intent on assessing present conditions for the purpose of engaging productively with the future. In addition, the link becomes dramatically stronger when viewed from the perspective of an architectural proposal for the simple reason that this kind of work requires the movement of great quantities of material and energy based on a prediction of needs in the present and the future. Therefore, the architect is the ultimate actor working to most effectively align the resources of construction with future needs. Clearly, the spectre of substantial uncertainty hovers between a future of great success or great waste.

Interestingly, the discussion of uncertainty and resource planning has prompted a reconsideration of the most fundamental statements of sustainable design by those working within industrial ecology. Because sustainable design is, by definition, simultaneously concerned with the present and the future needs of society, it is inherently involved in the business of envisioning a future state of affairs. One only need recall the most widely quoted statement of sustainable development:

> ...development that meets the needs of the present without compromising the ability
> of future generations to meet their own needs.
>
> World Commission on Employment, 1987

to realize that the prediction, or at least the envisioning, of a future state is strongly compelled by this idea. And yet, the notion that we could or should envision the future for those coming generations stands in opposition to a very important fundamental characteristic of natural ecologies - that of *adaptability*.

It has been shown, in the natural sciences, that ecologies are robust systems that possess significant capacity for adaptation to changing conditions (Bey 2001;Holling 2001). Recently, a paper in the *Journal of Industrial Ecology* noted the significance of this resilience in natural systems through the work of the noted ecologist C.S. Holling (Spiegelman 2003). This resilience lends backing to the argument that it may be more productive to step back from a process of attempting predictive visions of an ideal "sustainable" future. It may be more useful to embark on the diverse and design-oriented task of developing technologies, building form, building systems and other physical constructs that embody *adaptive capacities*.

Financial tools, such as the use of real option theory, have been applied to the valuation of a capacity to adapt to changing conditions. The statement, "Flexibility is of no value in the absence of the resources required for execution" (Kogut 1994) makes it very clear that the value of adaptation is mute without actual capacity to do so. For architectural proposals this involves actually designing physical systems such that a useful adaptation may be accessed at some undetermined point in the future. This may be as simple as allowing for the easy reclamation of components from a building enclosure for maximum recycling of materials. Or it may involve designing a structure such that it allows for the broadest possibilities of changing uses and adaptive reuse. In each case, both the actual *physical capacity* to adapt and the *option value* for adapting in the future are critical components of an architecture that strives for realistic service to future generations (Greden 2005).

In addition, the fact that ecologies tend to be fundamentally able to shift patterns of consumption to enable the continued use of valuable resources also means that industrial systems may be naturally "tuned" for maximum efficiency of resource exploitation. In fact, countering the generally benign notion of ecological systems, industrial ecologies may be driven to compete with the natural world for resources to the extent that the results conflict with the goals of sustainable development. That is, industrial ecologies may prove to be very good at maximum material consumption. If this is the case, then self-conscious design for managing resource exploitation will be a necessary aspect of building ecologies for responsible materials use (Spiegelman 2003;Schneider and Kay 1994).

The reality of adaptive capacities in industrial ecologies, and the opportunities for shaping those ecologies, will most likely allow for both positive and negative consequences. The adaptive capacities of industrial ecologies will present positive opportunities to refrain from having to predict the future while guiding the likely paths for future consumption. They will also allow for multiple possibilities and necessary design and engineering strategies for curtailing the "natural" consumption efficiencies of industrial networks that may result in rampant material and energy resource depletion. In either case, the future role of the architect is certain to be modulated by the need to engage with the future in a more active and direct way.

A Flourishing Design Future

John Ehrenfeld writes that the analogy of ecology as applied to human activities reaches its successful culmination when we can focus on providing the adaptive capacity such that all life will "flourish on the planet forever" (Ehrenfeld 2004). This is a very different notion of the goal of acting today so as not to compromise the possibilities for future generations. In essence, it places front and center the idea that adaptation, and therefore continuous reevaluation of the context and the choices that evolve, is the dominant mode for a humane and ecologically prosperous future. It also quietly maintains within itself the understanding that no future can be as blessed as the present with the material and energy resources currently available.

And therefore the real power of design resides in the potential inherent in the creative process of matching needs with form and material. An infinite set of possibilities characterizes the work of designers. It is this infinite set that lends promise to the possibility of a future in which all life will "flourish on the planet forever". An intriguing set of opportunities becomes evident. Architects are not only capable and responsible for designing buildings but also have the capacity for building ecologies - one building at a time.

General Notes

Before each one of the three major sections of this Bibliography, I note significant publications relevant to the topics discussed within. The list of publications includes important primary sources of general information, highly relevant specialized research findings published in architecture and building technology journals, significant papers from other types of journals, useful literature reviews, papers from edited compilations, working papers, books, and a small amount of material acquired from various sites on the internet. Discussions with knowledgeable persons are not separately identified but assumed to contribute to the overall content of the book, unless a specific point is being stressed. The sources are meant as supporting evidence to particular points made in the text, suggestions for further reading, and links to an expansion of the ideas covered narrowly here for the focused purpose of this book.

Websites are listed only when they fulfill two criteria. First, they must offer more than a simplified, or clearly prejudiced view of their subject matter. As author, I've taken responsibility for making judgments about oversimplifcation or the presence of distorted points of view. It is true that most trade group or association sites, such as the Nickel Development Institute, are by their very mandate, advocacy organizations that will take a particularly positive view of their client. For example, these groups are guaranteed to articulate a positive perspective on the sustainable charateristics of their respective materials. Clearly, these viewpoints need to be assessed critically with independent information sources. However, these sites are valuable in that they contain some of the best indications of the state of the industry, its direction and its concerns. Often these sites can also lead to important links and other information sources outside of the association. Individual companies sites, however, are even less likely to find a place in the references here. However, I have included several for the particularly detailed information they provide not only about the characteristics of the products and materials that they use but also the behavior of the product (and therefore similar products of other companies) in an architectural assembly. Therefore, manufacturers' sites that provide good MSDS (material data safety sheets) describing in detail the material contents of their products will be included here. Also, corporate sites that provide information using accepted and certified standards (such as ASTM test results) may also be included. Any tests not regulated by accepted standards are not included here.

The second criteria is one of stability. All of the sites chosen must be relatively stable sites, likely to remain at the same URL over the foreseeable future. It is understood that one cannot accurately predict whether a site will continue to publish and stay current. However, one suspects that sites such as www.steel.org and www.plastics.org will last for some time to come. This, again, is a difficult criteria for many corporations to fulfill. Unfortunately and for obvious reasons, large Fortune 500 companies with sites like www.dupont.com, www.3M.com etc. are more likely to be included here (assuming the other criteria are met) than the sites of smaller companies. Because innovation in materials and their diffusion into the marketplace is greatly influenced by the private, for-profit sectors, it is worthwhile including material from them. Every attempt has been made to render the state of the art in an equitable way such that this book does not support or advocate the use of any particular product from any single company. References to particular products have been done for the purpose of illustrating a larger trend or innovation and uusally implies the availability of similar products.

Prologue: Building Design

Literature included here on the technology of buildings is extensive, varied and the manifestation of the work of both architectural and engineering disciplines. Practicing architects that have written on the subject have often taken on the role of advocacy that best serves their design production. This is understandable due to the fact that the primary product of these persons is usually the built thing, not a written work. Other sources for the topic of technology in architecture have been the writing of some specialists, usually academics that have specialized in the history of technological innovation in architecture. Tom Peters' book *Technological Innovation during the Nineteenth Century* serves as a primary source for civil innovation during the rapld mobilization of large-scale machines engaged in projects of previously unheard of ambition and scope. Also, Cecil Elliot's book, *Technics and Architecture*, is an elegant and very useful history of the evolution of the technology of the primary building materials and modern building systems. The book is particularly useful as a description of the transfer and evolution of technologies to the United States as they were brought from England and adapted for use in the New World. Chapter

7 of Alberto Perez-Gomez's book, *Architecture and the Crisis of Modern Science*, provides great insight into the fitful relationship between science and technology at the inception of analytical techniques. Other important sources include Basalla, Kuhn, Cowan, Daniels, Frampton, Manzini and Turner.

Auer, G. (1995) Building Materials are Artifical by Nature. *Daidalos, Architektur, Kunst, Kultur,* June 1995, pp. 20-35.

Basalla, G. (1988) *The Evolution of Technology*. Cambridge University Press, Cambridge, UK.

Beukers, A. van H., Editor (1998) *Lightness: the inevitable renaissance of minimum energy structures*. 010 Publishers, Rotterdam.

Calvino, I. (1988) *Six Memos for the Next Millennium*. Harvard University Press, Cambridge.

Cornish E.H. (1987) *Materials and the Designer.* Cambridge University Press, Cambridge, UK.

Cowan, H. J., Smith, P. R. (1988) *The Science and Technology of Building Materials*. Van Nostrand Reinhold, New York.

Daniels, K. (1997) *The Technology of Ecological Building, Basic Principles and Measures, Examples and Ideas*. Birkhauser, Munich.

Daniels, K. (1998) *Low-Tech Light-Tech High-Tech, Building in the Information Age*. Birkhauser, Munich.

DiTomas, E. E. (1996) New Materials for the 21st Century. In: Ken P. Chong, ed., *Materials for the New Milennium*, Proceedings of the Fourth Materials Engineering Conference, Materials Engineering Division of the American Society of Civil Engineers, Washington, DC, November 10-14, Volume 1, pp.14-22.

Elliot, C. D. (1992) *Technics and Architecture: The Development of Materials and Systems for Buildings*. MIT Press, Cambridge.

Frampton, K. (1995) *Studies in Tectonic Culture: The Poetics of Construction in Nineteenth and Twentieth Century Architecture*. MIT Press, Cambridge, MA.

Frampton, K. (1999) Between Earthwork and Roofwork: Reflections on the Future of the Tectonic Form. In: *Form and Structure*, Lotus International 99, Rivistra trimestrale di architettura, pp. 24-31.

Gregotti, V. (1996) *Inside Architecture*. The MIT Press, Cambridge.

Groak, S. (1992)*The Idea of Building*. E & F Spon, London.

Kahn, L. (1944) Monumentality, from New Architecture and City Planning, a symposium edited by Paul Zucker.

LeCorbusier (1931) *Towards a New Architecture*. John Rodker, London.

Manzini, E. (1989) *The Material of Invention*. The MIT Press, Cambridge.

Mori, T. (2002) *Immaterial Ultramaterial: Architecture, Design and Materials*. Harvard Design School in association with George Braziller, New York.

Pallasmaa, J. (1994) Six themes for the next millennium. *The Architectural Review*, Volume CXCVI, No. 1169, pp. 74-79.

Pearson, C. A. (2001) Material Affairs, Tod Williams and Billie Tsien talk about going slowly and letting materials emerge from place, time, and process. *Architectural Record*, March: pp. 68-72.

Schwartz, M. (1996) *Emerging Engineering Materials*. Technomic, Basel, Switzerland.

Tenner, E. (1997) *When Things Bite Back: Technology and the Revenge of Unintended Consequences*. Vintage Books, New York.

Timberlake, J. (2001) *Transfer Technologies: Transfer Materials, Transfer Processes*. Latrobe Fellowship Status Report Talk given to the American Institute of Fellows: December 8, 2001.

Turner, R. G. (1986) *Construction Economics and Building Design*. Van Nostrand Reinhold, New York.

Wigginton M. H. J. (2002) *Intelligent Skins*. Butterworth-Heinemann, Oxford.

I Time

The first part of this book is generally influenced by work in the fields of the history of science and research and the development of industrial ecology. Chapter 1 outlines the rise of organized research initiatives that have had an impact in architectural materials. Chapter 2 is broadly indebted to the emerging discipline of industrial ecology (IE). Important sources in this area include books by Graedel, and both volumes by Kibert as well as many papers, mostly from the *Journal of Industrial Ecology* and several publications from the Wuppertal Institute and the World Resources Institute. On issues of material flows, Material Flow Analysis, national, regional and international material production and consumption data, industry material uses and other information relevant to the flow of materials in contemporary society these several key sources form the basis for conclusions reached in Chapter 2 Time and Materials. Other important sources for these chapters include; Chapter 1 - Bakis, Bentur, Elliot, Ford, Frampton, Fridley, Moavenzadeh, Perez-Gomez, Peters, Chapter 2 - Abramson, Ayres, Bringezu, Geiser, Lynch, Matos, Slaughter, Tilton,

Weizsacker and Wernick. The leading journal addressing the rich and ongoing discussion of industrial ecology is the *Journal of Industrial Ecology* published by the MIT Press.

1   Matters of Research

Abbott, C. (1996) Long Life Ambition. Nickel. NiDi, *The Nickel Development Institute*, Vol. 12(1), Autumn.

Alberti, L. B. [1550] (1999). *On the Art of Building in Ten Books*, Cambridge: MIT Press.

Allen, E. (2004) In conversation regarding the persistent intellectual distance between design and technology teaching. Cambridge, MA.

Ashby, M. F., Evans, E. G., Fleck, N. A., Gibson, L. J., Hutchinson, J. W., Wadley, H. N. G. (2000) *Metal Foams: A Design Guide*. Butterworth-Heinemann.

Bakis, C.E., Bank, L.C., Brown, M., Cosenza, E., Davalos, J.F., Lesko, J.J., Machida, S.H., Rizkalla, S.H., Triantafillou, T.C., (2002) Fiber-Reinforced Polymer Composites for Construction – State-of-the-Art Review. American Society of Civil Engineers, J*ournal of Materials in Civil Engineering*, Vol. 6, No. 2:pp. 73-87.

Basalla, G. (1988) *The Evolution of Technology*. Cambridge, Cambridge University Press: pp. 91-102, 128.

Bentur, A., (2002) Cementitious Materials – Nine Millennia and a New Century: Past, Present, and Future. American Society of Civil Engineers, *Journal of Materials in Civil Engineering*, Vol.1 4, No. 1: pp. 2-22.

Bernal, J.D. (1954) *Science in History: Volume 2, The Scientific and Industrial Revolutions*. The MIT Press: pp.412-414,562-3, 596-598.

Beukers, A. van H., Editor (1998) *Lightness: the inevitable renaissance of minimum energy structures*. 010 Publishers, Rotterdam.

Bijker, Wiebe E. (1995) *Of Bicycles, Bakelites, and Bulbs: Toward a Theory of Sociotechnical Change*. MIT Press, Cambridge.

Campbell, C., (1967) 1715-25, *Vitruvius Britannicus or The British Architect*, Vol. I, London 1715; Vol. II 1717; Vol. III, London 1725, reprinted, New York.

Coulomb, Charles-Auguste. (1773) Sur l'Application des Reglés de Maximis et Minimis à Quelques Problèmes de Statique Relatifs à l'Architecture In: *Collection de Mémoires Relatifs à la Physique*. Paris.

Cowan, R. S. (1997) *A Social History of American Technology*. Oxford University Press, New York, NY.

Elliot, C.D. (1992) *Technics and Architecture: The Development of Materials and Systems for Buildings*. The MIT Press, Cambridge, MA.

Fitchen, J. (1994) *Building Construction Before Mechanization*. The MIT Press, Cambridge, MA.

Fontana, C. (1694) *Il Tiempo Vaticano e Sua Origine*. Rome.

Ford, E. (1996) *Details of Modern Architecture, Volume 2*. Cambridge: MIT Press.

Frampton, K. (1996) The Owl of Minerva: An Epilogue. In: *Studies in Tectonic Culture: The Poetics of Construction in Nineteenth and Twentieth Century Architecture*. The MIT Press, Cambridge, MA: pp. 377-387.

Fridley, K.J. (2002) Wood and Wood-Based Materials: Current Status and Future of a Structural Material. American Society of Civil Engineers, *Journal of Materials in Civil Engineering,* Vol.14, No.2: pp. 91-96.

Gautier, H. (1727) *Traité des Ponts*. Paris: 1727-28.

Gregotti, V. (1996) *Inside Architecture*. The MIT Press, Cambridge.

Hartoonian, G. (1986) Poetics of Technology and the New Objectivity. *The Journal of Architectural Education*, Fall 1985, pp. 14-19.

Heyman, J. (1995) *The Stone Skeleton: Structural Engineering of Masonry Architecture*. Cambridge University Press, Cambridge, UK.

Heyman, J. (1998) *Structural Analysis: A Historical Approach*. Cambridge University Press, Cambridge, UK.

Heyman, J. (2002) Wren, Hooke and Partners. In: *Proceedings of the First International Congress on Construction History*. Instituto Juan de Herrera, Madrid, Spain.

Hill, J. (2003) Hunting the shadow – immaterial architecture. *The Journal of Architectural Education*, Vol.8: pp.165-179.

Hillig,W. B. (1976) New Materials and Composites. *Science*, New Series, Vol. 191, Issue 4228, 733-739.

Hitchcock, H. R. (1942) *In the Nature of Materials: 1887-1941 The Buildings of Frank Lloyd Wright*. Da Capo Press, New York.

Holton, G. (1996) On the Art of Scientific Imagination. In: Managing Innovation. *Dædalus, Journal of the American Academy of Arts and Sciences*, Spring, pp.183-208.

Hughes, T. P. (1989) *American Genesis: A Century of Invention and Technological Enthusiasm*. Viking, New York, NY.

Hurley, D. (1982) About Making. *Perspecta: The Yale Architectural Journal*, Vol. 19, pp. 83-86.

Intrachooto, S. (2002) Technological Innovation in Architecture: Effective Practices for Energy Efficient Implementation. Ph.D. Dissertation, Department of Architecture, MIT: pp. 195-205.

Jacob, M.C. (1997) *Scientific Culture and The Making of the Industrial West*. Oxford University Press, New York, NY.

JNMR (1998) The Newsletter of Japan's Engineered Materials Industry. *Japan New Materials Report,* Vol. XIII, No. 1, January-February, 1998. pp.2-16.

Keller, T. (2003) Use of fibre reinforced polymers in bridge construction. *Journal of the International Association for Bridge and Structural Engineering* (IABSE), ETH, Hönggerberg, Zurich.

King, R. (2000) *Brunelleschi's Dome: The Story of the Great Cathedral in Florence*. Pimlico, London, UK: pp. 154-159.

Kranzberg, M. S. Stanley, C. (1988) Chapter 4, Materials in History and Society. In: Forester, Tom, editor. *The Materials Revolution: Superconductors, New Materials, and the Japanese Challenge*. MIT Press, Cambridge, MA.

Kuhn, T.S. (1962) *The Structure of Scientific Revolutions*. Cambridge, Mass., The MIT Press: pp. 164-170.

Latour, B., Woolgar, S. (1986) *Laboratory Life*. Princeton University Press, Princeton, NJ.

Latour, B. (1987) *Science in Action*. Harvard University Press, Cambridge, MA.

LeCorbusier (1935). *Aircraft*. London: The Studio: p.13.

LeCorbusier (1927) *Towards a New Architecture*. trans. Etchells, F. Rodker, London.

Magee, J. H., Schnell, R. E. (2002) Stainless Steel Rebar. *Advanced Materials and Processes*. October, pp. 43-45.

Mark, R. Editor (1993) *Architectural Technology Up to the Scientific Revolution*. The MIT Press, Cambridge, MA.

Markaki, A.E. Westgate, S.A. Clyne, T.W. (2002a) the stiffness and weldability of an ultra-light steel sandwich sheet material with a fibrous metal core. Working paper to be published in Ghosh A.K., Claar T.D., Sanders T.H., editor, *Processing and Properties of Lightweight Cellular Metals and Structures*. TMS, Seattle, February. 17-21, 2002.

Markaki, A.E. Clyne, T.W. (2003b) Mechanics of ultra-light stainless steel sandwich sheet material, Part I. Stiffness. *Acta Materiali*, Vol.51. pp. 1341-1350.

Markaki, A.E. Clyne, T.W. (2003c) Mechanics of ultra-light stainless steel sandwich sheet material, Part II. Resistance to delamination. *Acta Materiali*, Vol.51. pp. 1351-1357.

McClellan III, J.E. Dorn, H. (1999) *Science and Technology in World History*. The John Hopkins University Press, Baltimore, Maryland.

Moavenzadeh, F., Editor (1990) *Concise Encyclopedia of Building & Construction Materials*. Cambridge, MIT Press.

NMAB (2000) *Materials in the New Millenium: Responding to Society's Needs*. National Materials Advisory Board, National Academy Press, Washington, DC.

Nicolaïdis E. Chatzis K. (2000) *Technological Traditions and national Identities: A Comparison between France and Great Britain during the 19th Century. Science, Technology and the 19th Century State*. Institut de Recherches Neohelleniques, pp. 13-21.

Pacey, A. (1992) *Technology in World Civilization*. The MIT Press, Cambridge, MA.

Palladio, A. (1570) *The Four Books on Architecture*. Venice: Dominico de' Franceshi.

Perez-Gomez, A. (1994) *Architecture and the Crisis of Modern Science*. Cambridge: MIT Press.

Peters, T. (1996) *Building the Nineteenth Century*. The MIT Press, Cambridge, MA.

Peters, T. (2003) Technological thought and theory, a culture of construction. In: *Proceedings of the First International Congress on Construction History*. Instituto Juan de Herrera, Madrid, Spain: pp.1629-1637.

Pevsner, N. (1968) *The Sources of Modern Architecture and Design*. London, Thames and Hudson: pp.9-20.

Restany, P. (1997) New craftsmanship as the catalyst of global communication. *Domus* 796, September 1997, pp. 109-112.

Robbin, T. (1996) Chapter 8: Materials. In: *Engineering a New Architecture*. Yale University Press, New Haven, pp. 100-115.

Sebestyen, G. (1998) *Construction: craft to industry*. E & F Spon, London.

Strike, J. (1991) *Construction into Design, The Influence of New Methods of Construction on Architectural*

Design, 1690-1990. Butterworth-Heinemann Ltd, Oxford.

Sivakumar, K. (2002) Discussion of "Cementitious Materials: Nine Millennia and a New Century: Past, Present, and Future." American Society of Civil Engineers, *Journal of Materials in Civil Engineering*, Vol. 15, No. 4, pp. 2-22.

Stearns, P.N. (1993) *Industrial Revolution in World History*. Westview Press, Boulder, Colorado.

Timoshenko, S.P. (1953) *History of Strength of Materials: With a brief account of the history of theory of elasticity and theory of structures*. McGraw-Hill Book Company, Inc., New York.

Turner, R. G. (1986) *Construction Economics and Building Design*. Van Nostrand Reinhold, New York.

Vitruvius (translated by Granger, F.) (1999a). *On Architecture: Books I-V*. Harvard University Press, Cambridge, MA.

Vitruvius (translated by Granger, F.) (1999b). *On Architecture: Books VI-X*. Harvard University Press, Cambridge, MA.

Von Meiss, P. (2000) The aesthetics of gravity. *Architectural Research Quarterly*, Vol. 4, No. 3, pp.237-245.

Watson, D. (1997) Architecture, Technology, and Environment. *Journal of Architectural Education*, ACSA,119-126.

Whitehead, A. N. (1925) *Science and the Modern World*. Macmillan, New York: pg. 98.

Williams, S. P. (2000) Invasion of the Design Lab Mutants. *The New York Times*, May 11.

Yoshino, M. (1990) Development of resin-coated stainless steel in Japan. *The Nickel Development Institute, NiDi Research Report*.

Zambonini, G. (1988) Notes for a Theory of Making in a Time of Necessity. *Perspecta 24, The Yale Architectural Journal*, pp. 3-23.

2   Time and Materials

Abramson, D.M. (2005) Discourses of Obsolescence. A talk delivered as part of the seminar: *The Culture and Politics of the Built Environment in North America,* delivered at the Charles Warren Center for Studies in American History, Harvard University on February 14, 2005 as part of the tenure of Mr. Abramson as a Warren Center Fellow.

Adriannse, A., Bringezu, S., Hammond, A., Moriguchi, Y., Rodenburg, E. and others (1997) *Resource flows - The material basis of industrial economies*. World Resource Institute, Washington D.C.

Allenby, B. R. (1999) *Industrial Ecology: Policy Framework and implementation*. Prentice-Hall, Englewood Cliffs, NJ.

Amato, I. (1997) *Stuff: The Materials the World is Made of*. Basic Books, New York.

Ayres, R. U. (1994) *Industrial Metabolism: Theory and Policy*. In: The Greening of Industrial Ecosystems, National Academy Press, Washington, DC, pp. 23-37.

Ayres, R. U. (2002) Industrial ecology and the built environment. In: Kibert, C., ed., *Construction Ecology: Nature as a basis for green buildings*. Spon Press, London, UK, pp.159-176.

Balkau, F. (2002) Construction ecology. In: Kibert, C., ed., *Construction Ecology: Nature as a basis for green buildings*. Spon Press, London, UK: pp. 220-226.

Bartelmus, P. (2002) Dematerialization and Capital Maintenance: Two Sides of the Sustainability Coin. Wuppertal Paper Nr. 120. *Wuppertal Institute of Climate, Environment and Energy*, pp. 7-17.

Bernardini, O., Galli, R. (1993) Dematerialization: Long-term trends in the intensity of use of materials and energy. *Futures*, pp.431-448.

Beukers, A. van H., Editor (1998) *Lightness: the inevitable renaissance of minimum energy structures*. 010 Publishers, Rotterdam.

Billington, D. (1985) *The Tower and the Bridge*. Princeton University Press, Princeton, NJ.

BNABOM (Bulletin of the National Association of Building Owners and Managers) (1930) Ask for more Equitable Obsolescence Allowance. In: *Chicago Office Buildings Demolished to Make Way for New Structures*.

Bolton, R.P. (1911) *Building for Profit: Principles Governing the Economic Improvement of Real Estate*. DeVinne Press, New York.

Brand, S. (1994) *How Buildings Learn: What Happens After They're Built*. Penguin Books, New York, NY.

Brand, S. (2000) *The Clock of the Long Now: Time and Responsibility: The Ideas Behind the World's Slowest Computer*. Basic Books, New York.

Bringezu, S. (2002) Construction ecology and metabolism. In: Kibert, C., ed., *Construction Ecology: Nature as a basis for green buildings*. Spon Press, London, UK, pp. 196-219.

British Geological Survey (2001) World Mineral Statistics, 1992-2000.

Brown III, W. M., Matos, G. R., Sullivan, D. E., (1998) Materials and Energy Flows in the Earth Science Century. *U.S. Geological Survey Circular 1194*, U.S. Department of the Interior, Washington D.C.

Bryson, J. R. (1997) Obsolescence and the Process of Creative Reconstruction. *Urban Studies*, Vol. 34, No. 9, Carfax, pp.1439-1458.

Burton, H. J. (1919) *Valuations and Depreciations of City Buildings: Extracts from Opinions from Leading Authorities*. National Association of Building Owners and Managers, Chicago.

Caples, S., Jefferson, E. (2005) Polycarbonate sheeting used as a wall material in large skylights. Excerpted from a lecture in the MIT Department of Architecture, April.

Chen, P., Chung, D. D. L., (1996) Carbon fiber reinforced concrete as an intrinsically smart concrete for damage assessment during static and dynamic loading. *ACI Mater. J.*, Vol. 93, No. 4, pp. 341-350.

Cheng, L., Subrahmanian, E., Westerberg, A. W., (2003) Design and planning under uncertainty: issues on problem formulation and solution. *Computers and Chemical Engineering*, Vol. 27, pp. 781-801.

Cleveland, C.J., Ruth, M. (1999) Indicators of Dematerialization and the Materials Intensity of Use. State of the Debate, *Journal of Industrial Ecology*, Vol. 2, No. 3, pp. 15-50.

Cornish, E. H. (1987) Chapter 11: Factors controlling the selection of substitute materials. In: *Materials and the Designer*. Cambridge University Press, Cambridge.

Daniels, P.L. (2002) Approaches for Quantifying the Metabolism of Physical Economies: A Comparative Survey, Part I: Methodological Overview. *Journal of Industrial Ecology*, Vol. 5, No. 4, pp. 69-93.

DelMonte, J. (1981) *Technology of Carbon and Graphite Fiber Composites*. Van Nostrand Reinhold: New York.

Douglas, J. (2002) *Building Adaptation*. Butterworth Heinemann, Oxford.

Fernandez, J. (2004) Design for Change, Diversified Lifetimes: Part 1. *Architectural Research Quarterly*, Cambridge, UK, Vol. 7 No.2, pp.169-182.

Foremans Buildings Ltd.: http://www.foremansbuildings.co.uk/

Formoso, C. T., Soibelman L., De Csare, C., Isatto, E. L. (2002) Material waste in building industry: main causes and prevention. *Journal of Construction Engineering and Management*, Vol. 128, No. 4, pp.316-325.

Geiser K. (2001) *Materials Matter: towards a sustainable materials policy*. The MIT Press. Cambridge, Massachusetts.

Goodland, R., Daly, H. (1993) Why Northern Income Growth is Not the Solution to Southern Poverty. *Ecological Economics*, Vol. 8, pp. 85-101.

Graedel, T. E., Allenby, B. R. (2003) *Industrial Ecology: 2nd Edition*. Prentice-Hall, Englewood Cliffs, NJ.

Gray, C. (2005) Once the Tallest Building, but since 1967 a Ghost. In: *Streetscapes*. The New York Times, January 2.

Grübler, A. (1996) Time for a Change: On the Patterns of Diffusion of Innovation. The Liberation of the Environment, *Dædalus, Journal of the American Academy of Arts and Sciences*, Summer, pp. 19-41.

Hebel (2005) AAC block literature. www.hebel.com.

Herman, R., Arkekani, A., Ausubel, J. H. (1989) Dematerialization. In: Ausubel, J.H., Sladovich, H.E., ed.s, *Technology and environment*. by National Academy Press, Washington, D.C., pp. 50-69.

Houghton, T. (1993) On the nature of real estate, monopoly and fallacies of 'monopoly rent'. *International Journal of Urban and Regional Research*, 17, pp. 260-273.

Kahn, E. (2005) Extreme Textiles. *I.D. Mighty Materials*, March/April, pp. 54-63.

Kesler, S. (1994) *Mineral Resources, Economics, and the Environment*. Macmillan, New York, NY.

Keymer, M. A. (2000) Design strategies for new and renovation construction that increase the capacity of buildings to accommodate change. Master of Science, MIT, Cambridge, MA.

Kibert, C. (2003) In conversation with Charles Kibert during the 11th International Rinker Conference on Deconstruction, May 2003, Gainesville, Florida.

Kibert, C.J. (1999a) *Proceedings of the First International Conference of CIB TG 16*. November 6-9, 1999, Tampa, Florida.

Kibert, C. Editor (1999b) *Reshaping the Built Environment*. Island Press, Washington DC.

Kibert, C. Editor (2002) *Construction Ecology: Nature as a basis for green buildings*. Spon Press, London, UK.

Klein, J.L. (1922) Depreciation and Obsolescence. In: *Proceedings of the Annual Convention of the National Association of Building Owners and Managers*.

Krausse, J., Lichtenstein, C. (1999) *Your Private Sky: R. Buckminster Fuller, The Art of Design Science*. Lars Müller Publishers, Zürich, Switzerland.

Kronenburg, R. (1997) *FTL, Tod Dalland, Nicolas Goldsmith - Softness Movement and Light*. Academy Editions, West Sussex.

Labys, W.C. Waddell, L.M. (1989) Commodity lifecycles in US materials demand. *Resources Policy*, Vol. 15, pp. 238-251.

Lamarche, F. (1976) Property development and the economic foundations of the urban question. In: Pickvance, C., ed., *Urban Sociology*. Methuen, London, pp. 85-118.

Liss, H. (2000) *Demolition, The Art of Demolishing, Dismantling, Imploding, Toppling & Razing*. Black Dog and Leventhal Publishers, New York, pp. 108-111.

Lynch, K. (2001) *What Time is this Place?* The MIT Press, Cambridge, MA.

Marx, K. (1984) *Capital, Volume 3*. Lawrence and Wishart, London, UK.

Matos, G., Wagner, L. (1998) *Consumption of Materials in the United States, 1990-1995*. USGS Report, Denver.

Maury, C.L. Jr. (1999) Framework to assess a facility's ability to accommodate change, application to renovated buildings. Master of Science, MIT, Cambridge, MA.

McDonough, W. (1992) *The Hannover Principles: Design for Sustainability*. William McDonough Architects, Charlottesville, VA.

Mikesell, R.F. (1995) The limits to growth, a reappraisal. *Resources Policy* Vol. 21, No. 2, 127-131.

Mines, U.S. Bureau of (1991) Materials shifts in the new society. *New Mat. Soc.*, Vol. 2: pp. 1-15.

Moavenzadeh, F. editor (1990) *Concise Encyclopedia of Building & Construction Materials*. Cambridge, MIT Press.

Mori, T. (2002) *Immaterial Ultramaterial: Architecture, Design and Materials*. Harvard Design School in association with George Braziller, New York.

Nireki, T. (1996). Service life design. *Construction and Building Materials*. Elsevier, Vol. 10, No. 5, pp. 403-406.

Patterson, M. (1998) No time to change: flexible facilities must regroup, reorganize, restructure in an instant. *Buildings*, 92(7): pp. 38-42.

Peters, T. (1989) An American Culture of Construction. *Perspecta 25, The Yale Architectural Journal*, pp.142-161.

Prins, M., Bax, F.T. (1993) Design and decision support systems in architecture. In: Timmermans, H. ed., A Design Decision Support System for Building Flexibility and Costs. Netherlands, Kluwer Academic Publishers, pp. 147-163.

Reynolds DB. (1999) Entropy and diminishing elasticity of substitution. *Resources Policy* Vol. 25, pp. 51-58.

Riley, T. (1995) *Light Construction*. The Museum of Modern Art, New York, 1995.

Roberts, J. (1930) *Obsolescence in the Marshall Field Wholesale Building. Bulletin of the National Association of Building Owners and Managers*, 150, September 1930: pg. 41.

Roberts, N.W. (2003) Design as Material Research: Building a Cathedral to Last 500 Years. *Architectural Research Quaterly*, Vol. 7, Numbers 3/4, pp. 333-351.

Sachs, W. (2000) Development: The Rise and Fall of an Ideal. *Wuppertal Paper Nr. 108*. Wuppertal Institute of Climate, Environment and Energy, pp. 25-27.

Schmidt-Bleek, F. (1993): MIPS - A Universal Ecological Measure? *Fresenius Envir. Bulletin* 2, pp. 306-311.

Schumpeter, J. (1950) *Capitalism, Socialism and Democracy, 3rd Edition*. Harper & Brothers, New York, NY:pg. 83.

Schwartz, J., Gattuso, D. J. (2002) Extended Producer Responsibility: Reexamining its Role in Environmental Progress. *Policy Study Number 293*. The Reason Foundation, Los Angeles, CA.

Slaughter, E. S. (2001) Design strategies to increase building flexibility, *Building Research & Information*, Vol. 29, No. 3, pp. 208-217.

Smith S.D. (2003) *USGS Statistical Summary*. United States Geological Survey, March 2003.

Soronis, G. (1996). Standards for design life of buildings: utilization in the design process. *Construction and Materials*. Elsevier, 1996, pp. 487-490.

Strongwell (2005) Various pultrusion material brochures. from www.strongwell.com.

Tilton J. E. (1979). Exhaustible resources and sustainable development, two different paradigms. *Resources Policy* Vol. 22, No.s 1/2, pp. 91-97.

Tilton J. E. (1983) Material Substitution: lessons from Tin-Using Industries. Resources for the Future, Inc. and Johns Hopkins University Press, Washington, DC, pp. 1-11.

US Census 2000. see http://www.census.gov/main/www/cen2000.html

USGS Minerals Reports, Various (see the USGS web site: www.usgs.gov)

Wagner, L. A., Sullivan, D. E., Sznopek, J. L. (2002) Economic Drivers of Mineral Supply. *USGS Report, U.S. Geological Survey Open File Report*, Denver, pp. 02-335.

Weizsacker, E. U. von, (1998) Dematerialization – Why and How? In: P. Vellinga, F. Berkout, and J. Gupta, *Managing a Materials World*. Kluwer, London.

Wernick I. K., Herman, R., Govind S., Ausubel J. H. (1996) Materialization and Dematerialization: Measures and Trends. In: The Liberation of the Environment. *Dædalus, Journal of the American Academy of Arts and Sciences*. Summer, pp. 171-197.

Wernick, I. K., Herman, R., Govind, S., Ausubel, J.H. (1996) Materialization and Dematerialization:

Wernick, I.K. (2002) Industrial ecology and the built environment. In: Kibert, C., ed., *Construction Ecology: Nature as a basis for green buildings*. Spon Press, London, UK, pp. 177-195.

Wolman, A. (1967) The Metabolism of Cities. *Scientific American*, Vol. 213, No. 3, pp. 178-193.

II   Material

The literature on materials for engineering, industrial and architectural uses is vast, decentralized and presented in a dizzying array of formats at every technical level. This part captures only a small segment of materials literature ouside of architectural applications. However, these sources - Ashby, Cornish, Davis, Gordon, Zahner and others - have been carefully chosen for their utility to the designer. For material properties and selection methodologies, the primary source for this part has been derived from materials science literature. In particular, all of the work of Mike Ashby clearly forms the core for the classification of material families and properties and the approach to materials selection. The materials selection software used to produce many of the graphs and some of the tables is the Cambridge Engineering Selector 4.5 (CES 4.5), available for purchase from Ashby's company, Granta Design Ltd, located in Cambridge, England (www.grantadesign.com). A version specifically designed for the selection of materials for buildings will be available for purchase during the second half of 2005 (a collaboration between the author and GrantaDesign Ltd). Ashby's several books, *Materials Selection in Mechanical Design, Engineering Materials I and II*, and with Kara Johnson, *Materials and Design*, provide the best outline of the array of techniques for the selection of materials for any design application, architectural or otherwise. For each material class, several types of sources were used, including literature from materials science, building science, building construction materials and methods, construction ecology, industrial ecology, and specialized books and papers on specific materials and building systems.

There is an extensive literature regarding the selection of engineering materials for various construction applications. A definitive method for buildings and architecture has not been established primarily because the factors to be considered in construction have not been organized for consideration in an existing methodology. This will hopefully change as the *Granta: Fernandez/Ashby Materials Selector for Buildings and Construction* is released. Therefore, for the purposes of this book the methodologies that have been offered cover a wide range of qualitative guidelines and rules of thumb as well as algorithms for using optimization, risk reduction and decision tree mapping.

Journals that entertain topics in materials for construction include *Building Information and Research, Construction and Building Materials, Cement and Concrete Composites, The Journal of Composites*, and the various journals of the American Society of Civil Engineers (ASCE). Most journal papers cited were found in these journals. It would benefit the architectural community globally, and especially in the United States, to have these journals more widely read and discussed by practicing design professionals. Today internet access to most of these journals is easy and inexpensive.

3   Material Properties and Classes

Allen, E. (1999) *Fundamentals of Building Construction: Materials and Methods, 3rd Edition*. Wiley & Sons, New York.

Ashby, M. F., Evans, A. G., Fleck, N. A., Gibson, L. J., Hutchinson, J. W., Wadley, H. N. G., (2000) *Metal Foams: A Design Guide*. Butterworth-Heinemann, Oxford.

Ashby M. F., Jones D. R. H. (2001a) *Engineering Materials I: an introduction to their properties and applications*. Butterworth-Heinemann.

Ashby M. F., Jones D. R. H. (2001b) *Engineering Materials II: an introduction to microstructures processing and design*. Butterworth-Heinemann.

Ashby M. F., Johnson K. (2002) *Materials and Design: The Art and Science of Materials Selection in Product Design*. Butterworth-Heinmann, Oxford.

ASM International (American Society of Materials): see http://www.asm-intl.org/

ASTM C 1018-97 (1998) *Standard Test Method for Flexural Toughness and First-Crack Strength of Fiber-Reinforced Concrete (Using Beam with Third-Point Loading)*. Vol. 4.02, Committee on Standards, ASTM, Philadelphia.

Baccini, P. (1991) *Metabolism of the anthroposphere*. Springer-Verlag, Berlin, Germany.

Barr, B., Gettu, R., Al-Oraimi, S. K. A., Bryars, L. S. (1996) Toughness Measurement – the Need to Think Again. *Cement and Concrete Composites*. Vol. 18, pp. 281-297.

Block, V.L. (2002) *The Use of Glass in Buildings: STP1434*. ASTM International, West Conshohocken, PA, USA.

British Geological Survey (2001) *World Mineral Statistics, 1992-2000*. See http://www.bgs.ac.uk/

Brock, L. (2005) *Designing the exterior wall: An architectural guide to the vertical envelope*. John Wiley & Sons, New York, USA.

Brown III, W. M., Matos, G. R., Sullivan, D. E. (1998) Materials and Energy Flows in the Earth Science Century. *U.S. Geological Survey Circular 1194*, U.S. Department of the Interior, Washington D.C.

Brunner, P.H. (2004) Materials Flow Analysis and the Ultimate Sink. *Journal of Industrial Ecology*, Vol. 8, No. 3, pp.4-7.

Callister Jr., William D. (2003) *Materials Science and Engineering*. Wiley & Sons, New York.

Cornish, E.H. (1987) *Materials and the Designer*. Cambridge University Press, Cambridge.

Cowan, H. J., Smith, P. R. (1988) *The Science and Technology of Building Materials*. Van Nostrand Reinhold, New York.

DiTomas, E.E. (1996) New Materials for the 21st Century. *Proceedings of the Fourth Materials Engineering Conference*, Washington, DC, Vol. 1, ASCE, New York, pp. 14-22.

Doran, D. K. Editor (1995) *Construction Materials Reference Book*. Butterworth-Heinmann, Oxford.

Ehrenfeld, J. R. (2004) Can Industrial Ecology be the "Science of Sustainability"? *Journal of Industrial Ecology*, Vol. 8, No. 1-2, pp.1-3.

Everett, A. (1998) *Materials, 5th Edition*. Longman, Essex, UK.

Gopalaratnam, V.S. (1995) On the characterization of flexural toughness in fiber reinforced concretes. *Cement and Concrete Composites*. Vol. 17, pp. 239-254.

Gordon, J. E. (1988) *The New Science of Strong Materials*. Princeton University Press, Princeton.

Graedel, T. E., Allenby, B.R. (2003) *Industrial Ecology: 2nd Edition*. Prentice-Hall, Englewood Cliffs, NJ.

Hagan, S. (1998) The good, the bad and the juggled: the new ethics of building materials. *The Journal of Architecture*, Vol. 3, pp.107-115.

Harper, C., Editor in Chief (2000) *Modern Plastics Handbook*. McGraw-Hill, New York.

Heyman, J. (1995) *The Stone Skeleton: Structural Engineering of Masonry Architecture*. Cambridge University Press, Cambridge, UK.

Hondros, E. D. (1988) Chapter 3, Materials, Year 2000. In: Forester, Tom, ed., *The Materials Revolution: Superconductors, New Materials, and the Japanese Challenge*. The MIT Press, Cambridge, MA.

Incropera, F. P, DeWitt, D. P. (2002) *Fundamentals of Heat and Mass Transfer*. Wiley & Sons, New York.

Kesler, S. (1994) *Mineral Resources, Economics, and the Environment*. Macmillan, New York, NY.

Kingery, W. D., Bowen, H. K., Uhlmann, D. R. (1976) *Introduction to Ceramics*. John Wiley & Sons, New York, pg. 5.

Lesko, J. (1999) *Industrial Design: Materials and Manufacturing Guide*. Wiley & Sons, New York.

Lifset, R. (2004) Probing Metabolism. *Journal of Industrial Ecology*, Vol. 8, No. 3, pp.1,2.

Moavenzadeh, F., Editor (1990) *Concise Encyclopedia of Building & Construction Materials*. Pergamon, Oxford, UK.

Ochsendorf, J. (2002) *Collapse of Masonry Structures*. PhD Dissertation, King's College, University of Cambridge, UK.

Pascoe, K. J. (1978) *An Introduction to the Properties of Engineering Materials*. Van Nostrand Reinhold, New York.

Reid, E. (1995) *Understanding Buildings: A Multidisciplinary Approach*. MIT Press, Cambridge.

Robbin, T. (1996) Chapter 8: Materials. In: *Engineering a New Architecture*. Yale University Press, New Haven, pp. 100-115.

Taylor, G. D. (2000) *Materials in Construction, 3rd Edition*. Longman, Essex, UK.

Trechsel, H. Editor (2001) *Moisture Analysis and Condensation Control in Building Envelopes*. ASTM, West Conshohocken, USA.

US Bureau of Mines: see http://pubs.usgs.gov/products/books/usbmcirc.html
USGS (United States Geological Survey): see http://www.usgs.gov/
Walker, P. M. B. General Editor (2001) *Materials Science and Technology Dictionary*. Chambers Harrap Publishers, Edinburgh, UK.
Wolman, A. (1967) The Metabolism of Cities. *Scientific American*, Vol. 213, No.3: pp. 178-193.

Websites
Matweb: Material Property Data Online: www.matweb.com
Granta Design Limited (materials selectors for design): www.grantadesign.com
Online Materials Information site: www.azom.com
National Institute of Standards and Technology (materials): www.nist.gov/srd/materials.htm
Mineral Information Institute (an industry education site): www.mii.org

3.1 Metals

Abdul-Wahab, S. A., Bakheit, C. S., Al-Alawi, S.M. (2003) Atmospheric corrosion of metals. *Journal of Corrosion Science and Engineering*, Vol. 5.
Aluminum Now (2005a) Aluminum Hydroforming. Vol. 7, No. 2, pg. 9.
Aluminum Now (2004b) Floor of the Future: Dutch Architect Koolhaas Brings Aluminum Flooring to US. Vol. 6, No. 6, pg. 18.
Aluminum Now (2005c) Blowin' in the Wind: aluminum facades aim to reveal invisible force of nature. Vol. 7, No. 2, pg. 18.
Aluminum Now (2004d) Simple Geometry: design firm touts structural, environmental benefits of modular aluminum housing. Vol. 6, No. 2, pp. 12,13.
Ashby, M. F., Evans, A. G., Fleck, N. A., Gibson, L. J., Hutchinson, J. W., Wadley, H. N. G., (2000) *Metal Foams: A Design Guide*. Butterworth-Heinmann, Oxford.
ASM International (2002) *Atlas of Stress-Strain Curves, 2nd Edition.* ASM international, Materials Park, Ohio.
Bargigli, S., Raugei, M., Ulgiati, S., (2002) A multi-scale and multi-criteria analysis of aluminium "greeness". *Working paper. Energy and Environmental Research Unit*, Department of Chemistry, University of Siena, Italy.
Bernal, J. D. (1954) *Science in History: Volume 2, The Scientific and Industrial Revolutions.* Cambridge, Mass., The MIT Press, pp. 412-13, 562, 596-98.
Cornish, E. H. (1987) Chapter 4: Properties of metals and alloys. In: *Materials and the Designer.* Cambridge University Press, Cambridge, UK.
Davis J.R., Editor (2001) *Alloying: Understanding the Basics*. ASM International, Materials Park, USA.
Degischer, H.P. (1997) Innovative light metals: metal matrix composites and foamed aluminium. *Materials and Design*, Vol. 18, No. 4/6, pp.221-226.
Domininghaus, H. (1988) *Plastics for Engineers*. Hanser Publishers, Munich.
Duocel (2005) *Aluminum Foam product publication now property of ERG Materials and Aerospace Corporation* (see www.ergaerospace.com).
Elias-Ozkan, S.T. (2003) Deconstruction of earthquake-damaged buildings in Turkey. *Deconstruction and Materials Reuse*. CIB Publication 287, *Proceedings of the 11th Rinker International Conference, TG39.*
Fewtrell, J. (2005) News Release - World produces 1.05 billion tonnes of steel in 2004. *International Iron and Steel Institute*, Brussels, Belgium, January 19, 2005.
Fleischman, R.B. Sumer A. (2003) Development of Modular Cast Steel Connections for Seismic-Resistant Building Frames. *Standardization News*, ASTM International, January 2003, pp. 40-43.
Gehry, F.O. (1995) Foreward. In: Zahner, L. W., *Architectural Metals: A Guide to Selection, Specification, and Performance*. Wiley & Sons, New York, NY: pg. xvii.
Geiser, K. (2001) Chapter 9: Recycling and Reuse of Materials. In: Geiser, K., *Materials Matter*. The MIT Press, Cambridge, MA, pp. 215-236.
Hart, S. (1999) Wood versus Steel: Two industries scuffle in a public relations battle for green bragging rights. *Architecture*, April, pp.134, 135.
Hitashi Metals (2002) High-Toughness Fire-Resistant Cast Steel (see www.hitachimetals.com).
Hoeckman, W. (2001) Bridge over the River Loire in Orleans, France. *Structure Engineering International*. Vol. 11, No. 2, pp. 94-98.

Honeycombe, R.W.K. Bhadeshia, H.K.D.H. (1995) *Steels, Microstructure and Properties, 2nd Edition*. Arnold, London.

Jobb, D. (2003a) Ultra-Light Stainless. In: *Nickel, the Magazine Devoted to Nickel and its Applications*. Vol. 18, No. 2, February, pp. 10,11.

Jobb, D. (2003b) Good as New. In: *Nickel, the Magazine Devoted to Nickel and its Applications*. Vol. 18, No. 3, June, pp. 8,9.

Jolly, J. L. (2003) The US Copper-base Scrap Industry and its by-products. *Copper Development Association*, Inc., New York, NY, pp. 14-29.

Kriner, S. (2004) Metal-the Big Green: Metal is a Big Player in the Green Building Movement. *Metalmag*, Vol. 5, No. 8, November/December, pp.64-66.

Knotkova, D., Boschek, P., Kreislova, K. (1995) Effect of acidification on atmospheric corrosion os structural metals in Europe. *Water, Air, Soil Pollution*, Vol. 85, pp. 2661-2666.

Kruger, J. (1990) Corrosion of Metals. In: Moavenzadeh, F. ed., *Concise Encycloperia of Building and Construction Materials*. Pergamon Press, Oxford, pp.151-156.

Llewellyn, D. T. (1994) *Steels - Metallurgy and Applications, 2nd Edition*. Butterworth-Heinemann, Oxford.

Magee, J. H., Schnell R. E. (2002) Stainless steel rebar. *Advanced Materials & Processes*. October, pp.43-45.

Materials Progress (2004) Bridge reinforced with stainless rebar to last for 100 years. *Advanced Materials & Processes*, ASM International Publication, Materials Park, Ohio, Vol. 162, No. 10, pp. 11.

Mikhailov, A. A., Suloeva, M. N., Vasilieva, E.G. (1995) Environmental aspects of atmospheric corrosion. *Water, Air Soil*, Vol. 85, pp. 2673-2678.

Mueller, B. (2005) Investment Casting. *Advanced Materials & Processes*. ASM International Publication, Materials Park, Ohio, Vol. 163, No. 3, pg.30.

NiDI (1996) Long Life Ambition. *Nickel Development Institute, Nickel*, Vol. 12, No. 1, Autumn 1996.

NiDI (2002a) *Stainless Steel in Architecture, Building and Construction: Guidelines for Corrosion Prevention*. Nickel Development Institute, NiDi: Nickel Development Institute. Reference Book Series No. 11, 24.

NiDI (2002b) A Stainless Showpiece. *Nickel Development Institute, Nickel*, Vol. 18, No. 1, October, pp. 12,13.

NiDI (2003) Oregon Bridge Uses Stainless. *Nickel Development Institute, Nickel*, Vol.18, No.2, Feburary, pg. 5.

Pease III, L. F. (2005) A Quick Tour of Powder Metallurgy. *Advanced Materials & Processes*, ASM International Publication, Materials Park, Ohio, Vol. 163, No. 3, pp. 36.

Pevsner, N. (1968) *The Sources of Modern Architecture and Design*. London, Thames and Hudson Ltd, pp. 9-18.

Polmear, I.J . (1995) *Light Alloys, 3rd Edition*. Arnold, London.

Ruth M. (1998) Dematerialization in five US metals sectors: implications for energy use and CO_2 emissions. *Resources Policy*, Vol. 24, No. 1, pp. 1-18.

Saito, M., Iwatsuki, S., Yasunaga, K., Andoh, K. (2000) Development of aluminum body for the most fuel efficient vehicle. *JSAE Review*, pp. 511-516.

Sampat, P. (2003) Scrapping Mining Dependence. In: Gardner, G., Project Director, *State of the World 2003*. W.W. Norton & Company, New York: pp. 110-129.

Sandberg, O., Jönson, L. (2003) Advances in Powder Metallurgy. *Advanced Materials & Processes*, ASM International Publication, Materials Park, Vol. 161, No.12, Ohio, pg. 37.

Sullivan, C.C. (1997) Designing with Aluminum Composites. *Architecture*, June 1997, pp.174-177.

Uhlig, H. H., Revie, R. W. (1985) *Corrosion and Corrosion Control*. John Wiley & Sons, Inc, New York, NY.

Smith S. D. (2003) *USGS Statistical Summary*. United States Geological Survey, March 2003.

Tilton, J.E. (1999) The future of recycling. *Resources Policy*, Vol. 25, pp. 197-204.

van Vuuren, D. P., Strengers, B.,J. De Vries, H. J. M. (1999) Long-term perspectives on world metal use - a system-dynamics model. *Resources Policy*, Vol. 25, pp. 239-255.

USGS Minerals Reports, Various (see the USGS web site: www.usgs.gov)

Walker, P. M. B. General Editor (2001) *Materials Science and Technology Dictionary*. Chambers Harrap Publishers, Edinburgh, UK.

Walp, M. S., Speer, J. G., Matlock, D. K. (2004) Fire-Resistant Steels. *Advanced Materials and Processes*, Vol. 162, No. 10, pp. 34-36.

Wilquin, H. (2001) *Aluminum Architecture, Construction and Details*. Birkhäuser - Publishers of Architecture, Basel, Switzerland.

Zahner, L. William (1995) *Architectural Metals: a guide to selection, specification and performance*. John Wiley & Sons, New York.

Websites

American Iron and Steel Institute: www.steel.org

ASM International (formerly American Society of Materials): www.asminternational.org

The Steel Alliance: www.thenewsteel.com

Nickel Development Institute: www.nidi.org and www.stainlessarchitecture.org

Copper Development Association: www.copper.org

International Aluminium Institute: www.world-aluminium.org

Key to Metals: A metals information website: www.key-to-metals.com

The Aluminum Association Incorporated: www.aluminum.org

Aluminum Anodizers Council: www.anodizing.org

Non-Ferrous Founders' Society: www.nffs.org

National Mining Association: www.minexpo.com

National Association of Architectural Metal Manufacturers: www.naamm.org

Metal Bulletin and Minmetals: www.metalbulletin.com

Metal Construction Association: www.metalconstruction.org

Steel Recycling Institute: www.recycle-steel.org

Bekaert: www.bekaert.com

Hitachi Metals: www.hitachimetals.com

Duocel SAF: www.ergaerospace.com

3.2 Polymers

Altschuler, K., Horst, S., Malin, N., Norris, G., Nishioka, Y. (2004) Assessment of Technical Basis for a PVC-Related Materials Credit in LEED®. *Public Review Draft, TSAC PVC Task Group*, U.S. Green Building Council, Washington DC.

Antonelli, P. (1995) *Mutant Materials in Contemporary Design*. The Museum of Modern Art, New York.

Barthes, Roland (1964) *Mythen des Alltags*. Frankfurt, Main 1964, Original: Edition du Seuil, Paris, 1957.

BASF News Release (2001) Strong sandwich polymer. November 27, 2001.

Berger, B.D., Anderson, K.E. (1992) *Modern Petroleum: A Basic Primer of the Industry, 3rd Edition*. Pennwell Books, Houston, TX.

Brookes, A. (1998) Moulding Architecture. *The Architects' Journal*, September 10.

Burnett, R. H. (1993) Defending Vinyl. *Environmental Building News*, Volume 2, No.5, September/October.

CES (2004) News Release: European Union Headquarters Restored Using Silicones for Aesthetics, Sustainability. Centre Europeen des Silicones, October 22.

Davis, J. R. (2001) *ASM Materials Engineering Dictionary*. ASM International.

Dietz, A. (1969) *Plastics for Architects and Builders*. Cambridge, MIT Press.

Dominighaus, H. (1988) *Plastics for Engineers*. Hanser Publishers, Munich.

Doran, D. K., Editor (1995) *Construction Materials Reference Book*. Butterworth-Heinmann, Oxford: pp. 46/1-46/17.

Driscoll, B., Campagna, J. (2003) Epoxy, Acrylic and Urethane Adhesives. *Advanced Materials and Processes*, ASM International, Materials Park, Ohio, Vol. 161, No. 8, pp.73-75.

EBN (1993) Problems with PVC. *Environmental Building News*, Volume 2, No.3, May/June.

EBN (2005) USGBC Releases Draft Report on PVC. *Environmental Building News*, Volume 14, No.1, January.

Fenichell, S. (1996) *Plastic: The Making of a Synthetic Century*. HarperCollins Publishers, New York, NY: pp. 133-223.

Finaldi, L. (1993) PVC Debate Continues. *Environmental Building News*, Volume 2, No.6, November/December.

Graedel, T. E., Allenby B. R. (2003) *Industrial Ecology*. Pearson Education, Inc. Upper Saddle River, New Jersey.

Hagighat, F., De Bellis L. (1998) Material Emission Rates: Literature Review, and the Impact of Indoor

Air Temperature and Relative Humidity. *Building and Environment,* Vol. 33, No. 5, pp. 261-277.

Harper, C., Editor in Chief (2000) *Modern Plastics Handbook*. McGraw-Hill, New York.

Hashem Z.A., Yuan R. L. (2001) Short versus long column behavior of pultruded glass-fiber reinforced polymer composites. *Construction and Building Materials*, Vol. 15, pp. 369-378.

Kahn, E. (2005) Extreme Textiles. *I.D. Mighty Materials*, March/April, pp. 54-63.

Kaltenbach, F. (2001) Artificial Transparency. Simple Forms of Building, *DETAIL*, Serie 2001, No.3, pp. 454-460

Kelley III, M. E. (2001) PVC Toxicity and Sustainable Materials. *Environmental Building News*, Vol. 10, No.11, November.

Lefteri, C. (2001) *Plastics: Materials for Inspirational Design*. RotoVision SA, Switzerland.

Malin, N. Wilson, A. (1994) Should We Phase Out PVC? *Environmental Building News*, Vol. 3, No.1, January/February.

NTC (2004) *Annual Reports, Research Briefs and Invesitigator Biographies*. National Textile Center, N. Bethlehem Pike, PA.

Makovsky, Paul (2000) TechnoGel. *Metropolis*, December 2000, pp. 114,115.

Lacey, M. (2005) Flower of Africa: A Curse that's Blowing in the Wind. *New York Times*, April 7.

Materials Progress (2004) Polyetherimide sheet forms entire cockpit of C17 plane. *Advanced Materials & Processes*, ASM International, Vol. 162, No. 11, pg. 16.

Novitski, B.J. (2000) Pentagon Battered but Firm. *ArchitectureWeek,* Page N1.2 . 03 October.

Reinprecht, L (2000) Biodegradation and treatment of Ancient Wood in Slovakia. *Technical University in Zvolen publication*.

Revkin, A.C. (2004) Just One Word for the Oceans: Plastics. *New York Times*, May 11.

Selke, S. E. (2000) Plastics Recycling and Biodegradable Plastics. In Harper, C., ed., *Modern Plastics Handbook*. McGraw-Hill, New York: pp.12.1-108.

Soroushian, P., Tlili, A., Alhozaimy, A., and Khan, A. (1993) Development and Characterization of Hybrid Polyethylene Fiber Reinforced Cement Composites. *ACI Materials Journal*, March-April, Vol. 90, No. 2, pp. 182-190.

Stevens, E. S. (2002) *Green Plastics: An Introduction to the New Science of Biodegradable Plastics*. Princeton University Press, Princeton.

Tenner, E. (1997) *When Things Bite Back: Technology and the Revenge of Unintended Consequences*. Vintage Books, New York.

Thompson, R.C. Olsen, Y. Mitchell, R.P. Davis, A. Rowland, S.J. John, A.W.G. McGonigle, D. Russell, A.E. (2004) Brevia: Lost at Sea: Where is all the Plastic? *Science*, May 7, Vol. 304, pg. 304.

Tukker, A., Kleijn, R. (1999) Using SFA and LCA in a Precautionary Approach: the Case of Chlorine and PVC. *Wuppertal Conference Proceedings, SFA and MFA, Part II*, pp. 64-71.

Walker, P. M. B., General Editor (2001) *Materials Science and Technology Dictionary*. Chambers Harrap Publishers, Edinburgh, UK.

Vest, H. (2001) Technical Options for the Recycling of Plastic Waste in Developing Countries. *Trialog 71, Zeitschrift für das Planen und Bauen in der Dritten Welt*, 4.

Wilson, A., Yost, P. (2001) Plastics in Construction: Performance and Affordability at What Cost. *Environmental Building News*, Volume 10, No.7, July/August 2001.

Additional references for Textiles, Films and Foils

AFMA (1988) Manufactured Fiber Fact Book. American Fiber Manufacturers Association, Inc.

Berger, H. (1999) Form and Function of Tensile Structures for Permanent Buildings. *Engineering Structures*, August, Issue 21, pp. 669-679.

Berger, H. (1985) The Evolving Design Vocabulary of Fabric Structures. *Architectural Record*, March 1985, Vol. 173, No. 3, pp.152-156.

Blum, R. (2002) Material properties of coated fabrics for textile architecture. In: Mollaert, M. ed., *The Design of Membrane and Lightweight Structures: From Concept to Execution*. VUB Brussels University Press, Brussels.

Braddock, S. E., O'Mahony, M. (1998) *Techno Textiles: Revolutionary Fabrics for Fashion and Design*. Thames and Hudson, New York.

Davey, P. (2000) *Equilibrium: Nicolas Grimshaw and Partners*. A supplement published by The Architectural Record, Phaidon, New York.

Gayle, S. R., Kolokotroni, M., Cripps, A., Tanno, S. (2001) ETFE foil cushions in roofs and atria. *Construction and Building Materials*, Vol. 15, pp. 323-327.

Kronenburg, R. (1997) *FTL, Tod Dalland, Nicolas Goldsmith - Softness Movement and Light*. Academy Editions, West Sussex.

Otto F., Rasch B. (2001) *Frei Otto, Bodo Rasch: Finding Form, Towards an Architecture of the Minimal*. Deutscher Werkbund, Bayern,

Mollaert, M. Editor (2002) *The Design of Membrane and Lightweight Structures: From Concept to Execution*. VUB Brussels University Press, Brussels.

Rein, A., Wilhelm, V. (2000) Membrane Construction. *DETAIL: Review of Architecture*, No. 6, September, pp.1044-1058.

Robbin, T. (1996) *Engineering a New Architecture*. Yale University Press, New Haven.

Small, D.J. Courtney, P.J. (2005) Fundamentals of Industrial Adhesives. *Advanced Materials & Processes*, Vol. 163, No.5, pp. 44-47.

Satkofsky, A. (2002) The Status of Degradable Plastics for Composting. *BioCycle, Journal of Composting & Organics Recycling*, March, pp.60-67.

Talarico, Wendy (2000) Designing with Structural Fabrics. *Architectural Record*, September.

Topham, Sean (2002) *Blowup: Inflatable Art, Architecture and Design*. Prestel, Munich.

Trechsel, H. Editor (2001) M*oisture Analysis and Condensation Control in Building Envelopes*. ASTM, West Conshohocken, USA.

Willmert, Todd (2002) Architects discover the flexibility of lightweight and durable fabrics: Advances in films and coatings make fabric an excellent alternative to glass. *Architectural Record*, Vol. 90, No.4, April, pp.141-150.

Yergin, D. (1991) *The Prize: The Epic Quest for Oil, Money and Power*. Free Press, New York, NY.

Additional uncited periodical references for polymers

Allen, I. (2001) A Taste of Eden. *Architectural Record* 22 February, pp. 30-39.

Ad Hoc Incident (1975) *Design* June: pp. 48 – 49

Battle, McCarthy (1995) Multi-source synthesis: atomic architecture. *Architectural Design,* January-February, pp. iii-vii.

Best, A. GRP: (1975) Those in favour. *Design* June, pp. 36-41.

Dawson, S. (2001) Rocket Science. *Architect's Journal,* Vol. 5 July, pp. 24 – 33

Knecht, B. (2001) Plastics finally get respect. *Architectural Record* December, pp. 107-112.

Pearson, C. A. (2001) Material Affairs. *Architectural Record* March, pp. 68 – 72

Plastics in architecture: Pandora's plastic box. (1975) *Progressive Architecture* September, pp. 86-91.

Plastics in architecture. (1970) *Progressive Architecture* October, whole issue.

Sheehan, T. (1995) Advanced construction materials. *Architects' Journal* July 13, pp. 37-38,41.

Stach, E. (2001) Leichtgewichte (Lightweights) *Architektur. Innenarchitektur und Technischer Ausbau* September – October, pp. 64 - 67

Websites

Introduction to polymer science: www.cem.msu.edu/~reusch/VirtualText/polymers.htm
Polymer library service: www.polymerlibrary.com
Centre Europeen des Silicones: www.silicones-europe.com
Dutch Polymer Institute (especially newsletters): www.polymers.nl
The Chemical Heritage Foundation (for polymer history): www.chemheritage.org
Recycled Polymer Exchange: www.go-polymers.com
MatWeb (Polymer manufacturer and trade name pages): www.matweb.com
CRC Polymers: A Property Database: www.polymersdatabase.com
Polymer Science online Journal resource: www.e-polymers.org
University of Florida Chemical Engineering Polymer links: www.che.ufl.edu/www-che/topics/polymers.html
Polymers information site including database of acronyms and numerous links: www.plastics.com
Dupont Plastics: http://plastics.dupont.com
Dupont's Teflon® pages: www.teflon.com
General Electric Plastics: www.geplastics.com
Bayer Material Science (plastics): www.bayerplastics.com, www.bayermaterialsciencenafta.com
Innovative Polymers Incorporated: www.innovative-polymers.com
Henkel: www.henkel.com
BASF: www.basf.com

Epoxy Systems, Inc.: www.epoxy.com
Dow Plastics: www.dow.com/plastics
Epoxy Technology: www.epotek.com
National Textile Research Center: www.ntcresearch.org

3.3   Ceramics and Glasses
Ceramics
Behling, S., Behling, S., Editors (1999) *Glass: Structure and Technology in Architecture*. Prestel Verlag, Munich.
Cardwell, S. (1997) New materials for construction. *Arup Journal*, Vol. 8, pp. 18-20.
Heyman, J. (1995) *The Stone Skeleton, Structural Engineering of Masonry Architecture*. Cambridge, Cambridge University Press, pp. 24-5.
ISE (1999) *Structural Use of Glass in Buildings*. Institution of Structural Engineers, December, London.
Nervi, P.L. (1956) *Structures*. F.W. Dodge, New York, pg. 29.
Ochsendorf, J. (2002) Collapse of Masonry Structures. PhD Dissertation, King's College, University of Cambridge, UK.
Rice, P., Dutton, H. (1995) *Structural Glass*. E & F Spon, London.
Spradling, D. M., Guth, R. A. (2003) Carbon Foams. *Advanced Materials & Processes*, November, pp. 29-31.

Fired clays
Foley, N.K. (1999) Environmental charateristics of clays and clay mineral deposits. *USGS Information Handout*, September: available at http://pubs.usgs.gov/info/clays/
Virta, R. L. (2001) Clay and Shale. In: *U.S. Geological Survey Minerals Yearbook, 2001*. United States Geological Survey, Reston, VA, pp.18.1-18.8.
Velde, B. (1995) Erosion, sedimentation and sedimentary origin of clays. In: Velde, B., ed., *Origin and mineralogy of clays*. New York, Springer-Verlag: pp.162-219.

Stone
Patton, J.B. (1990) Construction Materials: Dimension Stone. In: Moavenzadeh, F., ed., *Concise Encyclopedia of Building & Construction Materials*. Pergamon Press, Oxford, pp.119-124.
Kurtis, K.E., Dharan, C.K.H., (1997) Composite Fibers for External Reinforcement of Natural Stone. *Journal of Composites for Construction*, August, pp.116-119.

Concrete
(some of the following references have not been cited in the text but listed here for interested readers)
Aitcin, P.-C. (1998) High Performance Concrete. *E 7* FN Spon, London.
Aitcin, P.-C. (2000) Cements of yesterday and today, concrete of tommorow. *Cement Concrete Research*, Vol 30, pp.1349-1359.
Bentur, A., (2002) Cementitious Materials: Nine Millennia and a New Century: Past, Present, and Future. American Society of Civil Engineers, *Journal of Materials in Civil Engineering*, Vol. 14, No. 1, pp. 2-22.
Chen, P., Chung, D. D. L. (1996) Carbon fiber reinforced concrete as an intrinsically smart concrete for damage assessment during static and dynamic loading. *ACI Mater. J.*, Vol. 93, No. 4, pp.341-350.
Damtoft, J.S. (1998) Use of fly ash and other waste materials as raw feed and energy source in the Danish cement industry. *Proceedings of the CANMET/ACI International Symposium on Sustainable Development of the Cement and Concrete Industry*. Canada.
Dowd, W.M. O'Neil, E.F. (1996) Development of Reactive Powder Concrete (RPC) Precast Products for the USA Market, In: *Proceedings, Fourth International Symposium on the Utilization of High-Strength/High-Performance Concrete*, F. de Larrard, and R. Lacroix, eds. Presses de l'École Nationale des Ponts et Chaussées, Paris, FRANCE, 29-31 May 1996, pp 1391-1398.
Ductal (2005) see www.ductal.com and follow to the LaFarge site. Ductal has been jointly developed by LaFarge, Bouygues and Rhodia.
ECT (2003) Emerging Construction Technologies. Web site article: www.new-technologies.org
Glavind, M., Munch-Petersen, C. (2000) "Green" concrete in Denmark. *Structural Concrete*, Vol 1, No.1: pp.19-25.

Hoff, G.C. (1996) Toward rational design of concrete structures - Integration of structural design and durability design. In: Sakai, K., *Integrated Design and Environmental Issues in Concrete Technology*. E & FN Spon, London.

Jardine, K. Cameron, J. (1999) Building for Affordability and Energy Efficiency. *Fine Homebuilding*, Summer, No.123, pp. 82-87.

Lawrence, C.D. (2004) The production of low energy cements. In: Hewlett, P.C., ed., *Lea's Chemistry of Cement and Concrete; 4th Edition*. Butterworth-Heinemann, London: pp. 277-286.

O'Neil, E.F. (1995a) Reactive Powder Concrete: A Very-High-Performance Concrete Material, In: H.W. Jones, and B. D. Fehl, eds., *Proceedings, Corps of Engineers Structural Engineering Conference,* U.S. Army Corps of Engineers Engineering and Construction Directorate, San Antonio, TX. 28-30 August, pp 1195-1204.

O'Neil, E.F. Dowd, W.M. (1995b) Reactive Powder Concrete: A New Material for the Construction Industry, In: Ghosh, S.K. ed., *Proceedings, Third National Concrete and Masonry Engineering Conference*, National Concrete and Masonry Engineering Conference, San Francisco, CA. June 15-17, pp 43-50.

O'Neil, E. F., Dauriac, E. C., Gilliland, S. K., (1995c) Development of Reactive Powder Concrete (RPC) Products in the United States Construction Market, In: Bickley, J. A., ed., *High-Strength Concrete: An International Perspective*, ACI SP-167, J. A. Bickley, ed., American Concrete Institute, Farmington Hills, MI, November, pp. 249-262.

Richard, P. Cheyrezy, M. (1994) Reactive Powder Concretes with High Ductility and 200 - 800 MPa Compressive Strength", In: *Concrete Technology Past, Present, and Future, Proceedings of V. Mohan Malhotra Symposium ACI SP-144*, P. K Mehta, ed. American Concrete Institute, Farmington Hills, MI, March 1994, pp. 507-518.

Richard, P. Cheyrezy, M. (1995) Composition of Reactive Powder Concretes. *Cement and Concrete Research*, vol. 25, (7) (1995), pp. 1501-1511.

Parsons, J. (2000) Concrete for a Sustainable Future. *Architecture*, November 2000, pp.70-1.

Rostam, S. (1996) Service Life Design for the Next Century. In: Sakai, K., *Integrated Design and Environmental Issues in Concrete Technology*. E & FN Spon, London.

Sakai, K., (1996) *Integrated Design and Environmental Issues in Concrete Technology*. E & FN Spon, London.

Schlaich, J. (2001) A plea for Concrete Construction in Keeping with the Nature of the Material. *DETAIL, Concrete Construction*, Vol. 1, pp. 28,29.

Schiessel, P. (1996) Durability of reinforced concrete structures. *Construction and Buildings Materials*, Vol. 10, No. 5, pp. 289-292.

van Oss, H.G. Padovani, A.C. (2002) Cement Manufacture and the Environment, Part 1: Chemistry and Technology. *Journal of Industrial Ecology*, Vol. 6, No. 1, pp.89-105.

Wilson, A. (1993) Cement and Concrete: Environmental Considerations. *Environmental Building News*, Vol. 2, No. 2: (www.buildinggreen.com).

Glass

Amstock, J. S. (1997) *Handbook of Glass in Construction*. McGraw-Hill, New York, NY.

Bauer J. (1995) Switchable Glass Research Report. *Internal document, Polshek and Partners*, New York.

Behling, S., Behling, S., Editors (1999) *Glass: Structure and Technology in Architecture*. Prestel Verlag, Munich.

Compagno, A. (1999) *Intelligent Glass Façades*: Material, Practice, Design. Birkhauser, Berlin.

Elliot, C. D. (1992) *Technics and Architecture, the Development of Materials and Systems for Buildings*. The MIT Press, Cambridge, MA.

Fischer-Cripps, A.C. Collins, R.E. (1995) Architectural Glazings: Design Standards and Failure Models. *Building and Environment*, Vol. 30, No.1, pp.29-40.

Fierro, A. (2003) *The Glass State*. MIT Press, Cambridge.

Glass Association of North America, various publications.

Heyman, J. (1995) *The Stone Skeleton: Structural Engineering of Masonry Architecture*. Cambridge University Press, Cambridge, UK.

ISE (1999) *Structural Use of Glass in Buildings*. Institution of Structural Engineers, December 1999, London.

Lampert, C. M. (1999) Advances in materials and technology for switchable glazing. *Glass Processing Days*, 13-16, pp. 296-300.

Lefteri, C. (2002) *Glass: Materials for Inspirational Design*. RotoVision, Switzerland.

Mark, R. Editor (1993) *Architectural Technology Up to the Scientific Revolution*. The MIT Press, Cambridge, MA.

Oesterle E., Lieb R. D., Lutz M., Heusler W. (2001) *Double-Skin Facades*. Prestel, Munich.

Rice, P., Dutton, H. (1995) *Structural Glass*. E & F Spon, London.

Ruth, M., Dell'Anno, P. (1997) An industrial ecology of the US glass industry. *Resources Policy,* Vol. 23, No. 3, pp. 109-124.

Schittich C., Staib G., Balkow D., Schuler M., Sobek W. (1999) *Glass Construction Manual*. Birkhauser, Munich.

Schwartz, T. (2003) *Glass and Curtain Walls: Learning from the Past, Improving the Future*. Presentation to the Department of Architecture , MIT, February 10, 2003.

Wigginton, M. (1996) *Glass in Architecture*. Phaidon Press, New York.

Websites

Annual international conference on glass technologies: www.glassprocessingdays.com

3.4 Composites

(some of the following references have not been cited in the text but listed here for interested readers)

Bakis, C.E., Bank, L.C., Brown, M., Cosenza, E., Davalos, J.F., Lesko, J.J., Machida, S.H., Rizkalla, S.H., Triantafillou, T.C., (2002) Fiber-Reinforced Polymer Composites for Construction – State-of-the-Art Review. American Society of Civil Engineers, *Journal of Materials in Civil Engineering*, Vol.6, No.2, pp. 73-87.

Bannister, M., Herszberg, I., Nicolaidis, A., Coman, F., Leong, K.H. (1998) The manufacture of glass/epoxy composites with multilayer woven architectures. *Composites: Part A 29A*, No. 3, pp. 293-300.

Bowen, D. H. (1989) Applications of composites: an overview. In: Kelley, A. editor. *Concise Encyclopedia of Composite Materials*. Pergamon Press, The MIT Press, Cambridge, Mass, pp. 7-15.

Burford, N.K., Smith, F.W. (1999) Developing a new military shelter system: a technical study in advanced materials and structures. *Building Research & Information*, 27, No.2, pp. 64-83.

Callus, P.J., Mouritz, A.P., Bannister, M.K., Leong, K.H. (1999) Tensile properties and failure mechanisms of 3D woven GRP composites. *Composites: Part A 30*, No.11, pp.1277-1287.

Chajes, M.J., Thomson, T., Finch, W.W., Januszka, T. (1994) Flexural strengthening of concrete beams using externally bonded composite materials. *Construction and Building Materials*, Vol. 8, No.3, pp.191-201.

Chang, K. (2005) Tiny is Beautiful: Translating 'Nano" into Practical. *New York Times*, February 22.

Clyne, T. W., Withers, P. J. (1993) *An Introduction to Metal Matrix Composites*. Cambridge University Press: Cambridge.

Composites Worldwide (2001) 500-750% Growth Curve for FRP Composites Aiding Global Infrastructure Sector. News Release, July 2001. Composites Worldwide, Inc.

Cosenza, E. Manfredi, G. (2002) Research Needs and Unresolved Issues of Composites for Built Infrastructure. *Journal of Composites for Construction*, August, Vol.6, No. 3, pp.141,142.

DelMonte, J. (1981) *Technology of Carbon and Graphite Fiber Composites*. Van Nostrand Reinhold: New York.

ECT (2005) Emerging Construction Technologies: www.new-technologies.org

Feder, B. (2004) Tiny Ideas Coming of Age. *New York Times*, October 24.

Goldsworthy, W. B., Hiel, C. (1998) Composite Structures, *SAMPE Journal*, Vol. 34, No.1, pp. 24-30.

Hawthorne, C. (2003) Carbon Fiber Future. *METROPOLIS*. February 2003: pp. 66-123.

Hayes, M. D., Ohanehi, D., Lesko, J. J., Cousins, T. E., Witcher, D. (2000) Performance of tube and plate fiberglass composite bridge deck. *Journal of Composites for Construction*, May 2000, pp.48-55.

Matériaux composés - Composite Materials: Logements, Bordeaux. Techniques architecture, No.448: De la matière. pp. 83-87.

Hooks, J., Siebels, J., editors. (1997) *Advanced Composites in Bridges in Europe and Japan*. US Department of Transportation. Federal Highway Administration, Washington, DC, October 1997.

Hull, D., Clyne, T.W. (1996) *An Introduction to Composite Materials*. Cambridge University Press, Cambridge.

Keller, T. (2003) *Use of Fibre Reinforced Polymers in Bridge Construction.* International Association for Bridge and Structural Engineering, Structural Engineering Documents, No. 7, IABSE-AIPC-IVBH, Hönggerberg, Zurich, Switzerland.

Kelly, A., Editor (1989) *Concise Encyclopedia of Composite Materials.* Pergamon Press, Oxford.

Kiesling, T. C., Chaudhry, Z., Paine, J. S. N., Rogers, C. A. (1996) Impact failure modes of thin graphite epoxy composites embedded with superelastic nitinol. *Proceedings of the AIAA/ASME/AHS/ASC 37th SDM Conference,* Salt Lake City, UT, April 15-17.

Kuzumaki, T., Hayashi, T., Ichinose, I., Miyazawa, K., Ito, K., Ishida, Y. (1996) *Japan Instr.. Metals 61,* No. 9.

Kuzumaki, T., Hayashi, T., Ichinose, I., Miyazawa, K., Ito, K. (1998) *Journal of Materials Research,* Vol.13, No.9, pp. 2445-2449.

Moavenzadeh, F. Editor (1990) *Concise Encyclopedia of Building & Construction Materials.* Cambridge, MIT Press.

Moeller, M. (2001) New Materials, Stronger Buildings. *Blueprints,* Published by the National Building Museum No.1, Winter, pp. 6,7.

Mouritz, A. P., Bannister, M. K., Falzon, P. J., Leong, K. H., (1999) Review of applications for advanced three-dimensional fibre textile composites. *Composites: Part A 30A,* No.12, pp. 1445-1461.

Mouritz, A. P., Cox, B. N. (2000) A mechanistic approach to the properties of stitched laminates. *Composites: Part A 31,* No.1, pp. 1-27.

Overney, G. Zhong, W. Tomacek, D. (1993) *Phys. D 27,* No.93.

CDCC. (1998) *Durability of Fibre Reinforced Polymer (FRP) Composites for Construction,* CDCC'98. Sherbrooke, Canada, 1998.

Pochiraju, K., Chou T. W. (1999) Three-dimensionally woven and braided composites. II: An experimental characterization. *Polymer composites,* 20, No.6, pp. 733-747.

Raasch, J.E. (1998) All-composite construction system provides flexible low-cost shelter. *Composites Technology,* Vol.4, No.3: pp.56-58.

Ruan, X., Safari, A., Chou, T. W. (1999) Effective elastic, piezoelectric and dielectric properties of braided fabric composites. *Composites: Part A 30A,* No.12, pp. 1435-1444.

SEI. (1999) Advanced Materials: State of the Art Reports Canada. Europe, Japan, USA. *Structural Engineering International,* November.

Shaker, M., Ko, F., Song, J. (1999) Comparisons of the low and high velocity impact response of kevlar fiber-reforced epoxy composites. *Journal of Composites Technology and Research,* 21, No. 4, pp. 224-229.

SP (2003) SP Systems Guide to Composites. *Published by SP Systems: Composites, Engineering, Materials,* (www.spsystems.com).

Websites

The Composites Corner: www.advmat.com
Composite News Supersite: www.compositesnews.com
Composite Retrofit International: www.tyfofibrwrap.com
ConfibreCrete: www.shef.ac.uk/uni/projects/tmrnet/home.html
CONMAT: www.cerf.org/conmat/index.html
Creative Pultrusion: www.pultrude.com
Fiberline Composites: www.fiberline.dk
Glasforms: www.glasforms.thomasregister.com
Hardcore Composites: www.hardcorecomposites.com
ISIS Canada: www.isiscanada.com
Kansas Structural Composites: www.ksci.com
Marshall Industries Composites: www.c-bar.com
Martin Marietta Composites: www.martinmarietta.com
Master Builders: www.masterbuilders.com
Maunsell Structural Plastics: www.maunsell.co.uk
Sonderforschungsbereich 532: www.sfb532.rwth-aachen.de
Strongwell: www.strongwell.com
TopGlass pultrusions (Italian pultrusion manufacturer): www.topglass.it
XXsys Technologies: www.xxsys.com
3Tex Composites: www.3tex.com

3.5 Biomaterials and Loam

(some of the following references have not been cited in the text but listed here for interested readers)

Ashby, M. F., Jones, D. (2001) *Engineering Materials I: an introduction to their properties and applications.* Butterworth-Heinemann: London.

Ashby, M. F., Jones D. (2001) *Engineering Materials II: an introduction to microstructures processing and design.* Butterworth-Heinemann: London.

Aziz M. A., Paramasivam P., Lee S. L., (1981) Prospects for natural fibre reinforced concretes in construction. *The International Journal of Cement Composites and Lightweight Concrete*, Vol. 3, No. 2, pp.123-132.

CBIP (2000) Biobased Industrial Products, Priorities for Research and Commercialization. *Committee on Biobased Industrial Products, Board on Biology*, Commission on Life Sciences, National Research Council, Washington, DC: National Academy Press.

Emmott, B. (2003) Today the real surprise is how good things are, not how bad. Article in *The Times* (of London) Business Section, pg. 33.

Diamond, J. (2004) *Collapse, How Societies Choose to Fail or Succeed.* Viking Adult, New York.

Férnandez-Galiano, L. Cariño, G. (2000) *Fire and Memory: On Architecture and Energy.* The MIT Press, Cambridge, MA, pp. 17-22.

Gerngross, T. U. (1999) Can biotechnology move us toward a sustainable society? *Nature Biotechnology* Vol. 17, June 1999, http://biotech.nature.com.

Gram H. E. (1988) Chapter 4 - Durability of natural fibres in concrete. In: Swamy RN, editor. *Natural Fiber Reinforced Cement and Concrete*, London: Blackie and Son Ltd, London.

Hughes, J. D. (1975) *Ecology in Ancient Civilizations.* University of New Mexico Press, Albuquerque, NM.

Kurdikar, D., Laurence, F., Slater, S., Paster, M., Gergross, T.U., Coulon, R., Greenhouse Gas Profile of a Plastic Material Derived from a Genetically Modified Plant, *Journal of Industrial Ecology*, MIT and Yale University, Volume 4, Number 3.

Minke, G. (2000) *Earth, Construction Handbook, The Building Material Earth in Modern Architecture.* WIT Press, Southampton, UK.

Ponting, C. (1991) *A Green History of the World: The Evnironment and the Collapse of Great Civilizations.* Penguin Books, New York, NY: pg. 73-80.

Sampat, Payal (2003) Scrapping Mining Dependence. In: Gardner, G., Project Director, *State of the World 2003.* W. W. Norton & Company, New York, pp. 110-129.

Wernick, Iddo K. (2002) Industrial Ecology and the Built Environment. In: Kibert, C. J., Sendzimir, J., and Guy, G. B., ed., *Construction Ecology: Nature as the basis for green buildings.* Spon Press, London, pp. 177-195.

Sobral HS, editor. (1990) Vegetable Plants and their Fibres as Building Materials. *Proceedings of the Second International Symposium sponsored by RILEM.* London: Chapman and Hall.

Swamy R. N., Editor, (1988) *Natural Fiber Reinforced Cement and Concrete.* London: Blackie and Son Ltd.

Soroushian, P., Marikunte, S. (1992) Long-term durability and moisture sensitivity of cellulose fiber reinforced cement composites. In: Swamy RM, editor. *Proceedings of the Fourth International Symposium held by RILEM.* London: E & FN Spon.

Hannant, D. J., (1978) Fibre Cements and Fibre Concretes. NewYork: John Wiley & Sons.

Piggott M. R. (1980) *Load Bearing Fibre Composites.* Pergamon Press, Oxford, pp. 131-32.

Wood

Bignens, C. (1995) Plywood as Determinant of Form. In: *Magic of Materials, Daidalos*, no. 56, June, pp. 75-79.

(FPL) Forest Products Laboratory (1999) Wood handbook--Wood as an engineering material. Gen. Tech. Rep. FPL-GTR-113. Madison, WI: U.S. Department of Agriculture, Forest Service, Forest Products Laboratory.

Schniewind, A. P. (1990) Wood: Deformation under Load. In: Moavenzadeh, F., ed., Concise Encyclopedia of Building & Construction Materials. Pergamon Press, Oxford, pp. 642-3.

Giedion, S. (1944) *Space, Time and Architecture.* Cambridge, Mass., Harvard University Press, pp.347-355.

Haygreen J. G., Bowyer, J. L. (1998) Forest Products and Wood Science: An Introduction, Second Edition. Iowa State University Press, Ames, Iowa.

LeVan, S. L. (1998) Benefits from wood engineering research. Wood engineering in the 21st century - Research needs and goals, *American Society of Civil Engineers*, Reston, Va, pp. 1-4.

Mathews, E., Hammond, A. (1999) *Critical Consumption Trends and Implcations: Degrading Earth's Ecosystems*. World Resources Institute, pp.31-50.

NZS (1998a) *Engineering Design of Earth Buildings*. NZS 4297:1998, Standards, New Zealand.

NZS (1998b) *Materials and Workmanship for Earth Buildings*. NZS 4298:1998, Standards, New Zealand.

NZS (1998c) *Earth Buildings Not Requiring Specific Design*. NZS 4299:1998, Standards, New Zealand.

Solberg, B., et al. (1996) An overview of factors affecting the long-term trends in non-industrial and industrial wood supply and demand. *European Forest Institute Research Report*, No.6, pg.48.

(FAO) United Nations Forest and Agriculture Organization (2003) State of the World's Forests
Can be found at: http://www.fao.org/

United Nations (1997) *State of the World's Forests*. Food and Agriculture Organization of the United Nations, FAO, Rome, 1997, pg.55.

Victor, D. G., Ausubel, J. H. (2000). Restoring the Forests. *Foreign Affairs*, Volume 79, No.6, December.

Websites

Biopolymers: www.biopolymer.net

Biomaterials: www.nf-2000.org/home.html

FAOSTAT - Food and Agriculture Organization of the United Nations: apps.fao.org

US Department of Agriculture Forest Service: Forest Products Laboratory: www.fpl.fs.fed.us

American Wood Preservers Institute: www.preservedwood.com

Society of Wood Science and Technology: www.swst.org

Forest Products Society: www.forestprod.org

Cargill Dow LLC biopolymers: www.natureworksllc.com

III   Design

The literature on building systems is extensive, yet varied. This attests to the multi-disciplinary interest in the design and engineering of building systems. Architectural sources focus on the historical basis for systems design and the results of particular cultural movements. Engineering sources address the influence of better methods of analysis and understanding of the basic phenomena that formed the basis for technical solutions. Chapter 4 relates the method of multi-objective optimization as refined and presented by Mike. F. Ashby in his various publications and through the work of his company Granta Design Ltd. In Chapter 5, references have been separated into two sections; first, those sources related to the fabric research work and second, those sources pertaining to the NFRC research work.

4   Masterial Selection

Allen, E. (1981) *Stone Shelters*. The MIT Press, Cambridge,MA, pp.17-49.

Ashby, M. F. (1999) *Materials Selection in Mechanical Design, Second Edition*. Butterworth-Heinemann, Oxford.

Ashby, M. F., Johnson, K. (2002) *Materials and Design: The Art and Science of Materials Selection in Product Design*. Butterworth-Heinmann, Oxford.

Ashby M. F., Jones D. R. H. (2001) *Engineering Materials I: an introduction to their properties and applications*. Butterworth-Heinemann, Oxford.

Ashby M. F., Jones D. R. H. (2001) *Engineering Materials II: an introduction to microstructures processing and design*. Butterworth-Heinemann, Oxford.

Cornish, E. H. (1987) Chapter 11: Factors controlling the selection of substitute materials In: *Materials and the Designer*. Cambridge University Press, Cambridge.

Elliot, C. D. (1992) *Technics and Architecture, the Development of Materials and Systems for Buildings*. The MIT Press, Cambridge, MA.

Mowery, D. C., Rosenberg, N. (1998) *Paths of Innovation: Technological Change in 20th Century America*. Cambridge University Press, Cambridge.

Watson, D. (1917) Architecture, Technology, and Environment. *Journal of Architectural Education*, ACSA: pp. 119-126.

Wright, Frank Lloyd (1943) An Autobiography. Sloan and Pearce, New York, pp.337-49.

Websites
Granta Material Selectors: www.grantadesign.com
Granta Materials data site: http://matdata.net
American Society of Materials International: www.asminternational.org

5   Material Assemblies
Braddock, S.E., O'Mahony, M. (1998) *Techno Textiles: Revolutionary Fabrics and Design*. Thames and Hudson, New York, NY.
Brock, L. (2005) *Desgining the exterior wall: An architectural guide to the vertical envelope*. John Wiley & Sons, New York, USA.
Gregotti, Vittorio (1996) *Inside Architecture*. The MIT Press, Cambridge.
Mollerup, P. (2001) *Collapsible: The Genius of Space-Saving Design*. Chronicle Books, San Francisco, CA, USA.
Moritz, K. (2004) *DETAIL Praxis: Translucent Materials*. Birkhauser, Munich, Germany.
Topham, S. (2002) *Blowup: inflatable art, architecture and design*. Prestel-Verlag, Munich.

Project I: A multi-layered high performance textile exterior envelope
Project II: A laminated glass and high performance textile composite for an exterior envelope assembly
(some of the following references have not been cited in the text but listed here for interested readers)
McEvoy, M. (1999) *External Components*. Longman, Essex, UK.
Compagno, A. (1999) *Intelligent Glass Facades*. Birkhauser Publishers, Berlin.
Daniels, K. (1997) *The Technology of Ecological Building, Basic Prinicples and Measures, Examples and Ideas*. Birkhauser, Munich.
Daniels, K. (2000) *Low-Tech Light-Tech High-Tech, Building in the Information Age*. Birkhauser, Munich.
Fabric Skyscapers (1995) *Architectural Design*. Volume 65, No. 9, September–October, pp.49-50.
Foulger, S. H., Gregory R. (2000) Intelligent Textiles based on environmentally responsive fibers, *Research Report, National Textile Center,* University Research Consortium, M00-C07, November.
Gregory, R.V., Samuels, R.J., Hanks, T. (2000) Chameleon Fibers: Dynamic color change from tunable molecular and oligomeric devices, *Research Report, National Textile Center*, University Research Consortium, M98-C1.
HPF (1994) High Performance Fibers. *Entire issue of the Journal of The Textile Institute*, Volume 25, Number 3/4.
Lupton, E. (2002) *Skin, Surface Substance + Design*. Princeton Architectural Press, Princeton, NJ.
McEvoy, M. (1999) *External Components*. Longman Group, Essex, England.
Mills, G., Slaten, L., Broughton, R. (2000) Photoadaptive fibers for textile materials, *Research Report, National Textile Center*, University Research Consortium, M98-A10, June.
Muneer, T., Abodahab, N., Weir, G., Kubie, J. (2000) *Windows in Buildings: Thermal, Acoustic, Visual and Solar Performance*. Architectural Press, Oxford.
Riley, T. (1995) *Light Construction*. The Museum of Modern Art, New York, 1995.
Robinson-Gayle, S., Kolokotroni, M., Cripps, A., Tanno, S. (2001) ETFE foils cushions in roofs and atria, *Construction and Building Materials*. pp. 323-327.
Schittich, Staib, Balkow, Schuler, Sobek (1999) *Glass Construction Manual*. Birkhauser Publishers, Basel, Switzerland.
Structural Engineering International. (1999) *Entire issue of the Journal of the International Association of Bridge and Structural Engineering*, Volume 9, Number 4, November 1999.
Walsh W. K., Lin W., Buscle-Diller G., McClain A., Hudson S. (2000) Intelligent, stimuli-sensitive fibers and fabrics, *Research Report, National Textile Center*, University Research Consortium, M98-A16, June 2000.
Wigginton, M., Harris, J. (2002) *Intelligent Skins*. Butterworth-Heinemann, Oxford, UK.

Project III: Natural Fiber Reinforced Concrete
(some of the following references have not been cited in the text but listed here for interested readers)
ACI, Measurements of properties of fiber reinforced concrete. ACI Mater. J., 1988; 85(6): 583-93.
Adams W. M., (1990) *Green Development, Environment and Sustainability in the Third World*. London: Routledge.

Agopyan V., John V. M. Building panels made with natural fibre reinforced alternative cements. In: Swamy RN, editor. *Fibre Reinforced Cements and Concretes, Recent Developments,* London: Elsevier Applied Science. pp. 296-305.

Arntzen, C. J., et al. (2000) Biobased Industrial Products, Priorities for Research and Commercialization. *Journal of the American Academy of Arts and Sciences, National Academy Press,* Washington, DC: pp. 19-40.

ASTM C 1018-97, Vol. 4.02, Standard Test Method for Flexural Toughness and First-Crack Strength of Fiber-Reinforced Concrete (Using Beam with Third-Point Loading). *Committee on Standards, ASTM,* Philadelphia, 1998.

Aziz M. A., Paramasivam P., Lee S. L., (1981) Prospects for natural fibre reinforced concretes in construction. *The International Journal of Cement Composites and Lightweight Concrete* 1981; Vol. 3 No. 2, pp. 123-132.

Barr B., Gettu R., Al-Oraimi S. K. A., Bryars L. S., (1996) Toughness Measurement – the Need to Think Again. *Cement and Concrete Composites*, Vol. 18, pp. 281-297.

Bledzki A. K., Gassan J., (1999) Composites reinforced with cellulose based fibers. *Progress in Polymer Science*, Vol. 24, pp. 221-274.

Committee on Biobased Industrial Products (2000) Board on Biology, Commission on Life Sciences, National Research Council.

Coutts R. S. P., (1992) From Forest to Factory to Fabrication. In: Swamy RN, editor. *Proceedings of the Fourth International Symposium held by RILEM*, London: E & FN Spon.

Curtis, W. J. R. (1996) Chapter 31, Modernity, Tradition and Identity in the Developing World, In: *Modern Architecture Since 1900*. Phaidon, New York.

Eisenstadt, S. N. (2000) Multiple Modernities. In: Multiple Modernities. *Dædalus, Journal of the American Academy of Arts and Sciences*, Winter 2000, pp. 1-29.

Eisenstadt, S. N. Schluchter, W. (1998) Introduction: Paths to Early Modernities - A Comparable View. In: Early Modernities. *Dædalus, Journal of the American Academy of Arts and Sciences*, Summer 1998, pp. 1-18.

Fordos Z, (1988) Chapter 5 – Natural or modified cellulose fibres as reinforcement in cement composites. In: Swamy R. N., ed., *Natural Fiber Reinforced Cement and Concrete*. London: Blackie and Son Ltd, London.

Gassan J., (1999) Possibilities for improving properties of jute/epoxy composites by alkali treatment of fibres. *Composites Science and Technology,* Vol. 59, pp. 1303-1309.

Goodman L. J., (1979) Low-Cost Housing: Guidelines and Issues. In: Goodman, Pama, Tabujara, Razani, Burlan, editors. *Low-Cost Housing Technology - An East-West Perspective.* Oxford: Pergamon Press, pp. 15-24.

Gopalaratnam V. S., (1995) On the characterization of flexural toughness in fiber reinforced concretes. *Cement and Concrete Composites,* Vol. 17, pp. 239-254.

Gram H. E., (1988) Chapter 4 - Durability of natural fibres in concrete. In: Swamy R. N., ed., *Natural Fiber Reinforced Cement and Concrete*. Blackie and Son Ltd, London.

Gram H. E., (1988) Chapter 8 – Natural fibre concrete roofing. In: Swamy R. N., ed., *Natural Fiber Reinforced Cement and Concrete*. Blackie and Son Ltd, London.

Hannant, D. J., (1978) *Fibre Cements and Fibre Concretes*. John Wiley & Sons, NewYork, .

Hermann A. S., Riedel U., (1998) Construction materials based upon biologically renewable resources – from components to finished parts. *Polymer Degradation and Stability*, Vol. 59, pp. 251-261.

Lloyd E. (2000) Bast Fiber Applications for Composites. private communication.

MacVicar R., Matuana L. M., Balatinecz J.J. (1999) Aging mechanisms in cellulose fiber reinforced cement composites. *Cement and Concrete Composites*, Vol. 21, pp. 189-196.

Mallick P. K. (1988) *Fiber-Reinforced Concretes*. Marcel Dekker, New York.

Marusin S. L. (1995) Sample Preparation – Key to SEM studies of failed concrete. *Cement & Concrete Composites*. Vol. 17, pp. 311-318.

Mishra S., Naik J. B., Patil Y. P. (2000) The compatibilising effect of maleic anhydride on swelling and mechanical properties of plant-fiber-reinforced novolac composites. *Composites Science and Technology 2000*, Vol. 60, pp. 1729-1735.

Piggott M. R. (1980) *Load Bearing Fibre Composites*. Pergamon Press, Oxford, pp. 131-32.

Rehsi S. S. (1988) Chapter 7 – Use of natural fibre concrete in India. In: Swamy R. N., ed., *Natural Fiber Reinforced Cement and Concrete*. London: Blackie and Son Ltd, London, 1988.

Richardson, I. G. (2000) The nature of the hydration products in hardened cement pastes. *Cement & Concrete Composites*, Vol. 22, pp. 97-113.

RILEM 49TFR, (1984) Testing methods for fibre reinforced cement-based composites. RILEM Draft Recommendations. *Mater. & Struct.*, Vol. 17: 441-56.

Savastano Jr., H., Agopyan, V., Nolasco, A., Pimentel, L. (1999) Plant fibre reinforced cement components for roofing. *Construction and Building Materials*, Vol. 13, pp. 433-438.

Savastano Jr., H., Warden P. G., Coutts R. S. P. (2000) Brazilian waste fibres as reinforcement for cement-based composites. *Cement and Concrete Composites*, Vol. 22, pp. 379-384.

Savastano Jr., H., Agopyan, V. (1999) Transition zone studies of vegetable fibre-cement paste composites. *Cement and Concrete Composites*, Vol. 21, pp. 49-57.

Sobral, H. S., Editor. (1990) Vegetable Plants and their Fibres as Building Materials. *Proceedings of the Second International Symposium sponsored by RILEM*. London: Chapman and Hall.

Soroushian, P., Marikunte, S. (1992) Long-term durability and moisture sensitivity of cellulose fiber reinforced cement composites. In: Swamy R.N., ed., *Proceedings of the Fourth International Symposium held by RILEM*. London: E & FN Spon.

Swamy R.N., Editor (1988) Natural Fiber Reinforced Cement and Concrete. Blackie and Son Ltd, London.

Toledo, F. R. D., Scrivener, K., England, G. L., Ghavami, K. (2000) Durability of alkali-sensitive sisal and coconut fibres in cement mortar composites. *Cement and Concrete Composites*, Vol. 22, pp. 127-143.

Valadez-Gonzalez, A., Cervantes-Uc, J. M., Olayo, R., Herrera-Franco, P. J. (1999) Effect of fiber surface treatment on the fiber-matrix bond strength of natural fiber reinforced composites. *Composites: Part B*, Vol. 30, pp.309-320.

Valadez-Gonzalez, A., Cervantes-Uc, J. M., Olayo, R., Herrera-Franco, P. J. (1990) Chemical modification of henequen fibers with an organosilane coupling agent. *Composites: Part B,* Vol. 30, pp. 321-331.

Epilogue – Building Ecologies

The Epilogue has been influenced equally by journal papers and books. Because of the relative youth of the study of industrial ecology, journal papers are still the richest resource for the ongoing development of fundamental theory and methods. The leading journal is the *Journal of Industrial Ecology* published by the MIT Press. Also, books by Graedel and Allenby, Allenby, Kibert and several addressing uncertainty and decision-making theory are also important here.

Allenby, B. R. (1999) *Industrial Ecology: Policy Framework and Implementation*. Prentice-Hall, Inc., Upper Saddle, New Jersey.

Ayres, R. U. (1989) *Industrial metabolism. In Technology and environment*. Edited by J.H. Ausubel and H.E. Sladovich. Washington, DC:National Academy Press, pp. 23-49.

Ayres, R. Ayres, L. (1996) *Industrial Ecology: Towards closing the materials cycle*. Cheltenham, UK, Edward Elgar Publishing, Washington DC, National Academy Press.

Basalla, G. (1988) *The Evolution of Technology*. Cambridge, Cambridge University Press, pp.26-30.

Bell, D. E., Raiffa, H., Tversky, A. (1988) *Decision Making: Descriptive, normative, and prescriptive interactions*. Cambridge University Press, Cambridge, UK.

Bey, C. (2001) Quo vadis industrial ecology? *Greener Management International*, Vol. 34, pp. 35-42.

Black, F., Scholes, M. (1973) The pricing of options and corporate liabilities. *Journal of Political Economy,* 81 (May-June): pp. 637-659.

Daniels, P. L. (2002a) Approaches for Quantifying the Metabolism of Physical Economies: A Comparative Survey, Part I: Methodological Overview. *Journal of Industrial Ecology*, Vol. 5, No.4, pp. 69-93.

Daniels, P. L. (2002b) Approaches for Quantifying the Metabolism of Physical Economies: A Comparative Survey, Part II: Review of Individual Aproaches. *Journal of Industrial Ecology*, Vol. 6, No.1, pp. 65-88.

Ehrenfeld, J. R. (2004) Can Industrial Ecology be the "Science of Sustainability"? *Journal of Industrial Ecology*, Vol. 8, No. 1-2, pp. 1-3.

Graedel, T.E., Allenby B. R. (2003) *Industrial Ecology*. Pearson Education, Inc. Upper Saddle River, New Jersey.

Greden, L. (2005) Flexibility in Building Design: A Real Options Approach and Valuation Methodology to Address Risk. Thesis dissertation document, Department of Architecture, Massachusetts Institute of Technology.

Hindle, B. (1981) *Emulation and Invention*. New York.

Holling, C. S. (2001) Understanding the complexity of economic, ecological, and social systems. *Ecosystems*, Vol. 4, pp. 390-405.

Jolly, J. L. (2003) The US Copper-base Scrap Industry and its by-products. *Copper Development Association*, Inc., New York, pp. 14-29.

Keoleian, G. A., Menerey, D. (1993) *Life Cycle Design Guidance Manual: Environmental Requirements and the Product System*. EPA/600/R-92/226. Cincinnati: U.S. Environmental Protection Agency, Office of Research and Development, Risk Reduction Engineering Laboratory, January.

Kibert, C., Sendzimir, J., Guy, G. B. (2002) *Construction Ecology: Nature as the Basis for Green Buildings*. Spon Press, New York.

Lifset, R. (2004) Probing Metabolism. *Journal of Industrial Ecology*, Vol. 8, No. 3, pp. 1,2.

Mayr, E. (2001) *What Evolution Is*. Basic Books, New York, pp.210-219.

MII (2005) *Every American Born Will Need...* (Mineral Information Institute, Golden Colorado www.mii.org).

Morgan, M. G., Henrion, M. (1990) *Uncertainty: A Guide to Dealing with Uncertainty in Quantitative Risk and Policy Analysis*. Cambridge University Press, Cambridge, UK.

Schneider, E. D. Kay, J. J. (1994) Life as a manifestation of the second law of thermodynamics. *Mathematical and Computer Modeling*, Vol. 19, No.s 6-8, pp. 25-48.

Spiegelman, J. (2003) Beyond the food web: Connections to a deeper industrial ecology. *Journal of Industrial Ecology*, Vol. 7, No. 1, pp.17-23.

Trigeorgis, L. (2002) *Real Options: Managerial Flexibility and Strategy in Resource Allocation*. The MIT Press, Cambridge, MA.

USGS (2004) USGS Annual Mineral Commodity Summaries. (http://minerals.usgs.gov/minerals/pubs/mcs/)

World Commission on Employment (1987) *Our Common Future*. Oxford University Press, Oxford, UK.

Websites

Environmental Building News: www.buildinggreen.com
United States Green Building Council: www.usgbc.org
Center for Sustainable Systems (University of Michigan): http://css.snre.umich.edu
United States Geological Survey: www.usgs.gov
USGS Minerals Reports: http://minerals.usgs.gov/minerals/pubs/mcs

Photo Credits

All photographs, graphs, tables and other images and graphics are credited to the author unless noted otherwise.